Runaway and Freed
Missouri Slaves and
Those Who Helped
Them, 1763–1865

ALSO BY HARRIET C. FRAZIER
AND FROM McFARLAND

Lynchings in Missouri, 1803–1981 (2009)

*Death Sentences in Missouri, 1803–2005:
A History and Comprehensive Registry of Legal
Executions, Pardons, and Commutations* (2006)

Slavery and Crime in Missouri, 1773–1865
(2001; paperback 2010)

Runaway and Freed Missouri Slaves and Those Who Helped Them, 1763–1865

Harriet C. Frazier

McFarland & Company, Inc., Publishers
Jefferson, North Carolina, and London

The present work is a reprint of the library bound edition of Runaway and Freed Missouri Slaves and Those Who Helped Them, 1763–1865, *first published in 2004 by McFarland.*

LIBRARY OF CONGRESS CATALOGUING-IN-PUBLICATION DATA

Frazier, Harriet C.
Runaway and freed Missouri slaves and those who helped them,
1763–1865 / Harriet C. Frazier.
p.   cm.
Includes bibliographical references and index.

ISBN 978-0-7864-4678-0
softcover : 50# alkaline paper ∞

1. Slavery — Missouri — History.   2. Fugitive Slaves — Missouri — History.
3. Freedmen — Missouri — History.   4. Abolitionists — Missouri — History.
5. Slaves — Legal status, laws, etc. — Missouri — History.   6. Undergroud railroad — Missouri.
7. Missouri — History.   8. Missouri — Race relations.
9. African Americans — Missouri — History.   I. Title.
E445.M67F73   2010   973.7'115'09778 — dc22   2004006355

British Library cataloguing data are available

©2004 Harriet C. Frazier. All rights reserved

No part of this book may be reproduced or transmitted in any form or by any means, electronic or mechanical, including photocopying or recording, or by any information storage and retrieval system, without permission in writing from the publisher.

Cover photograph: Mr. and Mrs. Sam Harper,
runaway slaves from Bates County, Missouri, 1894
(Kansas State Historical Society, Topeka, Kansas)

Manufactured in the United States of America

McFarland & Company, Inc., Publishers
Box 611, Jefferson, North Carolina 28640
www.mcfarlandpub.com

For Mattie and Joey J.

Acknowledgments

My debt to others begins with the librarians at Central Missouri State University (CMSU), Warrensburg, Missouri. At my request the library purchased a multireeled microfilm edition of *The Register of Inmates, Missouri State Penitentiary, 1836–1931*. Without it I would never have known the large number of persons imprisoned for their abolitionist activities. I thank Doris Brookshier, Vanessa Chappell, Pat Downing, Lori Fitterling, Joyce Larson, Nancy Littlejohn, Wanda Moore, and Patti Morrison, some past and some present CMSU librarians, for their valuable assistance.

Lauren Boechmann, librarian, and Christine Montgomery, photographic specialist, at the Missouri State Historical Society, Columbia, Missouri, are thanked for their assistance.

Coralee Paull located vital documents housed at the Missouri Historical Society and the Office of the City of St. Louis Recorder of Deeds, St. Louis, Missouri.

Janice Schultz, astute librarian at Mid-Continent Public Library, Independence, Missouri, provided much appreciated assistance.

At the Kansas City Public Library, Kansas City, Missouri. I thank Mary Beveridge, Jeremy Drouin, Dennis Halbin, Brenda Hunnicutt, Judy Klamm, and Gary Tollison. I also thank the staff at the Westport Branch of this library.

At the Kansas City Public Library, Kansas City, Kansas, I thank Sue Cunningham and Georgia Slaughter.

My thanks also go to University of Missouri–Kansas City Law School librarians Lawrence MacLachlan and Nancy Morgan.

Dr. Shelly J. Croteau at the Missouri State Archives is thanked, among much else, for her knowledge, diligence and speed in sending me copies of pardons of abolitionist inmates at the Missouri State Penitentiary. Without her and her staff's help, this book would be far less informative.

I thank the staff of the Fort Madison, Iowa, Public Library for compiling a packet of materials concerning the Underground Railroad in Lee County, Iowa.

I thank Corinne Patterson and Janice Toms for their generous sharing of information about an ancestor. Corinne Patterson is the great granddaughter of Jeremiah McCanse, a Missouri slave who gained his freedom during the Civil War. Janice Toms is the great-great-granddaughter of Seneca T.P. Digges, the slave owner whose death at the hands of Slave John Anderson created an international incident.

Others who assisted me include Jeff Blackman, Selma Dreiseszun, Andy Hannas, Dody McKinley, Evelyn Moore, Martha Parker, Harry Penner, Betty Stack, Louise VanGallera, and Max Watson. I thank them all.

Crick Camera of Kansas City, Missouri, is thanked for its photographic excellence and its competent and pleasant personnel.

Finally, I thank Tom Fairclough, El Paso, Texas, for reading and correcting successive drafts of this book and discussing in great detail any and all aspects of it with cheerfulness, insight, and accuracy.

Contents

Acknowledgments   vii
Preface   1

1. The Myth of the Contented Slave   5
2. The Background of Slavery in Missouri   23
3. Legal Freedom: Winners and Losers   42
4. Free Negroes and Mulattoes   62
5. Runaways   87
6. Slave John Anderson and Canadian-English Justice   106
7. Abolitionist Prison Inmates   124
8. Missouri's Western Front   141
9. "The Excitement on It Continues"   152
10. The Underground Railroad on Missouri's Borders   168

Appendix 1. 1771 Spanish Census of Missouri   181
Appendix 2. 1794–95 Spanish Census of Missouri   182
Appendix 3. Missouri's Slave-Stealer (Abolitionist) Prison Inmates, 1838–1864   183
Appendix 4. Slave Population as a Percentage of Total Population in American Slaveholding Jurisdictions, 1820–1860   185
Abbreviations   186
Chapter Notes   187
Bibliography   201
Index   211

Preface

Despite the majesty and awe of the successive white rulers — French, Spanish, and American — of what is now the state of Missouri, no governing authority totally controlled its slave population. Despite the harsh slave codes of all three governments, the response of the braver and more daring of the oppressed was at least an attempt to end their servitude. Probably more fled the service of their masters by running away than managed to achieve their freedom within the system. However, from the start of French rule in 1720 through the state's abolition of slavery in 1865, liberty was always the goal of the vast majority of Missouri's enslaved people. Help from abolitionist outsiders acquired a physical presence when Elijah Lovejoy moved to St. Louis in 1833, but Mennonites and Quakers voiced their detestation of human bondage long before the United States existed. A number of devout persons served time in the Missouri state penitentiary for their abolitionist acts, or what the law termed "slave stealing." In the endgame stage of slavery in Missouri, the presence in eastern Kansas of a host of abolitionists from upstate New York and New England made slaveholding in western Missouri a risky business. Much as this state's slave owners may have believed that their human property was contented, the census figures tell quite another story. By 1860 Missouri had a smaller percentage of its population in human bondage than any other slave jurisdiction. The reason was geography: to the state's east was Illinois, to its north Iowa, to its northwest Nebraska, and to its west Kansas. Seventy-five percent of it adjoined free territories, which in due course became free states. This book tells the story of how those who could shook off their slavish yokes and of the help they received from others, including at least two foreign governments.

Chapter 1, "The Myth of the Contented Slave," looks at the widely-held belief in slave states, including Missouri, that African-Americans thoroughly enjoyed being owned. They only left their masters and mistresses, so the myth went, because abolitionists enticed them; otherwise, they were happy to remain enslaved. The grim reality of the Missouri slave's life is examined herein.

Chapter 2, "The Background of Slavery in Missouri," is a broad overview of attitudes toward slavery in the Louisiana Purchase, including early American abolitionist writings, the "peculiar institution's" protection in both the Articles of Confederation and the U.S. Constitution, and the federal government's passage of the Northwest Ordinance in 1787 — a law that prohibited slavery immediately east of Missouri, among other places. This chapter also examines Louisiana's Black Code, a document which governed the lives of Missouri's slaves from its publication in New Orleans in 1724 until it was superseded by Virginia's Slave Code, adopted as Missouri law in 1804. That Thomas Jefferson, a slave owner, was president when the United States acquired Louisiana, does not explain the continuation of slavery in this state. Its 80-year existence in Missouri fits well with its far longer tenure in the original southern colonies.

Chapter 3, "Legal Freedom: Winners and Losers," examines Spanish censuses of Missouri, and it finds that by 1800 96 percent of resident free persons of color were women and mulatto children. Almost certainly they were initially owned by white men, especially military officers who freed their concubines and biracial children before returning to Spain. The story of Esther, a mulatto woman freed in 1793 by her owner, Jacques Clamorgan, a St. Louis resident, illustrates the indomitable spirit of a good woman. York, a member of the Lewis and Clark expedition, requested his freedom as a reward for his lengthy service in the Corps of Discovery after he returned to St. Louis from the Pacific Ocean. His master, William Clark, later a successful territorial governor of Missouri, denied his request, at least during York's most productive years. Legal freedom was mostly the master's call, not the slave's. This chapter also details those circumstances under which Missouri courts granted slaves their freedom despite their owners' opposition and those in which the judges upheld bondpersons' continuing enslavement. The discussion of Missouri appellate case law concerning slave suits for freedom ends with the U.S. Supreme Court's decision in the Dred Scott case.

Chapter 4, "Free Negroes and Mulattoes," concerns bondpersons whose owners voluntarily freed them or their ancestors; no appeals courts were involved in this chapter's emancipations. It includes discussions of the following: Cyprian Clamorgan's book, *The Colored Aristocracy of St. Louis* (1858); Elizabeth Keckley, a St. Louis seamstress who became Mary Todd Lincoln's best friend after President Lincoln's assassination; Charles Lee Younger, a western Missouri resident and father, by Elizabeth, his slave woman, of two children who attended Oberlin College in Ohio under the terms of his will, a document wherein he also emancipated his biracial children; William Greenleaf Eliot, a St. Louis minister, who freed Archer Alexander, the model for the slave whom Lincoln frees in "Freedom's Memorial," a statuary group which today stands in Lincoln Park, Washington, D.C.; one Union Army soldier's freedom; and other interesting emancipated Missouri slaves.

Chapter 5, "Runaways," examines numerous advertisements for fugitive slaves which appeared in Missouri's newspapers between 1808 and the Civil War years. A great deal of advance planning was involved in bondpersons' decisions to leave the service of masters.

Chapter 6, "Slave John Anderson and Canadian-English Justice," concerns the Canadian government's refusal to extradite a runaway Missouri slave who, in the process of making his getaway, shot and killed a Howard County, Missouri, slave owner.

Chapter 7, "Abolitionist Prison Inmates," examines Missouri State Penitentiary records of 42 persons, including two women and five African-Americans, incarcerated between 1837 and 1865 for their abolitionist activities. The best known of these convicts, George Thompson, attended Oberlin College, and was greatly influenced by Theodore Weld, a famous nineteenth-century abolitionist.

This chapter also concerns the release between 1843 and 1865 of many of Missouri's prison's slave stealer inmates. Eight different governors issued these multiple pardons; the last-released convict gained his freedom after Missouri abolished slavery.

Chapter 8, "Missouri's Western Front," examines the consequences for western Missouri of the U.S. Congress's passage of the Kansas-Nebraska Act in 1854. This law turned a swath extending 60 miles west of the Kansas-Missouri border into a war zone for and against slavery. (Any area in Kansas much more than 60 miles beyond the Missouri border was fraught with danger for runaway slaves. Slave-owning American Indians inhabited most of Kansas, and they might re-enslave any escaping Missouri slave whom they captured.) Detailed herein are the near-lynching in 1855 of George S. Park, founder of Parkville, Missouri, by a pro-slavery mob; John Brown's "rescue" of 12 slaves in 1858 from Bates County, Missouri; his journey with them through eastern Kansas and eventually to Canada; and the coverage in the region's newspapers of Brown's hanging following his raid on Harpers Ferry.

Chapter 9, "The Excitement on It Continues," describes the 1859 apprehension, by a group of Missouri slave owners near Oskaloosa, Kansas, of Dr. John Doy and his companions, including 13 slaves owned in Missouri. All were brought back to Missouri. Once returned, Doy was nearly lynched, tried twice for slave stealing, and sentenced to a five-year term in Missouri's prison; but his Kansas abolitionist friends broke him out of jail in St. Joseph, Missouri. This chapter also details the near-lynching of another group of abolitionists in Independence, Missouri.

Chapter 10, "The Underground Railroad on Missouri's Borders," concerns the assistance escaping slaves received in St. Louis, western Illinois, and western Kansas, principally in the 1850s. The chief beneficiaries of the help extended by abolitionists in these locales were Missouri's slaves.

My primary sources for this book are handwritten prison records, pardon papers, trial court records, printed appellate case law, statutory law, old newspapers, and relevant scholarship. I found a variety of fascinating material in the process of researching this book, and I hope that my readers share my enthusiasm.

1

The Myth of the Contented Slave

A portion of Mark Twain's unfinished autobiography explains the mindset of the typical white resident of any slave state in the antebellum period. In the years immediately following his mother's death in 1890 and while Harriet Beecher Stowe was his close friend and neighbor on Forest Street in Hartford, Connecticut, Twain wrote about his Presbyterian mother. Jane Clemens was born, raised, and married in Adair County, Kentucky, and eventually became a long-term resident of Hannibal, Missouri.

> When slavery perished my mother had been in daily touch with it for sixty years. Yet, kind-hearted and compassionate as she was, I think she was not conscious that slavery was a bald, grotesque, and unwarrantable usurpation. She had never heard it assailed in any pulpit, but had heard it defended and sanctified in a thousand; her ears were familiar with Bible texts that approved it, but if there were any that disapproved it they had not been quoted by her pastors; as far as her experience went, the wise and the good and the holy were unanimous in the conviction that slavery was right, righteous, sacred, the peculiar pet of the Deity, and a condition which the slave himself ought to be daily and nightly thankful for. Manifestly, training and association can accomplish strange miracles. As a rule our slaves were convinced and content.[1]

Churches played a crucial role in convincing slaves that they were or certainly ought to be contented. Those with "branches in the South," as Quarles explains, were noted for "their timidity on slavery." For example, at the Methodist Episcopal Church's 1840 conference in Baltimore, its minister participants "voted to debar Negro church members from testifying against whites in ecclesiastical trials in those states in which law prohibited Negroes from testifying against whites."[2] Of even greater importance, members of the same denomination might hold wholly opposite views on slavery. As Murray describes the Southern point of view: "The basic proslavery argument from the Bible ran like this: Since slavery was directly sanctioned in the Old Testament, and was not condemned by Christ or the Apostles in the New Testament, then it could not be sinful for Christians in any era."[3]

As a subsequent chapter explains, during the time period in which three devout Presbyterians were inmates in the Missouri State Penitentiary for their abolitionist activity, others of this same religion were preaching a very different doctrine. The Reverend Daniel Patton, a Presbyterian minister who had many years of service in Missouri, gave an address at the courthouse in a western county, Clay, which the local newspaper

Missouri counties in 1860. The Missouri River flows south from extreme northwestern Missouri to northern Jackson County and then east to St. Louis. To its north are Clay, Ray, Carroll, Chariton, Howard, Boone, Callaway, Montgomery, Warren and St. Charles counties; to its south are Jackson, Lafayette, Saline, Cooper, Moniteau, Cole, Osage, Gasconade, Franklin, and St. Louis. The Mississippi river runs south and immediately east of Clark county to Pemiscot county at the State's southeastern tip. The Missouri River joins the Mississippi in St. Louis County. Based on a map in *A History of Missouri for High Schools*, 1944.

printed on its front page. Brother Patton told the assembled: "It would reflect dishonorably upon the Great Creator-Law Giver to suppose that He had failed or neglected ... to ordain human society. The relations existing in the great family of man are of divine appointment.... Slavery now existing in our country is in conformity with said appointment and in accordance with the Bible." He repeatedly assured the faithful that abolitionism was not God's plan, that Old Testament figures such as Abraham and those of the New such as Paul were not abolitionists. He concluded his "Discourse on Slavery": "Let God manage in his own way, this subject of African Slavery. It is too intricate, too high, too deep, for frail man to fathom.... Statesmen, Divines, Politicians ... let slavery alone."[4] Other ministers followed Patton in his Missouri preaching; they presented, as the newspaper noted, "beautiful, eloquent and truthful vindications of the Southern side of the slavery question." The revealed truth to these preachers and their listeners was clear: "African slavery was ordained of God, and that to attempt to disturb it, or rather to *break it up,* is to attempt to interfere with God's arrangements and to show ourselves wiser than God."[5] Further, and as other reverends assured their slave-owning parishioners: "God has, nowhere in his revelation to man, mentioned slaveholding as an evil.... Since legitimate human authority has sanctioned slavery, it cannot be evil."[6] Biblical texts such as Ephesians 6:5 — "Servants, be obedient to them that are your masters" — were embellished for most people, including slaves, who attended religious services in all American slave jurisdictions. Bondpersons were instructed in this manner:

Q. If servants suffer unjustly, what are they to do?
A. They must bear it patiently.
Q. Ought servants to rebel against the authority of their masters?
A. No. It is a sin against God and man.
Q. Should servants ever run away?
A. No. If they do, they sin against God and man.[7]

William Wells Brown, an ex-slave formerly owned in St. Louis, described the auctioneer at a slave market in that city in the late 1820s and early 1830s as hawking his female merchandise in these terms: "How much is offered for this woman? She is a good cook, good washer, a good obedient servant. She has got religion." Brown explained that in Missouri and throughout the slave states, the religious instruction "consists in teaching a slave that he must never strike a white man; that God made him for a slave, and that when whipped, he must not find fault; slaveholders find such religion very profitable."[8]

Brown identified the biblical basis of these instructions as passages such as Luke 12:47: "That servant, which knew his lord's will, and prepared not himself, neither did according to his will, shall be beaten with many stripes." Obviously, the Bible also teaches behaviors other than docility in the face of injustice. For the most part, bondpersons who might have discovered other truths through reading and interpreting the Bible for themselves could not. The danger was too great that they would not find the same celebration of their bondage in the Scriptures that their various owners' ministers discovered therein. Exodus 5:1 records that "Moses and Aaron went in, and told Pharaoh, Thus saith the Lord God of Israel, Let my people go." Exodus 21:16 advises, "He that stealeth a man and selleth him, or if he be found in his hand, he shall surely be put to death." In Galatians 3:28, Paul admonishes the faithful that "There is neither Jew nor Greek, there is neither bond nor free ... for ye are all one in Christ Jesus." Matthew 19:30 says, "Many that are first shall be last; and the last shall be first." The Golden Rule, found among other places in Luke 6:31, cautions, "And as ye would that men should do to you, do ye also to them." These were all dangerous precepts for slaves to read, or to hear, or worst of all, to believe.

As early as 1740, the colony of South Carolina prohibited teaching any slave to write or employing one in writing because doing so "may be attended with great inconvenience." Upon conviction, the punishment was a fine of 100 pounds.[9] At this early date, the most likely evil which this statute sought to prevent was the means for slaves to write their own passes. Doing so, assumed the South Carolina legislature, would allow them an unwarranted freedom of movement, and perhaps of escape. The lawmakers were not then concerned that rebellious ideas such as those contained in the Declaration of Independence might float into the slaves' consciousness. It would be another 36 years before Thomas Jefferson sat down alone and wrote this eloquent document.

However, when the spirit of liberty fostered a slave revolt on French-ruled St. Domingue in 1791, American slaveholders became fearful about what were previously unsuspected dissatisfactions among their slaves. In 1819 and perhaps even earlier, Virginia decreed that slaves assembled "in considerable numbers" at places of religious worship at night or "at schools for teaching them reading or writing ... if not restrained may be productive of considerable evil to the community." A slave's punishment for such unlawful activity was up to 20 lashes.[10] The harm contemplated by this statute appears to have been the coming together of large numbers of bondpersons, which might result in an insurrection.

Ten years later, black literacy was the subject of legislation when, in 1829, the state of Georgia prohibited any person from teaching a slave, a Negro, or a free person of color to read or to write.[11] In 1830, the state of Louisiana made it a crime to use language in public discourse which tended to produce discontent among the free colored population and to excite insubordination among slaves.[12] In 1837, Missouri's General Assembly prohibited the publication, circulation, or promulgation of abolition doctrines and punished those convicted of any variation of this crime with two years in the Missouri State Penitentiary for the first offense, not more than 20 years for the second, and a life prison term for the third.[13] Laws such as these which Virginia, Georgia, Louisiana, Missouri, and other slave states passed suggest their legislators understood that the slave's contentment was highly dependent on isolation and ignorance.

Missouri had adopted Virginia's slave code in 1804, curtailing from the start of American rule slave assembly, freedom of movement, and association with free blacks and whites other than owners or overseers. More oppressive laws, such as the 1837 anti-abolition legislation, were enacted in Missouri after Nat Turner became a dreaded household name throughout slaveocracy. Had he been born white in 1800 in Southampton County, Virginia, his name would have been *Nathaniel*, which in Hebrew means "the gift of God," but he was not, and instead was named *Nat*, a typical nickname for a male slave. He differed from other slave children in his ability to read and write; exactly who taught him is uncertain. His first owner, a devout Methodist, encouraged both his young slave's literacy and his study of the Bible. Turner never drank alcoholic beverages, felt no temptation to steal, and spent his leisure time either praying or reading books, especially accounts of Old Testament figures such as Moses, who liberated his people, and Ezekiel, whose prophecies concerned the destruction of his enemies. Another of his owners and his wife allowed young Nat his Sundays free to preach, and this gave him considerable freedom of movement. By the time this slave preacher was in his late twenties, he knew which blacks, either slave or free, were worthy of his trust. Though Virginia passed a law in April 1831 which made it a crime to teach slaves to read and write, enforcement of the law was lax. Some still learned reading and writing, and Nat Turner, who continued to preach, also kept meeting with his chosen lieutenants. His owner believed that this bright, hard-working, and well-behaved bondman needed little supervision.

In August 1831, Turner and his followers began a murderous rampage in their southeastern Virginia county which left 60 whites, including his owner, dead from stabbings and decapitations. The Southampton militia who pursued him came across scenes of unimaginable horror: 10 decapitated white children tossed together in a bloody pile. In all, what was perceived as a huge slave army attacked 15 different households where they murdered white people. As the "Prophet's" men were captured, tried, and hanged in late August and September 1831, "the great banditti chief," as newspapers referred to him, remained at large, with $1,100 offered for his capture. When he was finally caught in late October and appeared before a court; he told the judges, "I am in particular favor with heaven." When asked by a white man what had happened to all the money he had stolen from his white victims, he replied that he had taken 75 cents, and he said to a free Negro, "You know money was not my object." He was tried November 5; found guilty of conspiracy to rebel and making insurrection; valued at $375, which amount the Commonwealth of Virginia presumably eventually paid his owner's estate; hanged November 11, 1831; and his body was given to physicians for dissection. In all, in addition to the 60 whites who died, more than 200 African-Americans, rightly or wrongly believed to be associated with or inspired by him also lost their lives.

Slave owners were confident that Nat Turner and his free black and slave followers were motivated by religious fanaticism and the spirit of abolitionism which, coincidentally, William Lloyd Garrison (1805–1879) and others like him were advocating in some of the Northern states. That Nat Turner had neither heard of Garrison nor seen a single issue of his newspaper, *The Liberator*, was not the point. White Southerners could not comprehend that their own oppressive treatment of people of color, both slave and free, had bred the first successful armed rebellion of slaves in American history.[14] They continued to believe that others were to blame for any slave insurrection.

Because of his pertinacity, Garrison would become the abolitionist most detested in the South. In 1829 he began insisting, as he would throughout the remainder of slavery in America, "I will be heard." On July 4th of that year, in Boston, he delivered his first of many public attacks on slavery. In his address, he called for the "immediate and complete emancipation" of slaves. On January 1, 1831, he began publication of *The Liberator*, which he continued to publish weekly for the next 35 years. It called for the swift and total destruction of slavery, and, though its circulation never exceeded 3,000 subscribers, from the Southern point of view Garrison quickly became and remained Public Enemy No. One.[15]

In the fall of 1831, partially in reaction to Nat Turner's bloodletting, the corporation of Georgetown, D.C.; a vigilance association in Charleston, South Carolina; a grand jury in Raleigh, North Carolina; and the state of Georgia all targeted Garrison and his newspaper. In Georgetown, any free black who received a copy through the post office could be fined $20 or imprisoned for 30 days, and if the fine and jail fees were not paid, the subscriber could be sold as a slave for four months. In Charleston, a reward of $1,500 was offered for the arrest and conviction of any white person circulating *The Liberator*. In Raleigh, Garrison was indicted for publishing and circulating his weekly;

and in Georgia, the legislature offered a $5,000 reward for the arrest and conviction of, among other persons, the editor or publisher of the paper.[16] This flurry of legal and financial activity regarding him stemmed from his repeated violation of laws which the various Southern legislatures had passed against speaking and writing about incendiary ideas such as the immediate emancipation of slaves. It did not matter that Garrison always opposed any violence to achieve his goal of ending slavery; his advocacy of such ideas sufficed.

The slave states believed that they could best stifle thoughts of insurrection and/or freedom among bondpersons by suppressing black literacy and religious worship. In March 1832, Virginia passed statutes which strengthened the penalties for anyone teaching blacks to read and write, disallowed any religious services conducted by black preachers, and banned all forms of writing which encouraged persons of color within Virginia to make insurrection or rebellion.[17] Missouri enacted similar laws during the next decade.

In that state, Nat Turner's and his followers' violent reaction to their enslavement changed the views of few if any slaveholders about what was actually in the hearts and minds of their human property. In September 1831, one Missouri newspaper attributed Turner's motivation to "only a desire to plunder."[18] "It is generally supposed that [Turner and his followers] had no definite object in view, but were stimulated with the desire of plunder."[19] Several months later, it carried this brief account of his death: "Nat, the ringleader of the Southampton insurrection, has been tried and executed, in company with several other slaves concerned with him in his murder."[20] The average white Missourian continued to believe that the subservient-appearing slaves he encountered were content in their God-ordained inferiority.

However, to be on the safe side and with no known incident in the state prompting its General Assembly to act, an 1845 Missouri law decreed that if an apprentice were colored, "it shall not be the duty of the master to cause [him] to be taught to read or write, or a knowledge of arithmetic."[21] In 1847, Missouri's General Assembly prohibited any person from teaching any Negro or mulatto to read and write, and the new law also disallowed any black religious services unless some "sheriff, constable, marshal, police officer, or justice of the peace was present during all the time of such meeting or assemblage in order to prevent all seditious speeches and disorderly and unlawful conduct." Since all these various officers in Missouri were white, any black meeting for worship without an official white presence was illegal. Any person who violated the act could be fined up to $500 for each offense and imprisoned for up to six months.[22]

These harsh new laws were put in place to insure the illiteracy of both free and enslaved African-Americans. They probably reflected both the fact that Turner's followers included free blacks and the increasing number of free persons of color in border states such as Virginia and Missouri. The free Negro population of Virginia increased in every federal census. Though the non-slave black population in Missouri declined between 1810 and 1820, small as were the numbers it almost tripled between 1830 and 1840, going from 569 free Negroes to 1,574.[23] Whites in Missouri, as elsewhere in the slave states, perceived free blacks as having, at best, an unwholesome influence on their slaves; the more repressed free persons of color were, the logic must have been, the easier the management of bondpersons. The resulting legislation in Missouri of the 1840s sought to remove any imagined source of slave restlessness. As the legislature saw it, the bad example of free "niggras," the subversive speech and writing of outsiders, and abolitionists' enticements of other men's property were the causes of slave discontent. By their very nature, bondpersons were happy; all that was required to keep them smiling and laughing was strict racial control. It was key to the continuing white belief that any person in bondage was, as Oates puts it, "a submissive, feeble-minded Sambo, [a] 'banjo-twanging, hi-yi-ing happy Jack.'"[24]

A Missouri law of 1855 dealt especially severely with persons charged with raising an insurrection of slaves, free Negroes, or mulattoes. Conviction for any aspect of this crime, either the substantive act of rebellion or insurrection, or entering any agreement to rebel, or aiding or assisting such a rebellion, carried a death sentence. Any person who published, circulated, spoke, or displayed any picture or device which, among other matters, had "the tendency ... [t]o excite any slave, or other colored person in this State, to insolence or insubordination toward his master ... or to escape from his master" was, upon conviction, sent to prison.[25] Though some unlucky inmate may have served time for *exciting* a slave to escape from his owner, there were no death sentences carried out under these statutes. As a subsequent chapter explains, most if not all abolitionists were imprisoned in the Missouri State Penitentiary under other statutes for *enticing* a slave to escape and the like. These 1855 laws appear to have been passed to insure that troublesome alien influences would be kept from this state's otherwise contented bondpersons.

The press in rural Missouri assured readers that the slave was "the happiest laborer in the world," and published arguments for the continuing enslavement of Africans such as "Slavery is the highest state of Civilization the negro has ever enjoyed in the history of the world. In Africa he is a brute.... In the slave states he has a home; ... has the protection of the laws; has friends and associations among the most refined of the land; has religious instruction."[26] Most of the state's antebellum newspapers ran no stories on the actual living conditions of the typical slave. For a field hand, which most were, the odds greatly favored a life that was exhausting, dangerous, and short.

The difference in longevity between nineteenth-century whites and slaves can be found in out-of-the-way places, such as information about life insurance which appeared in Missouri's press during the 1850s. Though this industry was unregulated in Missouri until after the Civil War, a number of companies sold insurance, and some ran detailed ads in various newspapers. One company used the headline, "INSURE YOUR SLAVES." The smaller print spelled out that insurance was not available for any under 14 years of age or over 40 years old; and no slave's life could be insured for more than one year. For a benefit of $100 upon the insured chattel's death, the annual rate increased every year between 14 and 40. It ranged from a low of one dollar for a 14-year-old bondperson to a high of $3.30 for one aged 40 years.[27] In contrast, whites could be insured for one year, five years, and for life.

Even more indicative of the discrepancy between the life expectancy for whites and slaves were the differences between the premiums for the same benefits which another insurance company offered. Because both white and slave infants and children died young, this company did not advertise any life insurance for any person under 15 years of age. Its tables, contained in its ads, clarified that for a $100 policy, a white 15-

year-old could be insured for 77 cents per year for one year; the premium for a slave of the same age was $1.84 per year for that same $100—2.389 times more. According to these figures, the white 15-year-old was more than twice as likely to reach his 16th birthday as the slave. A 33-year-old white's insurance for one year cost $1.14; for a slave of the same age for the same time period it was $3.21, or more than 2.395 times more for the $100 death benefit. At the opposite end of the table, a 60-year-old white could be insured for $4 for one year, while a 60-year-old slave's premium was $10.44, or 2.600 times more for the $100 death benefit. According to these figures, from age 15 on a slave was at least twice as likely to die as a white person, and the more both demographic groups aged, the greater the likelihood that the slave would die sooner than the white.[28]

The forms of the first eight federal censuses further illuminate the discrepancy between the value of white and slave life and the difference in the longevity between white and slave. No census taken between 1790 and 1860 contains even one slave's name. In the first six, bondpersons were counted in the same enumeration as whites. In 1790, only free white males were divided into age categories: "Of Sixteen Years and upwards" and "Under Sixteen Years." Under "Slaves" the total owned in each household was all this first census contained. In subsequent enumerations between 1800 and 1840, free white inhabitants, both male and female, were divided into more age groups than slaves. For example, in the 1830 and 1840 censuses, free white persons were placed in 13 age ranges and slaves in six. At the upper limits whites were classified as being "40 & under 50," "50 & under 60," and so on by decade until "100 & upwards." In contrast older slaves were enumerated in much larger age groups: "36 & under 55," "55 & under 100," and "100 & upwards." In the 1850 and 1860 censuses, enslaved persons were separately counted in documents entitled "1850 Slave Schedule" and "1860 Slave Schedule."[29] Only the owner's name was listed. All we know for certain of those in bondage in 1850 and 1860 is their color, sex, and age. Had enslaved persons lived as long on average as their white masters, the age categories for the owners and the owned would be identical. In a word, the federal census forms reflect the same facts as life insurance policies of the antebellum period. The anticipated longevity of whites vastly exceeded that of slaves.

Though the pre-Civil War press of Missouri from 1808 onward contained numerous and at times detailed obituaries about whites, there were almost none for bondpersons. Nor were there news stories about slaves who died of non-contagious natural causes. To be sure, Missouri's press covered the deaths of any killed by contagious diseases, because whites could contract the same deadly illnesses. Thus, accounts such as this appeared: "Cholera—Two negroes belonging to Dr. Wilson Brown, died of Cholera at Jefferson City, last week. No other cases have been heard of, nor have we heard of any nearer approach of this fatal disease."[30]

Newspapers usually published the names of slaves who were executed or lynched, but when a slave died by his or her own hand, the press at times included the name and at others did not. If a slave's cause of death was accidental, the story typically omitted the name of the deceased. Instead, the usual account of his passing included the cause and manner of death and the owner's name: "A negro boy belonging to Mr. James M. Keller, of [Clay] County, was drowned in the river at Missouri City on Sunday last. He was bathing."[31] In *Huckleberry Finn*, for ironic effect, Mark Twain explores the typical white reaction upon learning of the accidental death of an African-American. When Huck tells Aunt Sally that the steamboat on which he was a passenger blew out a cylinder-head, she inquires, "Good gracious! Anybody hurt?" Huck answers, "No'm. Killed a nigger." A relieved Aunt Sally responds, "Well, it's lucky; because some times people do get hurt." [32] Obviously, to Aunt Sally and her kind, Negroes were not anybodies; they were not people. Twain also remembered that "once when a white man killed a negro man for a trifling little offence everybody seemed indifferent about it — as regarded the slave — though considerable sympathy was felt for the slave's owner, who had been bereft of valuable property by a worthless person who was not able to pay for it."[33] A Missouri news story furnished this example of a loss to the white owner: "Negro Killed — On Christmas day, Dr. Reese Davis, of Milton, had a very valuable negro (worth $1200) killed while chopping in the woods. One tree lodged against another, and in cutting the last, the first one fell upon his head and mashed it, killing him instantly."[34] The slave's name, age, and survivors, if any, were unmentioned.

Comparisons are available of the coverage of the death of a slave with that of whites from similar causes. One newspaper reported that "The clothes of a negro girl living at the hotel of General Smith took fire a few nights since and burned her so badly that she died but a few days later. She belonged to Col. Murphy of Wright County. Gen'l Smith, in his efforts to save the girl, had his hands badly burned."[35] The story's emphasis is on her white lessee's damage to his hands and to another man's property. When the fatal victim of burns was a white woman, coverage included such detail as "Mrs. Eustace, wife of the Reverend Eustace, died as a result of burns received when a lamp exploded. Her husband, Thomas, was a Presbyterian minister."[36] Or "Ann Ravell, a young lady, was burned to death at the home of Mrs. Reilly.... She had returned from church, and she stood too near the fireplace."[37]

Though most slaves died at younger ages than most whites, fanciful stories regarding the unbelievable longevity of an occasional slave appeared in Missouri newspapers. One concerned Negro Sam, who died on the plantation of his master in Georgia in 1860. Sam believed that he was 40 years old when captured in Africa in 1760. From unnamed reliable persons and "the negro's own statement, he is supposed to have been over one hundred and forty years old at the time of his death."[38]

Such accounts often concerned bondpersons allegedly owned by the family of President George Washington. One was 191 years old, formerly the property of Augustine Washington, father of our first president. She was on display at the Museum and Gallery of Fine Arts in Louisville: "It is said that unquestionable certificates of her age can be shown."[39] Another former nurse of General Washington, aged between 140 and 160 years, a news story related, had been exhibited in New York: "She ... lies in bed, eating or smoking her pipe. Her pulse is full, strong and regular and near 80 in a minute. She tells many interesting anecdotes in relation to the early childhood of General Washington."[40] Eighteen years later, General Washington's sole surviving slave, a male aged 124 years, was being transported to the World's Fair and put on display near a contribution box for the Washington Monument.[41]

Mark Twain's essay, "General Washington's Negro Body-Servant," describes newspaper accounts of the death of Washington's famous servant, whose name was also George, at age 95. These stories, Twain notes, date from 1809 until 1864, including one which appeared in the *St. Louis Republican* in 1840. The humorist went to the heart of the matter when he wrote, "The longer [George] lived the stronger and longer his memory grew.... Allowing that when he first died, he died at the age of 95, he was 141 years old when he died last, in 1864."[42] Most likely, none of these many fanciful stories mention that President Washington's last will and testament gave his wife, Martha, a life estate in all 150 slaves he owned, and she freed all of her inherited human property before her death in 1802. Even if, miraculously, they might have been alive decades after their former owners' deaths, all were long since ex-slaves; all were free women and men.

Surely, few who read these tall tales believed the reported ages of these slaves to be accurate, nor were they likely to credit their purported intimate association with the family of Washington; but these accounts, if somewhat exaggerated, showed how beneficial slavery must had been for those who enjoyed well over a century of being owned by prominent white persons who took such good care of them. Whites chuckled as they read these stories, and in addition to the human interest of such accounts, readers were thereby assured that slavery helped to promote the longevity of the featured bondpersons. Persons who lived to these wonderfully advanced ages must be content. That unhappy people die much sooner was the sound moral of these reports about the slaves of George Washington more than 60 years after his death.

What of the birth of slaves? Their beginnings may or may not have been recorded. It is unimaginable that many illiterate parents knew the exact day, month, and year of any child's nativity, and if they did, they had no means to write down this information. Some owners kept accounts of increases among their slaves; others did not. Many runaway advertisements prefixed the age of the missing slave with "about," described him or her as being "between" two ages, or gave a range of years, such as 30 to 35, 35 to 40, and the like. Though most slaveholders who placed these ads probably did not know the precise years of their slaves, it was to any owner's advantage for his bondpersons not to know their actual ages. When sold they could be passed off as younger than they were because no slave could be truthful about what he never knew. In contrast, white life was not for sale and inherently valuable. The birth of a white infant was recorded in a family Bible.

In Missouri, there were few official records of any births and deaths outside the city of St. Louis until well after the Civil War, and there was no compulsory statewide issuing of birth or death certificates until the twentieth century. Such records in the antebellum period were mostly a private matter. Presumably, then as now, birthdays of white children were observed. Without written records of the births of slaves and little to prompt parents' memories of their children's beginnings, the celebration of their birthdays would have been difficult, if not impossible. The famous black abolitionist, Frederick Douglass, a runaway slave from Maryland, resented the fact that he never knew his birth date. He wrote, "I have no accurate knowledge of my age, never having seen any authentic record containing it. By far the larger part of the slaves know as little of their age as horses know of theirs."[43]

Did slaves reproduce more often than whites? Nothing suggests that they did. Large families were the order of the day for most women. King describes the high mortality among slave infants and children in the nineteenth century: "Mothers, white and black, came to live with the reality that some of their children would not live to maturity. The dread reality was even more real for slave mothers, whose children died at greater rates than white children."[44] King attributes the death of large numbers of slave infants and children to, among other causes, the poor prenatal and postnatal diets of breast-feeding slave mothers and the drudgery which their owners required of them. The reality of child bearing for enslaved women at times occasioned great sadness and anguish.

In Missouri, as in all places of American slavery, the mother's status, not the father's, conveniently determined whether their offspring were slave or free. Though documenting such matters is difficult, the fact that the 1850 and 1860 slave censuses faithfully listed whether the bondperson was black or mulatto suggests just how many white men fathered children with slaves, some owning the very children they fathered. Pregnancy and childbirth under such circumstances could only have been a sorrowful experience for the women who knew that they were bringing slave children into a world where power belonged to white men.

Missouri newspaper coverage of slave birth was as illusionary as accounts of slaves living to ages well beyond 100 years. A 42-year-old woman had 41 children and was pregnant with her 42nd or possibly her 43rd "as she frequently had doublets."[45] Another news story concerned a 49-year-old slave who gave birth to twins: "has had five children in less than five years, and altogether 24 children."[46] Another, headlined, "Negrophilia," concerned a slave mother who gave birth to four "fine healthy 'little niggers' in the period of eleven months and four days. A few more such, and a man would soon become quite rich and comfortable."[47] Yet another, headlined "A grandmother at 26 years," dealt with a slave child who gave birth to a girl when she was 14 and her daughter "improved upon the example of her mother," and had a daughter when 11 years old.[48]

Absent from any of these semi-imaginary accounts of the birthing feats of slave women was any mention of the fathers of these many infants or follow-up accounts of just how many of these babies lived long enough to become productive laborers for their owners. Again, the logic of the recounted prolificacy suggests that these prodigious feats of childbearing were the result of good care on the part of owners, happy family life, and contented parents and children. The truth is that a sizable number of known cases of slave mothers attempting to murder or actually murdering one or more of their children survive from slavery's tenure. The abolitionist William Lloyd Garrison attributed the epidemic of slave women killing their young to their desire to relieve their infants and children of "the curse of involuntary servitude."[49] Toni Morrison's novel *Beloved* (1987) is a fictional tale based on an actual runaway from Kentucky who murdered her daughter, Beloved, by slitting her throat, to prevent her growing up a slave. Thus speaks the actual record of fine healthy "little niggers," their happy mothers, and their proud fathers.

Beginning as early as the 1820s but significantly increasing in coverage in the 1850s and early 1860s, Missouri newspapers carried stories of slaves who loved, above all else, their enslavement. The earliest of these accounts available in a Missouri newspaper concerned a black barber from Charleston, South Carolina, himself the owner of several slaves, who sailed for Sierra Leone where he, his family, and other free blacks intended to settle in 1821. He offered his slaves the choice of joining him in freedom or remaining in America and being sold. Only one of his bondpersons accompanied him to Africa.[50] A sentimental story came from Richmond, Virginia, in 1845 that concerned, as its headline proclaimed, "An Old School Negro" owned by John Marshall (1755–1835), first Chief Justice of the U.S. Supreme Court. This unnamed "favorite body servant" of Marshall "is but a nominal slave now, preferring like many others here not to be free."[51] The old former slave insisted that he take the hat of, fill the water glass of, and perform other services for Marshall's successor, Chief Justice Roger B. Taney.

By the 1850s, a few of the news stories about slaves who disliked freedom concerned bondpersons owned in Missouri. An unnamed bondwoman, owned in Weston (Platte County), had, while passing through Elmira, New York, with her mistress some two years earlier, been detained "against her will — and by force by some zealous Negrophilist." When her former mistress visited her at the home of the "kind and excellent family where she was well cared for," the former slave privately told her Platte County owner that "she would rather live one year as a slave than two as a free girl," and she was allowed to return to Missouri.[52] A slave from Carroll County, north of the Missouri River in the central section of the state, ran away in 1856. He returned two years later because he could not support himself on the meager wages he had received in Ohio, Michigan, and Canada. The newspaper related that he told his master that "he wanted to receive a good whipping and serve him the rest of his days."[53]

Most of these tales, however, were set in out-of-state locales. One 1856 account of a Southern Negro's opinion of the free blacks up North was almost certainly apocryphal. Its headline was "A Savannah Slave Airing Himself up North — His Estimation of the Free Blacks," and it was presented as excerpts from a letter which he wrote from Saratoga Springs, New York, to his Savannah, Georgia, owner, whom he addressed as "Dear Old Mistress." He related to her, "I came near striking one of the darkies in New York for calling me a Southern slave. I told him that I would buy him ... and take him home to plant rice ... for I believe he needed it."[54] Since Georgia law had made it a crime to teach any African-American, slave or free, to read and write in 1829, it seems unlikely that any black or mulatto actually wrote letters to his former Georgia mistress more than 25 years later.

Other accounts appeared in Missouri newspapers in the 1850s. One, headlined "Dissatisfied with Freedom," related the aftermath of a Louisville, Kentucky, widow's freeing 10 or 11 slaves and renting lodgings for them in Cincinnati, Ohio. A year later, they returned to Kentucky and "expressed themselves as heartily tired of freedom. One old woman said she ... would rather be put at auction and sold to the highest bidder, even to the devil himself, sooner than go back to freedom as she found it."[55] "Not Fond of Freedom," proclaimed another story's headline about 17 Negroes transported from Mississippi to California for purposes of emancipating them. They also preferred slavery at home to freedom elsewhere.[56] Two women returned to their Virginia owners. One came back after 10 years of freedom and "applied for the privilege of again becoming a slave at the Richmond Circuit Court."[57] The other, a runaway whose story was headlined "Sick of Freedom," voluntarily returned to her minister-owner in Lynchburg after nearly starving among her "pretended friends" in Boston. She said of her several months of freedom that she would "never again leave old Virginia, where, she says, the negro is ten time as free and happy as in the North."[58]

Probably many of these stories, if exaggerated, were not complete fabrications. One enterprising Southerner, as a Missouri newspaper related the matter, opened an office in Canada to assist the return of fugitive slaves to their masters. He proposed furnishing them with the cost of their transportation to the South in the company of an agent, in the hope of reimbursements from their owners.[59] From early in the nineteenth century, Canada consistently refused to return fugitive slaves to their masters, and never established an extradition treaty for these purposes with the United States. Therefore, the only way Southern masters could retrieve their bondpersons from north of the border was by their slaves themselves choosing to return. Most likely, some did.

The psychotherapist Erich Fromm wrote an influential book, *Escape From Freedom* (1941), about the psychological phenomenon of persons avoiding freedom. He wrote: "Whistling in the dark does not bring light. Aloneness, fear, and bewilderment remain; people cannot stand it forever.... They must try to escape from freedom altogether." Fromm understood that the slave comes to believe that the person who rules over him is "wonderful or perfect," and he reasons "then I should not be ashamed of obeying him. I cannot be his equal because he is so much stronger, wiser, better, and so on than I am."[60] Throughout their lives, bondpersons were taught that white persons, especially their masters and mistresses, were their betters; some believed what they were taught. When they were either emancipated from or ran away from the security of being owned, they faced the hardships of freedom. Some slaves blinked and returned to their owners; similarly, some, in Missouri and elsewhere in the slave states, remained with their masters after the Surrender. These were mainly the timid, the infirm, and the elderly. They were not the young, bright, and energetic.

However, the truth was, especially in Missouri with its multiple free borders, that most opted for freedom with all its trials and uncertainties. The state's rural press, heavily dependent for its readers and advertisers on a slave-owning and a slave-owner-admiring population, infrequently published this truth. Its out-of-state news stories concerning slavery mostly came from the newspapers of other slave states, especially Virginia, Kentucky, Tennessee, and the Carolinas, or those regions which were the birthplaces of most of Missouri's rural residents. The newspapers of these states minimized the successes of those who ran away, principally through their collective silence on the subject. Instead, especially in the 1850s, they constantly glorified multiple aspects of slavery. They promoted the institution with, among much other puffery, accounts of slaves who chose their masters over freedom. They presented exceptions to the rule that bondpersons desired their liberty; instead they presented tales of the returned runaways and emancipated slaves to their enslavement as if these isolated instances were the rule.

Late in the antebellum period, the press in St. Louis, with its large German and Irish population and its generally non-slave-owning readers and advertisers, reported the facts of massive slave migration to the North far more accurately and fully than did its rural counterparts. One of these stories, with a Chicago date line, related that 106 fugitive slaves had left that city for Canada on a train. It estimated that over 1,000 former slaves had arrived in Chicago in the previous six months and that most had left following the recent enforcement of the Fugitive Slave Law, which resulted in the arrest of five slaves owned in St. Louis County.[61] This front-page St. Louis newspaper story was an elaboration of the earlier account taken from the *Chicago Journal* of April 8, 1861. Its headlines, "Great Negro Exodus. Flight of Over One Hundred Fugitives from Chicago. The Stampede for Canada. Scenes at the Depot," make clear that the reporting was sympathetic, and the lengthy coverage accurate.

According to the story, four boxcars were chartered from the Michigan Southern Railroad by persons whom the paper never named, presumably because doing so would subject them to criminal penalties under the Fugitive Slave Law. Into these four cars, 106 ex-slaves, their household goods, their clothing, and sufficient provisions for their journey such as crackers, bread, beans, dried beef, dried apples, and barrels of water, were tightly packed. Here was no mythology. Instead, the newspaper confirmed the same information derived from the runaway ads in Missouri newspapers, a subject extensively examined in a later chapter: "The larger proportion of the fugitives were ... men, ... many of them well-dressed.... Some of the party were old, but most of them were young men in their prime, as the class most likely to run the risk of fleeing from slavery. There were a number of young families going to save the children."[62] In keeping with the clandestine nature of the exodus, the newspaper omitted all names of former slaves, their previous residences, and the names of their owners. Such departures of former slaves for Canada were not exceptions to the rule that said most slaves cherished their bondage. Rather, freedom was the prevalent wish, if not the accomplishment, of most bondpersons.

The most convincing evidence that slaves were not made happy creatures by their enslavement is to be found in census information. Though there are no figures available regarding the actual number of persons of color who were slaves in Missouri when the institution was abolished on January 11, 1865, the figures of Missouri's State Auditor from 1860 shows that 114,000 slaves declined to 73,000 in 1863, a reduction of 35 percent.[63] In addition, many events after the beginning of 1863 must have fueled an increase in the number of Missouri slaves who left their masters.

President Lincoln issued the Emancipation Proclamation on January 1, 1863, and it freed all slaves held in most of the Confederacy, a would-be nation which Missouri never joined. On February 24, 1864, the Thirty-Eighth Congress mandated the drafting into the Union Army, and simultaneous freeing, of all able-bodied male persons of color between the ages of 20 and 45. Loyal masters were to be compensated for their former slaves at rates not exceeding $300 per man.[64] On June 28, 1864, this same congress repealed all legislation which required federal authorities to facilitate the return of fugitive slaves to their owners.[65] On October 23, 1864, Confederate General Sterling Price, a former governor of Missouri, lost an important engagement with Union troops in the Battle of Westport, in western Missouri.

Slavery in Missouri was going, going, and when it was finally gone, most likely an additional 40,000 slaves at least had already either run away from their owners during 1863 and 1864 or been freed by joining the Union Army. Fellman describes the Missouri slave owners' position during the war years: "The world was turning upside down. They were losing their property and their means to future wealth; they were losing their traditional control over blacks.... For them ... the top rail was going to the bottom and the bottom rail to the top."[66] Probably fewer than 33,000, mostly women, children, and old men, gained their freedom when Missouri officially ended their enslavement in January 1865. However, as Trexler wrote, "The escape of the slave was a problem in Missouri throughout the whole slavery period."[67] Had the majority of slaves ever actually been content, their owners could have dismissed the departures of the dissatisfied few as good riddance to bad rubbish. Doing so was not possible because those who fled their bondage were not the lame, the halt, and the blind; rather, they were the most financially valuable because they were the most vigorous, the most adventuresome; that is, they were the best and the brightest.

Despite all the propaganda concerning the happy slave, and the frequency with which the clergy, the rural Missouri press, and the owners insisted on just how well off this state's enslaved persons were, the majority of bondpersons never believed this rubbish. Powerful white persons probably convinced themselves that their human property believed what their betters taught them. However, the *Oxford English Dictionary* defines the word "slave" as "One who is the property of, and entirely subject to, another person, whether by capture, purchase, or birth." It is not credible that most persons held in this powerless condition were satisfied.

This is not to suggest that there were no contented slaves in Missouri. Of course there were. However, if one compares the percentage of Arkansas' population which was slave in 1860, 25 percent, with Missouri's 10 percent, it could appear that slaves in Arkansas were more than twice as satisfied as those in this state. Such thinking is arrant nonsense. The difference between these jurisdictions, both originally parts of a single unit of government under the French, the Spanish, and the Americans, was the absence of any free (that is, non-slave) borders in Arkansas and the presence of four free borders in Missouri: Kansas to the west, Nebraska to the northwest, Iowa to the north, and Illinois to the east. In Missouri, slaves had the opportunity to vote with their feet, and thousands left their owners. A run for freedom there was doable in a way that it was not in Arkansas, a state bordered by Texas, Indian Territory, Missouri, Tennessee, Mississippi, and Louisiana, all slave jurisdictions.

The narrative of William Wells Brown offers a valuable insight regarding Missouri's runaway phenomenon. Thanks to the abolitionist Elijah Lovejoy, a newspaper publisher and editor in St. Louis who at one time leased Brown and taught the capable young man to read and write, this former Missouri slave wrote, among much else, his own story about his experiences as the property of white men. He was born in Lexington, Kentucky, between 1814 and 1816, of a slave mother and a white man, a relative of his owner. When Brown was a small boy, his master, Dr. John Young, moved from Kentucky to St. Charles County, Missouri. In 1820 Young represented Montgomery County, then recently formed from St. Charles, in the General Assembly. In 1827, Brown's owner moved to the city of St. Louis, where he repeatedly leased his slave William to various persons, including Lovejoy.

While out and about on errands for his lessees, Brown learned about Canada "as a place where the slave might live, be free, and be protected." Among those he worked for was a trader who bought slaves in St. Louis and transported them by steamboat to New Orleans, where he sold them. William helped prepare them for market. Old men's whiskers were shaved, their grey hairs plucked out of their heads, and their heads blackened. They were also taught how old they were; typically they learned that they were 10 to 15 years younger than their actual ages. To increase their fitness for sale, as Brown described the various slave behaviors: "Some were set to dancing, some to jumping, some to singing, and some to playing cards. This was done to make them appear cheerful and happy."

William knew early that he would run away. His first attempt was in the company of his mother. They purchased "some dried beef, crackers, and cheese." At first they had no guide but the North Star; however, 150 miles east of St. Louis in Illinois, they began traveling by day. Soon thereafter slave hunters captured them and returned them to their masters, collecting a $200 reward which was paid by their different owners. Brown and his mother were returned to Missouri, which he termed "the land of whips, chains, and bibles." She was sold and put on a steamboat, and he last saw her chained to another woman in a gang of 50 or 60 other slaves. Her last words to him were, "Try to get your Liberty."

After Brown's return, Dr. Young sold him to a merchant-tailor in St. Louis who had previously leased him. His new owner never knew that Brown was an unsuccessful runaway, and the tailor eventually sold him to Enoch Price, a steamboat owner and St. Louis resident. Price assessed the likelihood of Brown's running away if employed as a steward on a steamboat. He asked him if he had ever been to a free state, and he replied, "Oh yes.... I have been in Ohio; my master carried me into that state once, but I never like a free state." He convinced Price that it was safe to allow him to travel on steamboats and soon took the opportunity to escape across the Ohio River from Covington, Kentucky, to Cincinnati in 1834. He was between 18 and 20 years old, the age of many runaway males whose flight was featured in Missouri's newspaper ads.

When Brown left the steamboat, he was distrustful of all men. He described his reaction to others: "I had long since made up my mind that I would not trust myself in the hands of any man, white or colored. The slave is brought up to look upon every white man as the enemy to him and his race." Instead, as he related the matter, "I welcomed the sight of my friend,—truly the slave's friend—the North Star," a conspicuous heavenly body near the end of the handle of the Big Dipper, which illiterate slaves could easily locate in the sky of the Northern Hemisphere. Eventually, wondering in Ohio, his cold and hunger became so intense that he approached a white man, who happened to be a "devoted friend of the slave," a Quaker, who fed and sheltered him for nearly two weeks, and bought him a pair of boots. He kept his slave name *William* and adopted the Quaker's name, *Wells Brown*. He eventually reached Cleveland, working first as a waiter in that city and later as a steward on a Lake Erie steamboat. Though he visited Canada several times, he was never a Canadian resident. Between May and December 1842, he helped 69 fugitives cross Lake Erie to Canada. Soon after arriving in the North, he subscribed to William Lloyd Garrison's *The Liberator*.[68] Later he became a regular letter-writer for this newspaper.

His *Narrative of William W. Brown, A Fugitive Slave, Written By Himself* was published in 1847, the same year the Missouri legislature made it a crime to teach a slave to read and write. Its place of publication was Boston, where it went through at least four printings. From its first appearance and through successive editions, *The Liberator* carried favorable reviews of it from other anti-slavery newspapers. Its author became an agent of the Massachusetts Anti-Slavery Society, and Garrison's newspaper faithfully published Brown's New England lecture schedule.[69] Additional editions of Brown's book were published in London beginning in 1849. In 1850 a Dutch translation was published as well.

He married a free black woman, and they were the parents of two daughters, both of whom were educated primarily in France and England, thus avoiding segregated schools. Throughout his life, Brown lectured in both the United States and Europe on the evils of slavery, the institution he knew first hand, primarily in Missouri. Among the famous people of the day whom he knew were Victor Hugo and Alexis de Tocqueville. At the time Brown was received at a soirée given by the de Tocquevilles, the Marquis was the French Minister of Foreign Affairs. Among the many dignitaries he met, however, the one he appeared to hold in the highest esteem was Harriet Beecher Stowe. He first saw her when her husband, Calvin Stowe, spoke at an abolitionist meeting attended by 5,000 in May of 1853 at Exeter Hall in London, a building erected for non-sectarian uses, among them, anti-slavery gatherings.

In a letter to Garrison, Brown wrote, "*Uncle Tom's Cabin* has come down upon the dark abodes of slavery like a morning sunlight," and he described Mrs. Stowe's entrance into Exeter Hall: "Her Grace, the Duchess of Sutherland, came in, and took her seat ... and an half hour after, a greater lady (the authoress of *Uncle Tom*) made her appearance and took her seat by the side of the Duchess."[70] Another famous woman of his day, who became his friend as they frequently shared lecture platforms, was Susan B. Anthony (1820-1906). She was the daughter of a Quaker abolitionist, an abolitionist herself, and one of the mothers of the women's rights movement in this country.

Apart from his first unsuccessful run for freedom, which revealed to his then owner this family's discontent with enslavement, Brown's various lessees and owners believed that he, like other well-behaved bondpersons, was a contented slave. Had he not been adept at outwitting his last owner, the river merchant Enoch Price, he would never have been permitted to travel by steamboat on the Ohio River, the body of water which separated the slave state of Kentucky from the free state of Ohio. Had his owner suspected his slave's intention, his route to freedom and his rewarding life would never have been open to him. Given Brown's status as a slave, honesty was the worst policy when it came to his owners, lessees, and most other whites in Missouri.

As in Brown's case, it was often vital to the slave's well-being that he or she deceive the master. Mark Twain may or may not have written accurately about the slaves he knew as a child in Hannibal when he described them as "content." Though his family's straitened financial conditions made ownership of any great number of bondpersons impossible, one named Jennie, whom his parents brought with them when they moved from Tennessee to Missouri, was later sold because the family could not afford to own her.[71] Twain recalled that as a child he objected to the noise Sandy, a young slave whom the family leased, made with his "singing, whistling, yelling, whooping, and laughing." Sam went to his mother and demanded that she silence him. She replied, "Think, he is sold away from his mother; she is in Maryland a thousand miles from here, and he will never see her again. When he is singing it is a sign he is not remembering and that comforts me. It would break my heart if Sandy should stop singing." His mother's compassionate explanation removed the irritation of the slave's racket, and young Sam Clemens was no longer bothered by it.[72]

The fact remains that Sandy's sounds of jubilation masked a deep distress. Mark

Twain, like other whites in pre-Civil War Missouri, surely at times mistook the appearance of contentment among the slaves he knew for its reality. Their existence was generally made easier insofar as they convinced their masters and mistresses that they were well-satisfied with their lot. When slaves achieved their freedom as runaways, they mostly did so by fooling their owners and convincing these persons of power that *their* slaves were untroubled, well cared-for, and mighty pleased to have such fine "massas."

As the next chapter makes clear, the early records of slavery in the Louisiana Purchase, including those from territorial times in Missouri, contain no mention of the contentment of bondpersons. When the slave states decisively held the balance of power in the federal government and abolitionists were few in number and those few were solo voices, there was no need for a myth that those in bondage were happy. However, as the numbers of free states joining the Union increased and the abolitionist movement became a force to be reckoned with, slaveholders and their admirers began believing their own propaganda. Slavery in Missouri began at a time when all the later nonsense about the institution was unnecessary and absent.

2

The Background of Slavery in Missouri

A slave's long lifetime before the birth of a new nation, human bondage was already well established in what eventually became the state of Missouri. The French were its original white inhabitants, and in 1720 a Frenchman, Philip François Renault, purchased Missouri's first African-Americans in a French colony, St. Domingue (Haiti), and transported them to the southeastern portion of the state to labor in its lead mines.[1] Initially whatever governed the lives of the servile black workforce was entirely generated by the steadfast power, self-interest, and caprice of the miners' white owners.

In New Orleans, the capital of what later became the Louisiana Purchase, some African slaves arrived even earlier; precisely when and in what numbers are unknown. By 1712 there were only 20, but in 1720 and again in 1721, 500 were imported each year. Their number had increased to more than 2,000 by 1724. As early as 1722 Louisiana was inhabited by free blacks, because one, free Negro Raphael, was convicted of stealing, whipped, and jailed.[2]

White persons of power reacted to, among other factors, the unique position of the African-American population in both New Orleans and the French colony's far-flung provinces, including the slave miners in southeastern Missouri. The authorities believed, as Matas noted, that written regulations were needed "to break the spirit of those rebellious Negroes, who remembered all too clearly their days of freedom in Africa."[3] As a result and at the request of his colonial ministers and slave owners, in March 1724, the French king, Louis XV, issued a 55-article document, "Edict Concerning the Negro Slaves in Louisiana," usually known as the "*Code Noir*" or "Black Code." It was published in New Orleans and remained the law for black slaves throughout French rule of Louisiana.[4] Spain acquired the vast territory from France in 1763, but the Spanish never repealed this code. It continued as law for African-Americans until the United States, under President Thomas Jefferson, doubled in size by purchasing Louisiana in 1804.

Because the Black Code remained slave law for the first 80 years of the white man's rule of Missouri, it merits careful inspection. Its first article contains a seemingly unlikely provision requiring that a French edict of 1615 be applied to Louisiana. By it, as Hertzberg explains, Marie de Medici, acting as queen-regent for her son, Louis XIII, had decreed that all Jews were to be expelled from France on grounds that they were "sworn enemies of the Christian religion." Such an edict had behind it the concept that "the state existed to be the servant of the Christian faith."[5] The 1724 law echoed the 1615 edict's language by requiring the expulsion of all Jews, "declared enemies of the Christian name,"[6] from Louisiana within three months, subject to the loss of both their property and lives. Obviously, race was not the Code's only basis for legal discrimination; religious bigotry had long been a potent and a familiar part of the Christian European landscape. That the first concern of French lawgivers was to rid Louisiana of any Jews within its borders was but a manifestation of the virulent anti-Semitism which plagued countries such as France and Spain from an early date. In addition, eliminating present or future Jewish settlement was intimately related to one of the Black Code's prime purposes.

As its Preamble stated, its law and certain rules were promulgated "to maintain ... the discipline of the Catholic Apostolic Roman Church." Article 2 required that all slaves in the province "shall be educated in the Apostolic Roman Catholic religion, and be baptized." Colonist-purchasers of recently imported slaves were required to have them instructed in Roman Catholicism and "baptized within a reasonable time, under pain of an arbitrary fine," (i.e., one that is discretionary and not fixed). Article 3 forbade the practice of any religion other than Catholicism; it required that "those who violate this, shall be punished as rebels." All meetings for practicing any other religion were "unlawful and seditious assemblages, subject to the same penalties inflicted upon the masters who shall permit or suffer it with respect to their slaves." Article 4 required the punishment of any overseer of bondpersons who was not Catholic and the confiscation of his Negroes. Article 11 ordered that the owner bury baptized slaves in consecrated ground, but it required that those who died without being baptized were to be buried at night in a "field adjacent to the place of their decease." Article 5 prohibited all persons, including slaves, from laboring on Sundays and holy days from midnight to midnight "in the culture of the soil ... under penalty of a fine." It also allowed, probably for repeat offenders, discretionary punishment for the masters and forfeiture of their human properties. With one exception — the masters' "privilege of sending their slaves to market"— all labor was required to cease on those days. In other words, the Catholic Apostolic Roman Church as the true and only church underpinned all facets of this 1724 Black Code which regulated the lives of African-Americans, mainly slaves, throughout Louisiana.

Article 6 made the intermarriage of whites and blacks unlawful. It also prohibited both whites and free blacks from "living in a state of concubinage with slaves." When such cohabitations resulted in children, the master who permitted such living arrangements was required to pay a fine of three hundred livres. In addition to the fine, the master was deprived both of his slave(s) and of the children that resulted from the prohibited liaisons. The offspring became the property of an entity known as the Hospital of the District and could never become free. However, if a black man, who was unmarried during his cohabitation with *his* slave, married her "according to the forms prescribed by the church," the code freed her and made her children free and legitimate. This provision, which allowed free black males who owned slaves to free them and their children through marriage, ultimately affected a sizable portion of the population.[7] However, what mattered and applied to the majority of residents was the criminal nature of marriage between white and black, a legal prohibition which commenced under the French in 1724, continued under Spanish and American rule of Missouri, and remained the law in a number of former slave states. Theoretically, no door to freedom opened in French Louisiana for any slave who married a white person and remained in the colony. It was closed, and it would remain slammed shut in Missouri and other slave states throughout the period of American human bondage and beyond.[8]

One route to freedom for slaves under French rule was spelled out in Article 50. Masters who were at least 25 years of age, the age of majority for both French and Spanish colonial males, could free their bondpersons while the master was alive and in health or in "causa mortis," that is, in contemplation of approaching death. The Code noted that "masters are often found sufficiently mercenary to fix the liberty of their slaves at a certain price." As a result, it stated that bondpersons eager to buy their liberty "frequently ... commit theft and robbery." To avoid such criminal behaviors, the law prohibited masters from freeing slaves without prior permission of the Superior Council. This five- to seven-member institution, first created by royal decree in 1712 as the highest law court in French Louisiana, in due course took on both administrative and legislative functions. It became and remained throughout French and early Spanish ownership of Louisiana the colony's governing body.[9] Without the Superior Council's agreement, a "permission ... granted without cost, when the reasons assigned by the master appear legitimate," there was no freedom for the slave.

The only exception to the requirement that the Superior Council's permission be obtained in the freeing of any slave appeared in Article 51. Slaves who were appointed by their masters as "guardians of their children" the code considered "persons affranchised," that is, free. Presumably the word *their* modified the joint offspring of the male master and the female slave. However, the master retained the choice about the appointment of any slaves as the guardians of any of his children. Not surprisingly, under Article 10, "if the father be free and the mother a slave, the offspring shall be slaves likewise."

Several of the code's provisions restricted the ability of the slave to earn money. Article 15 prohibited bondpersons from selling "any sort of commodity, ... fruits, greens, firewood, ... clothes or goods, without express permission from their masters, evidenced by a pass, or well-known marks." Probably the latter was a distinctive master-label on any commodity proffered for sale. Without clear evidence of the master's ownership of the sold item(s), he could reclaim same without restoration of the price to the "thievish receivers." The fine for the unwary purchaser of questionable goods ranged from a low of six livres to a high of 1,500 livres; the latter amount was the largest fine authorized in the code. Article 16 required either the Superior Council or inferior justices to appoint two persons as examiners of the wares and merchandise brought to each market by slaves. The appointees were required to verify that the goods bondpersons offered for sale bore "the letters and marks of their masters." Article 17 allowed "all our subjects ... to seize everything with which they may find said slaves laden when they are without any passes or known marks of the masters." The contraband articles were to be returned to the masters. Article 22 also discouraged the self-employment of any slave. It declared that bondpersons could neither own, transfer, nor will any property. Likewise, they could not be parties to any contract, as Article 22 concluded, because they were members of "a race incapable of transferring and contracting by their own free will."

These anti-commercial and anti-contractual statutes were not in the code to reduce or punish the property crimes of slaves. Other articles, for example 29 and 30, decreed that slaves were not to steal horses, mules, oxen, cows, sheep, goats, swine, poultry, peas, beans, "or other greens and provisions," and they also specified the allowable punishment for any slave(s) convicted of these crimes. The prohibitions against slave entrepreneurship were joined with those of Article 19. It forbade the master from releasing his bondpersons to labor a certain day in the week on their own account. Rather, under Article 18, owners were required to furnish their human chattel with food weekly and clothing annually.

The intent of these prohibitions against the slave as a businessperson seems clear. Industrious bondpersons allowed to labor on their own behalf one day a week could grow more food, weave more cloth, and build more furniture than their family required, sell the surplus, and eventually buy their freedom. As a result, the free black population of French Louisiana would experience an undesirable increase. For persons of color, slavery was the proper condition, the code implied at its every turn.

Article 13 prohibited the gathering together of slaves who belonged to different masters in both the day and nighttime. That the assemblage might be under "the pretense of attending weddings, or otherwise" or "at the abode of their masters, or elsewhere either in the highways or by-places" was irrelevant. Congregating slaves were to be whipped and branded; repeat offenders "may be punished with death." Under Article 14, masters who allowed slave assemblies were fined 30 livres for the first offense and 60 livres for "a repetition thereof." Additionally, owners were required to "repair every damage suffered by their neighbors on account of said gathering."

Though Article 12 prohibited slaves from "wearing of any offensive arms, or heavy clubs," the code did not envision the slave rebellions which later generations of owners so feared. The assembly prohibitions of Articles 13 and 14 were put in place to maintain the peace, not to prevent a slave takeover of the colony. Likewise, this early law contained no prohibitions against bondpersons being taught to read, write, and cipher. At this time the successful revolt of slaves in Haiti in 1791 and the unsuccessful insurrections of Pointe Coupée, Louisiana, in 1791 and 1795 were all in the future. Freedom was not perceived as achievable, during this early period, through open and organized rebellion.

The imagined route to freedom for the French slaves of the 1720s was by running away. The code, often general and vague in its permissible punishments, was specific in its treatment of the apprehended runaway. Under Article 32, the slave who had been absent for one month when taken into custody was punished by having both ears cut off and being branded on one shoulder with the fleur de lis, the ancient symbol of the French monarchy. For a second offense, he "shall be hamstrung and branded with a fleur de lis on the other shoulder." Matas observed that "physicians and surgeons on the Continent ... assist[ed] in the torture of prisoners, [but] the infliction of brutal punishments — which included cutting off hands and ears — was customarily left to the executioner." Doctors were only involved "to keep the prisoner alive until he had confessed."[10] Any surgeon assigned to a district hospital or military post in Louisiana might have helped torture captured fugitives, thereby aiding the authorities' efforts to foil runaway plots. As for actual lopping of bondpersons' ears and apparently slicing their tendons, thereby disabling the fugitives, these grisly tasks were left to the public hangman, usually a black prisoner on probation. Despite these lurid punishments and the likely ancillary torture of runaway offenders, the code specified that the third offense of running away was punished with death. The third time he/she made another runaway attempt, a disfigured, branded, and crawling slave made yet another try for freedom.

To speed up the punishment of repeat offenders, Article 33 allowed ordinary judges to pass sentences of hamstringing and death on runaways "without it being necessary for such judgments to be confirmed by the superior council." Under Article 26 all other crimes of which slaves were found guilty, including a number that also involved death sentences, could be appealed to the Superior Council. For the French and later the Spanish colonials, the frequency with which slaves committed the crime of *marronnage*, i.e., running from the service of their masters, was a seemingly insoluble problem. As Kerr describes the escaped slave or *marron*, he ran from his owner's plantation to the swamps and forests where he lived as a fugitive, sometimes in bands, sometimes alone. Ultimately the runaways' best chance for living as free persons was by hiding in the swamps surrounding New Orleans and supporting themselves by killing game and stealing crops, stock, or any other commodities. Such modes of survival discomforted New Orleans' general population.[11] All things considered, the matter of decreasing, if not halting, the multitude of slaves who fled the service of their masters was too urgent to waste time with an appeal. Likewise, apprehending escaped bondpersons was open to any individual owner or his hiree. Article 35 stated, "We freely permit our subjects ... who shall have runaway slaves in any place whatsoever, to institute a search ... in such manner as they deem proper, or to make such search themselves as shall seem best."

Article 34 dealt with those persons who assisted escaping runaways. It assumed that those who aided and abetted fugitive slaves were primarily free blacks. The code decreed that "Negroes, freeborn or manumitted [freed] who shall harbor in their dwellings fugitive slaves, shall be sentenced to bodily service for the master in a fine of thirty livres for each day of such harboring." Negroes unable to pay this sizable fine were to be "reduced to slavery and sold; and if the proceeds of the sale exceed the fine, the surplus shall be given over to the hospital." This article also assessed a fine of ten livres upon "other free persons who shall have afforded [fugitive slaves] such a refuge." The precise identity of these "other free persons" is unclear; perhaps they were *white* servants whose skin color made them ineligible for enslavement but for whom a ten-livre fine was immense. Clearly the slave owners for whose benefit the 1724 Black Code was written had no fear of latter-day abolitionists. Their audacious and meddling ways were to plague future generations of slave owners, not Louisiana's French colonists.

Finally, a provision spared the master any financial loss when his slave was condemned to death upon the victim-owner's accusation, either because he was a thrice-captured runaway or because he had committed another capital offense against his owner. For example, under Article 17 the slave who struck "its master, mistress, the husband of its mistress, or their children, so as to bruise, draw blood, or upon the face, shall be punished with death." Under these circumstances, Article 36 required that, prior to execution, the condemned slave be appraised "by two respectable inhabitants, to be nominated for that duty by the judge, and the amount of the appraisement shall be paid [to the owner]." The Superior Council provided for the appraised amount of the condemned bondperson by fixing a "tax upon the head of every negro," a tax mostly paid by slave owners, but nothing in the code limited this source of revenue to enslaved persons. Presumably free blacks also contributed their share to compensate slaveholders when the gallows or another contrivance of death deprived them of their bondperson(s). The 1724 Code established a seeming win-win situation for French colonial slave owners or other colonial masters who might inhabit the territory.

At some point in their rule of Louisiana, the French began enslaving American Indians. As early as 1721, a census for New Orleans showed 51 Indian slaves, although by 1736 they numbered only 26.[12] Eventually, Louisiana's next white owners, the Spanish, decided that the ownership of indigenous people was not in accord with the pious laws of Spain and gradually abandoned the practice. As a part of phasing out Indian bondage, the Spanish required the enumeration of all enslaved Indians in Missouri. These censuses are preserved from St. Louis and Ste. Genevieve, dated respectively May 28 and July 12, 1770. They show that most owned Indians were women, children and infants; 28 in Ste. Genevieve and 66 in St. Louis.[13] Though this form of bondage had fallen into desuetude by the 1770s, the Supreme Court of Missouri ruled on the lawfulness of Indian slavery as late as 1838.

French rule of Louisiana ended as a result of the European Seven Years' War, a military campaign known in America as the French and Indian Wars. This conflict concluded when France, Great Britain, and Spain all signed the Treaty of Paris in 1763. Under the terms of this document, France lost her North American possessions: she ceded territory east of the Mississippi River to England, and that west of the river to Spain, including the present states of Louisiana, Arkansas, and Missouri.

However, power changed hands slowly. The first Spanish governor came to Louisiana in 1766, and not until 1769 did the implementation of Spanish law truly begin, shortly after the arrival of Governor-General Alejandro O'Reilly, an Irishman in the employ of the Spanish government. Once more a change of ownership occurred when, after more than 40 years of Spanish rule of Louisiana, Spain retroceded the territory to France in 1803, the year of the Louisiana Purchase. However, the Spanish continued to govern until the purchase was concluded, and her colonial law remained in place for the first seven months of American ownership of the land. Neither O'Reilly nor any of his successors repealed the 1724 "Edict Concerning the Negro Slaves in Louisiana." Actually, O'Reilly required that it be translated into Spanish and "observed with exactitude."[14] The code went hand-in-glove with slave control by Spanish Catholic owners as it had earlier met the convenience and power requirements of French Catholic masters.

Not surprisingly, O'Reilly supplemented the 1724 "Edict Concerning the Negro Slaves in Louisiana" with his own substantive and procedural ordinances and instructions for the governance of the Louisiana Territory. Though he abolished the Superior Council, the governing bodies which he put in its place, including the *Cabildo*, or city council, were not democratic institutions. Their particulars have been explained elsewhere[15]; of chief importance, Spanish rule continued the appointment of all officials and the absence of elections and jury trials. As one might expect, Spanish rule neither relaxed the harsh rules for slaves nor disestablished the official religion of the French. In fact, O'Reilly's "Ordinances and Instructions,"[16] in name if not in observance, strengthened the already strong grip of Catholicism. Under Section I, "new converts to our holy faith" were ineligible for appointment to any governing office. Section V (1), "Of Punishments," began, "He who shall revile our Savior, or his mother, the most holy Virgin Mary, shall have his tongue cut out, and his property confiscated." Another of the punishment provisions (9) decreed, "he who shall be guilty of fornication ... with a professed nun ... shall be punished with death." Yet another (15) provided, "He who shall steal the sacred vessels in a holy place shall suffer death." The Irish Governor-General who ruled Louisiana for the Spanish did so in the name of the Church Militant.

O'Reilly gave to an ancient Spanish religious order, the brothers of the Santo Hermandad, authority concerning fugitive slaves in Louisiana Territory. The *hermandades*, as Henry Charles Lea noted, can be documented in Spain as early as 1282. They were, in his words, "brotherhoods or associations for the maintenance of public peace and private rights," and they carried out their policing roles during the heyday of the Spanish Inquisition and beyond.[17] Though the order's primary responsibility in Spain and in Spanish Louisiana was peacekeeping, as the "Ordinances and Instructions" explained, "the brothers of the St. Hermandad shall have the right of arresting, either within or without the city, all runaway negroes" (Section III, 9). When we link the duties concerning fugitive slaves which O'Reilly gave to the Hermandad to the numerous persons the Code Noir charged with apprehending runaways, it seems that most white males had some responsibility to halt the endless flight of yet another and another absconding slave.

The losses which slave owners suffered when runaways managed to escape were clearly extensive. In fact they were so great that, in 1773, the city council (Cabildo) of New Orleans began compensating owners whose slaves were killed in attempting to escape the service of their masters. These financial arrangements continued throughout Spanish rule of Louisiana. Kerr writes that "Petitions to the Cabildo for payment of compensation for slaves shot while escaping ... are numerous.... Countless fugitive slaves were killed in pursuit with no written record of their deaths ever occurring."[18] Arnold, an authority on colonial Arkansas under the Spanish, adds: "The slaves of the Arkansas unfortunately led virtually unrecorded lives, except for an occasional lamentation in a letter complaining of their having run away."[19]

The lives of blacks who were, at least briefly if not permanently, no longer bondpersons during Spain's rule of Louisiana can best be analyzed through the prism of the multiple Spanish criminal records which Kerr compiled and translated into English.[20] Though he includes at least 300 criminal cases, those discussed herein concern only the colony's freed, rebellious, and runaway African-Americans. The sheer number of cases dealing with these people speaks volumes about the inability of whites to either prevent an increase in the free Negro population or halt the large numbers of bondpersons from at least attempting to end their servitude. Many of these would be civil cases today.

The smallest group concerns non-slave defendants charged with either taking slaves from white owners or assisting their departure from their masters. In 1771, in Ste. Genevieve District, Chickasaw Indians were charged with the theft of an unspecified number of slaves. Most likely the bondpersons merely changed masters: many Indians owned slaves themselves. Indeed, the Chickasaws were among the tribes, as Abel noted, "anxious to join the southern Confederacy"[21] in the early stages of the Civil War, some 90 years after the Ste. Genevieve early record. Other accused (1786, 1793, 1795, and 1798) were charged with inciting slaves to flee, or harboring a fugitive slave, or encouraging slaves to rebel, or receiving them illegally. The defendants, two of whom were free mulattoes, were all persons with French or Spanish Christian and surnames, and their punishments ranged from a high of four years in prison, through exile from the colony, to a dismissal of charges upon the payment of court costs. That only five of Spanish Louisiana's approximately 300 colonial cases concern outsiders either taking the enslaved from their owners or assisting the bondpersons' quest for freedom demonstrates the insignificance of any abolitionist movement at this time and place.

The number of alleged crimes by free male persons of color under Spanish colonial rule is a large one. Many were charged with theft of items, including clothes, flour, hens, potatoes, a pirogue (dugout canoe), small amounts of money, and documents; in the document case the defendant was freed from charges and released. Assault, gambling, receiving stolen goods (pots), slander, abuse of a white man in a bulletin, sedition, and libel make up the bulk of the other offenses which persons described as free Negro, free mulatto, and free pardo (brown or dark) were charged with committing. Of interest in these many charges is that any matter in a bulletin would be in writing. In addition, the crime of *libel* (Latin for little book) always involved a *written* defamation. Further, sedition ranged from speaking to *publishing* words which excited discontent and contempt for the government. Therefore, it seems clear that no Spanish colonial laws made it a crime to teach persons of color to read and to write. The white authorities had not yet linked black literacy with black rebellion. None of these cases concerning free male persons of color were capital offenses; most were not crimes against persons. When physical force was alleged to have been used, usually the crime was assault: one case involved a free mulatto, Juan Weit, hitting another free mulatto overseer, Constanzio Tardif, because the defendant refused to work with slaves. When Jorge Felipo, a free Negro, beat up Lorenzo LaFontaine, a fiddle player, employed at Coquet's dance hall, the fine involved only damages for loss of wages. These records indicate that free males of color were not a criminal class especially to be feared. Free male persons of color as victims of crime involved several offenses at the hands of slaves, among them theft and assault. When Manuel Chovas had paid his owner the agreed sum for his freedom but was refused his liberty, the court found in favor of the ex-slave. Chovas was freed, and his former owner was required to pay court costs.

Free female persons of color appeared in these records almost as frequently as their male counterparts. The only capital case involving a freed woman concerns a quadroon (the offspring of a black grandparent, a white and a mulatto parent), Maria Glass. She and her husband, John Glass, a British Army deserter, were found guilty of the murder of a white child, Maria Elena, and both were hanged for the homicide. Otherwise, free women of color were arrested for essentially the same crimes as the men. One, Pelecy, free Negress, was charged with the theft of a small amount of money and found not guilty. Another, Ursula Bernarda, free Negress, was convicted of the theft of silverware and sent to prison for two years. One free mulatta, Marta Delille, was found guilty of selling contraband cloth goods and sentenced to pay court costs. The free mulatta Modeste Morales was charged with the illegal sale of liquor to slaves. Several free women were apprehended for assault; in three of these cases, both the perpetrator and the victim were persons of color. Slander was the crime charged when parties, among other matters, disagreed regarding the costs of furniture or a house. One free Negress, Juliana, was taken into custody after resisting arrest in a dispute with a tavern owner. She was jailed for 15 days and ordered to pay court costs. Other cases involved free females of color as victims. One woman, as had Manuel Chovas, petitioned the court for her freedom on grounds that she had made payment to her owner. She lost her case and was sentenced to silence on the subject. Another, Magdalene, was murdered by her ex-lover, Pedro de la Cabanne, a carpenter. The outcome of this case is unknown. Theft, slander, and assault were the crimes also committed against free women of color. One 1795 case was referred to the Supreme Council of War. In it the mulatta Catalina Durand charged that three soldiers, members of the Louisiana Regiment, had stolen two handkerchiefs from her.

As with the free male persons of color, except for one free woman as the perpetrator of murder and another as a victim of this crime, contemporary records show that the general population had little to fear from free women of color under Spanish rule. The relatively mild punishments meted out to them as perpetrators and the equally insignificant punishments of fines, court costs, and medical expenses, which were given to most of the perpetrators against them, make clear that free persons of color, both men and women, were not the chief concern of the Spanish under their rule of Louisiana.

Slaves who joined in rebellion or even planned to join in insurrection against their owners were a wholly different matter to the Spanish authorities; these bondpersons received the most severe punishment. In 1791, 16 slaves were sent to New Orleans from Pointe Coupée, Louisiana, for trial on charges that they were rebellious; their fate is unknown. Four years later and from this same area — a place where slaves greatly outnumbered their white owners — at least 60 were taken into custody on word of a plot involving an uprising set for the first Friday after Easter. Many more were imprisoned and executed for this abortive rebellion than for any other criminal act during the 1766–1803 Spanish rule of Louisiana Territory. At least 23 bondpersons were hanged, 22 received 10 years at hard labor, and 9 received 5 years. This event has been discussed in detail elsewhere.[22]

The severity of Spanish law can be seen most clearly when the subjects of the punishments were fugitive slaves. As with the Missouri bondpersons under American rule who fled the service of their masters, most of the runaways under Spanish rule were men. One woman fared extremely well: the charges against Margarita were dismissed; she had emancipation papers. Another woman, Maria, slave of a widow, ran away with the Indian Gabriel; the outcome of this case is unknown. One case involving numerous fugitives began in 1781 and continued into 1783. The defendants' crime against property involved the theft of some cows, but more importantly, they were runaways. Nine were hanged; six were branded with the letter *M* (for *marron* or runaway slave); others received punishments of either 200 or 300 lashes. In another case which dates from 1786, a fugitive, Carlos, was given 200 lashes, put in solitary confinement, and placed in irons for two years. He had stolen five handkerchiefs from a merchant. When six runaways, four men and two women, were taken into custody and charged with robbery and assault with intent to kill, two of the men were hanged and two received 200 lashes and were returned to their masters in irons. The women were merely whipped 200 times and returned to their masters. One slave who had murdered his master, a planter, escaped the harsh fate awaiting him when he was taken into custody by committing suicide. Another slave, Fam, was killed while escaping. The known outcomes of cases involving rebellious and runaway slaves record not only the most pitiless and unusual punishments of the many preserved criminal records from Spanish rule of Louisiana Territory; these penalties were also the most unchristian.

If any resident of Louisiana under either French or Spanish rule of the colony believed slavery was reprehensible, no written record of this sentiment survives. There was, however, Continental French criticism of human bondage. It was general, indirect, satirical, and muted during the *ancien régime*, a time when the country's absolute monarchy profited from both the slave trade and the use of slave labor. Imprisonment was the Crown's remedy for writers who expressed opinions displeasing to the state. Nonetheless, one such thinker, Charles Montesquieu (1689–1775), wrote of slavery in his influential *Spirit of Laws*, 1748:

> Slavery ... is the establishment of a right which gives to one man such a power over another as renders him absolute master of his life and fortune. The state of slavery is in its own nature bad. It is neither useful to the master nor to the slave: Not to the slave, because he can do nothing through a motive of virtue, nor to the master, because by having an unlimited authority over his slaves he insensibly accustoms himself to the want of all moral virtues, and thence becomes fierce, nasty, severe, choleric, voluptuous, and cruel.[23]

In 1726 Voltaire (1694–1778) served time in the Bastille for his outspokenness. When he wrote *Candide* (1759), he used satiric humor to attack, among much else, the method of punishing runaway slaves in colonial locales such as French Louisiana. He exaggerates its already great cruelty and sets the scene, not in any French possession, but in Surinam, a Dutch colony in northeast South America where, between 1675 and 1863, approximately 325,000 slaves were imported from Africa to raise, among other crops, sugar.[24] The traveler, Candide, speaks in Dutch to a Negro who is missing a left leg and a right hand and asks him, "What are you doing ... in that horrible state I see you in?" The slave responds, "When we work in the sugar mills and we catch our finger in the millstone, they cut off our hand; when we try to run away, they cut off a leg; both things have happened to me. It is at this price that you eat sugar in Europe."[25]

Sugar growers in the Americas were not confined to Dutch, French, and Spanish slave drivers. The British imported bondpersons to work in North America more than 100 years before the French began their rule of Louisiana. In 1619, the first bondpersons were brought from Africa to labor on the farms and plantations in the English colony of Virginia. From Virginia, slavery spread to other southern British colonies such as the Carolinas and Georgia, places where the climate suited the raising of sugar, tobacco, rice, and eventually cotton — all labor-intensive crops.

Almost 80 years after the English began their importations of African bondpersons to what became the United States, in 1688 Mennonites in Germantown, Pennsylvania, signed the first known written denunciation of slavery published on American soil. Protestors against human bondage in the American British colonies were less fearful of the more diffuse authority of the British Crown and thus more direct in their condemnation of slavery than their French counterparts. A small religious group, the Mennonites had suffered at the hands of the Turks in what is now Germany, then a part of the Hapsburgs' Austrian empire. Their petition read in part:

> How fearful and fainthearted are many on sea, when they see a strange vessel — being afraid it should be a Turk, and they should be taken, and sold for slaves into Turkey. Now what is this better done, as Turks doe? Yea, rather is it worse for them, which say they are Christians.... There is a saying, that we shall doe to all men like as we will be done ourselves; making no difference of what generation, descent or color they are [3].[26]

Other voices of protest followed; all of the early ones were rooted in religious objections to one person owning another. The Puritan Samuel Sewall (1652–1730) had been one of the judges at the Salem witch trials in 1692, which resulted in the hanging of 19 innocent people. He repented his role in these trials, and in 1700 he denounced slavery in the pamphlet "The Selling of Joseph: A Memorial." In it he wrote:

> The numerousness of Slaves at this Day in the Province, and the Uneasiness of them under their Slavery, hath put many upon thinking whether the Foundation of it be firmly and well laid.... It is most certain that all Men, as they are the Sons of Adam, are Co-heirs, and have equal Right unto Liberty, and all other outward Comforts of life.... Joseph was rightfully no more a Slave to his Brethren, than they were to him; and they had no more Authority to Sell him, than they had to Slay him [10–11].

Like the Mennonites in Germany, the Quakers (the Society of Friends) broke with the established church in England; both sects came to the United States in search of religious freedom. However, many Friends in America subsequently profited from the slave trade, as merchants and ship owners. Following a considerable period of disagreement among them regarding the righteousness of slavery, in 1754 John Woolman (1720–72), a Quaker New Jersey tailor, wrote "Some Considerations on the Keeping of Negroes." In it he stated:

> If I purchase a Man who hath never forfeited his Liberty, the natural Right of Freedom is in him; and shall I keep him and his Posterity in Servitude and Ignorance? How should I approve of this Conduct, were I in his Circumstances, and he in mine?... To seek a Remedy by continuing the Oppression, because we have Power to do it, and see others do it, will, I apprehend, not be doing as we would be done by [74].

The year before France officially relinquished ownership of Louisiana to Spain, a Quaker schoolmaster from Philadelphia, Anthony Benezet (1713–84), published his

"Pamphlet on Negroes in Africa" (1762). In it he continued the early abolitionist emphasis that Christians should treat others as they would wish to be treated:

> Our blessed Redeemer has enjoined us to do unto others as we would they should do unto us.... If they seldom complain of the unjust and cruel Usage they have received, in being forced from their native Country, it is not to be wondered at; as it is a considerable time after their Arrival amongst us before they can speak our Language, and, by the Time they are able to express themselves, they cannot but observe, from the Behavior of the Whites, that little or no Notice would be taken of their Complaints [89–91].

Benezet continued his crusade to end slavery, both within the Quaker community and outside it, through such writings as "An Account of Guinea" (1771), dealing with that part of Africa from which Africans were sold and carried into slavery. In his "Account," he observed that "instead of making slaves of the Negroes, the nations who assume the name and character of Christians, would use their endeavors to make the nations of Africa acquainted with the nature of the Christian religion" (163). Benezet's abolitionist writings continued throughout his life; they included his correspondence with people like John Wesley, the English founder of the Methodist Church. In 1774 Benezet wrote Wesley that the "Laws of Virginia ... [among other colonies] tend ... to promote a murderous disposition in the Masters towards their poor slaves; quite abhorrent of that universal brotherhood so strongly enjoined by the Gospel. These worse than Savage-laws, the slave-holders apprehend necessary for their safety, and to keep their Slaves in awe" (315). In due course, Upper Louisiana[27] would adopt Virginia's slave code in its entirety.

In 1773 in New Haven, Connecticut, two months after the Boston Tea Party, two ministers, Ebenezer Baldwin and Jonathan Edwards Jr., son of the famous preacher and writer, began a series of essays on slavery. They wrote in "Some Observations upon the Slavery of Negroes":

> Has it not a[n] ... appearance of inconsistence, to make a loud outcry against the British parliament for making laws to oblige us to pay certain duties, which amount to but a mere trifle for each individual; when we are deeply engaged in reducing a large body of people to complete and perpetual slavery? If it be lawful and right for us to reduce the Africans to a state of slavery, why is it not as right for Great Britain, France or Spain, not merely to exact duties of us; but to reduce us to the same state of slavery, to which we have reduced them? [294].

Among the descendants of Jonathan Edwards Jr. was Theodore Weld (1803–95), a man who eventually had an enormous influence on, among many others, the best-known abolitionist ever incarcerated in the Missouri State Penitentiary. Weld and his convict-disciple, George Thompson, were nineteenth-century opponents of slavery.

In the late eighteenth century as in earlier times, many abolitionists were ministers or former judges, whose torrents of words were little more than voices crying in the wilderness. However, not all who detested slavery and wrote about their detestation of it were outside the mainstream of colonial politics. On the eve of the American Revolution, the Philadelphia physician and signer of the Declaration of Independence,

Benjamin Rush (1745?–1813), wrote "An Address to the Inhabitants of the British Settlements in America upon Slave-Keeping" (1773). In it he insisted:

> Christianity will never be propagated by any other methods than those employed by Christ and his Apostles. Slavery is an engine as little fitted for that purpose as Fire or the Sword. A Christian Slave is a contradiction in terms.... In many places Sunday is appropriated to work for themselves. Reading and writing are discouraged among them.... Husbands have been forced to prostitute their wives, and mothers their daughters, to gratify the brutal lust of a master. This — all — this is practiced — Blush, ye impure and hardened monsters, while I repeat it — by men who call themselves Christians! [228].

Other prominent persons shared Benjamin Rush's opinion of slavery. Benjamin Franklin, Alexander Hamilton, John Jay, and Gouverneur Morris were all opposed to it. Starting with Vermont (1777) and New Hampshire (1779), the state constitutions of some jurisdictions ended the institution. Massachusetts, in a state Supreme Court decision, abolished it in 1783. The legislatures of Pennsylvania (1780) and Rhode Island (1784) passed statutes which outlawed it. Connecticut (1784) passed a gradual emancipation plan. As Ellis writes after listing these Northern places which ended slavery, "Abolition in the North was more a question of when than whether."[28] To these non-slave former colonies should be added New York and New Jersey: both states passed legislation that emancipated most slaves between 1804 and 1827.[29]

However, the 13 colonies that united to fight and defeat the British during the eight-year struggle to win independence (1775–1783) included jurisdictions wherein slavery had and would retain a strong hold. It is unimaginable that without the active participation of patriots from Delaware, Georgia, Maryland, North Carolina, South Carolina, and Virginia — all well-established places of slavery — the American Revolution would have ended in the defeat of the British. The undisputed leader of the colonial troops was George Washington (1732–1799), himself among the most prominent of Virginia's slaveholders. Patrick Henry (1736–1799), another of Virginia's great patriots and the owner of 67 slaves at his death, asked in his famous speech of 1775 before the Virginia Convention, "Is Life so dear or peace so sweet as to be purchased at the price of chains and slavery? Forbid it, Almighty God. I know not what course others may take but as for me, give me liberty or give me death." At first blush these words could be ascribed to one who detested slavery. However, in 1773, Henry responded to the antislavery argument of the Quaker Robert Pleasants, "Would any one believe that I am master of slaves, of my own purchase: I am drawn along by the general inconveniency of living without them."[30] The great eighteenth-century English moralist and writer Samuel Johnson understood well that persons such as Patrick Henry, so vocal in their insistence on their own freedom, were accomplished at denying it to others. Dr. Johnson's pithy remarks in 1777 on slaveholding American patriots capture this paradox: "How is it that we hear the loudest yelps for liberty among the drivers of negroes?" Johnson continued his opposition to slavery by observing, "An individual may, indeed, forfeit his liberty by a crime; but he cannot by that crime forfeit the liberty of his children.... No man is by nature the property of another."[31]

To be sure, among the colonists who fought for American independence were those who endorsed Samuel Johnson's views on the owning of slaves, but many Americans wholeheartedly embraced human bondage. The 13 colonies were held together between 1777 and 1789 by the Articles of Confederation. Though this document, like the U.S. Constitution which superseded it, contained no mention of slavery, the "peculiar institution" was well protected within it. Among the Articles' provisions was, "The free inhabitants of each State ... shall be entitled to all privileges and immunities of free citizens in the several States" (Art. 4, sec. 1). The implied converse was clear: slave inhabitants of each state were entitled to neither privileges nor immunities in any state. As in Louisiana's "Black Code" (1724–1804), the legislatures of the southern colonies made the slave's act of running away from the service of his/her owner a crime. The Articles provided, "If any person guilty of, or charged with [a] ... felony, or other high misdemeanor in any State, shall flee from justice, and be found in any of the United States, he shall, upon demand of the governor ... from which he fled, be delivered up, and removed to the State having jurisdiction of his offence" (Art. 4, sec. 2). Though this language lacks the specificity of Article IV, section 3 of the U. S. Constitution and subsequent fugitive-slave enactments of the U.S. Congress, it emphatically included the required return of any runaway slave found in another jurisdiction.

A third aspect of the Articles applied to, among much else, the elaborate slave codes of the Southern states. It read: "Full faith and credit shall be given, in each of these States, to the records, acts, and judicial proceedings of the courts and magistrates of every other State" (Art. 4, sec. 3). With only minute changes in language, this provision became a part of the U.S. Constitution, and a part of it which protected slavery. The word *white* appeared only once, in this context: the land forces which each state was required to contribute to the United States were to be "in proportion to the number of *white* inhabitants in such state"(Art. 9, sec. 5; italics added).[32] Otherwise, one would never know from reading this seminal document that there was more than one race in any state. All reference to the already contentious issue of slavery, even the most remote, was omitted in the Articles of Confederation, a document which was finally ratified by all 13 states on July 9, 1778.

Under its authority, the Continental Congress (1774–1789) governed the United States. Among the delegates' accomplishments were deciding on the author of the Declaration of Independence, raising armies, prosecuting the Revolutionary War to a successful conclusion, and agreeing to the terms of the Treaty of Paris in 1783, the official paper which ended the conflict. As Fehrenbacher's exhaustive research shows, the Confederation Congress approved a clause in the peace treaty with England which provided that the withdrawal of British forces from the United States was to take place without "carrying away any negroes or other property of the American inhabitants." He writes of it "Thus, almost casually, in the founding document that confirmed American independence, Negro slaves were recognized as property by the United States government.... From 1783 onward, Congress repeatedly instructed its diplomatic emissaries abroad to seek satisfaction for the thousands of slaves carried off in disregard of the treaty."[33] From the start of the new nation, America's slave interests were center stage front.

In addition to its responsibilities regarding independence, war, and peace, the Continental Congress acted under the authority of the Articles of Confederation to pass

2. The Background of Slavery in Missouri

the Ordinance of 1787. This important legislation established the Northwest Territory. Among other things, it settled the ownership question regarding the four states, Virginia, New York, Massachusetts, and Connecticut, which held territory in the lands that now make up the present states of Ohio, Indiana, Illinois, Michigan, Wisconsin, and part of Minnesota. It required that these four eastern colonies cede their western lands to the federal government. It also established a form of territorial government by which subsequent Western territories, including Missouri, were created and later admitted to the Union as states. Most importantly for purposes of this book, on the motion of a member of the Continental Congress from Massachusetts, Nathan Dane,[34] the Ordinance prohibited slavery in the Northwest Territory. Equally importantly, to assure the law's approval by Southern slave interests, Dane amended the law to allow slaveholders to capture their human property who escaped into the Northwest Territory. Article 6 reads:

> There shall be neither slavery nor involuntary servitude in the said territory, otherwise than in punishment of crimes whereof the party shall have been duly convicted: Provided always, that any person escaping to the same, from whom labor or service is lawfully claimed in any one of the original states, such fugitive may be lawfully reclaimed and conveyed to the person claiming his or her labor or service as aforesaid.[35]

When the delegates from the 13 nascent states that passed the Northwest Ordinance met in Philadelphia during the summer of 1787, their announced intentions were to amend the Articles of Confederation. After slightly more than 10 years under the articles' limitations, it was clear that changes must be made in the country's method of ruling itself. The central government had little authority; Congress was dependent on the states for its funds; unanimous rule among all 13 states made impossible the passage of any act desired by 12 of the 13; and the conduct of foreign affairs was severely hampered by the government's inability, among much else, to enforce treaty obligations.

During the meetings of 55 convention delegates who attended at one time or another between May and September of 1787, it became obvious that the Articles of Confederation were inherently flawed and a new governing document must replace them. It was equally apparent that the problems which slavery had already created between those who favored and those who opposed it could not be settled that long hot summer. Bowen wrote, "No delegate had come to Philadelphia hoping for anything so drastic as to outlaw slavery from the United States, even those who hated it most.... It was the business of delegates to create a Constitution for the country as it existed."[36]

With slavery on the agenda as a matter to be settled among the delegates, there could never have been a governing document which all 13 colonies endorsed. We the People of the United States would never have written and ultimately agreed to be ruled by the Constitution of the United States. It not only governed the 13 states which *formed* the union, it also decided the rules for the many which subsequently *joined* it. The unity and its corollary, the strength, of the country, were the objectives of these delegates. In order to achieve both, as in the earlier Articles of Confederation, the word *slavery* never appears in the U.S. Constitution drafted at Philadelphia in 1787 nor in any of the first 10 amendments, the Bill of Rights, which became a part of it in 1791. The convention delegates danced around this taboo subject as they gingerly accommodated the slave and non-slave interests at stake. Whenever the unmentionable was discussed and made its way into the Constitution, the fingerprints of compromise are everywhere apparent. Wiecek maintains that the Constitution supported slavery in no less than ten clauses;[37] but all of this support was stated indirectly.

The first non-mention of slavery is probably the most infamous. It occurred early in the document, and it dealt with counting, by adding "to the whole Number of free Persons, including those bound to Service for a Term of Years, and excluding Indians not taxed, three fifths of all other Persons" (Art. I, sec. 3). This new arithmetic was agreed to, not as a way of saying that African-Americans were only worth 60 percent of white persons, but as a means of partially increasing both the number of electors for president and members of the U.S. House of Representatives from the slave states. The Southern states wanted their burgeoning slave populations counted as whole persons for purposes of increasing the numbers of their congressmen and presidential electors. The Northern states wanted slaves excluded from this count. The compromise between these seemingly irreconcilable positions divided each slave into five portions and allowed the South to count three of the slave's portions as a whole person. By doing so the Southern states gained both members in the Congress and electors for president, but not nearly as many as had slaves been counted as whole persons.

The second non-mention of slavery occurred as a curb on the legislative branch. It required that "The Migration or Importation of Such Persons as any of the States now existing shall think proper to admit, shall not be prohibited by the Congress prior to the Year one thousand eight hundred and eight" (Art. 1, sec 9). This circumlocution refers to the slave trade. Northern delegates would have ended American importation of bondpersons effective immediately. Southern delegates would have left the matter to the states. The Constitution allowed any binding decisions regarding the importation of slaves to be postponed at least 20 years. As Fehrenbacher notes of this clause, it "implicitly confirmed federal regulatory power while explicitly suspending it until 1808."[38]

When the delegates agreed that "Full Faith and Credit shall be given in each State to the public Acts, Records, and judicial Proceedings of every other State" (Art. IV, sec. 1), slavery was not only being left to the states, as indeed it had been in the Articles of Confederation, it was also being recognized as a viable institution by all the states. On the plus side, the delegates achieved another source of unity among the states. On the minus, the roots, trunk, and branches of slavery were once more validated in the supreme law of the land.

Another clause of Article IV had first appeared in the Ordinance of 1787. When the Second Continental Congress prohibited involuntary servitude in the Northwest Territory, it also allowed slave owners to capture their human properties who had fled there and return them to their houses of bondage. The U.S. Constitution explicitly affirmed the same benefits. It reads, "No Person held to Service or labor in one State, under the Laws thereof, escaping into another, shall, in consequence of any Law or Regulation therein, be discharged from such Service or labor, but shall be delivered up on Claim of the Party to whom such Service or labor may be due" (Art. IV, sec. 3). It could be argued, if only feebly, that not only would enslaved African-Americans be returned to their owners under this provision, but white indentured servants would also find no refuge in the non-slave states.

Abolitionists such as William Lloyd Garrison fulminated against the U.S. Constitution as "the devil's pact" and exclaimed, "What a travesty on the mathematics of justice to announce excitedly that two and two make six, to argue a bit about it, and then to shake hands on the number five."[39] Ellis writes of the matter, "The circumlocutions required to place a chronological limit on the slave trade or to count slaves as three-fifths of a person for purposes of representation in the House, all without ever using the forbidden word, capture the intentionally elusive ethos of the Constitution." He continues, "The underlying reason for this calculated orchestration of non-commitment was obvious: Any clear resolution of the slavery question one way or the other rendered ratification of the Constitution virtually impossible."[40] Finkelman comments of the Southern convention delegates, "The limited nature of federal power and the cumbersome amendment process guaranteed that as long as they remained in the Union, their system of labor and race relations would remain free from national interference. On every issue at the Convention, slave owners had won major concessions from the rest of the nation."[41]

One of the most important slave owners, Thomas Jefferson (1743–1826), was absent from the Constitutional Convention. He had succeeded Benjamin Franklin as the American minister to France in 1785 and remained in Paris through 1789. Nonetheless, his importance to the birth of a new nation cannot be underestimated. If he had only penned the Declaration of Independence, his place in the pantheon of great Americans would probably be secure. In this mighty document, he wrote, "We hold these truths to be self-evident; that all men are created equal; that they are endowed by their creator with certain unalienable rights, that among these are life, liberty, and the pursuit of happiness."

Did Jefferson think that slaves were equal to their owners? No. That proposition waited for presidential belief until Abraham Lincoln enunciated it. Paradoxically, when Jefferson was a member of the Continental Congress, he introduced legislation in 1784 which would have prohibited slavery after 1800 in all the western territories; however, it failed to receive the necessary votes to become law.[42] Did this mean that he was an abolitionist? No. Jefferson owned approximately as many slaves as George Washington, or about 200.[43] In 1790 when Jefferson's daughter Patsy was married, the father of the bride gave the newlyweds 1,000 acres and twelve families of slaves as a wedding gift.[44] His generosity to his daughter on the occasion of her marriage was in keeping with his penchant for spending vast sums on whatever suited his fancy. His slaves were retained if for no other reason than the vain hope that he might someday pay off his debts with their labors.[45]

Of equal if not greater importance to any assessment of Jefferson was the sexual liaison he maintained over a number of years with his mulatto slave, Sally Hemings, a relationship which may have begun as early as the mid-1780s when 14-year-old Sally was sent to Paris in 1786 to care for Jefferson's daughter Polly. In 1789 Sally returned to America with her owner. Starting with Tom in 1790, continuing with Harriet, then

Madison, and ending with Eston in 1808, she conceived at least seven children when Jefferson was in residence at Monticello, and these seven conceptions resulted in live births. As early as 1802, after he was elected our third president, the rumor of Jefferson's illicit sexual relationship first appeared in print in a Richmond, Virginia, newspaper: "It is well known that the man *whom it delighteth the people to honor* keeps and for many years has kept, a concubine, one of his slaves. Her name is Sally.... The name of her eldest son is *Tom.* His features are said to bear a striking, although sable resemblance to those of the President himself."[46] The story remained a rumor, one that was largely ignored throughout most of America's subsequent history. Then DNA was discovered, and through its analysis in 1998, scientists concluded that Jefferson was the father of at least one of Sally Hemings' children, Eston, born in 1808, a man who bore a striking resemblance to our third president and became a member of white society in Madison, Wisconsin, as Eston Hemings Jefferson.[47] The truth of Eston Jefferson's paternity, confirmed 180 years after his birth, speaks loudly and clearly of Jefferson's extraordinary powers to mean one thing when he wrote, "All men are created equal," and quite another when he fathered slaves.

It was during his presidency that a financially drained France offered to sell Louisiana to the United States. Had John Adams not signed the immensely unpopular Alien and Sedition Acts in 1798, he might have been elected to a second term and been president when Louisiana was for sale. An opponent of slavery, not one who had no memory of ever being without bondpersons, would have been president when the United States purchased Louisiana under a treaty concluded in Paris on April 30, 1803. If Adams, not Jefferson, had been president, would slavery have ceased to exist in Louisiana, Arkansas, and Missouri? Not likely. Finkelman overstates the case when he argues that "After acquiring Louisiana, [Jefferson] did nothing to ban slavery in that vast territory. He might have used his influence to prohibit slavery throughout the territory, or at least limit it to what became the state of Louisiana."[48]

Not only was the peculiar institution protected at every significant turn in both the Articles of Confederation and the U.S. Constitution, it also had a more than 80-year history in the lands that were about to became a part of the United States. Moreover, the Eighth U.S. Congress, which passed the laws that enabled the president to take possession of the territories ceded by France to America, was weighted in favor of the slave states by the three-fifths rule for apportioning members. As early as 1790, when two Quakers presented petitions to the House requesting that the federal government end the African slave trade immediately, the members concluded that these petitions should not be heard. John Adams, as presiding officer of the Senate, concurred in the silence.[49] Finally in 1836, the U.S. Congress formalized its usual practice by passing its first "gag rule," a method whereby petitions dealing with the unmentionable subject of slavery were neither printed nor discussed in either the Senate or the House.[50]

From the signing of the Declaration of Independence in 1776 through at least the first 70 years of the United States, slavery had the upper hand. Though the Northwest Ordinance of 1787 disallowed human bondage in western lands north of the Ohio River, it increased the slave population of western places such as Missouri. Slaves and their owners could not live in Ohio, Indiana, Illinois, Iowa, or Wisconsin; therefore they migrated to areas where slavery was permitted. In 1804 Amos Stoddard, the first territorial governor of Missouri, counted the number of free persons and slaves in Upper Louisiana. He enumerated 7,876 whites and 1,497 blacks for a combined total of 9,373 inhabitants.[51] In other words, 19 percent of the population was made up of persons of color, the great majority of whom were slaves. Moreover, these bondpersons were mostly owned by the wealthy French residents whom President Jefferson was eager to accommodate. In the "Treaty Ceding Louisiana to the United States," it was agreed that the residents of the ceded lands shall enjoy "all the rights, advantages, and immunities of citizens of the United States; and in the meantime they shall be maintained and protected in the free enjoyment of their liberty, property, and the religion which they profess."[52] Thus the new French-American citizens retained their freedom, their Catholicism, and their slaves.

When it came to the actual rule of Upper Louisiana, Jefferson reappointed the same men to govern it whom Adams had initially appointed to oversee the Indiana Territory when it was created in 1800: William Henry Harrison, John Griffin, Henry Vanderberg, and William Clark. When Clark died, Jefferson replaced him with a man who knew the area well; Thomas Terry Davis had visited it before the Purchase. Governor Harrison and Judge Griffin were from Virginia, Judge Davis from Kentucky, and Henry Vanderberg from New York: all three states were then places of slavery. The Eighth Congress, not the president, delegated to these presidential appointees the responsibility to write the laws for Upper Louisiana.[53] When we remember that Virginia law was the model for Kentucky's slave code when it became a state in 1792, it is no surprise that the almost verbatim source of the "Law Respecting Slaves" (1804) was Virginia's slave code. Influential French slave-owning residents of St. Louis, such as August Chouteau, had been concerned that the Americans might relax the "Edict Concerning Negro Slaves in Louisiana," the Black Code which had governed their human property since 1724. These powerful French residents need not have worried. The new "Law Respecting Slaves" was no less repressive, actually more so in certain respects, than either the French or Spanish legislation which ruled the lives of most persons of color before the Louisiana Purchase.

3

Legal Freedom: Winners and Losers

All free persons of color who remained in Missouri during the time of slavery had been set free by law, either French, Spanish, or American. A bondperson gained legal liberty either because he/she was part of a small group the courts ruled was entitled to it, or because the owner, with a court's approval, voluntarily freed his human property. The earliest proof of the legal freeing of persons of color is not American. The count of Missouri's population made by Governor Amos Stoddard in 1804 did not distinguish between free and enslaved persons of color. In some districts and Arkansas Settlement, he listed the number of *slaves* and whites; in others he listed the number of *blacks* and whites.

The Spanish were diligent census takers, and their detailed records of Missouri's inhabitants supply the necessary documentation. Under Governor O'Reilly's instructions dated February 17, 1770, the lieutenant governors of the villages of St. Louis and Ste. Genevieve were required to "make a general list of the inhabitants" and send it to the governor-general annually. The first census from 1770 counted whites and slaves, males and females. Whites were divided into three age categories: up to 13 years inclusive; from 14 years to 50 years; and from 50 upwards. For slaves there were no age distinctions, only "Useful for Work" and "Useless for Work." These divisions stood roughly for those too young to work, those of working age, and those too old to work. All numbers were small. The total population of both St. Louis and Ste. Genevieve was 102, 51 in each village. Most were young; only four persons, all of them white, were 50 years of age or older. White males slightly outnumbered white females, but there were twice as many slave men as slave women. Those "Useful for work" were double the number of those "Useless for work."[1] This first Spanish count from 1770 listed neither freed mulattoes nor Negroes. Given the small number of Missouri's inhabitants at the beginning of Spanish rule, free persons of color may not have been separately counted.

A 1791 count of the inhabitants of Ste. Genevieve and St. Louis Districts named heads of households. It documented the presence in the former locale of two families with neither slaves nor white members. Jazmin's family included 14 free persons of color and Babeta's family nine. Jazmin's raised 100 bushels of wheat, 200 of corn, and 400 pounds of tobacco. Babeta's mined 10,000 pounds of lead. In St. Louis, three families had neither whites nor slaves in them: the family of Neptuno, a sailor who died in St. Louis at the age of 92, included 5 colored persons; Widow Juana's had six and Carlos Leveille's three. Neptuno's raised 20 bushels of wheat and 10 of corn, Widow Juana's 20 bushes of corn, and Carlos Leveille's 100 pounds of tobacco.[2]

The Spanish census of Upper Louisiana in 1794–95 counted, without naming, the residents of six villages, and it divided all persons into three age groups: First (up to 14 years); Second (from 14 years to 50 years), and Third (from 50 years upward). White males continued to outnumber white females by three to two. Separate and uniform categories exist in this census for whites, free mulattoes, free Negroes, mulatto slaves, and Negro slaves; the entire slave population was enumerated as 604. Though only four mulatto slaves out of 138 were 50 years of age or older, among the 466 enumerated Negro slaves, 52 were 50 years of age or older, or 11 percent. More than three-fourths of slaves (77 percent) were Negro.[3]

The change in the counted number of free persons of color between 1770 and 1794–95 is dramatic. In 1770 there were few or none in Missouri; 25 years later, there were 63, and of this number 56 (88 percent) were either children under 14 years of age or women. No free mulattoes were 50 years old or older, but almost one-half (30) were 13 years of age or younger. Six free Negroes, one man and five women, were listed as 50 years of age or older, and 48 of the 63 free persons of color, 76 percent, were mulatto.

The Spanish General Census of 1800 for Upper Louisiana continued the same categories as those listed in that of 1794–95: men and women, three age divisions, whites, free mulattoes, free Negroes, slave mulattoes, and slave Negroes. The numbers were once more larger than in the earlier censuses. Seventy-seven persons of color were free by 1800, and 74 of them (96 percent) were either children under 14 years of age or women. Free persons of color included 62 who were mulatto, or more than 80 percent. There were no free Negroes, either male or female, under 14 years of age. Only three Negro males were listed as free; one was between 14 and 50 and two were 50 years of age or older. However, 12 Negro women were free, five in the second age group and seven in the third. Among slaves, 264 were mulatto and 927 were Negro. Of the 1,191 slaves in Missouri, 80 percent were Negro. With 5,643 whites enumerated and 1,191 slaves, out of a total population of 6,911,[4] 17 percent were slaves. Like the extant 1794–95 census, that of 1800 included no names.

What do all these numbers and the percentages which can be extrapolated from them mean? They begin to make sense when we combine them with the recorded concern of Governor Ulloa, the first Spanish Captain General, who in 1767 worried that the settlers "must be watched carefully to see that they not introduce the vice which is generally reigning in the colony, ... the detestable crime of concubinage with the negro and mulatto slave women."[5] A 1779 document from Ste. Genevieve District illustrates the reality of Ulloa's vexation. It deals with the pseudo-emancipation which Jean Louis de Noyon granted to his Indian slave Jeanette, a woman known for her high moral qualities, the record asserted. Her owner freed her, but it was on condition that she continue to live with him throughout his life, almost certainly in concubinage without marriage.[6]

In a preserved letter which also dates from 1779, the Bishop of Louisiana, a Spaniard, expressed dismay that "the military officers and a good many of the inhabitants live almost publicly with colored concubines. And they do not blush at carrying the illegitimate issue they have by them to be recorded in the parochial registries as their natural children."[7] In all the preserved Spanish censuses the white men considerably outnumbered the white women. Clearly the demand for white women was far greater than the supply: there were never enough to go around. Therefore, white male residents of Missouri — including Spanish soldiers, especially officers, who were better paid than the enlisted men — could afford to purchase a slave girl or a woman. She provided her officer-master with sex, companionship, housekeeping, and nursing during his illnesses throughout his military service in an unfamiliar wilderness. When he completed it and returned to Spain, she and their children were left behind. March observed, "Although Spain controlled the territory for more than thirty years, hardly more than a handful of Spaniards settled there. Even the Spanish soldiers who had been sent up the river from New Orleans left when their tours of duty were finished."[8]

The fathers of these mulatto children were mostly officers, and they were mostly gentlemen enough to free their own children and their children's mothers. Some probably sold their offspring and their former concubines when their military duties in Missouri ended. It is too much to expect that all Spanish soldiers freed their biracial families when they left Missouri, but most did the right thing. The Black Code made a Spanish soldier's granting of freedom to his concubine and their children relatively easy because its Article 51 considered slaves whom masters appointed as "guardians of their children ... persons affranchised." Clearly, many women of color and their Spanish-African offspring were freed. Otherwise the Spanish censuses from Missouri would not document that 88 percent of free persons of color in 1794–95 and 96 percent in 1800 were women and children. Of greatest significance, all free children were mulatto; not one Negro child is listed as free in the Spanish census of Upper Louisiana for 1800.

The exact number of free persons of color in Missouri at the time of the Louisiana Purchase is unknown. Most likely it was between 100 and 200 persons. No aspect of the law which the governor and judges of the Indiana Territory adopted for Missouri in 1804 re-enslaved persons who were previously freed under either French or Spanish law.

The first known record of the emancipation of slaves who later moved to Missouri took place in Cahokia, Illinois, when a French priest, Father Francis Forget, requested of the Commandant that he "authorize granting freedom to the negro slaves of this mission, for the care and good services they rendered my predecessors and to myself, to wit: a negro named Appollo, aged about sixty years, his wife, Jeannette, thirty eight, and his youngest child, Anselmo, three years and a half." The request was made on November 4, 1763, and the slaves "enfranchised" eight days later.[9] Gilbert concludes that Jeannette, a free woman of color who owned property in St. Louis in 1765, was probably the same Jeannette whom Father Forget emancipated two years earlier in nearby Cahokia, Illinois.[10]

St. Louis documents, dated June 2 and June 3, 1770, explain the mechanism by which one Louis Villars, Lieutenant of Infantry in the Battalion of Louisiana, set free his Negro slave named Julie, about thirty years of age. He stated "that she has rendered him great services for a number of years, especially during two severe sicknesses.... The zeal and attachment she exhibited in his service having completely ruined her health, he desires to set her at liberty with a view to its restoration." Captain of Infantry of the Regiment of Louisiana and its Lieutenant-Governor Don Pedro Piernas granted his officer's petition by declaring Julie "from this day free and enfranchised, to enjoy, she and the children of early age she may have, all the rights and privileges granted to the enfranchised ... on the condition that said Julia bring by her good conduct, respect and honor on said Mr. Villars, on pain of being returned to her first condition of servitude."[11] Most likely, Julie (also Julia) remained a free person.

At least 10 free persons of color, most of them women, owned sizable amounts of real estate in St. Louis under the Spanish.[12] This group includes Jeannette, probably freed in 1763; Flore, an owner of her home and other property; Carlos Leveille, whose name as head of household appeared in the 1791 census of St. Louis; and best documented of all, Esther, a free mulatto. Because the properties to which these free persons of color acquired title under Spanish rule remained subjects of dispute well into the nineteenth century, their names crop up in a number of appellate decisions written by both the Missouri and the United States Supreme Courts.[13]

According to Gilbert, Esther (1753?–1833) came to Kaskaskia, Illinois, from Virginia with the Ichabod Camp family in 1784 when what is now the state of Illinois was a county in Virginia. Camp borrowed money from Jacques Clamorgan (1730?–1814),[14] a native of the West Indies who became, among many other things, a St. Louis merchant. Foley describes Clamorgan as a "slave dealer, fur trader, merchant, financier, and land speculator."[15] When the entrepreneur lent Camp money, the latter's slaves were used as collateral. When Camp's debt was past due, the creditor claimed Esther and brought her to St. Louis. Then in her early thirties, she became her new owner's concubine and business partner. In a writing signed and sealed before the Spanish Lieutenant Governor Don Zenon Trudeau on July 14, 1793, he freed her in order to transfer some of his property to her, hoping to protect it from creditors.[16] In 1793 he also sold Esther her own daughter, Celée, on condition that she serve her mother Esther for life.[17] However, prior to Clamorgan's selling Celée to her mother, Esther's daughter gave birth to Edward, a child alleged to have been sired by a visiting English nobleman. As a result, Clamorgan technically owned Esther's grandson; he freed him for $100 paid him by the child's reputed English father, Lord Edward Howard.[18]

Initially all appears to have been harmonious between Jacques Clamorgan and Esther. We know that Gabriel Dodier and Joseph Brazeau, French residents of St. Louis, transferred to Esther 40 arpents, or acres, of land on Little Prairie, adjoining the town of St. Louis, on November 4, 1793; and that she in turn transferred the land to Clamorgan on September 3, 1794. She was approximately 40 years old when this transfer occurred, and as she grew older, Clamorgan's interest in her as a sexual partner apparently waned.[19] Instead of continuing his amorous relationship with Esther, he fathered at least four biracial children by three other women of color, and he freed all three and their mutual offspring. Hélène bore him a son, St. Eutrope, on April 30, 1799; Susanne gave birth to his daughter Apoline on February 7, 1803; and Judith bore two sons, Cyprian Martial, born in June 1803, and Maximin, born early in 1807.

The first of the three slave playmates whom Clamorgan manumitted was almost certainly "the negress" Anna, also known as Susanne. Most probably the court record of his freeing her was no longer extant by the early twentieth century. In a French writing, probably simultaneously translated into English, Jacques Clamorgan acknowledged that he had received at Apoline's birth "a certain sum of money" paid to him "by the negress named Anna, otherwise called Susanne." This document acknowledging the 1803 payment is dated September 6, 1809. It restates the earlier emancipation of Apoline because "the change in government since that time" [February 1803] ... might cause or presume some defect to be found in the formality used under the preceding Spanish Government — or as the laws and usages of the United States relating to the liberation of slaves have not been known among us." It continues that "by virtue of the compensation paid" by Susanne, "Apoline is to be exempt from serving both me and my heirs." It is signed J. Clamorgan and witnessed by M.P. Leduc and Pierre Chouteau Jr. Under the Black Code's Article 51, the French and the Spanish considered slaves appointed by masters as "guardians of their children" to be "persons affranchised." Equally important, under its Article 22, slaves were "incapable of transferring and contracting by their own free will." Therefore, Susanne was already a free person when she made the agreed-upon payment to Jacques Clamorgan for the manumission of her daughter Apoline.

The early twentieth-century historian Harrison Trexler saw some papers dated September 12, 1809, among the records of St. Louis. He wrote of them, "Colored mistresses are known to have been freed by their owners, a familiar case being that of J. Clamorgan who in 1809 manumitted two such negresses who were mothers of his children."[20] Though Trexler never names these women, they could only have been Hélène, mother of St. Eutrope, and Judith, mother of Cyprian and Maximin.

In one contract between J. Clamorgan and Hélène, he declares her son St. Eutrope "free, independent, and liberated from all bondage." In another between J. Clamorgan and Judith he specifies that her sons, Cyprian Martial and Maximin, are "both ... free, independent, and liberated from all service." Both writings, witnessed by L.P. Leduc and Pierre Chouteau Jr., are dated September 16, 1809, or four days after J. Clamorgan formalized that he had already liberated Hélène and Judith. All three contracts, the one between J. Clamorgan and Susanne dated September 6, 1809, and two others dated September 16, 1809, one between J. Clamorgan and Hélène and the other between him and Judith, survive.[21]

All of the legal activity J. Clamorgan undertook in September 1809 on behalf of his sexual partners and their children may have been the catalyst which changed his relationship with Esther. In October 1809 she brought a lawsuit against him to recover money she alleged that he owed her and had promised to pay her for her years of service. Multiple documents from this suit survive. It lasted through the terms of two presiding judges and two sheriffs of St. Louis District. We know that she could neither read nor write because she signed all necessary papers in this suit with her X. The flavor of Clamorgan's defense can be gleaned from an extant deposition which James Mackay, a Scotsman, gave in behalf of the defendant on March 18, 1811. He and Clamorgan were associated at least as early as 1795, and both served as judges on the first court of quarter sessions — a body made up of people who were not attorneys — in St. Louis in 1804.[22]

Six questions were asked of Mackay concerning Esther. Among them was, "While the above said mulatto woman Esther was in my service do you know if she absented herself without my leave?" Answer: "I believe she absented herself when she pleased for

I know that she has been absent some times without permission." Another question: "While the said mulatto woman was in my service do you know whether or not I have furnished her and her family with all their clothing and other necessities with liberality?" Answer: "Yes I do, and I never saw a family of slaves or servants treated with more generosity and lenity than they have been by you." Another asked, "Do you know whether or not I have been at great expense with one of her grandchildren named Edward, at the request of her, the said mulatto woman, in sending him to the United States for his education?" Answer: "I know that you have been at great expense and trouble about the said Edward." Another question asked: "From the knowledge you have of the treatment the said mulatto woman and her family received at my hand, do you or do you not consider her conduct to have been ungrateful?" Answer: "I do." Finally Mackay was asked, "Do you or do you not know that the said mulatto woman while in my service gave me several causes of provocation and vexation by her insolent conduct?" He answered "I do know it."[23]

Not surprisingly, Esther produced her own witnesses to prove that Clamorgan became angry with her, struck her, and ordered her out of his house. When she departed, according to her witnesses, she complained that he would not permit her to bring away her clothes. She became suspicious that any document that he wished her to sign would waive her rights to any property she might be entitled to, and she refused to mark it with her X. According to one of his witnesses, Joseph Brazeau, Clamorgan complained, "that wench meaning the plaintiff will take away one half of my orchard." The surviving documents do not clarify whether or not she won her suit against him. According to Gilbert, Esther was cheated by Clamorgan and believed the lawyer she hired to sue him also defrauded her. However, she managed to retain a house in St. Louis and a tract of land, and she continued to litigate her claims until her death in 1833. She left her property and lawsuits to her grandchildren who sold their inheritance to a real estate agent for $10,000.[24]

When Clamorgan died, his will, written shortly before his death, left his entire estate to his natural children and appointed none other than Esther as the guardian of his minor children. Winch writes, "Why he did not leave them with their mothers is unclear. They may have died;... Esther proved a faithful guardian, raising Clamorgan's children and not defrauding them of the money she claimed Clamorgan owned her.... She had other property and was far from destitute."[25] None of Clamorgan's offspring enjoyed longevity, but they and some of their children and grandchildren remained in St. Louis. His son St. Eutrope worked as a hairdresser and married a former slave, Pelagie Aiotte, on April 20, 1820, when he was 20 and she was 17; he died in 1824. Jacques' son Maximin died at age 18 on June 7, 1825, and Cyprian Martial died at age 23 in February 1827. His daughter Apoline died in late April or early May 1830; four children, all fathered by white men, none of whom she could marry, survived her.[26] Her son Cyprian Clamorgan (1830–1906?), named for his mother's half-brother, wrote and published *The Colored Aristocracy of St. Louis* (1858). This book deals with a number of free persons of color who lived in St. Louis in the 1850s, including a mulatto child of a white U.S. Supreme Court justice. It is discussed in the next chapter.

The free descendants of Jacques Clamorgan, so long ignored in histories of Missouri, immensely enrich its past. The saga is quite a tale: Clamorgan obtained Esther as collateral on a defaulted loan in 1784 in Illinois; he shortly purchased her daughter Celée, and both lived with him in St. Louis. In 1793 he freed Esther and her daughter, and he later educated Esther's grandson Edward in the United States. By 1807 he had fathered four children by three other women of color. Three of them were born under Spanish rule of Missouri and the youngest under American ownership. He freed all of his children and their mothers, most under American rule, including Maximin, born when he was 73 years old. Esther took him to court in at least one bitterly contested property dispute in 1809. Nonetheless, five years later he appointed her the guardian of his minor children, and she properly raised these young persons whose birth mothers were probably her rivals.

Four years before Jacques Clamorgan's death in 1814, the 1810 census for Missouri documents that 607 free colored persons were residents.[27] Most likely this number represents both a natural increase from the 77 free colored persons counted by the Spanish as Missouri residents in 1800 and persons freed by their owners after 1800. Clearly, former slaves obtained their freedom under the newly adopted American law. How did the process work?

The "Law Respecting Slaves" for Upper Louisiana, which Governor Harrison and Judges Davis, Vanderburgh, and Griffin adopted effective October 1, 1804, followed Virginia's slave law. In both codes, any person could free a bondperson either in his/her last will and testament or by "any other instrument in writing." The document had to be witnessed by two persons and come before a court in the district or county in which the emancipator lived. In this manner former owners could and did "set free his or her slave, or any of them, who shall ... enjoy full freedom." Not unexpectedly, there were restrictions. If the freed slave was not (1) "in the judgment of the court of sound mind and body"; or was (2) "above the age of forty-five years," or a male under the age of twenty-one or a female under the age of eighteen years, "the person so liberating them" was required to support and maintain those whom he/she freed from bondage if the need arose. The neglect or refusal to provide such support for the owner's now freed but indigent slave would, upon application, cause the court to issue an order which allowed the sheriff or another officer to seize and "sell so much of the person's estate, as shall be sufficient for that purpose," of maintaining the impoverished former bondperson.[28] In Clamorgan's case we know that he transferred property to his children. As Winch's research makes clear, "in 1803 Clamorgan sold much of his real estate in St. Louis and several of his slaves to his friend, Joseph Brazeau, for a nominal amount. That same day Brazeau gave the land and the slaves to Clamorgan's children."[29]

The enslaved persons whom Jacques Clamorgan emancipated numbered at least 10: Esther, Celée, Edward (Esther's grandson), Susanne, Hélène, Judith, and the emancipator's four children born of three of his slave women between 1799 and 1807. Under American law, a few avenues of freedom were legally open to slaves irrespective of the master's permission. However, no aspect of French, Spanish, or American law required Clamorgan or most other owners to free even one of their human properties. Slaves might deserve freedom and actually achieve it, but whether or not any person held in bondage merited his/her liberty was the master's call, not the slave's. Freedom was a chance, but slavery was sure.

3. Legal Freedom

If any slave stands out as conspicuously worthy of his freedom, it is William Clark's York (1770–1832?). Clark's father had owned York's father, and Clark and York grew up together first in Virginia and later in Kentucky. Both became members of the Corps of Discovery when they joined Meriwether Lewis's party in October 1803 in Clarksville, Indiana Territory. After wintering in St. Louis during 1803–04, the party headed west on the Missouri River in May 1804, and, against all imaginable odds, came back to St. Louis in September 1806. They managed to cross the country to the Pacific Ocean and return from it, traveling by river, rapids, prairies, and mountains through a world of danger and adventure.

On March 3, 1807, the U.S. Congress passed a private law which granted to all white members of the Corps of Discovery considerable compensation. Lewis and Clark were given 1006 acres each, and to the estate of Charles Floyd (the only member of the party who died) and the 30 other surviving white men, this special law awarded 320 acres of land on the west side of the Mississippi River. In addition, the enlisted men received double pay for "the time he or they may have served, in the late enterprise to the Pacific Ocean, conducted by Messrs. Lewis and Clark."[30] Following the U.S. Congress's generosity toward the white members of the expedition — generosity that York as a St. Louis resident knew about in detail — he began asking Clark for his freedom. He believed that he had earned it by his exemplary service as a member of the Lewis and Clark Expedition. Ambrose relates that York's wife now belonged to a Louisville, Kentucky, owner, and he wished to join her, if need be by hiring himself out and sending the money to Clark in St. Louis. Clark allowed York to visit his wife, but he insisted upon *his* slave's return to him in St. Louis. York continued to request that Clark free him, but his request was denied. By May 1809 York was once more in St. Louis, and Clark complained of him in a letter to his brother which Ambrose quotes: York "is here but of very little service to me, insolent and sukly [*sic*], I gave him a Severe Trouncing the other Day and he has much mended." After quoting from this revealing letter Ambrose writes, "York had helped pole Clark's keelboat, paddled his canoe, hunted for his meat, made his fire, had shown he was prepared to sacrifice his life to save Clark's, crossed the continent and returned with his childhood companion, only to be beaten because he was insolent and sulky and denied ... his freedom."[31]

It is highly unlikely that Clark ever freed York. The first known statement that he had done so came late in Clark's life, and its source was Washington Irving (1783–1859), the New York author of "The Legend of Sleepy Hollow," "Rip Van Winkle," and other fanciful tales. In 1832, after a 17-year absence from the United States, Irving toured the West. In St. Louis he visited William Clark, who had earlier (1813–1821) served with distinction as Missouri's territorial governor. Irving gives this account of Governor Clark as emancipator:

> His slaves — set them free — one he placed at a ferry — another on a farm, giving him land, horses, etc. — a third he gave a large wagon & team of 6 horses to ply between Nashville and Richmond. They all repented & wanted to come back. The waggoner was York, the hero of the Missouri expedition & adviser of the Indians. He could not get up early enough in the morn — his horses were ill kept — two died — the others grew poor. 'Damm this freedom,' said York, 'I have never had a happy day since I got it.' He determined to go back to his old master — set off for St. Louis, but was taken with the cholera in Tennessee & died.[32]

Irving uncritically accepted Clark's word that at unspecified times he granted all his slaves their freedom. This much we know, however: in 1816 Clark offered a $100 reward for the return of his runaway slave, Juba.[33] Within three years, Clark's slave Scipio shot and killed himself in April 1819 because he feared being transported to New Orleans and sold.[34] Clark's will, dated April 14, 1837, or 16 months before his death on September 1, 1838, names 11 slaves and refers to others as children.[35] Clark, as his will clarifies, looked on all his property as that with which "Almighty God ... has been pleased to bless me." It is not credible that he would free all his slaves, surely all thoroughly trained, no later than 1832, only to purchase an entirely new batch in his last years. Those he already owned knew exactly how he wanted his breakfast eggs prepared, his clothing laundered, his household managed, his horses and other valuable livestock cared for, and his gardens and other lands tilled and tended. Obviously, Clark never freed many of his slaves. Of equal if not greater importance, Missouri law, as already discussed, imposed restrictions on the emancipation of bondpersons. In York's case his age was an impediment. Beside copious statutory law regarding the emancipation of bondpersons more than 45 years old, the Constitution of Missouri, adopted in 1820, gave the legislature the power to pass laws, among other matters, "to permit the owners of slaves to emancipate them, saving the right of creditors, where the person so emancipating will give security that the slave so emancipated shall not become a public charge."[36]

No present-day writer who speculates that Clark freed or probably freed York mentions Missouri law, including the statutory restrictions on the emancipation of bondpersons because of their age. Betts confirms that York remained Clark's slave as late as 1811.[37] By this time York was 40 or 41 and nearing the cut-off age for freedom independent of his owner's support. The odds overwhelmingly favor that, just as York began life as a slave when born to a slave mother on a Virginia plantation, so also did he probably die enslaved in approximately 1832.

In 1999, a magnificent and immense monument to the Lewis and Clark Expedition was unveiled and dedicated at a city park overlooking the Missouri River in Kansas City, Missouri. As expected, its figures include Meriwether Lewis and William Clark, but among the six additional figures of the Corps of Discovery is York, the slave who almost certainly never achieved freedom in life. If his imagined likeness in a larger-than-life statue is not the only sculpted depiction of an enslaved person that stands or has ever stood on Missouri soil, then it is one of the few.

Though York never qualified, there were carefully delineated circumstances under which a slave owned in Missouri was entitled to freedom irrespective of the wishes of his owner. These conditions are best understood by examining the legal basis of suits for freedom. With the help of a $175,000 federal grant, the Missouri State Archives has located and preserved 283 freedom suits filed in St. Louis courts between 1806 and 1865.[38] In all instances, the petitions for liberty which the state's highest court decided were contested. The slave filed suit in the belief that he/she should be free, while his/her putative owner had contrary views.

Although both the French and the Spanish rulers of Missouri enthusiastically supported African or Negro slavery, Spanish efforts to curb and end Indian slavery began soon after Spain commenced its rule of the Purchase in the late 1760s. The legal battles of Marie Jean Scypion and her descendants to achieve their freedom were based on their maternal Indian ancestry. As Foley relates the matter, it began in the 1740s when Marie Jean's mother, a Natchez Indian woman known as Marie or Marietta, was taken captive and sold into slavery under the French in what is now the state of Illinois. Marie Jean's father was a Negro slave named Scypion. She was owned by a French priest until he made a gift of her to his cousin, Madame Marie Boisset. Her owner's daughter, who married Joseph Tayon, inherited this Indian-African slave, and the Tayons brought her to St. Louis. There she gave birth to three daughters, Celeste, Catiche, and Marguerite, and there she also died in June 1802.

Under all applicable law, French, Spanish, Virginia, federal, and territorial Missouri, the mother's status, free or slave, determined her children's right to freedom or her owner's right to enslave them. Marie Jean Scypion's daughters filed writs for freedom based on their *maternal* Indian heritage as early as 1806, and their courtroom battles, which lasted more than 30 years, took place in three different Missouri counties: St. Louis, St. Charles, and Jefferson. The defendants in these suits stressed the women's Negro ancestry while the plaintiffs argued their maternal grandmother's Natchez Indian heritage. Additional plaintiffs in these cases included at least 15 persons, all of them great- and great-great-grandchildren of Marie or Marietta, the Indian ancestor first enslaved during French rule of what is now Illinois. The defendants became the Chouteaus; they were members of the wealthiest, most powerful, and probably the most extensively slave-owning family in territorial Missouri.

Over more than 30 years of court battles, the case went to the United States Supreme Court twice; in 1830 and again in 1838 the high court let stand the Missouri Supreme Court decision on grounds that the federal court lacked jurisdiction.[39] Thus, almost 70 years after Spanish Governor General O'Reilly began his efforts to eradicate Indian slavery, the Missouri Supreme Court by a divided vote ruled that it was unlawful to hold Indians, or their *maternal* descendants, as slaves.[40]

This victory before Missouri courts over a 30-year period was a small one. Many of the original plaintiffs had died, and scores of other Missouri slaves who might have benefited had no way of proving that they had a maternal Indian ancestor. Virginia law made no provision for the offspring of a Negro and an Indian.[41] It defined a mulatto as a person with one Negro grandparent, and it decreed the bloodline adequate for perpetual slavery. Missouri adopted Virginia law and made no reference in its statutes to Indian slavery. As a result the only beneficiaries of the 30-year court battle were the living descendants of the Natchez Indian woman enslaved in Illinois in the 1740s. Foley concludes that nothing is known of the surviving Scypions as free persons.[42]

Another related group of freedom suits in Missouri courts was based on the question of whether or not Negro slavery existed in Lower Canada (Quebec) in 1768. If it did then the children of Rose, a Negro born in Montreal about 1768, were the proper subjects of slavery. If, on the other hand, slavery was illegal in Lower Canada in 1768, then Rose was a free woman and her children were likewise free. No definitive proof of the existence or nonexistence of Negro slavery in Lower Canada could be established by either side to the satisfaction of the judges hearing the case. Rose's son Pierre and her daughter Charlotte were pitted against the same powerful family that Marie Jean Scypion's descendants battled in the courtroom, the Chouteaus. Pierre began the fight

Detail from statuary group, "The Lewis and Clark Expedition," located at 8th and Jefferson streets, Kansas City, Missouri, a locale with a superb view of the Missouri River. York is in the center foreground, with the dog Seaman. (Photograph by the author.)

for his freedom and his sister Charlotte continued it. Six times the Supreme Court of Missouri ruled on the matter; whoever won, the other side appealed. The first of these appellate decisions was decided in Chouteau's favor in 1845, but in the last three, decided between 1855 and 1862, Charlotte won. Chouteau complained in 1859 of the all-white male jury hearing the case that one "collected from the city [St. Louis] will necessarily include many who, from prejudice of birth and education, are not a fair or unprejudiced jury for the determination of the issues in this cause." He wanted the trial judge to decide that slavery had existed in Canada in 1768; the court left the decision to the jury, who found that there was no legal slavery in Canada "at the time when the ancestress of the plaintiff" was in Canada, and the Supreme Court of Missouri upheld the lower court.[43] The beneficiaries of this 17-year legal controversy were the living descendants of Rose in 1862, by which time the Civil War engulfed Missouri.

A third group of freedom suits concerned the slave's stay in the Northwest Territory. The Continental Congress first passed legislation regarding this area in 1787 under the authority of the Articles of Confederation. In 1789 the First U.S. Congress reenacted the identical legislation under the authority of the new Constitution. The law stated that slavery and involuntary servitude were illegal within the Northwest Territory. This line of cases is the most important because from it ultimately came the U.S. Supreme Court's *Dred Scott* decision.

An early suit in this group concerned the petition of Matilda, a free black girl under the age of 21, for leave to sue as a poor person for her freedom. It was filed on her behalf in the Superior Court of Missouri Territory for the Northern Circuit on March 28, 1816. It set forth the facts and the law regarding plaintiff's request that the court grant her plea for liberty. She was brought to Indiana Territory from one of the United States, which one was unknown to her, sometime between 1807 and 1809 by Elisha Mitchel. She resided "in said territory for a long time under the care of the said Mitchel." He sold her or — to use the language of the petition — she was "seized while living in said territory ... under the pretense of her being a slave" by one John Rector, and brought to St. Louis, she believes, in May 1808. Rector sold her to William Christy, and Christy sold her to Isaac Van Bibber, a resident of St. Charles County "in whose hands and possession she has remained ever since."[44]

Matilda's petition stated that "in consequence of an ordinance of Congress for the government of the Northwestern Territory ... if she had been a slave before her being brought to the said territory [she] was by virtue of the said ordinance entitled to freedom." In other words, because she "resided in said Territory for *a long time*," her residence in it freed her. Matilda asserted that federal law entitled her to her liberty, and because Isaac Van Bibber denied it to her from June 19, 1814, until March 28, 1816, she requested damages from him in the amount of $1,000. Van Bibber, the petition alleged, had "beat, bruised, and ill treated her, the said Matilda, and kept and detained her in prison ... at Saint Louis." The assertion of assault, battery, and false imprisonment which Matilda charged that her putative owner inflicted upon her remained the specific language of slave suits for freedom. Many years later Dred and his wife, Harriet Scott, also charged that those who claimed them as their slaves assaulted, battered, and falsely imprisoned them.

A deposition taken at the request of Matilda's lawyer in Monroe County, Illinois Territory, of William Everett, an acquaintance of Elisha Mitchel, supplies the necessary detail regarding the plaintiff's residence within the Northwest Territory. Since Matilda was black, she could not testify in her own behalf because she would do so against a white person. Missouri law from its inception in 1804 declared that persons of color were incompetent to testify against whites. As a result, William Everett's testimony was essential to establishing Matilda's stay in Illinois Territory. His preserved deposition states that when Elisha Mitchel moved to Monroe County, an area southeast of St. Louis, he had with him a Negro woman named Liddy and two children, one named Matilda and the other Lavina. They lived with Mitchel and his family throughout their residence in Monroe County, Illinois Territory. Afterwards, Mitchel and his family " moved on the west side of the Mississippi and there said Mitchel departed this life." Two months later Mitchel's widow sold John Rector the "two Negro girls." When William Everett, the deponent, first saw Matilda she was five years old, and "he heard said John Rector say afterwards that he had sold Matilda to Major Christy of St. Louis." (Christy was later, among other accomplishments, the state of Missouri's first auditor of public accounts. Van Bibber, an early settler of St. Charles County, had served as a Captain in the War of 1812.[45])

The key to whether or not Matilda was freed by being within the Northwest Territory depended on whether her stay in it was transient or one of intended permanent residence. Court papers filed in her name describe it as "near four months," "near five months," "a long time," and always as a matter of *residence*, never as a temporary stopping-off place. Though the extant court documents in her case do not contain the court's ruling on her freedom, the likelihood is great that she won her suit for freedom. However, she almost certainly would have been denied her request for $1,000 in damages.

Perhaps of greatest interest in this early suit for freedom, based on the solid grounds of residence in the Northwest Territory, was the attorney who represented a young black woman because the Superior Court of the Northern Circuit of Missouri appointed him Matilda's lawyer. He was Mathias McGirk, born in Tennessee about 1785, who studied law there and arrived in Missouri Territory as a talented young attorney in 1814. By 1815, when he was approximately 30 years old, he represented St. Charles County in the Legislative Council.[46] The next year he became the court-appointed attorney for Matilda. From the extant court documents in her case, it is clear that he represented her with warm zeal. On her behalf he spent an entire work week in Monroe County, Illinois Territory, where he took depositions in order to prove that she had *resided* there; and almost certainly he won her freedom for her.

Meanwhile, as Matilda probably gained her liberty, the contentious issue of slavery as it pertained to the admission of Missouri to the Union as a state bubbled and boiled in the U.S. Congress. After several years of bitter debate regarding human bondage, this body finally agreed, in legislation best known as the Missouri Compromise (1820), that, except for the state of Missouri, there should be no slavery north of latitude 36 degrees 30 minutes within the remainder of the Louisiana Purchase, or the northern boundary of Arkansas. The present-day states that border Missouri from which the Missouri Compromise excluded slavery are Oklahoma, Kansas, Nebraska, and Iowa.

As in the 1787 and 1789 versions of the Northwest Ordinance, however, it was agreed that slaves who fled the services of their masters in slave jurisdictions would not be freed by escaping into northern areas of the Purchase.[47] This federal statute settled the issue of where slavery could and could not exist on this state's borders for the next 34 years. Shortly after its passage, Missouri joined the Union.

When it became the 24th state in 1821, Governor McNair's first appointment to the three-member Supreme Court of Missouri was Matilda's court-appointed attorney, 35- or 36-year-old Mathias McGirk. Although the pro-slavery judge Robert Wash served on this court from 1825 to 1837, all other early members of it except McGirk served four years or less. McGirk remained on the Court longer than any other of its antebellum judges, and his longevity gave him an influence on the Court that his brethren never achieved. He sat as a Missouri Supreme Court judge for 21 consecutive years, 1820–1841, and when he resigned in 1841, he probably left the court because of ill health. He died August 14, 1842.[48] During his more than 20 years on the state's highest court, he wrote or joined most of the decisions dealing with suits for freedom based on the petitioner's stay in the Northwest Territory.

Not all slaves whose feet touched the soil of that territory were freed by virtue of their stay within it, however. The Missouri Supreme Court decided at least three cases against the bondperson's freedom based on their presence within the area.

In the first of these, the plaintiff based his right to liberty on the following facts. In 1816 Pascal Cerré, a St. Louis resident, wished to sell his slave, François, to a buyer who would remove him from St. Louis. M. Cerré did not choose Pierre Chouteau; instead he sold the plaintiff to Pierre Menard, a citizen of Illinois then living in Kaskaskia, for $500. Menard was acting as a middleman for Chouteau and never intended that the purchased slave live in Illinois. The bondman was employed at a mine, as a hand on a keel-boat, and as a boat unloader, all within slave jurisdictions. His stay in Kaskaskia, Illinois, was never one of permanent residence because it was only for a few days. The Court held, "the owner of a slave, who is merely passing through the country with him, or who may be a resident in Illinois and may choose to employ him in Missouri ... in boats or vessels that occasionally lade and unlade their cargoes ... within the state [of Illinois] does nothing toward engrafting slavery upon the social system of the state."[49] Judgment for Chouteau was affirmed.

Another denial of slave freedom was based on the birth of a slave in Prairie du Rocher, Illinois, in 1782. He remained there until brought to St. Louis in 1809. Since the plaintiff was born earlier than the passage of the Northwest Ordinance and the slave's owner was protected in his property by the state of Virginia's Act of Cession which held that the inhabitants of their former colony [Illinois] shall be protected in their rights and liberties, that is their right to own slaves, the present owner derived his title from the slave's original owner.[50]

A third situation which did not entitle the slave to freedom was based on the following facts. Though the owner moved from Missouri to Illinois, he leased his slave out in Missouri. The slave Nat ran away from Missouri to Illinois and hired himself out there, but his owner never received income from his runaway slave's independent hiring-out arrangements. The slave lost his bid for freedom that was based on his Illinois residence. As the Court held, "The slave must abide in the state of Illinois by and with the consent ... of his owner long enough to induce a jury to believe that the owner intended to make that country the place of the slave's residence."[51]

Had William Clark's slave York petitioned a Missouri court for his liberty based on his fall 1803 sojourn in Indiana Territory with his master, Missouri courts would have found in favor of his owner. Clark's purpose in being with York on the north side of the Ohio River in Indiana Territory was not to reside there with his slave. Rather he was staying there with his older brother, General George Rogers Clark, because he was awaiting the arrival of Meriwether Lewis. The latter floated down the Ohio River with his Newfoundland dog, Seaman, from Pittsburgh, Pennsylvania, past Wheeling, Virginia, past the state of Ohio and on to Clarksville, Indiana Territory. Once Lewis reached Clarksville, Clark and York left with him for St. Louis; there the white men assembled most members of the Corps of Discovery. From St. Louis the party embarked on their expedition to the Pacific Ocean in the spring of 1804 and returned to Missouri, a slave territory, in mid-September 1806.

Success rather than failure characterized a much larger number of slave suits for freedom based on the bondperson's residence in the Northwest Territory. Winny moved from Carolina to Illinois with the Whitesides at the end of the eighteenth century, and she resided with them there for three or four years before they moved to Missouri. The Court held (1824) that "Congress had both the power to acquire the [Northwest] Territory and to forbid the introduction of slaves.... If by a residence in Illinois [Phebe Whitesides] lost her right to the property in [Winny] that right was not revived by a removal of the parties to Missouri."[52] Likewise, when the mother of a slave who sued for his freedom was held as a bondwoman in what is now Illinois for approximately 36 years, the Cession Act of Virginia did not permit the enslavement of her son John. At the time of his birth he was not property. Judge McGirk wrote for the Court: "John is free.... The [Northwest] Ordinance is positive, slavery cannot exist."[53]

Vincent gained his freedom when it was established that he was hired to labor at the Illinois Saline near Shawneetown from 1817 until 1825. The Illinois Constitution of 1818 allowed slaves to be hired to work at the Saline if the duration of their hire did not exceed 12 months at a time.[54] Vincent was entitled to his liberty first because he was hired in 1817, the year before the Illinois Constitution was adopted, and second because he remained a laborer there until 1825. The Ordinance of 1787 controlled, and his presence in St. Louis could not re-enslave him.[55]

An appeal on the part of the putative owner to the United States Supreme Court of a decision by the Missouri Supreme Court in 1831 did not succeed. Aspasia, a woman of color born after 1787 in Illinois and held as a slave there until 1821 and afterwards brought to St. Louis, was not re-enslaved. The Missouri court held, "Aspasia was not a slave, but free."[56] The U.S. Supreme Court's determination that it lacked jurisdiction to decide her case allowed the Missouri Supreme Court's decision freeing Aspasia to stand.

There are still other suits in which the person of color gained his freedom based on his residence in the Northwest Territory. An owner who permitted his slave to hire his own time at, among other places, the lead mines in Galena, Illinois, beginning in 1814 or 1815 and continuing for a number of years, could not re-enslave him once the bondman returned to Missouri.[57] Likewise, an owner purchased a slave, Julia, in Kentucky and moved with her to Pike County, Illinois, and there bought land in 1829. The mistress kept her bondwoman in this locale at least one month and exercised "the ordinary acts of ownership and dominion over her, which are usually exercised by masters over their slaves." That she later hired her out in Louisiana, Missouri, and then sold her to the defendant in St. Louis did not re-enslave her. The case explained that the introduction of slavery in Illinois, based after 1819 on Article 6 of the Illinois Constitution, wrought an emancipation of the slave. Owners who were merely passing through a portion of the Northwest Territory were permitted to carry their human property with them, but if the owner *resided* there for as short a time as one month, by such residence his/her slaves were freed. Judge McGirk wrote for the court, "Something more than mere inconvenience ... of the emigrant ought to intervene to save him from a forfeiture ... swollen streams of water ... serious illness of the family, broken wagons ... would be a good cause of delay ... if the journey is resumed as soon as these impediments are removed, provided also due diligence is used to remove them."[58]

Rachael (1836) gained her freedom, ruled the Missouri Supreme Court, because her owner, an army officer, took her with him when he was transferred to Prairie du Chien, then in Michigan Territory. Judge McGirk wrote, "Though it be true that the officer was bound to remain where he did, during all the time he was there, yet no authority of law or the government compelled him to keep the plaintiff there as a slave."[59] There was only convenience in retaining Rachael as a slave in Michigan Territory, and necessity is not the same as convenience. Rachael's freedom was required, ruled the Court, by the Northwest Ordinance of 1787, the Missouri Compromise of 1820, and the laws and constitutions of non-slaveholding states.

Another case clarified that a slave suit for freedom could not be defeated by shipping the slave south. When an owner attempted to evade the law by causing his bondman to be put on a steamboat, the circuit court judge, at the behest of the slave's appointed attorney, ordered the sheriff to seize the slave and ordered both the slave and his owner to appear before him. The owner was required to pay court costs, his slave was in all likelihood freed, and the St. Louis trial judge's actions were upheld by the Missouri Supreme Court.[60]

Missouri law would appear to have been wholly clarified regarding the conditions under which a slave suit for freedom succeeded or failed when it was based on a stay within either the Northwest Territory or, excluding Missouri, north of 36 degrees 30 minutes and within the Louisiana Purchase. Missouri trial courts had heard repeated variations on slaves being within these regions of freedom. On the whole, the Missouri Supreme Court affirmed that the plaintiff slave, by virtue of *residing* in a free state or territory with his owner's permission and approval, was a freed person.

Then came additional freedom suits; they appeared routine, those of Harriet and her husband, Dred Scott. Their owner, Dr. Emerson, won these separate suits at trial; appeals were taken, and no final judgment in either party's favor came from the Supreme Court of Missouri's first decisions regarding the Scotts in 1848.[61] Four years later Missouri's highest court revisited its Harriet and Dred Scott decisions. It was a different bench than the court that had earlier frequently ruled in favor of the slave in his or her quest for freedom based on residence in non-slave jurisdictions. McGirk and his fellow liberal judges were gone, and in their places there were no new appointees of Missouri's governors. Instead the Missouri legislature decreed that, beginning in 1851, the three members of the state's highest court were to be elected.[62]

A Missouri Supreme Court popularly elected by the only residents who could vote, white males aged at least 21 years, once more decided Dred Scott's suit for freedom. It was based on his residence with his owner, Dr. Emerson, a surgeon in the U.S. Army. The doctor's duty stations had taken him, and with him his slave Dred Scott, to Rock Island, a military post in the state of Illinois, and also to Fort Snelling, Minnesota, a military post then in Wisconsin Territory, later shifted to Iowa Territory, and a place within the Louisiana Purchase and north of 36° 30'. The suit of Harriet, Scott's wife, and their children was inextricably bound with that of the father-husband. She belonged to a Major Taliaferro, who took Harriet with him to Fort Snelling where he sold her to Emerson. The Scotts' first child, Eliza, was born north of Missouri on a steamboat on the Mississippi River, and their second daughter, Lizzie, was born at Jefferson Barracks in St. Louis. From times much earlier than any preserved law on the subject, the mother's status, whether slave or free, determined the freedom or the enslavement of her children.

At stake when the Missouri Supreme Court delivered its second decision in the Scott case was the freedom of four persons, the Scotts and their two daughters. Judging from the previous case law in which Missouri's highest court had decided in favor of the slave seeking freedom based on his/her residence north and east of Missouri, one would logically expect a ruling favorable to the Scott family. The elected Supreme Court of Missouri did not rule as had the earlier appointees of various Missouri governors to this court.

One would never know by reading the 1852 Missouri Supreme Court decision in the Scott case that the Court had previously decided a considerable body of case law which carefully laid out the circumstances under which a slave's stay within either the Northwest Territory and/or the non-slave portions of the Louisiana Purchase entitled the bondperson to freedom. Judge Scott, for the majority, swept away nearly three decades of Missouri Supreme Court decisions favorable to the slave's suit for freedom when he wrote, "Times now are not as they were when the former decisions on the subject were made. Since then not only individuals but States have been possessed with a dark and fell spirit in relation to slavery, whose gratification is sought in the pursuit of measures, whose inevitable consequence must be the overthrow and destruction of our government."[63]

Judge Scott's "dark and fell spirit in relation to slavery" is a murky concept, but he surely was concerned about the increase in the number of free states and, with their greater numbers, their greater power in the halls of government. The list is impressive: Ohio in 1803, Indiana in 1816, Illinois in 1818, Michigan in 1837, Iowa in 1846, Wisconsin in 1848, and California in 1850 joined the Union as free states. By 1852 only two slave jurisdictions had become states in the previous decade, Florida and Texas, both in 1845; and they were the last slave states admitted to the Union. Looking ahead to Nebraska Territory in 1854 (admitted as a state in 1867), Minnesota in 1858, Oregon in 1859, and Kansas in 1861, all of these jurisdictions joined the Union as free states. Further, Kansas, Nebraska, Iowa, and Illinois made up approximately 75 percent of Missouri's borders. From the vantage point in 1852 of elected members to Missouri's highest court, freedom, or the loss of a man's property, was in the air.

Though the St. Louis jury hearing Scott's suit for freedom found for him under jury instructions based on case law written by Judge McGirk and his colleagues, the Missouri Supreme Court set aside this abundance of earlier law and reversed the St. Louis trial court's decision favorable to Scott. It opined, "Judgment reversed and remanded. No State is bound to carry into effect enactments conceived in a spirit hostile to that which pervades her own laws."[64] The Court continued, "The consequences of slavery ... are much more hurtful to the master than the slave.... We are almost persuaded that the introduction of slavery among us was in the providence of God, ... a means of placing that unhappy race within the pale of civilized nations."[65]

The Missouri Supreme Court had ignored at least two enactments of the U.S. Congress when deciding in 1852 that Dred Scott was not entitled to freedom based on where he lived with his peripatetic master, Dr. Emerson: the Northwest Ordinance of 1787, reenacted by the First Congress in 1789, and the Missouri Compromise of 1820. Following the U.S. Supreme Court's ruling in Dred Scott's case in 1857, the Missouri Supreme Court decided no further freedom suits based on the slave's residence within either the Northwest Territory or northern portions of the Louisiana Purchase.

Meanwhile, soon after the Supreme Court of Missouri denied Dred Scott his freedom, he changed owners. Dr. Emerson died, and his widow sold her slave to her brother, John F.A. Sanford, a resident of New York City. Scott's supporters seized on the residence of the new master as a means of getting the case into federal court on grounds of the diversity of state citizenship. The U.S. Constitution extends its judicial power to, among a number of other matters, "all Cases ... between Citizens of different States."[66] In 1854 Scott's case was tried before the U.S. Circuit Court for the District of Missouri in St. Louis, and the judge decided the suit in favor of the defendant, Sanford. Scott's lawyers filed an appeal from this unfavorable ruling to the U.S. Supreme Court, and it accepted his case. Any reader interested in a full account should consult Don Fehrenbacher's excellent book, *The Dred Scott Case: Its Significance in American Law and Politics* (1978).

For our present purposes, what matters is that Chief Justice of the United States Roger Taney wrote in *Scott v. Sanford* what is arguably the best-known decision in the history of the U.S. Supreme Court. His name is forever besmirched by his penning of these offensive words: "The language used in the Declaration of Independence show[s] that ... slaves ... whether they had become free or not were not then acknowledged as a part of the people.... They had no rights which the white man was bound to respect; and ... the Negro might justly and lawfully be reduced to slavery for his benefit."[67]

The precise ruling of the high court was that "Dred Scott was not a citizen of Missouri within the meaning of the Constitution of the United States, and therefore he remained a slave who was not entitled to sue in its courts." The Court might have limited its decision to its conclusion that Scott was not a citizen and therefore had no right of access to the federal courts. It might have avoided a briar patch of almost unimaginable controversy had it announced that other issues had been raised in his appeal, but they did not merit discussion. However, the Court rose to the bait, going even further in its destruction of law that in any way impeded the extension of slavery. The opinion declared that both the Northwest Ordinance's prohibition of slavery within its borders and the Missouri Compromise were unconstitutional and therefore void. The

Court concluded "that neither Dred Scott himself, nor any of his family were made free by being carried into this territory; even if they had been carried into this territory by their owner, with the intention of becoming a permanent resident."[68]

One concurring opinion, Justice John Catron's, is of special interest. He reasoned that Dred Scott remained a slave because the Missouri Compromise of 1820 was unconstitutional. He wrote: "Scott was Dr. Emerson's lawful property; he carried his Missouri title with him." Slaves were, in this jurist's view, the citizen's "most valuable and cherished property ... parts of his family in name and in fact."[69] These are indeed lofty sentiments about slavery. They were written by a man whose unacknowledged son, 30-year-old James Thomas, was a free mulatto and a St. Louis resident when his high and mighty white sire helped decide *Dred Scott*. (There is further discussion of this jurist's miscegenation in Chapter 4.)

The uproar that greeted this 7–2 ruling in which John Catron concurred is well known. The abolitionist senator from Massachusetts, Charles Sumner, denounced it as being "as absurd and irrational as a reversal of the multiplication table."[70] Our history textbooks have included among the causes of the Civil War the U.S. Supreme Court's 1857 *Dred Scott* decision. To undo what the High Court decided in this infamous case required not one but two amendments to the U.S. Constitution. The 13th Amendment, passed in 1865, used the language of Article 6 of the 1787 Northwest Ordinance to abolish slavery and involuntary servitude within the entire United States, or any place subject to its jurisdiction, and gave the U.S. Congress the power to enforce the article by appropriate legislation. The 14th Amendment, which became law in 1868, declared, among a number of other provisions, that "All persons born or naturalized in the United States, and subject to the jurisdiction thereof, are citizens of the United States and of the State wherein they reside." Therefore Dred Scott and all similarly situated persons *were* free men, women, and children, and they were also citizens of

Dred Scott's tombstone, Calvary Cemetery, St. Louis. Beside it is a marker for his wife, Harriet, which reads in part: "Harriet Scott ca. 1815–1860/American patriot/ wife of Dred Scott/mother of Eliza and Lizzy/ plaintiff in the historic Dred Scott case." In 1999 the Lovejoy Society placed Harriet Scott's marker beside her husband's remains. Her actual place of burial is unknown. (Photograph by Mary Seematter.)

both the United States and the state wherein they resided. Further, they were not to be denied access to either state or federal courts. However, before the U.S. Constitution included its 13th and 14th Amendments, the North had to win an extraordinarily bloody war. The Union survived, and with it the U.S. Supreme Court as the final arbiter of what is and what is not constitutional.

As for the man Dred Scott, he did not die a slave. John F.A. Sanford, Scott's owner, died in an insane asylum shortly after the U.S. Supreme Court decision in his favor. His sister, the former Irene Emerson, had married Congressman Calvin C. Chaffee, and the Chaffees, Scott's owners, quitclaimed the now famous slave to his longtime St. Louis benefactor, Taylor Blow, who manumitted Dred Scott and his family in May 1857. However, their freedom was short-lived. Scott had consumption and died in September 1857; his wife and daughter Eliza survived him by only a few years. In 1957 Taylor Blow's granddaughter provided a granite headstone for Dred Scott's grave in Calvary Cemetery, to which Taylor Blow had arranged for its removal from St. Louis Wesleyan Cemetery in 1867.[71]

That Scott was finally set free was not because of any appeals court action by either the Supreme Court of Missouri or the U.S. Supreme Court. Likewise, none of the persons discussed in the next chapter received their liberty outside the law. The freedom of all was legally acquired.

4

Free Negroes and Mulattoes

The "Law Respecting Slaves," which the governor and judges of the Indiana Territory adopted in 1804 for Upper Louisiana, dealt briefly and matter-of-factly with free persons of color. Under it, no Negro or mulatto, slave or free, could testify against a white person. If free, each who was a householder was permitted to keep one gun, powder, and shot. Though his association with slaves was limited, the statute also forbade any white person to meet with bondpersons or to hire the enslaved without the owner's consent. No Negro or mulatto, bond or free, was allowed to "lift his or her hand to any person not being a negro or mulatto." Emancipated bondpersons were required to carry a copy of the instrument of his or her emancipation "when traveling out of the district [county] of his residence."[1] Otherwise, the earliest American law governing its non-white population dealt, as its title indicated, with slaves.

As the numbers of free non-whites increased throughout most of the United States so also did white detestation of free mulattoes and Negroes. This was especially evident in the slave states. There the fear lurked that free persons of color would set unacceptable examples for the enslaved.[2] How could a bondperson remain properly submissive to his white owners when he saw that his equally black brothers had shaken off the shackles of their servitude? In 1847 the Missouri Supreme Court expressed well the current belief about the pernicious influence of free Negroes on slaves. Their presence, wrote the pro-slavery judge William Napton, tended "only to dissatisfy and corrupt those of their own race and color remaining in a state of servitude."[3] It was clear; slaves must be protected from such harmful influences. The movement to exclude free persons of color from Missouri began early.

Missouri's first state constitution of 1820 gave the legislature the *duty* to pass laws, among other matters, "To prevent free negroes and mulattoes from coming to and settling in this state, under any pretext whatsoever."[4] According to the 1820 federal census, there were 10,222 slaves and 347 free Negroes in Missouri; ten years later this census listed 25,091 slaves and 569 free persons of color as Missourians.[5] The state's slave residents had increased during the decade but so had its free non-whites. Obviously, legislative measures were called for to slow, if not abruptly halt, the increase in this highly undesirable segment of Missouri's population.

In 1835, the Missouri General Assembly did its duty in magnificent style to discourage free black immigration to the state. It passed "An Act Concerning Free Negroes and Mulattoes," which with additions and modifications remained the law throughout the state's slave times. The first section of this law defined a mulatto as being at least one-eighth Negro, that is, having one black grandparent; all other forebears might be Caucasian.[6] The remainder of this major legislation's 27 sections contained a number of restrictions on free persons of color in Missouri; chief among these was the requirement that they obtain a license if they wished either to settle or to remain in the state. Section 10 provided that a license was available to those who could produce evidence they were "of the class of persons ... of good character and behavior, and capable of supporting [themselves] by lawful employment." Section 9 limited the license to those who (1) resided in Missouri in 1825 and continued to do so; or (2) were emancipated or born free within the state; or (3) were between ages seven and 21 years and had completed service as an apprentice or a servant; or (4) were the free husband or wife of a slave who married with the consent of the owner. Section 11 required that the license be issued by a county court and that it describe the applicant "by his name, age, size, personal appearance and occupation." Section 14 specified that if the licensee moved from one county to another, he was required to produce his license and be registered in the new county. Section 15 required that the applicant pay 50 cents for the initial license and 12.5 cents for each registration of it in another county. Section 16 specified that all persons whose right to freedom accrued from their residence outside the state, for example in either Illinois or northern portions of the Louisiana Purchase, were subject to the licensing requirements. Section 3 required that, regardless of his birthplace, any colored person who owned "any gun, firelock or weapon of any kind, or ammunition" must be licensed, and it encouraged any informer against the weapon-owning colored person to come forward by permitting the snitch to keep the seized contraband arms and ammunition for his own use. Section 17 required the forfeiture of the license if its holder was convicted of "any felony or infamous crime, or of keeping a gaming house, bawdy house, or disorderly house." Section 4 specified that any person of color who served an apprenticeship "in company of a free white apprentice" could only be taught the trade or occupation if the parents or guardian of the white apprentice gave permission. Section 18 required that every sheriff, coroner, and constable be on the lookout for any "negro or mulatto acting as a free person," arrest him/her, and bring him/her before "some justice of the peace." Section 19 required any justice of the peace who "shall receive satisfactory information that any Negro or mulatto, not entitled to residence in this state, is within his county" to issue an arrest warrant for his/her appearance before him. Section 20 provided that the presiding justice of the peace or other magistrate be satisfied that the arrestee brought before him was free; otherwise, the law required that the magistrate commit the Negro or mulatto to jail as a runaway, a subject dealt with in the next chapter.

Section 21 mandated that the justice of the peace impose a fine of between ten and one hundred dollars on any free-appearing person of color unable to establish his right to residence within the state by either producing a license "granted pursuant to the provisions of this act, or a certificate ... evidencing that he is a citizen of the United States." (The act explained neither how any person of color became a citizen of any of the United States nor how he proved his out-of-state citizenship.) The magistrate could jail any arrestee unable to pay this sizable fine until it and costs were paid and then order him/her "immediately thereafter to depart the state." Section 22 allowed any justice of the peace to sentence the free person of color unable to establish his right to residence within the state to between ten and twenty lashes *and* either require his immediate departure from Missouri or order the sheriff to rent out "such person for such time as shall be sufficient to raise from the hire, the fine and costs and the expenses of imprisonment." Section 23 required a five-hundred-dollar bond of anyone employing the apparently free Negro or mulatto as security that he would keep the person in his service, feed, clothe, and lodge him, and "not permit or suffer him to go at large and deal as a free person." Section 24 allowed all free Negroes and mulattoes not entitled to residence in Missouri three days and "one additional day for every twenty miles he must travel to depart this state" after their discharge from arrest or service. Section 25 mandated a fine of five dollars per day for anyone who employed any unauthorized free Negro or mulatto unless, as section 26 specified, the hire was for no longer than three months and he/she was "employed on board any vessel, or as a wagoner or messenger, or as a servant of a traveler." Section 27 allowed a fine of one hundred dollars upon any person who brought any unauthorized free Negro or mulatto into the state. Finally, section 28 exempted both "masters of vessels" who employed the unlicensed on their boats and persons traveling through the state with free Negroes and mulattos as servants. However, the maximum time of such employment of free blacks within the state was six months.

It is difficult to imagine that any additional legislation on the subject could be more restrictive of any rights free blacks and mulattoes might have, or could make life more difficult for them, but subsequent enactments of the Missouri General Assembly continued to turn the screw. In 1841 the city of St. Louis was the scene of what still remains the largest mass execution under state authority in Missouri's history: three free Negro residents of St. Louis and one slave, whose owner lived in the state of Louisiana, were convicted of the April attempted robbery of a bank and the murder of two white male clerks, aged 22 years. In July 1841 the four culprits were hanged on Duncan's Island, an area approximately a mile south of the St. Louis Courthouse; crowd estimates of those wishing to watch them die range as high as 20,000 persons.[7] Nothing about these sensational events and their massive press coverage made life easier for any of the more than 1,500 free persons of color who were then St. Louis residents and uninvolved in this crime, its trial, or its punishment.

In 1843 the legislature stepped up the pressure on free persons of color. Its enactments disallowed any colored apprentice in company with a free white to be taught any trade or occupation.[8] Further, it no longer exempted any free colored person who could produce a certificate of citizenship from any of the United States from acquiring a Missouri license in order to live there. All out-of-state free persons of color were required to obtain a license in order to reside in the state. Under section 10 of the 1843 statutes, the applicant for a license was required to post a bond of up to one thousand dollars as security for his good behavior. Except when traveling, no longer could licenses be carried on the person of mulattoes or Negroes. Under section 15, free papers found in their possession were confiscated, and under section 16, if they refused to surrender their free papers, a justice of the peace could sentence them to receive up to 30 lashes. Under sections 17 and 18, any violation of law, no matter how trivial, subjected the free black to forfeiture of his/her license and removal from the state. Under section 22, any person who brought a slave into the state "entitled to freedom at a future period" was guilty of a misdemeanor and could be fined up to five hundred dollars and imprisoned for up to six months. Theoretically, if not in practice, this meant that slaves brought to Missouri from elsewhere could not buy their freedom from their owners, or as it were, buy themselves. Likewise section 25 made it a crime for any person to "employ, harbor, or entertain [hire]" any free person of color brought within the state. Doing so was a misdemeanor punishable with a fine of not less than 50 dollars or more than 200 dollars. Section 24 gave to the recorder of the city of St. Louis all the powers and duties that justices of the peace in Missouri's other counties had concerning free Negroes and mulattoes. Otherwise the 1835 version of the law remained the same.

As white Missourians grew more fearful, the restrictions under which non-whites lived grew more galling. As mentioned in Chapter 1, in 1847 the General Assembly passed "An Act Respecting Slaves, Free Negroes and Mulattoes." It disallowed teaching persons of color to read and write, and it banned religious assemblages for Negroes or mulattoes unless at least one white law enforcer was present throughout the meeting or assembly, in order to prevent all uppity speech, and disorderly and unlawful conduct of every kind. It also dispensed with the licensing requirement, stating: "No free negro or mulatto shall, under any pretext, emigrate to this State, from any other State or Territory." It allowed a five-hundred-dollar fine and/or jailing for up to six months for the violation of the act, and it disallowed the binding out as apprentices of any free Negroes and mulattoes who were under age 21 and not entitled to receive a license to remain in the state.[9] Despite the almost insurmountable difficulties of living in Missouri for free blacks and mulattoes, their numbers there increased from 1,574 in 1840 to 2,618 in 1850, or by 40 percent; between 1850 and 1860 the enumerated free colored persons climbed to 3,572, or an additional 27 percent. Various legislative attempts late in the antebellum period to exclude *all* free persons of color from residence in Missouri failed; the governor vetoed them.[10]

Though city ordinances could never allow the non-slave Negro or mulatto any freedom denied him by the extensive state statutes which governed his life, any municipality could add laws which paralleled or even exceeded those of the state in restricting the pariahs' activities. For example, in 1855, the City of Kansas, now Kansas City, enacted a curfew for free Negroes and mulattoes. They were not allowed to leave their "place of abode" between 10:00 p.m. and 4:00 a.m. "unless going to or coming from some lawful place of business or assemblage." Violators were to be fined between one and ten dollars.[11]

The restrictions under which free persons of color existed can be amply shown in surviving documentation. As early as 1837 the Supreme Court of Missouri rejected the argument that the "seizure of any free person, simply because he has negro blood in his veins, is in violation of the 4th, 5th, 6th, and 7th Amendments to the U.S. Constitution." The court ruled that it was an indictable offense for a free Negro or mulatto to come into the state, and it also upheld the lawfulness of the St. Louis mayor's sentencing the accused to a fine of $100 and jailing him until he paid both the fine and its costs.[12] In another decision this same court disallowed attorney's fees for a St. Louis lawyer who submitted a bill for his services to the city in the amount of $450. Of this total, $350 dealt with these items: (1) "professional services and attention to two hundred cases before the recorder of St. Louis, of free negroes arrested for being in the State of Missouri without a license, at one dollar per case—$200"; (2) "professional services and attention before the County Court of St. Louis County for two weeks in cases of free negroes applying for licenses to remain in this State—$100"; and (3) "attention to the case of a free negro (Charles Lyons) in an application by him to judge of the St. Louis Circuit Court for discharge—$50." The court held that the plaintiff's professional services "were either such as the duties of his office imposed upon him, or if not, that the mayor had no authority to bind the city for the payment of his fees."[13]

So standard were fines and license applications for free Negroes and mulattoes in St. Louis that, unlike most court records of the period which were handwritten, these were printed. No time was to be wasted in writing out the offense; only a few blanks need be filled in. One form read:

> Whereas *James Davis* a free negro hath this day been brought before the undersigned, Recorder of the City of St. Louis, and whereas, in as much as it appears to the satisfaction of the Recorder of said City, that *James Davis* is a free person, living in the State of Missouri contrary to the provision of an act of the said State, entitled "An Act concerning free Negroes and Mulattoes," approved March 14th, 1835, it is adjudged that the said *James Davis* a free negro aforesaid, pay a fine of *twenty* dollars to the State of Missouri, and *two and 25/100* dollars, costs; and that he stand committed until the fine and costs are paid, and that he immediately thereafter depart this State. These are therefore to command you to take the body of the said *James Davis* into your custody, until the said fine and costs are paid; and until then, you are hereby authorized to commit the body of said *James Davis* to the safe keeping and custody of the gaoler of the county gaol of St. Louis.[14]

The paperwork accompanying this case documents that, before the state's criminal justice system finally spat out the accused, he was charged $29.87. In this fashion and under the auspices of the State of Missouri, James Davis and hundreds of other free men and women of color were fleeced of sizable sums, arrested, jailed, and required to leave the state because their skin was the wrong color.

Another printed form dealt with those seeking a license to reside within the State of Missouri.

> The State of Missouri, ... Know ye that *Emily Mason* aged *about thirty one years light complexion five* feet *two inches* high and by occupation *a washerwoman* having on the *fourth* day of *May* in the year of our Lord eighteen hundred and forty *three* produced satisfactory evidence before the County Court of said County, that he[sic] is of the class of free negroes and mulattoes who are authorized by law to be licensed by said Court, to reside within the State of Missouri; that he [sic] is of good character and behavior, and capable of supporting *her* self....These are therefore to license and authorize the said *Emily Mason* to reside within the State aforesaid, so long as he [sic] shall be of good behavior and no longer.

Her application, as the extant form makes clear, was granted June 3, 1843,[15] or about a month after she paid $5 for the privilege of living in St. Louis County and officially supporting herself by washing dirty clothes.

Yet another printed form dealt with the necessary bond following the revision of the law in 1843. Up to one thousand dollars was required as security for a free person of color who sought a license to reside in Missouri. On one example of it was handwritten the name of

> The principal, *Dred Scott*, and *Taylor Blow* as securities are held and firmly bound unto the State of Missouri in the just and full sum of ten hundred Dollars, lawful money of the United States, for the payment of which we bind ourselves, our heirs, executors and administrators, firmly by these present,.... Dated this 4 day of May A.D. 1848.

The printed portion continued that if the "said Dred shall be of good character and behavior during his residence in the State of Missouri, then this obligation to be void; else of full force and virtue."[16] At this time, Scott had won in St. Louis circuit court, but his freedom was short-lived. Subsequent court rulings declared that he continued as a slave for life. However, as noted in Chapter 3, Taylor Blow eventually freed him and his wife in 1857.

Consequently, Dred Scott's name appears on an especially intriguing document, an extant "List of Free Negroes, Licensed [in] ... St. Louis County."[17] Though most of the information contained within it is printed, many of its entries are handwritten. It consists of the names, ages, heights, occupations, and granting dates of licenses for more than 700 free persons of color who applied for them before the County Court of St. Louis County between 1841 and 1859. There is variation in the spelling of their surnames; among many others, there are entries for Emily Macon [*sic*], washer (1843); Charles Lyon [*sic*], fireman (1846); Dred Scott, steward (1858) and his wife Harriet Scott, washer (1858). Probably there were earlier lists now lost, of free colored licensees, especially for St. Louis County, because Missouri enacted its first draconian code concerning free Negroes and mulattoes in 1835.

Other societies have also singled out minorities for special affliction. The Nazis passed the Nuremberg Laws in 1935. These statutes defined the Jew, stripped him of German citizenship, disallowed his voting, prohibited marriage and sexual relations between Jews and Germans, and encouraged Jewish emigration out of Germany.[18] One hundred years earlier, fear of the harmful influence of free persons of color on Missouri's slaves had trumped both the rationality and the humanity of most white Missourians. The Nazis attempted to obliterate the achievements of 50 generations of Jewish literacy; Missouri's laws were enacted, among a variety of other reasons, to prohibit colored Missourians, slave or free, from attaining literacy. Despite the state's deplorable legislation concerning free Negroes and mulattoes, it nevertheless failed to prevent the remarkable adventures and achievements of many colored Missourians.

Fehrenbacher calls attention to the fact that, despite the numerous restrictions imposed upon them, free Negroes and mulattoes actually had a few civil liberties. He writes, "In some respects, such as property rights, a black man's status was superior to that of a married white woman, and it was certainly far above that of a slave. He could marry, enter into contracts, purchase real estate, bequeath property, and ... seek redress in the courts."[19] The immense variety of ways by which free persons of color earned their livings is splendidly documented in the extant "List of Free Negroes" licensed by the County Court of St. Louis County. It contains more than 40 occupations of free male persons of color who obtained their licenses to live in Missouri in the 1840s and 1850s: barber, blacksmith, boatman, boat furnisher, bricklayer, carpenter, carriage driver, carrier [porter], carman [cart driver], coachman, collier [seller of coal], cook, cooper [maker and repairer of casks, buckets, and tubs], drayman [driver of a cart used by brewers], engineer, farmer, fireman, gardener, hack [carriage] driver, mechanic, miner, minister, musician, ostler [caretaker of horses at an inn], physician, preacher, plasterer, porter, rectifier [instrument adjuster], room cleaner, saddler [a saddle maker or dealer], servant, shoemaker, slate [record] keeper, soldier, steward, teamster [driver or owner of a team], trader, tinner [tinsmith], tobacconist, vegetable dealer, waiter, and whitewasher [painter]. Not surprisingly, no steamboat captains, pilots, or mates were included; these exalted positions were reserved for white men.

The occupations of free women of color were much more restricted; in all, only eight were listed. From the most prestigious to the least they were as follows: mantua maker (3), seamstress (10), dressmaker (1), housekeeper (4), cook (2), chambermaid (21), nurse (5), servant (24), and washer (229). That only two were cooks meant this profession was dominated by men; 42 males gave cook as their profession on the 1841–1859 list. Because nurses were as young as 16 years of age they were not today's educated professionals. Both men and women listed their occupation as servant. That washer was the official métier of 77 percent of female licensees is primarily explainable, as Lowry notes, by the fact that white women did not do laundry for hire in the slave states during the antebellum period.[20] Among those listed as proprietors of laundries in 1859 was Harriet Scott, presumably a listing that she was sufficiently successful to buy.[21] With few exceptions the lot of the free black and mulatto women who earned their own livelihoods was one of unrelenting drudgery.

Despite almost insurmountable obstacles, by the 1850s in St. Louis, among this large group of free blacks and mulattoes, there existed a sufficient number of successful persons that one of them, Cyprian Clamorgan (1830–1906?), wrote and published *The Colored Aristocracy of St. Louis* (1858). Among its 41 listed heads of household and their family members, only 10 can be identified — and a few only tentatively — as obtaining licenses between 1841 and 1859. Most likely, the majority of persons gossiped about in this slender volume obtained their licenses before 1841. The law appears to have exempted no resident free person of color. Though Harriet Clamorgan, wife of Cyprian's half-brother Henry, is the only Clamorgan on the "List of Free Negroes," (1841–1859), most likely many other members of this clan obtained their living-in-Missouri licenses between 1835 and 1841.

The author, Cyprian Clamorgan, was probably an early successful applicant for a license. His little book would be of interest under any circumstances, but it is more so because, as noted in Chapter 3, he was a grandson of Jacques Clamorgan. Cyprian's mother was Jacques' only daughter, Apoline, who died in 1830 when she was only 27 years old. Her death left her infant son Cyprian, whose father was white, without a mother. However, as Winch notes, "Eventually his white guardian had sent him out of his home state, and away from all that he had known, in order to get him an education" (4).[22] She identifies Charles Collins as the guardian of the young Clamorgans, and she also clarifies that Collins sent his wards to Illinois for their schooling (27). That the mulatto author was richly steeped in the humanities evinces itself in his book at every turn.

Though Cyprian never knew his fabulous grandfather, who died in 1814, he strongly identified with him. The grandsire had no choice about his religion under Spanish rule of Missouri: between its throne and its altar, the mother country decreed that all persons in its North American colony, Louisiana, should be Catholic. Cyprian was likewise Catholic, and his religious preference probably explains why no preachers or ministers are listed among his colored aristocrats. After all, from the author's point of view, no matter how great their achievement, they were mere apostates. Whenever he identifies the religion of any of his aristocrats, invariably it is Catholicism.

At a time when it was a crime in Missouri to teach any Negro or mulatto to read and write and the U.S. Supreme Court had just decided that the black man had no rights which the white was bound to respect, the far-ranging knowledge demonstrated in Clamorgan's writing is remarkable. Literary, historical, biblical, and mythological allusions abound in his work. He had read Shakespeare with great care; echoes of *A Midsummer Night's Dream, Romeo and Juliet, The Merry Wives of Windsor, Hamlet, Othello,* and *Macbeth* reverberate in his descriptions of his aristocrats. Likewise he alludes to the Bible books of Genesis, Judges, and Matthew, to Roman and Greek mythology, to Cervantes, Alexander Pope, Thomas Gray, Lord Byron, and to English and French history with equal ease and familiarity.[23] Perhaps the biggest surprise in his literary references is to Herman Melville's recently published long short story, "Benito Cereno." It first appeared in *Putnam's Monthly Magazine* in 1854, and was republished as a part of *Piazza Tales* in 1856. Its subtle account of the slave takeover of the ship *San Dominick*[24] would have appealed to any literate free person of color. In his story Melville writes:

> There is something in the negro which, in a peculiar way, fits him for avocations about one's person. Most negroes are natural valets and hair-dressers; taking to the comb and brush congenially as to the castanets, and flourishing them apparently with almost equal satisfaction.... [The barber Babo tells the ship captain] Master knows I never yet have drawn blood.[25]

Clamorgan writes:

> A majority of our colored aristocracy belong to the tonsorial profession; a mulatto takes to razor and soap as naturally as a young duck to a pool of water...; they certain make the best barbers in the world, and were doubtless intended by nature for the art. In its exercise, they take white men by the nose without giving offense, and without causing an effusion of blood [54].

The preponderance of Cyprian Clamorgan's 41 named aristocrats are barbers, and should one wonder why they were not refused licenses to practice barbering, the answer is simple. Other than the occupations associated with alcoholic beverages and the law, which state statutes barred any black or mulatto, slave or free, from practicing, Missouri's licensing requirements for physicians, embalmers and funeral directors, barbers, pharmacists, and other professions commence only in the 1880s, at a time when slavery had long ended.

The author describes the numerous barbers and barbershop and bath owners, all of whom were male, as a "dealer in steel and soap," "one of the most expert chin scrapers in the city," "peels off the beard like a dairy-maid skimming cream," a "knight of the razor," and the like. Many of his men were also stewards on steamboats, persons who attended to the comfort of passengers. Other professions of the men included, as the occupations on the 1841–1859 "List of Free Negroes" suggest, coffeeshop owners, butchers, cattle dealers, providers to steamboats of such items as meat and vegetables, peddlers of fruits and vegetables, restaurant workers, porters, and handymen. Many if not most had more than one profession. For example, as travel by steamboat gave way to travel by railroad, men who had earlier been steamboat stewards likely became merchants or porters.

The great majority of Clamorgan's named aristocrats were men; they dominated the prestigious occupations reserved for blacks and they earned more money than women. He lists three married couples, and the merits of the wives are included: "Mrs. Sawyer is one of the most fascinating ladies of the city.... Her mind is equally gifted with her person.... Her father ... bestowed a world of pains upon her education" (55); "Mrs. Cox is a fine-looking woman, and was wealthy previous to her marriage" (57); and Mrs. Taggert "is very amiable, and is a pattern of a wife" (58). Nine aristocratic entries are of women, and most are great beauties, very rich, or both. The flavor of Clamorgan's descriptions of them can be gleaned from the following: Pelagie Nash "owns nearly the whole block in which she resides" (49); Sarah Hazlett "possesses a comfortable fortune of seven thousand dollars" (49); Mary Obuchon "owns the property upon which she resides, and is worth about nine thousand dollars, [and] has been very useful in times past as a sick nurse" (50); Mrs. Pelagie Foreman "can command the cool sum of one hundred thousand dollars" (59); the Misses Reynolds are Mary Louise and Rebecca, the former "amiable, accomplished and intellectual" and the latter "handsome, ... sings like a nightingale, and is one of the brightest ornaments of society" (61–62); and finally, he describes Harriet Johnson as "an accomplished and fascinating young lady, and quite intelligent"; her sister Julia "is pretty" (63).

Though a nickname may be used in the text of Clamorgan's discussion of his aristocrats, he never lists them by their diminutives. Unlike the names of slaves discussed in the next chapter, without exception none of the women whom Clamorgan discussed are *Hattie, Becky, Lou,* and the like. Likewise, his men are *Samuel* not *Sam, Richard* not *Dick, William* not *Bill, Henry* not *Hank, Robert* not *Bob,* and so on and so forth. His own first name, *Cyprian,* is that of a saint in the early Catholic Church,[26] and the Christian name of three of his aristocratic women, *Pelagie,* is French; it derives from the Greek masculine *Pelagios*.[27] Slaves did not have the privilege of naming their children; free persons of color did, and their dignified choices are reflected throughout Clamorgan's book.

The prior residence, previous condition of servitude, and color of Clamorgan's aristocrats are worth noting. Despite the intent of the Missouri General Assembly's many laws concerning free Negroes and mulattoes, all its legislation did not keep persons of color who wished to live in St. Louis from moving to this bustling, growing, and exciting city. Illinois, Kentucky, Ohio, Pennsylvania, South Carolina, Tennessee, and Virginia are the listed out-of-state origins of the group; Virginia greatly outnumbers all the other places from which his worthies moved to Missouri. Clamorgan identifies this jurisdiction as "the prolific old State of Virginia, the mother of Presidents and mullatos [sic]" (58). As the voluminous "List of Free Negroes" (1841–1859) demonstrates, these out-of-state free persons of color were subject to the indignity of obtaining a license to live in Missouri. The author glides over this demeaning aspect of life.

Clamorgan's discussion of slavery is for the most part general. In his introduction, he writes, "According to the decision of Chief Justice Taney, a colored man is not a citizen of the United States, and consequently has no political rights under the Constitution. His life is all that he is entitled to, and in some States he holds that merely because he is useful to his master" (47). Shortly thereafter, he also observes of "the wealthy free colored men of St. Louis … [that] "the abolition of slavery in Missouri would remove a stigma from their race" (47). Otherwise, human bondage is not a topic which permeates his sketches. Usually he is silent regarding the conditions of previous servitude of his aristocrats and their ancestors.

He is aware, as would be any colored person of his day, of the skin shade of his patricians. His descriptions include "a tall, pompous black man" (54); "is nearly white, and looks more like a Mexican than anything else" (56); "in her younger days a fascinating lump of yellow flesh" (60); "is a large, fine-looking man … nearly dark in color" (61); and "a thin yellow man." More interesting than the author's comments about the racial characteristics of his nobility is the discovery Winch makes about the census-takers' opinions of Clamorgan's aristocrats. Today, the enumerated are asked to state their race or racial mixture. In the nineteenth century, the census-taker eyeballed those he enumerated, and he listed his opinion without consulting them. One of Clamorgan's families counted in the 1850 census as white was listed in the 1860 census as mulatto (88); another aristocrat described as white in 1830 had become a mulatto by 1860, and he and his entire family were once more white in 1870 (90). A family enumerated as black in 1850 consisted of mulatto parents with black children by 1860, and by 1870 the husband-father was black and his wife was a mulatto (92). In another family the father, listed as a mulatto in 1850, had a son, daughter-in-law, and all three grandchildren described as white by 1870 (103). Obviously, far more than beauty was in the eye of the census-taker; so was the skin color of the enumerated. When it paled, as Winch notes, usually the wealth of the family had increased (54).

The ages of Clamorgan's aristocrats ranged from teenage girls to prosperous mid-fifties men and women, at the time he wrote and published his book. One, Nancy Lyons, is of special interest. Whether or not she was born free or a slave is not clarified in the extant records. However, her birth in Illinois of an Indian father and an African-French mother in 1815 means she was approximately 12 years old when Judge McGirk wrote for his court that the child of a slave was free when he was born in Illinois, regardless of the status of his mother: "The [Northwest] Ordinance is positive, slavery cannot exist."[28]

Her family name was Washinga (perhaps a corruption of Washington), and she and other members of it lived first in Kaskaskia, Illinois, until 1844 and then two years in Belleville, Illinois. They moved in 1846 to St. Louis, where she married George Doré, the father of her only son, Felix Doré. Her first husband died in 1849, and she later married Charles Lyons. His name appears in both the "List of Free Negroes" and a previously discussed Missouri Supreme Court decision dealing with attorney's fees of $50 to get him out of jail. Prior to obtaining his license in December 1846, he was an unlicensed free black living in Missouri; doing so was a criminal act, and he was imprisoned because of it. He died in 1853; his widow survived by 69 years, dying in 1922.

Several newspapers ran her obituary with her undated photograph. It is of a very old person. One account described her as "a devout Catholic [who] attended mass every morning until she fell and suffered a fracture of one hip six years ago. She recovered from this injury."[29] Another stressed her travels as a trained nurse; she visited Europe, Asia, and Africa, with, among others, the family of Ethan Allan Hitchcock, later President McKinley's Secretary of the Interior. This newspaper appropriately noted, "She had lived under the reign of nine Popes,"[30] A third paper contained details about her descendants. At her death she was living with her 87-year-old son, Felix Doré, himself a great-grandfather.[31] All news stories mention that she was nearly blind for the last 10 years of her life, but she otherwise enjoyed good health until a few days before her death. All accounts of her passing emphasize, either as fact or probability, that she was St. Louis' oldest resident at the time of her death.

It is indeed remarkable that anyone born in 1815 lived until 1922. Her life spanned the administration of 26 presidents. When she was born, James Madison was president; at her death, Warren Harding. As Chapter 1 makes clear, advocates for slavery claimed that the servitude of persons of color increased their longevity, but in a case wherein the very long life of a colored Missourian can be documented, the aged person was free. Clamorgan writes of her when she had 63 years of additional life: "She was ... raised in ... [Illinois]. Living among the French inhabitants she, of course, learned their language, and was educated in the tenets of the Catholic Church." He also notes that she "keeps an aristocratic boarding house.... Her husband died in California, leaving her the mistress of a fortune of twenty-five thousand dollars, most of which was accumulated by herself "(54).

Perhaps the most dominant feature of Clamorgan's aristocrats is their wealth. Winch demonstrates that he often exaggerates their assets by listing five- and six-figure sums when their financial worth was actually much less. Occasionally he underestimates their riches. It is now difficult to know if his emphasis on their money is explainable by the many indignities all persons of color, either slave or free, suffered at the time and place he wrote his book, or if Cyprian Clamorgan, like Midas, just loved money. He spent years involved in unsuccessful lawsuits relating to his grandfather Jacques Clamorgan's real estate claims.

In any case, the author definitely underestimates the riches of one of his aristocrats, James Thomas, at $15,000. Winch believes that Thomas was by 1870 "the richest person of color in Missouri." She continues, "One report put his wealth at half a million dollars" (96). The father of James Thomas, John Catron (1786–1865), as noted in Chapter 3, was eventually a member of the United States Supreme Court. Earlier, Catron was Chief Justice of the Tennessee Supreme Court. When the father of a six-year-old slave child, James Thomas, Catron upheld the colonization provisions of an 1831 Tennessee statute. It conditioned the freeing of any slave in a last will and testament on either the executor-administrator signing security bonds to guarantee the support of the freed person or the manumitted being transported out of the United States, preferably to Liberia on the coast of Africa. Justice Catron approved of the colonization provisions of this law when he wrote for the court in 1834:

> Degraded by their color and condition in life, the free Negroes are a very dangerous and most objectionable population.... Their condition has and will preclude intermarriage and close association. The [free] black man ... sinks into vice and worthlessness.... He is ... an outcast and his fancied freedom a delusion.... Generally, and almost universally, society suffers and the Negro suffers by manumission.[32]

The "List of Free Negroes" licensed by the County Court of St. Louis includes the name of James Thompson, aged 28 years, identifies his occupation as servant, and dates the issuance of his license as October 1855. Most likely *Thompson* should be *Thomas* because the other aspects of the entry match this unacknowledged child of a U.S. Supreme Court justice, a son who became a huge success.

All we know about James Thomas' conception is that his sire was not also his master. His mother and brother were among the 42 slaves owned by a Virginia planter, Charles Thomas, at his death in 1825. His mother was brought to Nashville, the capital of Tennessee and the residence of his father, Justice Catron, sometime thereafter. At the time of his birth, October 1827, he was an asset of the Thomas estate, which remained unsettled until 1835. Its executor, John M. Martin, a relative of the deceased, was a great spendthrift. Aunt Sally, as Thomas' mother was known, accurately predicted that Martin would sell anything because he would always need money. Sally consulted Ephraim H. Foster (1794–1854), a prominent Nashville attorney who, among other accomplishments, served in the U.S. Senate. Foster helped a number of slaves, including Thomas, obtain their freedom. He learned that Martin was asking $400 for six-year-old James. His mother had managed to save $350 from her work as a laundress of fine linen, and she proposed that Foster buy her son and not sell him to her until she could pay him the additional $50 of his purchase price. Eventually she was able to buy herself for an additional $200.[33]

Foster became Thomas' technical owner in January 1834, and the young slave remained the attorney's property for the next 17 years. When the County Court, at the request of Foster, approved the emancipation of 23-year-old Thomas, as a preserved court document clarifies, he "was placed in a barber's shop where he remained until he learned his trade well; and having followed it ever since, he is now adept in his business and profitably employed therein." Tennessee law of 1842 permitted an emancipated person of good character, capable of posting sufficient bond and of proving his Tennessee residence prior to 1836, to remain in the state. With Ephraim Foster and one E. A. Raworth as his securities, Thomas gave bond in the amount of $500 and the free mulatto, James Thomas, was permitted to remain a resident of Nashville, Davidson County, Tennessee, effective March 1851.[34]

When he died at the age of 87 on December 17, 1913, he was buried in St. Louis. The passing of this prominent Catholic and long-time resident was mentioned in the St. Louis newspapers. One listed his cause of death as bronchitis, and it noted his burial permit.[35] Another's headline read, "Former Friend of President Polk Dies," and though this was surely a stretch, the fact that he was survived by four children, one of whom was a physician, was not.[36] A third mentioned that his funeral took place on Thursday, December 18, 1913, at St. Vincent de Paul Catholic Church.[37]

Between his birth as a slave in Nashville in one century and his death in St. Louis as a devout and philanthropic Catholic in another, James Thomas led a life rich in incident in a variety of geographic locales with periods of great wealth and ultimately great poverty. He traveled from Nashville to New Orleans in 1855, to Central America and Wisconsin in 1856, to Louisville, Kentucky; Keokuk, Iowa; and Topeka, Kansas, in 1857. By 1858 he was working as a waiter and barber on a steamboat which made monthly trips between St. Louis and New Orleans. During his time off he worked in the busy barbershop of Henry Clamorgan, grandson of Jacques and half-brother of Cyprian. At this establishment Thomas was promoted from barber to head barber to full partner. Through his work in this prosperous barbershop, he met, among many members of free black society, 20-year-old Antoinette Rutgers, the daughter of the wealthy Pelagie Rutgers, the first person profiled in *The Colored Aristocracy of St. Louis*. Cyprian Clamorgan estimated Mrs. Rutgers' wealth at $500,000, and her will stipulated, as Winch observes, that her daughter Pelagie's inheritance would be "for her sole, separate & exclusive use, free from the control, and from all liabilities of any husband."[38]

Pelagie Rutgers was born a slave, bought herself for $3, and at age 17 married her first husband, the 20-year-old hairdresser St. Eutrope Clamorgan (1799–1824), son of Jacques Clamorgan and his slave companion Hélène. Although Pelagie was born a slave and married the son of a slave, nonetheless she objected to James Thomas as a son-in-law because he also was born and lived his early life in bondage. Pelagie refused to allow her daughter, Antoinette, child of her second husband, Louis Rutgers, a free black, to marry a former slave. As a result, the marriage of Antoinette Rutgers and James Thomas took place at least 10 years later than it would have were it not for his slave background. When this couple finally married in 1868 at St. Vincent's Catholic Church, after Pelagie Rutgers' death, the bride and groom each held assets of approximately $400,000.

Like many of the early free persons of color in Missouri who can be identified because they were property owners, James Thomas, while continuing to work as a barber, began buying, selling, renting, and leasing real estate, as Schweninger notes. By 1870 his accumulated fortune made him the richest person of color in St. Louis. He lost most of his assets through a market downturn in 1893 and the devastations of an 1896 tornado which struck his inadequately insured properties. As yet another blow, his wife, Antoinette, died in

Photograph and obituary of Mrs. Nancy Lyons, *St. Louis Post-Dispatch*, March 22, 1922. (Used by permission, State Historical Society of Missouri, Columbia. All rights reserved.)

1897.³⁹ When he was still very prosperous, he traveled to Europe in 1873. Later he began and eventually completed his autobiography. In its first chapter he explains that he learned to read and write while a child in Tennessee: "The authorities allowed a school to be kept for teaching the children of free persons. In that school I learned to read and write" (31–32).

His book, written when he was in his seventies, is not the work of an astute critic of society. His education was inadequate for such an undertaking, and most likely as he aged, the anger he probably experienced as a younger man dissipated. However, Thomas describes his great white father: "He presided over the Supreme Court Ten Years (of Tennessee) but he had no time to give me a thought. He gave me twenty five cents once. If I was correctly informed, that was all he ever did for me" (60).

What comes through in his awkward, improperly capitalized, and at times tedious prose is his enjoyment of his occupations, the arts, architecture, people, and travel. His nostalgia for barbering is clear: "The old time Barber shop was the best of all places to learn the ways and peculiarities of the old time gentlemen" (73). As Schweninger explains, it was while a barber at Henry Clamorgan's St. Louis shop that Thomas saw Dred Scott pass by almost every day. Thomas writes about the famous case: "One of the finest pieces of Engineering was getting the Dred Scott Case before Judge Taney. The Negro has no rights that the white man is bound to respect" (81).

Thomas understood well his success as a barber. He writes:

> [Should] a white man attempt to wait on a southern country gentleman in the capacity of barber, he would go into spasm. If a white man came towards him to shave him, he would jump out of his chair. In Charleston a gentleman would not let a white shoemaker measure him for a pair of shoes, nor could a white tailor measure him for a suit of clothes. It was not a white man's place to play the part of srv't [89–90].

In his discussion of steamboats on the Mississippi, Thomas comments that "In the early days all the stewards, with very few exceptions, were colored men" (115). However, he gives credit to a superior writer on this same subject: "Mark Twain, in his Life on the Mississippi, has fairly covered the ground" (117). Twain's *Life on the Mississippi* was first published in 1883 when Thomas was 56 years old. From his comments about it and other worthwhile books, it is evident that Thomas read a great deal.

His account of his travels in Europe in 1873 provides one of the most interesting chapters of his book. His pride in obtaining his passport is touching: "That document gave the person named the right to travel where he chose and under the protection of the American flag" (180). He went by ship from New York to Liverpool, England, and then to London. There, among other outings, he visited the Tower of London and thought it "was the most interesting place I had ever seen" (182); but he also enjoyed musical performances at Drury Lane and Covent Garden and his visit to Westminster Abbey. While in Paris, he determined that "Notre Dame was one of the places of great interest to church people" (186). From Paris he went to Geneva, Switzerland. There he was among a group who dined with the American minister on the fourth of July; he thought "at the time it was the most distinguished party I had ever sat at the same table with" (187). From Geneva, he journeyed to Milan, Florence, Rome, Naples, and other splendid Italian cities. He wrote of his visit to St. Peter's that the "Supreme Pontif [*sic*] ... must be acknowledged the most conspicuous figure in the human family" (188). After touring other countries, including Germany and Austria, he returned to the United States and the intractable realities of segregation:

> Every colored man may or ought to know, although he has been eating and riding with Americans and treated as a companion, as the vessel approaches American soil, all that comes to an end. Each is supposed to take his regular place. Custom, which has a heap to say, has so ordered it [195].

This statement ends the autobiography of a remarkable man. James Thomas, onetime child slave, successful entrepreneur, caring husband and father, devout and generous Catholic, was in all ways the antithesis of his white father's opinion of free Negroes and mulattoes.

Other free persons of color associated with St. Louis include John Berry Meachum (1789–1854) and Elizabeth Keckley (1818–20?–1907). Neither is included in Clamorgan's *Colored Aristocracy of St. Louis* and only Keckley's name appears on the 1841–1859 list of St. Louis's free negroes. Meachum achieved his freedom, and most probably his license to live in Missouri, before 1841.

He made contributions in three different areas. As N. Webster Moore describes the man: "first he purchased slaves, trained them and set them free; second, he began the education of Negroes in St. Louis; and third, he was the town's first black preacher and founded the First African Baptist Church (First Baptist), the oldest Protestant black congregation in St. Louis."[40] He was born a Virginia slave in 1789, and thanks to an apprenticeship he learned carpentry and cabinet- and barrel-making. He saved sufficient money to buy his own and his father's freedom. Meanwhile he moved from Virginia to Kentucky where he married Mary, a slave woman; he followed his wife's owner to Missouri. Soon he purchased her and their children and moved with them to St. Louis.

In 1818 Meachum met an influential white Baptist missionary, John Mason Peck of Connecticut. That same year Peck met with Governor William Clark, and with the governor's approval began religious and literacy instruction of Negroes. Peck's able assistant was John Berry Meachum, eventually ordained a minister in the First African Baptist Church of St. Louis in 1825 when he was in his mid-thirties. Meachum continued his ministry in this same church for the next 38 years. His flock consisted of 220 members, 200 of whom were slaves whose masters approved of Meachum's preaching. By 1836 he had purchased 20 slaves, taught them his own skills of carpentry and coopering, and allowed them to buy their freedom on the installment plan. No slave was able to buy himself or herself until the purchaser was also self-reliant, frugal, and industrious.

At least one of Meachum's purchased Negroes was not content to remain a bondwoman, and she sued her new black owner for her freedom in St. Louis Circuit Court. Although he employed the capable attorney Charles D. Drake, she won her suit for freedom against Meachum, and the Missouri Supreme Court upheld the lower court.[41] Though the appellate decision concerns only the admissibility of a Negro witness's testimony in behalf of Julia Logan, the transcript of proceedings in December 1834, in the circuit court in St. Louis before Judge Luke E. Lawless, makes clear just how routine suits for freedom based on the plaintiff's residence in the Northwest Territory had become. In the 1820s, Judy was a slave of Benjamin Duncan in Daviess County, Kentucky, and her master carried her to Indiana, where he hired her out to labor as a slave for one month. He then returned her to Kentucky and sold her to one James Newton, a white man, who sold her to Berry Meachum, a Negro, in Missouri. Meachum permitted Judy to hire her own time on paying him $12 per month, and she hired herself in the state of Illinois for about one month at Galena with his full knowledge and consent. In her suit for freedom before the all-white male jury which heard her case, she asked for $500 in damages. The jury found for the plaintiff, granting her freedom, but it awarded her only one dollar. The Court ordered "that the said Judy be liberated and entirely set free from the said Berry Meachum," and it assessed court costs against him.[42] The details of this 1836 case, contained in handwritten court records, reveal a less attractive side of Meachum than the one usually presented. Despite his shortcomings, however, he did a great deal for his own people.

In the basement of his church, Meachum operated a school wherein he clandestinely taught colored people, slave and free, reading and writing. (Included among his students was James Milton Turner, then about 12 years old; later, among other accomplishments, he was the first black member of the American Foreign Service. In 1871 President Grant appointed Turner the American minister to Liberia.[43]) Local St. Louis legend maintains that when the sheriff disrupted Meachum's school, the preacher moved it out of the state of Missouri—onto a steamboat equipped with a library. On it and on the Mississippi River, he and his slave employees supplied other steamboats with provisions. In the process his employees became sufficiently wealthy to buy themselves, and Meachum was also to purchase two houses in St. Louis and a farm in Illinois.

In 1847 the legislature banned the instruction of Negroes and mulattoes; however, it could do so only within the *state* of Missouri. As early as 1796, the Fourth U.S. Congress passed legislation which made the navigable rivers of the country public highways.[44] No state could charge tolls or otherwise obstruct the travel of any watercraft upon them. Subsequent congresses retained federal control of the nation's waterways. In 1811, the Eleventh Congress specified that all the navigable rivers and waters of Orleans and Louisiana shall be and forever remain public thoroughfares.[45] As a result, the federal government, not the state of Missouri, then owned the Mississippi River. Meachum built another steamboat, anchored it in the middle of the river, and transported his students to his boat from the riverbank in the morning, taught them reading, writing, and arithmetic on board, and returned them after classes were completed for the day. He did this in total compliance with Missouri law because his school and his instruction in that school were outside the state. Today he would qualify for a presidential medal of freedom; then the authorities were required to tolerate him. He spent a lifetime teaching patience, forbearance, and preparation for freedom, never insurrection or violence. He died as he had lived, while preaching. He fell dead in his pulpit on February 19, 1854, and was buried two days later in Bellefontaine Cemetery, St. Louis.[46]

Though John Berry's name does not appear on the 1841–1859 "List of Free Negroes," five other Meachums do, and most were probably his children: Patsey Meachum, age

22, mantua maker, and Clemson Meachum, aged 24, cooper, both licensed May 1843; Maria Meachum, aged 24, washer, licensed December 1846; Berry Meachum, aged 27, boat hand, and Washington Meachum, no age given, cook or steward, licensed May 1859. As for Cyprian Clamorgan's aristocrats, no Meachums appear among them. The head of household, John Berry Meachum, was almost certainly excluded because he died five years before this little book was published; even if alive, he might have been omitted because he was a prominent non-Catholic preacher.

Another name which appears on the 1841–1859 "List of Free Negroes" was that of Lizzie Keckley, aged 39 years, height, 5'2", occupation, mantua maker. As Jennifer Fleischner explains, "in the hierarchy of dressmaking, Lizzy soon rose to the top and could legitimately advertise herself as a mantua maker. Not all dressmakers could sew the complicated and popular mantua, a dress whose bodice was made to fit snugly through vertical pleats stitched in the back."[47] This talented seamstress obtained her license to live in Missouri in May 1859. She was born a slave on a Virginia plantation in February 1818, the daughter of a white man, Armistead Burwell, and his slave, Agnes Hobbs. Both Lizzie's mother and her slave husband, George Pleasant Hobbs, were literate.[48] The daughter learned sewing from her mother, and at age 14 she moved to Hillsborough, North Carolina, as the slave of her owner's oldest son. There, like her mother before her, she unwillingly became pregnant by a white man, a neighbor of her owner, Alexander Kirkland. Her son and only child, George Kirkland, eventually enlisted in the Union Army as a white man and died in the Battle of Wilson's Creek in Springfield, Missouri, on August 10, 1861. After the Civil War, with the help of Owen and Joseph Lovejoy, congressmen and both brothers of Elijah Lovejoy, she received a pension of $8 per month because she was a widow whose only son was a war casualty.[49]

Keckley left North Carolina and moved back to Virginia, where she joined the household of a daughter of her owner, Anne Burwell. When Anne married Hugh Garland, Slave Lizzie came with her and her family when they moved to St. Louis. (Garland was a St. Louis attorney who represented Dred Scott's owner in various aspects of this famous suit for freedom.) While a resident of St. Louis, Lizzie married a Mr. Keckley whom she believed to be both free and sober. He was neither; rather he was an alcoholic slave, and after eight years of marriage, he died. Meanwhile and more importantly, she managed to raise the $1,200 necessary to purchase her own and her son George's freedom from Hugh Garland effective August 10, 1855. The clerk of St. Louis Circuit Court duly recorded their manumission in November 1855.

In the spring of 1860 Mrs. Keckley moved to Washington, D. C. Her first important customer as a seamstress was the wife of then U.S. Senator Jefferson Davis, later president of the Confederacy. Soon, however, Mary Todd Lincoln interviewed and hired her, and it is as Mrs. Lincoln's modiste, that is a person who makes or deals in fashionable clothes for women, that Elizabeth Keckley is chiefly remembered. She began her employment at the White House in 1861, and by spring and early summer 1862, Keckley had made 15 or 16 dresses for the 43-year-old First Lady. One was the magnificent gown in which Mathew Brady photographed her in November 1861. Mrs. Lincoln wore it at a White House party February 5, 1862, to which 500 guests were invited. Her seamstress was present when the President saw his wife in this stunning outfit. She quotes him as saying on his first sight of the dress, or rather his wife in it,

"Whew! Our cat has a long tail tonight," and when Mrs. Lincoln made no reply, her husband added, "Mother, it is my opinion, if some of that tail were nearer the head, it would be in better style."[50] The President's whimsical objection, as subsequent biographers of him, such as David Herbert Donald, have commented, was to Mrs. Lincoln's "remarkably low décolletage."[51] This was a wonderful moment in the lives of the Lincolns, and we know about it because her modiste later wrote about it.

This talented seamstress remained an employee — and after the president's murder, frequently an unpaid employee — until Keckley wrote about her employer in *Behind the Scenes*, published in 1868. Jean Baker, capable biographer of Mary Todd Lincoln, describes it as "a ghostwritten exposé that Mary Lincoln considered a breach of their intimacy."[52] Jennifer Fleischner credits Elizabeth Keckley with writing this book herself. She considers James Redpath, the journalist and early biographer of John Brown previously assumed to have written Keckley's memoir, to have been Lizzie's collaborator, editor, and the person able to get the book published, not its author.[53]

When her book appeared, Robert Lincoln, the cruel and only surviving son of his parents, persuaded its publisher to recall it; further, all available copies were purchased by "friends of Mr. Lincoln." The author received no royalties from her book, lost customers in her business as a seamstress, and finally died following a stroke on May 26, 1907. On November 11, 1935, a story by the Associated Press credited a Washington newspaperwoman, Jane Swisshelm, with writing *Behind the Scenes*. It denied the very existence of Elizabeth Keckley, but within a few days a Lincoln biographer, John E. Washington, set the record straight in the *Washington Evening Star*.[54]

There is probably no better source about Mary Todd Lincoln between 1861 and 1868 than Elizabeth Keckley's narrative. She was with the Lincolns during the death of their son Willie in February 1862, and she was also in the White House when the President was nominated for and won a second term in summer and fall 1864. She traveled with them to Richmond after the city's capture by Union troops spelled the end of the Confederacy in March 1865. The next month, as so often during the Lincoln presidency, Mrs. Keckley dressed Mrs. Lincoln on April 14, the night she and her husband attended a performance of *Our American Cousin* at Ford's Theater. Afterwards the President's widow was asked, "Is there no one Mrs. Lincoln, that you desire to have with you in this terrible affliction?" She responded, "Yes send for Elizabeth Keckley. I want her just as soon as she can be brought here."[55] Her seamstress remained the confidante and chief prop of a long troubled and now distraught widow. The two women — one a former slave and the other a former First Lady traveling incognito as Mrs. Clarke — met in New York when Mrs. Lincoln tried to sell her luxurious clothes in order to raise money. (At the time, pensions for widows of presidents were not automatic.) When Mrs. Lincoln left New York for Chicago, Keckley remained behind and continued her efforts to help her employer, a person now unable to pay her. One of a number of letters included in *Behind the Scenes* written to her by Mrs. Lincoln — "M.L." as she signed herself— ended: "I consider you my best living friend, and I am struggling to be enabled someday to repay you. Write me often as you promised."[56] Though Mrs. Keckley continued her correspondence with Mrs. Lincoln, she also wrote about her in *Behind the Scenes: Thirty Years a Slave, and Four Years in the White House*. Between the aftermath of its publication in 1868 and Mrs. Lincoln's death in 1882, the two women were never reconciled.

Today no biographer of either Abraham or Mary Todd Lincoln ignores Keckley's narrative. David Herbert Donald's best seller *Lincoln* (1995) cites it twice, and Jean H. Baker's popular *Mary Todd Lincoln: A Biography* (1987) refers to it or some other aspect of Elizabeth Keckley 28 times. *Behind the Scenes* was in its day, and remains, a fascinating read. In addition, the Smithsonian houses a purple velvet gown which Keckley made for Mrs. Lincoln about 1864. A photograph of it on a mannequin together with a short biographical sketch of its creator appear in a recent publication of the museum.[57] The inclusion of this former slave's magnificent dress for a former First Lady continues to enhance Elizabeth Keckley's reputation. The latest tribute to her is Jennifer Fleischner's *Mrs. Lincoln and Mrs. Keckly* (2003), a wonderful biography which gives equal attention to the lives of both women.

More is known about free persons of color in St. Louis than in any other locale within the state. Although most Missouri counties in both the 1836 and the 1848 state censuses listed one or more non-slave persons of color as residents,[58] information about the great majority of them is not readily available. One other area of the state which contains accessible detail about the lives of free Negroes and mulattoes is western Missouri.

One is a tale of three counties, St. Clair, Jackson, and Cass, with an out-of-state connection to Oberlin College in Ohio, a school long celebrated as first to admit women as students, educator of abolitionists, and early pioneer in interracial education. A history of the college, written in the 1940s, makes oblique reference to two students:

> In 1855 a slaveholder of Osceola, Missouri sent his quadroon children (a boy and a girl) to Oberlin to be brought up and educated. They were taken into the home of an Oberlin white woman and, after a period of study in the common schools, were enrolled in the Preparatory Department of Oberlin College, the girl living for a while in Ladies Hall and becoming an accomplished musician.[59]

Nearly 60 years passed before a diligent local records field archivist with the Missouri Secretary of State's Office completed several years of research regarding this boy and girl and published her compelling account of their lives.

Charles Lee Younger is best known as a grandfather of two outlaw bands who terrorized Missouri and its bordering states from the close of the Civil War until the 1890s, the Younger brothers and their cousins, the Daltons.[60] He was born December 28, 1783, in Hampshire County, Virginia, and he married twice. First, when only 14 years old, he wed Nancy Toney in Garrand County, Kentucky; her death in 1807 left him with two young children. Next, he married Sarah Sullivan Purcell of Little York, Indiana, and from his union with his second wife five children were born. His third cohabitation was with Parmelia Wilson, and during the course of his liaison with this common-law wife, he sired seven children. However, it was from his lengthy living arrangement with his mulatto slave Elizabeth that the two children, Catherine and Simpson Younger, came into being.

In February 1852 their father, then 66 years old, and owner of many acres and slaves[61] in Jackson County, Missouri, made a will. In it he provided for his numerous progeny, including the freedom of his slave Elizabeth and his two children by her, Catherine and Simpson Younger. Charles Lee Younger died on November 11, 1854,[62] by which time he had moved from Jackson to St. Clair County, where he lived with Elizabeth. The day before he died, he added a codicil to his will which included generous provisions for the upbringing and education of his two quadroon children.

Strife among his surviving wives surely explains why, within a month of his burial in St. Clair County, his wife Sarah (grandmother of the Younger gang) had his remains exhumed and removed for reburial in Jackson County; but a third burial probably placed him in the Ragan family plot in the Orient Cemetery in Harrisonville, Cass County, Missouri. Sarah Younger managed to get the administration of her husband's estate transferred from the Probate Court of St. Clair County to that of Jackson County. This feat was accomplished through an act of the Missouri General Assembly passed January 29, 1855. In his will, Charles Lee Younger made ample provision for his daughter Adeline, his child by his common-law wife Parmelia, but he specifically excluded Adeline's husband, Lewis Dalton, father of the Dalton gang.

Despite the obvious displeasure of Sarah Younger, Parmelia Younger, and the numerous children of the deceased by both these white women, the Probate Court of Jackson County upheld the codicil regarding his slave children by Elizabeth. Younger's will named Waldo P. Johnson, a St. Clair County attorney, as executor, and this document specified in pertinent part "that after my death, the following slaves belonging to me, be manumitted and forever set free from slavery or service or bondage to any man, to wit, Elizabeth, aged 22 years, of Mulatto Colour, and her two children named Catherine and Simpson." The codicil required that after the testator's death the executor Waldo Johnson transport Catherine, then about six years old, and her brother Simpson, then about eight, to "a free state and place them in a respectable school where they shall be well clothed, and cared for in every respect, and their morals particularly guarded, until they arrive at the age of twelve each." It also specified that at the age of 12, Catherine and Simpson were to become students in a "college of high grade, where each may receive a thorough classical education." Their expenses were to be paid by their father's estate, and, upon arriving at the age of 21, each was to receive $3,000, and if either did not reach this age, the survivor was to receive $6,000 on his/her twenty-first birthday. Accordingly, after their father's death, Johnson took the children from their mother, Elizabeth, and she did not see her son again until he was 21 years old. (She later married a black man, and they had five children.) The Younger estate paid Delia Shepard $130 twice a year to care for Catherine and Simpson in her home in Oberlin, Ohio, where they were educated in preparatory schools until they were old enough to attend the college there.

Catherine was an Oberlin College student in 1861–62 and 1866–69. Meanwhile, before he attended college, her brother, Simpson, at the age of 13, enlisted in the 27th United States Colored Troops as one of the youngest members of the Union Army. Today his name is displayed on Plaque B-43 at the African American Civil War Memorial in Washington, D. C. After the war Simpson attended Oberlin College between 1866 and 1870, and during those years he made his mark as the pitcher on the college Resolute Baseball Team. After his years at Oberlin he taught school, learned the trades

Members of the Resolute Base Ball Club, 1868, Oberlin College, Oberlin, Ohio. Simpson Younger is second from left, front row. (Courtesy Oberlin College Archives, Oberlin, Ohio.)

of marble cutting and tile setting, married a woman of color, Grace Carter, in 1879, divorced her in 1889 after a lengthy separation, and in 1890 married another colored woman, Florence Higgerson, in Kansas City, Missouri, where they resided.

In 1888, the light-skinned Simpson purchased orchestra seat tickets for a performance at the Ninth Street Theater in Kansas City, Missouri, but because the woman accompanying him was a darker color than he, the usher refused to seat them in the orchestra section of the theater; it was reserved for whites. An angry Simpson Younger filed suit in Jackson County Circuit Court against the owner of the theater. He alleged that his rights under the Equal Protection Clause of the 14th Amendment to the U.S. Constitution had been violated. The trial court found for the defendant theater owner, and Simpson then took an appeal from this decision to the Supreme Court of Missouri. It upheld the right of the theater owner to segregate members of his audience on the basis of their skin color. The Court wrote, "Such separation does not necessarily assert or imply inferiority on the part of one [race] or the other. It does no more than work out natural law and race peculiarities."[63] (Four years after the Missouri Supreme Court interpreted the 14th Amendment's Equal Protection Clause in Simpson Younger's case, the U.S. Supreme Court enunciated the infamous doctrine of "separate but equal" regarding the segregation of white and black passengers in railroad cars.[64]) Simpson Younger lived until May 1943. He died in Wichita, Kansas, while staying at his daughter's home. The *Sedalia Democrat* (Pettis County, MO) described him as the last living Civil War veteran of the county. His life was lived as a man of color, and there was more in it, including his lawsuit for civil rights, to be enjoyed than to be endured.

His sister Catherine chose a different course. She returned to St. Clair County,

African-American Civil War Memorial, 10th and U streets, N.W., Washington, D.C.: Statuary group and portion of roster—see facing page—including Simpson Younger's name. (Photographs by Eric Chelline.)

Missouri, and in January 1878 she married a white man, Speed Warren, and in due course they became the parents of five children. He died in 1898, and she was left with the care of her elderly mother-in-law and the children. At times Catherine resided in Oklahoma, but she always returned to St. Clair County, Missouri. Though she could and did pass as a white woman elsewhere, in her home county it was widely known, and it would never be forgotten, that she was the daughter of a slave. Apparently she was accepted by neither white nor black, and her life was largely one of unhappiness. She aspired to be something she was not, a white person. She died in her 90s in January 1941 at her farm in St. Clair County in the care of her son, Edward Warren. Extant contemporary newspapers of her county make no mention of her death.[65]

Details of the life of one additional black person conclude this chapter; his name was Jeremiah McCanse. He was born a slave in Lawrence County, Missouri, in 1847, owned in Vernon County, Missouri, valued at $600 as a child, freed in 1863, and at age 15 became a drummer in an all-black infantry unit of the Union Army. After the Civil War he moved to Spring Hill, Kansas, where as a barber, married father of six, and school board and Republican Party member, he was prominent in his community until his death in 1904. When his daughter Jessie McCanse (Campbell) graduated from Spring Hill High School in 1897, her father signed the gigantic diploma (21¾" by 17") graduates then received. It certifies "that Jessie M. McCanse has honorably completed the Course of Study, as prescribed for the High School, and by her intellectual attainments and correct deportment is entitled to receive this."

Two structures which Jeremiah McCanse built in Spring Hill still stand. On his original limestone marker in the Spring Hill Cemetery in southwest Johnson County, Kansas, his name is misspelled McCause. (Likewise his name is misspelled McCants in his Union Army papers.) Almost a century after his death, the Bruce Funeral Home in Spring Hill donated a new headstone, and descendants of Jeremiah McCanse and those of the family who owned him came together to dedicate it. The new one spells his name correctly. About 200 people attended the ceremony as speakers celebrated diversity and asked forgiveness for the sin of slavery. The great granddaughter of Jeremiah McCanse, Corinne Patterson, who attended the dedication of her ancestor's new tombstone, summed up her great grandfather's legacy this way: "You can come from nothing and make a ton. You can live a dignified life even when everything conspires to make you fail. Hate can never win."[66]

4. *Free Negroes and Mulattoes*

The many obstacles that any person of color, slave or free, faced in Missouri during the antebellum period were considerable. However, as has been shown, they were not insurmountable. Whether those who made their mark were children or grandchildren of a Jacques Clamorgan, U.S. Supreme Court Justice John Catron, landowner Charles Lee Younger, or illiterate bondpersons, those whose lives are mentioned herein achieved a great deal, and

Top: Tombstones of Jeremiah McCanse, Spring Hill, Kansas, Cemetery. The new stone in the foregound was donated by Bruce Funeral Home, Spring Hill, and dedicated in August 2002. (Photograph by the author.) *Bottom:* Graduating class, Spring Hill (Kansas) High School, 1897, with teacher (second from left, front row). Jessie McCanse (Campbell), daughter of former slave Jeremiah McCanse, is second from left, back row. (Photograph courtesy Corinne Patterson, great granddaughter of Jeremiah McCanse.)

all achieved their freedom with perfect legality. As the next chapter explains, an even greater number of persons removed the restraints of slavery by escaping. Seventy-five percent of Missouri was bordered by free territory, and this accidental fact of geography explains much about the mass exodus of the enslaved.

5

Runaways

Any slave owner lived with the likelihood that his/her bondpersons might run away. That there were always escaped and escaping slaves seems a given of human bondage, and the frequency with which owned persons absconded presented a seemingly insoluble problem for both the master and his government. As discussed in Chapter 2, the French first introduced the Black Code in 1724, and its multiple articles were applicable throughout what later became the states of Louisiana, Arkansas, and Missouri. Under its provisions, running away from the master *(marronnage)* was a crime only slaves committed; colonial judges determined both the guilt of accused runaways and their sentences. Though the Spanish never repealed the code, there are no documented cases involving runaways under either French or Spanish rule of Missouri. After the area passed to American control the runaways may have headed north toward a free state, but during most of the eighteenth century there was neither a United States of America nor free jurisdictions within it. Kerr's research documents that Spanish colonial authorities authorized payment to the owners of runaway slaves who died while escaping. He observes that "All fugitive slaves killed in attempting escape would be paid at [200 pesos]. Each slave owner was to pay a pro rata fee of four reales [50 cents] per slave into a general fund in order to pay the compensation for slaves killed or executed."[1] This fund also covered the costs of catching or attempting to catch the runaways. Kerr's table "Payments Received for Fugitive Slaves 1774–1788" lists 14 different reimbursements whereby various owners received compensation from the Spanish government because their slaves were killed in flight.[2] Nonetheless, slaves ran from their owners under French, Spanish, and American ownership of the Purchase.

Once Upper Louisiana became a territory of the United States, the legislative authority adopted Virginia law to govern slaves. The 1804 Law Respecting Slaves contained several prohibitions for free persons in their dealings with bondpersons which were intended to hinder slave flight. If any white, free Negro, or free Mulatto hired any slave without the consent of his or her owner, a justice of the peace heard the case, and upon conviction the offender was either fined $3 plus court costs or received 20 lashes on his or her bare back. Any person convicted of the theft of a slave suffered death; but since the only recovered court records concern the 1804–1805 indictment of an already deceased defendant, John Pickens, yeoman, it seems unlikely that slave stealers were tried, convicted, and executed under the authority of the United States in territorial Missouri. Today any American criminal case is mooted by the death of the defendant, but under the law of territorial Missouri, restoration of the stolen property to the rightful owner was a part of the penalty for the crime. John Pickens' supposed victims, Pascal Cerré and Antoine Soulard, two prominent French residents of St. Louis, stood to benefit financially if John Pickens, alive or dead, was found guilty of the theft of slaves whom Cerré and Soulard alleged they owned.[3] The outcome of this case is unknown.

Several newspaper items about a 45-year-old slave woman named Ginny, who her supposed owner alleged was stolen from him in Cape Girardeau District in 1809, suggest that property disputes were settled with reference to the 1804 capital statute. Other particulars appeared concerning the ownership of Ginny. One story stated that her thief had been arrested and discharged, and the other that the accused had lawfully purchased her.[4] By the time Missouri became a state, the theft of a slave was no longer a death-penalty crime.

The 1804 law also contained a specific section dealing with runaways. Taken almost verbatim from a 1792 Virginia statute, the Missouri law required any two justices of the peace of the district containing slaves "lurking in swamps, woods, and other obscure places" to issue warrants wherein, if known, the slave(s) and owner(s) were named. These court orders empowered the sheriff to search for such slaves, and, if he found them, to commit them to the district jail.[5] From the start of American government in Missouri, the fee for jailing runaways was the responsibility of the slave owner. The legislative authority anticipated that bondpersons in significant numbers would run from their owners and adopted laws which aided them in recovering their fugitive property, providing the masters reimbursed their government for its assistance.

The 1804 statute required the sheriff of the district to commit any apprehended runaway to the jail of his district "for further trial." This language probably required, as most likely did identical language in the 1792 Virginia runaway statute, that the owner prove he owned the fugitive. Because the law did not list any punishment for the absconding slave, almost certainly as early as 1804 in Missouri the slave's flight from his owner was not a crime. This was not true in earlier times in other areas of what became the United States. Wiecek summarizes South Carolina law concerning runaway slaves under a 1696 statute:

> A mere runaway was given forty lashes for the first offense, branded with an *R* on the right cheek for the second, forty lashes and an ear sliced off for the third; for the fourth, if a male he "shall be gelt" and a female branded *R* on the left cheek and her left ear slit off; and for the fifth offense, death or the cord of one of the slave's legs to be cut above the heel.[6]

North Carolina law of 1714, according to Kay and Cary, permitted "any person or persons" to "kill any Runaway Slave that hath lyen out two months; ... such person or persons shall not be called to answer for the same if he give Oath that he could not apprehend such Slave but was constrained to kill him." Its 1741 modification eliminated any waiting period prior to the use of deadly force to apprehend fugitive slaves. It allowed their catchers "to kill and destroy such slave or slaves by such Ways and Means he or she shall think fit, without Accusation or Impeachment of any Crime for the same."[7] Further, North Carolina colonial statutes provided that the colony would compensate the owner of any runaway when his human property was killed while fleeing the service of his master.[8]

Mutilations and outright murder of slaves which the older slave states inflicted on their runaways were barred in the territories because of the application therein of the U.S. Constitution. There, no *state* law was in place to disallow any number of rights if the case involved a slave. Only federal law applied, and the 1791 Bill of Rights to the Constitution mandated a number of rights for the defendant in any *criminal* case. The Eighth Amendment prohibited cruel and unusual punishments; the Fifth and Sixth Amendments mandated indictments by grand juries, jury trials, the privilege against self-incrimination, and compulsory process for obtaining witnesses in the accused's behalf. Further, under legislation passed by the First Congress which George Washington signed in 1790, in any capital case all persons, including slaves, were guaranteed the right to two attorneys. These were all requirements of prosecuting *crime* in any territory of the federal government. Of equal importance, once American rule of Missouri began, owners were never compensated when their slaves escaped their bondage and survived as free persons, as they probably had been under Spanish authority.

Under American rule of Upper Louisiana, the slave who ran from his master was always a fugitive, but he/she was not a criminal. Neither territorial nor state law in Missouri ever provided for the prosecution and punishment of the *act* of the slave running from his owner any more than it provided for indictments and trials for strayed livestock. Upon any owner's establishing proof, were it contested, of his right to his lost property in a court of law and paying costs, the owner reclaimed his chattel. Always the substantial risk remained that the departed human property would not be found and the owner's loss would be permanent. The many changes in runaway laws make clear that Missouri's lawmakers never devised any effective means to halt the multitude of slaves who ran from their masters.

In 1817 the Third Territorial Legislature passed a statute which supplemented the 1804 law. It presumed that any slave traveling without a token or written pass from his owner was a runaway. It required any person apprehending such a slave to take him or her before a justice of the peace. In the event the slave(s) were not residents of the county wherein they were found, the finder was required to run a 90-day advertisement in a Missouri newspaper. The owner was responsible for payment for the ad as well as for a reward of at least $5 plus the finder's expenses, or $10 if offered by the owner. In addition, the owner was also responsible for his runaway's lawful expenses. If no owner claimed such slaves after 90 days, the sheriff of the county holding them was empowered to sell them to the highest bidder. This official could deduct the fees for the sale as well as the cost of jailing the runaways. The surplus, if any, was to be deposited in the county treasury and made available to any owner able to establish his or her ownership of the sold slave(s) before any court of record in Missouri Territory.[9]

The change in the law between 1804 and 1817 suggests that by the late territorial period the apprehension of runaways had become too labor-intensive to remain the sole responsibility of the sheriff and those he deputized. The large number of runaway ads in St. Louis's earliest newspaper also indicates that the sheer volume of absconding slaves was immense. In 1808 the Board of Trustees of the town of St. Louis passed two ordinances within a month of each other aimed at curbing slave freedom. The first,

"Ordinance Concerning Slaves in the town of St. Louis," prohibited slave public drunkenness, and it required the owner's permission for any slave, among other activities, to assemble with three or more other slaves and associate with any whites, free Negroes, and free mulattoes. The purpose of the second, "An Ordinance Regulating Patrols in the town of St. Louis," was the enforcement of the new slave ordinance and general policing duties. Either the chairman of the town Board, any two judges, or any two justices of the peace could order an armed patrol "whenever circumstances shall require." A patrol consisted of no fewer than four persons, including a captain. All male inhabitants of the town aged 18 years and older, or their substitutes, were required to serve on patrol for a four-month period. Among other tasks, the patrol was ordered to "arrest all slaves found after nine o'clock in the streets or public highways … and conduct them to their masters or mistress," who either whipped their misbehaving properties or were fined because they did not.[10] Both of these early St. Louis ordinances and a Virginia law of 1819 were the sources of an 1822 Missouri statute which remained in effect throughout slavery.

The purpose of that law was preventive, and its passage underscored heightened anxiety in the state's slave-rich counties that bondpersons might either revolt against or run from their white owners. At its discretion, each county was allowed to appoint for one year in each township within its borders, a captain of the patrol and up to four additional patrollers. These men spent no less than twelve hours each month on the lookout for suspicious slaves. Any member of the patrol was allowed to administer up to 10 lashes on the bare back of any slave "found strolling about from one plantation to another, without a pass from his or her master, mistress, or overseer."[11] A justice of the peace could permit the application of up to 39 patroller-administered lashes on the back of the strolling or unlawfully assembled slave. Assignment to the patrol was of sufficient importance to exempt its members from both jury and militia duty.

Williams' extraction of the appointment and payment of patrol companies between 1823 and 1850 in Ralls County, which bordered the Mississippi River in northeastern Missouri, illuminates extensive white citizen concern with its human chattel. That the task was immense is illustrated by both the original legislation and the detailed record of patrol appointments and payments. In this county more than 100 men were appointed as patrollers between the 1820s and the 1850s, and the county paid them hundreds of dollars for the performance of their duties.[12] Presumably other counties, with slave populations equal to or larger than Ralls, also appointed patrollers and paid sizable sums to them. Such surveillance was motivated by white fear that slaves would not remain docile; its only objective was their control. The 1822 statute specified that the lashes which patrollers were allowed to administer were not as punishment for a crime, because a jury trial and other legal niceties were required before a slave could be punished for criminal act(s). As late as 1860 the city of Liberty considered forming a patrol to prohibit Negroes from congregating at meetings without the presence of white police. Its newspaper complained of the "distracted condition of the country, and the fact that the country is full of disguised abolitionists."[13] Early and late in slavery's Missouri tenure, slave flight remained a persistent problem.

In 1835 the General Assembly provided that, in the event a justice of the peace committed a person who was not a runaway to jail, a court of record could order the wrongly jailed colored person's release. However, any black or mulatto had considerable difficulty establishing that he/she was free. The law was clear: color was prima facie evidence of slavery. This put the burden of proving that any black or mulatto was free on the inmate, and he was not entitled to an attorney because Missouri law never classified running away as a crime. Lawyers were only appointed for slaves in *criminal* cases. Nonetheless, if any free person of color could prove that he/she was not a slave, the state paid all expenses of supporting the prisoner and jailer's fees. The 1835 law also required that the state pay the keep of any slave committed as a runaway who died in jail.[14] In 1848, a man, probably white, who was incarcerated for stealing goods beat a runaway to death in the Clay County jail in Liberty.[15]

The initial "Act Concerning Freed Negroes and Mulattoes" which the legislature passed in 1835 required that free persons of color carry their licenses on their persons. It changed, and its revisions are explainable by the increased volume of runaways. By 1843, unless the licensee was traveling, free papers were required to be deposited with the clerk of the county court of residence of the free person of color. A justice of the peace could sentence any free black who refused to surrender his or her free paper to up to 30 lashes. Obviously any skilled runaway might obtain free papers, the legislature reasoned, and pass himself off as a person without a master. However, the traveling runaway might have stolen the license of the free person of color and still make good his getaway.

In 1845, the legislature increased the slave catcher's reward for arresting runaways. This law was taken in part from a Virginia statute of 1819 which required the reimbursement of slave hunters for the distances they journeyed in order to apprehend and return runaways.[16] The 1845 Missouri law based rewards on both the age of the fugitive and the catcher's travels. If the capture was made outside Missouri of a slave above the age of 20 and he or she was delivered either to the master or the sheriff of the master's county, the hunter received $100. If a slave captured out of state was under age 20, the reward was $50. If a fugitive slave of any age was apprehended within the state, the sum was $25, plus whatever the owner offered as a reward. The owner's time for claiming his runaway prior to the sheriff's sale of the slave was reduced from a year to three months. The sheriff was now required to advertise in three newspapers in different areas of Missouri, describing as fully as he could his runaway-slave prisoner(s). In addition to his usual remittance for jailing and selling the slave(s), he received "a fee of ten dollars to himself." The 1845 act contained another feature which indicated the general direction of slave flight. The law required the governor of Missouri to publish the runaway legislation in two Illinois newspapers for three months and thereafter to publish it annually. The state treasurer was authorized to pay the expenses for such publication.[17] With minor exceptions such as shortening the time period between the fugitive slave's capture and sale still further to two months, the 1845 legislation remained runaway law in Missouri throughout the tenure of slavery.

Other laws about runaway slaves made their way into the statute books and the courts. They tell us a great deal about the means of transportation bondpersons used when they made their getaways. Most probably walked, but not all. In 1817 the first steamboat traveled on the portion of the Mississippi which borders the state of Missouri; in 1819 the first made its way from St. Louis to Franklin, Missouri, on the Missouri River.[18] Shortly, a number of runaways discovered that they could speed up their journeys to freedom by traveling by commercial watercraft. In 1822 the Missouri General Assembly reacted. At this early date it did not envision all the opportunities which travel by steamboat afforded runaways. The legislation merely required that "any ferryman or other persons who may be convicted of crossing any slave from the state across the Mississippi ... shall forfeit and pay to the owner ... all damages and costs ... and the full value of such slave.[19] This statute was aimed at inhibiting the journeys of slaves *across* the Mississippi River, not *on* it. Subsequent enactments of the legislature continued the liabilities of ferrymen who transported fugitives across the Mississippi from Missouri to Illinois, but it also gave "Any master, commander or owner of a steamboat, or any other vessel" the duty to be on the lookout for fugitives from labor and not "transport or carry away any servant or slave out of this state without the consent of the owner.[20] Though many suits brought by slaveholders against steamboats were filed in St. Louis County, they also arose in other counties which bordered either the Mississippi or the Missouri River.

In 1844 the *Wapello*, which had been docked overnight at Glasgow (Howard County), picked up a Negro passenger at Boonville (Cooper County). The captain examined his boarding passenger's license to reside in Missouri, and it bore the seal of the clerk of Howard County. The examining captain believed it described its bearer, Pompey Spence, a traveling free Negro who properly had his license with him. However, a runaway slave named Charles had stolen both a horse to ride from Glasgow to Boonville and Pompey Spence's license. The steamboat transported Charles to St. Louis where he disappeared, presumably into a free state. His owner successfully sued the captain for the value of Charles in Howard County Circuit Court; in 1846 the Supreme Court of Missouri affirmed the judgment against the captain of the steamboat. Judge Scott wrote for the Court:

> The greater portion of our eastern frontier, being only separated by a navigable stream from a non-slaveholding state, inhabited by many who are anxious and leave no stone unturned to deprive us of our slaves; our interior being drained by large watercourses ... render it necessary that the strictest diligence should be exacted from all those navigating steamboats on our waters in order to prevent the escape of our slaves.[21]

As the statute was written in 1835 and remained on the books until repealed in February 1864, the standard of care required of masters of vessels came close to absolute liability on the part of boat owners when their vessels transported Missouri runaways on their journeys to freedom. Eventually, the Supreme Court of Missouri reasonably relaxed it. In a Ray County case (one of the few involving a female runaway on a steamboat), the Court held that the plaintiff-owner of the now lost slave was required to show that those in charge of the steamboat had been negligent. The care required, wrote the Court, was "such ... as thoughtful and prudent persons would have taken in navigating a boat in the midst of a slave population, to prevent the escape of slaves upon it, if the property endangered had belonged to themselves instead of belonging to others."[22]

However, the demand for extra workers was constant on commercial river vessels.

Steamboats were often short of hands to "wood," that is, to feed pieces of timber into the fire from which the steam was made, and runaways frequently "wooded" in exchange for the price of their fare. It is from cases decided by the Missouri Supreme Court that we know steamboats such as the *Bates, Ben Franklin, El Paso, General Leavenworth, Harry of the West, Reindeer, Timoleon, Utility*, and others unwittingly transported Missouri's slaves for at least a portion of their journey to freedom. Twain lists the *Ben Franklin* and *Reindeer* among steamboats which completed their antebellum trips on the Ohio and Mississippi Rivers in record time.[23] The runaways on board these fast watercraft likely knew about their speed.

Late in the antebellum period, fugitive slaves began riding on railroads. In a vain effort to halt yet another mode of runaway transportation, the legislature passed a law in 1855 which allowed the owner to recover double the value of his slave if the railroad transported him without his master's consent.[24] In four of Missouri's interior counties — Osage, Cole, Pettis, and Macon — owner suits against railroads were appealed to the Missouri Supreme Court between 1864 and 1866. In each, the owner alleged that the railroad transported his runaway slave without his consent.[25] Their outcome is not clear; however, that the act was repealed in February 1864 and slavery abolished in 1865 did not settle railroad liability, if any.

Missouri's many statutes concerning runaways never prevented bondpersons from leaving the service of their masters; rather, each new enactment underscores the increasing ineffectiveness of the state's runaway legislation. Whether slaves walked, were carried, ran, rode stolen horses, were concealed in the beds of mule-drawn wagons, made their way by steamboat or railroad, or used some combination of these modes of transportation, the statutes and the lawsuits about their departures were but stage props for the human drama which played itself out in this border state.

Stories about fugitives were featured in Missouri newspapers primarily in the 1850s. Earlier, there were mostly advertisements. Those examined appeared in the state's newspapers between 1808 and 1860, and their analysis reveals a great deal about the owners and the owned. Always the advertiser wished to capture the fugitive, or reunite him with his owner, never to aid his flight to a safe haven. Sometimes the sheriff or jailer advertised, but more often the slaveholder purchased the ad. The success or failure of the slave to achieve permanent freedom cannot be ascertained from the ad. Usually, the failure is confirmed in the slave's later mention in a court record, a newspaper, or a history of the county involved.

Most Missouri newspaper advertisements concerning runaways described *men* between the ages of 18 and 50 who ran solo from their owners. One of the earliest concerned a mulatto man named Anthony who ran from the advertiser, presumably his owner, on October 4, 1807, at Nashville, Tennessee. The ad contained no age for the runaway, but it included his height, 5'7" or 5'8", his clothing, a blue coat and pantaloons, and his manner, "crafty and cunning." The riveting detail "branded *R* on each cheek"[26] suggests that Anthony had earlier broken the law of a Deep South state such as South Carolina. That state's statutes gave judges wide discretion in punishing slaves for a number of non-capital offenses, including absconding from their owners or enticing other slaves to leave their masters. Nose slitting, hand or face burning, forehead or cheek branding with hot irons, ear severing, and other horrors were all court-authorized punishments for the better ordering and governing of Negroes in eighteenth-century South Carolina.[27] A physician was indicted in that state in 1799 for the misdemeanor of branding a Negro with a hot iron on his forehead. Though his indictment was reversed on appeal because it had not been filed in a timely fashion,[28] this doctor's fault was apparently in not using the courts to obtain the desired punishment for his slave. Despite Anthony's cruel and unusual punishments for a crime such as running from his owner, he also ran from his Tennessee master, perhaps, the advertiser believed, to or near the town of St. Louis.

Almost certainly, the branding of human beings was never a penal measure under the authority of the United States, including the Territory of the United States South of the River Ohio which was created in 1790 and became Tennessee in 1796, the first state formed from national territory. In 1790, the First Congress did not include branding as a punishment in a major crime bill which specified a number of other penal measures for a variety of crimes. Effective 1791, the cruel and unusual punishments prohibitions of the Eighth Amendment forever excluded its federal use. Nor did Virginia, at least during the time period of the Nashville ad, employ it. Rather it permitted the sheriff of any Virginia county which lodged unclaimed runaways to "put an iron collar, stamped with the letter *F* round his neck" and hire him out for his keep.[29] Probably the letter *F* stood for *Fugitive*, and the legislation which permitted the iron collaring of captured runaways was an enlightened improvement over the law of South Carolina or other Deep South states which punished bondpersons more severely for their unsuccessful flight(s).

When Anthony's owner offered a $20 reward plus expenses for his slave's capture and deposit in any jail in the country, the master, a resident of Nashville, was relying on the support of the federal government, not a loose arrangement for the return of fugitive slaves agreed upon between one state and another. Both the Northwest Ordinance passed in 1787 and an act passed by the U.S. Congress in 1793 required that any state or territory either south or northwest of the Ohio River return any fugitive slave to his owner. The 1793 law permitted the owner, or his agent, or his attorney "to seize and arrest such fugitive from labour," and take him before either a federal, state, or territorial judge, where, upon a showing of sufficient proof, including oral testimony, the hearing judge issued a court order which authorized the captured slave's removal to the state or territory "from which he or she fled."[30] This enactment of the U.S. Congress and its far better known successor, the Fugitive Slave Act of 1850, were both passed under the authority of the U.S. Constitution's Article IV. As noted in Chapter 2, Article IV, section three specifies: "No Person held to Service or Labour in one State, under the Laws thereof, escaping into another, shall, in Consequence of any Law or Regulation therein, be discharged from such Service or Labour, but shall be delivered up on Claim of the Party to whom such Service or Labour may be due." Whether or not the existence of this impressive array of legal authority as early as 1807, and the many enforcers and rewarded volunteers who hunted fugitive slaves, ever returned the twice-branded Anthony to his owner is unknown.

The great majority of advertisements examined which appeared in Missouri newspapers concerned slaves who absconded from their Missouri masters, not owners who lived in other states such as the bordering jurisdictions of Kentucky and Tennessee. None of the advertisements contained photographs; photography in the United States was a development of the second half of the nineteenth century. Some ads showed a crude cartoon of a running black; men were in trousers and women in long skirts; in both sketches the runaway carried a knapsack on a stick. Both early and late the fled slave ads relied almost entirely on the written word.

The descriptions usually included the approximate age, height, and weight. Among male fugitives the teeth, burns, and scars were often mentioned as identifying features: "has a scar on the outside of his right leg ... occasioned by a burn"; "his teeth before are defective"; "has a remarkable scar across his nose"; "has on one of his arms a deep scar occasioned by a burn"; "has a large mark from a scald on the left arm below the elbow and a small piece off the left ear"; and "One of his front teeth of the upper jaw is broken."[31] Theodore Weld, an immensely influential opponent of slavery (his book against the institution sold 100,000 copies in 1839, the year it was published), asserted that slaves "have some of their front teeth torn out or broken off, that they may be easily detected when they run away."[32] Clearly, hard manual labor alone did not explain the disfigurements so carefully detailed in the advertisements: "has been badly whipped" and "has a scar on his forehead and one above his left eye and the scar of a burn below his left elbow — a few marks of the whip on his back."[33]

For the most part, the ads described men who had been worked and worked: "has lost the little toe off the right foot." The mishandling of the ax, one of the major instruments for cutting down trees and removing their stumps, appeared in several: "has a remarkable scar ... on his back just below one of his blade bones ... 2 or 3 inches long, occasioned by the stroke of an ax"; "his left leg is stiff, occasioned by a cut from an ax"; "an ax cut on the instep of his left foot"; and one female had "a remarkable scar on the outside of one heel ... caused by an axe falling from her shoulder and hitting on the heel."[34]

The great majority of persons described in these ads had only first names. Among male slaves, *Juba* the name of two kings of Numidia in North Africa in the First Century B.C.[35] The Bible accounted for *Aaron, Abraham, Andrew, Daniel, David, Gabriel, Isaac, John, Jordan, Joseph, Matthew, Peter, Sampson, Shadrack, Stephen,* and *Thomas. Jupiter* derived from Latin mythology; *Anthony, Dennis, George, Harry,* and *William* were proper Christian masculine names. Surnames used as first names explained *Anderson, Bailor, Barnett, Booker, Claiborne, Hampton, Murphy, Reece, Squire, Wesley,* and *Willis*. However, nicknames predominated in these male runaway ads: *Ben, Bill, Bob, Dave, Davy, Dick, Frank, Ike, Jack, Jim, Jo, Joe, Lige, Matt, Rafe, Sam, Sie, Steve, Tom,* and *Zack* all ran from their owners.

Among the smaller group of women runaways were the standard American first names such as *Betsey, Catherine, Ellen, Eliza, Louisa, Mary, Rose, Sylvia,* and *Sophia.* Virgil's *Aeneid* was apparently the basis of *Dido*; the Bible provided the concept of *Charity*, and the names *Esther, Judah* and *Jude*, the latter two masculine names of slave women. *Fancy* came from a lively imagination. *Diner* may be a phonetic misspelling of *Dinah*, and *Annice* probably derived from *Annis*, a medieval vernacular form of *Agnes*.[36] Though *Doll, Fan, Judy, Patsy, Peggy,* and *Sukky* were nicknames, among females there was not the lengthy list of diminutives so prominent among Missouri's male slave population. Perhaps their owners did not fear their female slaves because of their lesser strength and size, and they less frequently diminished them with nicknames than their stronger and larger male counterparts.

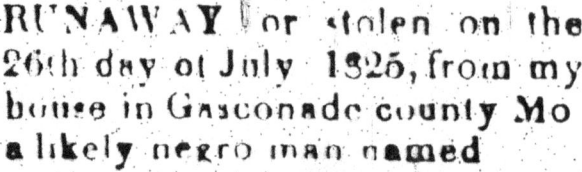

$80 Reward.

RUNAWAY or stolen on the 26th day of July 1825, from my house in Gasconade county Mo a likely negro man named **TOM**, about 23 years of age, ordinarily black, 5 feet 8 inches high, well made, converses fluently, can read and write a little, and has one heel less than the other, from a burn or frost bite; would weigh 160 or 165. ALSO—two of his sisters to wit: the older named PATSY 20 years old, low and heavy built, the younger named JUDE, about 18 years of age, slenderly made, and toes of both feet considerably cramped, a knot of the bigness of a partridge egg on one of her wrists, it is thought they will endeavor to go to Jesse Starky's, living in Madison Co. Illinois. The above reward will be given if delivered at my house, or secured in a jail so that I can get them again

JOEL STARKY, sr.

August 1—5t.

Runaway-slave advertisement, *Missouri Republican* (St. Louis), Aug. 22, 1825. (Used by permission, State Historical Society of Missouri, Columbia. All rights reserved.)

Some ads mentioned the fugitive's occupation or special skills: of male runaways, "speaks English and French"; "is a good hand in a brickyard, tending on a mason, and a tolerable plasterer"; "can play the fiddle"; "plays on the fiddle"; "has been and still professes to be a Methodist and has occasionally preached"; "is a tolerable good blacksmith, and very ingenious at any kind of mechanical work"; "by trade a blacksmith"; "converses fluently, can read and write a little"; "pretends to be religious and can read a little"; "is a good boot and shoe maker by trade"; "said Negro has worked some at the blacksmith's trade"; and "plays the fiddle, blacks shoes and boots."[37] The ads describing the women's abilities included "naturally active and quick, speaks French nearly as well as English"; "is a first rate house servant and seamstress and a good spinner"; and "remarkably brisk and quick in actions."[38]

The youngest solo runner in the advertisement sample was 14-year-old Fancy, who her master believed "has been stolen by some white man."[39] Most female runaways were in their twenties, and male fugitives were in their twenties and thirties; the oldest fugitive of both sexes in the ads examined was aged 45 to 50 years. The configuration of groups who left their master(s) included two sisters, one aged 18 and the other 20, who ran with their 23-year-old brother from their common owner; and three brothers, aged 20, 22, and 24, who together left their owner. Almost all who ran with a non-family member were males in their twenties. Only one pair of unrelated women was located in the inspected ads, and they were young adults who ran with a ten-year-old boy and a young adult male from joint owners. The ads mentioned few children under the age of 14; none ran alone, and most owner-subscribers did not include the name(s) of the young. No adult male runaway in the examined ads was the sole companion of a child. Rather, each youngster was accompanied by an adult female, usually his or her mother. Judah ran with her two-year-old. Peter and his wife Fran ran with "their two children," undescribed as to age or sex. Dave and his wife Judy ran with their son John, aged nine years and "cross-eyed."[40] Catherine ran with her two children while pregnant with a third.

The most complete account of disrupted family life to be gleaned from the ads concerned this last-named slave. Catherine's owner, Antoine Chenie, had posted a recognizance bond to guarantee her appearance on November 4, 1811, at the Court of Quarter Sessions for St. Louis District to answer a charge of assaulting one Catiche, a black woman, the slave of Manuel Lisa.[41] Both Chenie and Lisa were sufficiently important St. Louis residents to have signed a petition to Congress concerning the government of territorial Missouri. On June 27, 1812, Catherine, a 35-year-old pregnant mother of two, ran with her children from her owner, Antoine Chenie, and he offered a $30 reward for her return. The previous month, he had placed a "for sale" newspaper ad concerning "a Negro man, aged about 43 years, named Cupid, fit for many kinds of work, strong and healthy." Cupid, as Chenie's runaway ad for Catherine advised, was her husband and most likely the father of her children. He was purchased by a resident of Illinois Territory, and Catherine attempted to join her spouse, but she was captured and returned to M. Chenie. He sold her to Jourdan Labrose, probably another resident of St. Louis. She ran from him in May 1814, and he advertised a $5 reward for her return. In the 1814 ad she was called *Mourning* or *Catherine*; it contained no mention of any of her children.

It seems a certainty that the Catherine of the 1811 criminal record and the Catherine who ran from her owner in 1812 and 1814 was the same slave; her four different owners, two before Antoine Chenie and one after him, were listed in one or more runaway advertisements concerning her.[42] Chenie's sale of her husband made life in his household intolerable for her. She ran to join her husband encumbered by their offspring while expecting another. As such she was the easiest of targets for any slave catcher. She may have been called *Mourning* by 1814 because she mourned the loss of her husband and three children. Like cheek-branded Anthony, Catherine was a person of courage, strength, and determination; and we know nothing of her ultimate fate.

Scant salacious detail appeared about the woman who fled, but one ad described 25-year-old Sophia as having "left a husband and children, and from circumstances taken up with a white man whose very countenance is sufficient to hang him."[43] Included in some of the ads which described male runaways was mention of the fugitive's ability to lie: "a remarkably flippant liar"; "very plausible in his tales"; "can make a plausible story"; "he is artful and full of lies"; and "addicted to lying."[44] Perhaps runaways so described knew a great deal about the secret and scandalous lives of their owners, who discredited their bondpersons' truthful tales about them in advance. Other ads stress the alleged alcoholism and criminality of their male runaways: "fond of liquor which he will use to excess"; "fond of talking and drinking"; "is fond of spirits and will steal anything upon which he can lay his hands"; "is apt to become intoxicated"; "is bound over to appear at the next term of court at St. Louis for theft committed here"; and "was put in ... jail for attempting to commit a rape upon a white woman."[45] A few, and these subscribers were primarily attorneys, included the cautionary legalisms: "the public are hereby cautioned against dealing or harbouring him at their peril" and "All persons are forbidden to harbour the said Negro."[46] Often the ad described the skin shade: "too black to be called dark Mulattoes"; "dark Mulatto"; "of a black complexion"; "complexion agreeable as to colour"; "very black"; "of a yellow complexion"; "is a light-coloured Negro, though I believe has no white blood"; "very black skin"; "of a brownish complexion"; "of a light brown colour"; "has very much the features of a white man"; and "ordinarily black."[47]

Many advertisements described the male runaway as smiling, stuttering, stammering, and displaying other physical manifestations of lifelong servitude: "assumes a smiling countenance when alarmed or spoken to"; "smiles when spoken to"; "stutters in speaking"; "stutters or stammers when discovered or taken by surprise"; "he is very apt to stammer con-

$100 REWARD.

RAN AWAY from the subscriber, living in Boone county, Mo. on Friday the 13th June,

THREE NEGROES,

viz DAVE, and JUDY his wife; and JOHN, their son. Dave is about 32 years of age, light color for a full blooded negro—is a good boot and shoe maker by trade : is also a good farm hand. He is about 5 feet 10 or 11 inches high, stout made, and quite an artful, sensible fellow. Had on when he went away, coat and pantaloons of brown woollen jeans, shirt of home made flax linen, and a pair of welted shoes. Judy is rather slender made, about 28 years old, has a very light complexion for a negro; had on a dress made of flax linen, striped with copperas and blue; is a first rate house servant and seamstress, and a good spinner, and is very full of affectation when spoken to. John is 9 years old, very likely and well grown; is remarkably light colored for a negro, and is cross-eyed. Had on a pair of brown jeans pantaloons, bleached flax linen shirt, and red flannel one under it, and a new straw hat.

I will give the above reward and all reasonable expenses, if secured any where out of the State, so that I can get them again, or $50 if taken within the State—$30 for Dave alone, and $20 for Judy and John, and the same in proportion out of the state. The above mentioned clothing was all they took with them from home, but it is supposed he had $30 or $40 in cash with him, so that he may buy and exchange their clothing.

WILLIAM LIENTZ.
Boone county, Mo. June 17, 1834:   52-2

Runaway-slave advertisement, *Missouri Intelligencer* (Columbia), June 28, 1834. (Used by permission, State Historical Society of Missouri, Columbia. All rights reserved.)

siderably when spoken to"; "lisps much when speaking"; "is apt to smile when spoken to"; "has a remarkable habit of closing his eyelids in rapid succession when in conversation"; "has a guilty bashfulness when addressed, averting his eyes, glancing them rapidly from object to object"; "when he speaks he holds down his head"; and "walks very erect, and might be termed a stargazer by walking with his head back and looking aloft."[48] Little in these descriptions of the fled slave's demeanor distinguished him from his counterparts who remained with their owners. Bolster's study of antebellum African-American seamen also documents that "some enslaved sailors stuttered."[49] Likewise, Kay and Cary found mention of bondmen's speech impediments in eighteenth-century North Carolina runaway ads, and they cite other studies of male slave stutters in eighteenth-century Virginia and South Carolina newspaper ads.[50]

In sharp contrast, the female runaway ads generally omitted negative descriptions of deportment. Those examined contained "of a good countenance"; "answers very pleasantly when spoken to"; "very full of affection when spoken to"; "naturally active and quick" and "very talkative."[51] Why the difference? One likely reason was that male slaves encountered patrollers whenever they left their owners' real estate, and their masters often sent them off the premises on errands and for work. Females had no such freedom of movement; they were kept at home. The male bondperson's significantly greater range of mobility made for more constant threat of abusive contact with unfamiliar white men, and the result was a terrorized male slave, as reflected in his speech and demeanor.

Clothing descriptions were unexpectedly prominent for the male, but not the female. Their lower range included "He is almost naked"; "sorrily clothed, having none but those on him, viz a big coat of plains dyed brown, the under part of the sleeves of a drab colour"; "he had on a pair of white cotton trousers, deerskin, moccasins, and an old fur hat"; and "had on when he left, brown jeans coat and pantaloons, and a dark cap without a brim."[52] Most likely the owners of these runaways were themselves hard workers and plainly attired. At the other end of the male clothing spectrum were the following elaborate descriptions of fine men's wear: "he had amongst other clothing a coat particularly valued by him for its graceful fashion of a dark green color, having plated buttons"; "when he left me, he had on a blue cloth coatee, a red flannel shirt, and a pair of light colored cloth pantaloons"; "his clothing was a dark brown cloth coat and pantaloons with gilt buttons"; "he has a blue linsey hunting shirt, two linen shirts, a pair of fine shoes, a pair of velvet pantaloons, and a purple silk vest"; "had on when he ran away a strait-bodied blue cloth coat and a frock coat of a brown color, with a velvet collar"; "had on and took with him a variety of clothing among which was a black frock coat, a white Marseilles vest, a striped yellow and white one, and a black silk one"; "he took with him a variety of good clothing amongst which are summer vests of different patterns, a number of fine linen and cotton shirts, a number of white cravats, and a black neck handkerchief."[53] It seems likely that the owners of these elegantly attired male runaways were themselves fashionable and careful dressers.

Among the much smaller sample of ads concerning female runaways, many contained no mention of their clothing, and those including it gave less detail and described it far less elaborately than the attire of the male runaways: "had on when she disappeared a calico dress of a red background, took with her two pair of shoes, two pair of hose, one woolen, one cotton, and three handkerchiefs"; "had on a blue striped frock, and took with her a brown cloth greatcoat or woman's habit"; "had on when she left a linsey dress, calico sun bonnet. She left without shoes"; "the above-mentioned Negro took with her the greatest part of her clothes, and a part of her bedding."[54]

The ads for women runaways which their owners placed included either the name(s) of their previous owners or the likely destination of their flight: "was raised near the falls of Ohio in Kentucky, and it is supposed she will try to get there again or to Natchez"; "was formerly the property of Philip Fine and Samuel Hammond"; "formerly the property of Calvin Adams"; "has been seen and now is supposed to be in Bonhomme Bottom in the county of St. Louis"; and "will endeavor to go to Jesse Starkey's, living in Madison Co. Illinois."[55] The frequency with which female runaway ads contain mentions of previous residence and/or previous owner suggest that they often ran not so much to escape as to be reunited with their own family, the family of a previous owner, or both. However, some women slaves were strictly runaways for freedom.

Because of its large free black population, the city of St. Louis offered escaped slave women a safer haven than any rural Missouri area. The runaway ads reflect its lure: "She [45- to 50-year-old Betsey] has been seen several times in different parts of the city, and I am induced to believe harbors generally with the free women of color, who live by washing, and she has been also seen going to the steamboats with clothes." And "I have been informed that a negro woman of the above name and description has been seen in the city of St. Louis, passing as a free woman, and probably having forged papers to that effect."[56] Another slave woman owned in the city of St. Louis found employment for several days as a cook in the St. Louis Arsenal, but when she ventured into the city a St. Louis policeman recognized and detained her, and she was soon handed over to her owner.[57]

On average, women runaways were probably less successful in achieving freedom than the men, who appeared far more often to be running toward any freedom available rather than returning to their families and/or the families of their previous owners. In excess of 50 runaway ads which owners placed in Missouri newspapers regarding males who ran either alone or with one partner contain no mention of either their previous owners or likely destination. Some owner-placed ads contained probable routes of escape for male runaways. Six mentioned the territory or the state of Illinois, and the subscriber was often concerned that his male runaway had a forged pass or free papers. One owner speculated that his slave Shadrack "may have free papers and try to make his way to Canada."[58]

Of the more than 100 Missouri newspaper ads and stories examined concerning at least 200 runaways over the more than 50 years between 1808 and 1860, weather and climate were important factors in the timing of the slave's departure. As expected, the least popular months for running were November, December, and January, or the late fall and winter season of the year. Likewise, February, one of the coldest months, and July, one of the hottest, were equally unpopular for escaping. June, August, September, and October were the most likely times for slaves to leave their owners, and the frequency with which runaway ads appeared during these pleasant-weather months suggests that considerable advanced planning went into the slave's runaway decision. Men, women, and children wished to be free, and they risked the dangers of that freedom over the security of their enslavement early and late in slavery's tenure in Missouri.

Nothing in these newspaper advertisements suggests that the social, economic, or political position of the slave's owner bound his human chattel to him. Among the subscribers who placed ads in Missouri newspapers during territorial and early statehood years were many well-known persons. John B.C. Lucas, an appointee of President Jefferson to the territorial Superior Court and commissioner to settle land claims, offered $10 for the return of his slave Sam in 1810. Antoine Chenie, a "highly respected Frenchman," as his 1840 obituary described him,[59] was the owner of Catherine, who ran from his household with her two children while pregnant with her third in 1812. Silas Bent, First Justice of the Court of Common Pleas and appointed by President Madison to the territorial Superior Court, offered $20 for the return of one of his slaves, Zack, in 1814 and $30 for the return of another, Bailor, in 1817. John Rice Jones, an influential delegate to the Missouri Constitutional Convention in 1820 and one of the first judges on the Missouri Supreme Court, offered $25 for the return of his slave Ben in 1815. William Clark, Missouri territorial governor, when Juba ran from him, offered $100 for his return in 1816. Since Juba does not appear in Clark's will written 22 years later, perhaps he made good his escape; equally possible was his death, either while enslaved or as a free man. Antoine Soulard, captain of the militia and assistant mayor of St. Louis under Spanish colonial rule, offered a "handsome reward" for the return of his slave Alexis in 1820; and Alexander Stuart was judge of the St. Louis Circuit Court when he offered a "reward" for the apprehension of Bob in 1826. These slaves, and surely a multitude of others owned by great persons, were not content to live in the reflected glory of their prominent owners, and they ran from their enslavement as surely as did the human property of obscure owners.

When we turn to news stories about runaways, mainly of the 1850s, we find these narratives concerned both the slaves' successful escapes and/or their apprehensions. Usually the accounts included the slaves' owners, perhaps their value in dollars, and the county of the action regarding them. At times the paper merely reported the arrest of "a negro man, woman, and a lot of children ... bound for 'sweet Illinois.' They escaped from ... Lafayette County."[60] At others, the story detailed the successful escape of a particular slave, Negro Ike for example, who was owned in Clay County and at press time had not been recaptured.[61] At times the story included a crime such as robbery as an incident related to the escape of a recently captured fugitive.[62] However, the big changes between the 1850s and earlier times were the larger numbers of slaves who absconded in groups, the direction of their travel, and the violence of the engagement between the hunters and the hunted: "Negro shot — the Negro man, Hiram, who recently ran away from Mr. ... Rollins ... was shot and killed the other day in Naples, Illinois. Three persons (Illinoisans) attempted to arrest him; he resisted, fired upon and wounded two of them, whereupon one of the party shot and killed him. Mr. Rollins [of Boone County] had offered $1,000 for his apprehension."[63] The headline of a story of Missouri runaways in Iowa read, "Capture of Eleven Runaway Negroes — Thirty Revolver[s] Recovered from them." The story itself said, "The leader of the Negroes fired three times without effect when he was shot down.... It was not ascertained whether or not he was fatally wounded."[64] "Stampede of Negroes from Lewis County" included the facts that ten slaves, five males and five females, owned by seven different persons and valued at no less than $10,000, stole a boat and crossed the Mississippi River from Lewis, a county bordered by the river, to the Illinois side. By press time an additional slave in the same county had effected his escape, making eleven in all.[65] Another story concerned the escape of a Negro man owned in Pike County, which also bordered the Mississippi River. It suggests a certain inevitability about the slave's departure: "It is supposed he crossed the river at this place, as he was seen on the other side of the river opposite here."[66]

These accounts of absconding slaves all appeared in Missouri newspapers after the Thirty-First Congress passed the Fugitive Slave Act in September 1850. It was a supplement to the 1793 federal act, "Persons Escaping from the Service of Their Masters." Because an 1842 U.S. Supreme Court decision held that state judges were not required to hear cases arising under the 1793 law dealing with fugitive slaves,[67] the 1850 federal act omitted mention of any state officials and authorized the judges of both the U.S. Circuit Courts and the Superior Courts of all organized territories to both appoint commissioners and enlarge their numbers should the demand require such in order to implement the new law. Both federal judges and the newly appointed federal commissioners were authorized to grant certificates to claimant slaveowners "upon satisfactory proof being made" that captured blacks were the property of their alleged owners; these certificates allowed the owner or his agent personally to retake his slaves. The hearing official, either a judge or a commissioner, could sign a warrant upon an owner's, authorized agent's, or attorney's application which required U.S. marshals and their deputies to return the fugitives from labor to the state from whence they fled, or to their owners. As under Missouri statutes, the federal law required that the owner pay several fees. The federal costs involved those of the U.S. marshal and his deputies for "the arrest, custody, and delivery of the fugitive to the claimant, his agent, or his attorney"; the commissioner's fee; and the expense of "keeping the fugitive in custody and providing him with food and lodging during his detention."[68]

Commissioners were entitled to a $10 fee if they ruled in favor of the owner and only $5 if they held the owner's evidence insufficient to issue a certificate or to sign a warrant. The testimonial incompetence of blacks against whites, which was the law of most if not all slave states, continued in the 1850 federal legislation, which expressly barred any alleged fugitive from labor from testifying at the hearing regarding him or her.[69] Likewise, as in all of Missouri's runaway slave statutes under American rule, so too under the 1850 federal act, the slave committed no crime in running from his owner and hence no part of the federal Bill of Rights, including the right to a trial by jury, applied in his or her case. The Fugitive Slave Act gave federal aid to slaveocracy in its quest to recapture its human property, and the law remained on the books, if only selectively enforced throughout its tenure but especially after the Civil War began, until the Thirty-Eighth Congress repealed it in June 1864.[70]

Obviously this law facilitated the return of some slaves to their Missouri owners. In 1859 an out-of-state newspaper reported that three fugitive slaves from Missouri were returned from Chicago to St. Louis.[71] Likewise an in-state paper ran separate stories, in April and May 1862, of the arrest in Kansas of one and two fugitive slaves and their return to their Clay County, Missouri, owners.[72] However, Slave Steve's and Slave Jerry's cases were far more typical of the effectiveness of the federal law. In 1861, Steve, owned in Clay, a western Missouri county, was arrested in Kansas, on a warrant issued by a U.S. Commissioner in Leavenworth, and charged with being a fugitive slave. During the hearing he escaped and drove off in a buggy beyond the reach of arresting officers.[73] Likewise, William Henry, nicknamed Jerry, escaped from his owner, John McReynolds of Marion County, Missouri, which bordered the Mississippi River. Though a U.S. marshal arrested him in Syracuse, New York, and hauled him before a U.S. Commissioner in September 1851, before his hearing was completed a crowd had rescued this former slave and sent him to Kingston, Ontario, where he lived until his death.[74]

We know about the life of one runaway Missouri slave, Archer Alexander (1828–1880?), who later achieved his freedom and remained in Missouri, because William Greenleaf Eliot (1811–1887) wrote a small book about Archer.[75] Eliot moved to St. Louis from New England in 1834 as a minister in the Unitarian Church. As early as his arrival in St. Louis, he favored the gradual emancipation of slaves. Later, among other accomplishments, he served as president of the St. Louis school board, founded Washington University, and became its president. He achieved posthumous notice as the grandfather of the American-English poet, T. S. Eliot.

A reminder of former slave Archer Alexander exists in a statue which still stands in Lincoln Park in Washington, D.C., "Freedom's Memorial." It was unveiled April 14, 1876, and is a representation of President Lincoln, as Eliot phrased it, "in the act of emancipating a Negro slave, who kneels at his feet to receive the benediction, but whose hand has grasped the chain as if in the act of breaking it, indicating the historical fact that the slaves took an active part in their own deliverance."[76] The face of the sculpted bondman is Archer's. This is so because Eliot happened to meet the American sculptor of this piece, Thomas Ball, in Florence, Italy, in 1869, and later sent the artist photographs of an actual, not an idealized, slave, Archer Alexander. The result was a likeness to Archer in the face and form of the freed slave as accurate as that of the murdered president. Eliot believed that Archer's apprehension in March 1863 was the last successful capture of a runaway slave in Missouri. This cannot be verified because so many court records, especially from western Missouri, are now lost. The identity of the actual last fugitive slave captured in this state is not susceptible to proof; it may or it may not have been Archer Alexander.

He, like a number of other bondpersons, came to Missouri with his owner and his owner's family when they moved from Virginia. The move took place in 1833, and in the process the slave was forever separated from his mother. After a number of years of faithful service, Archer's owner sold him to a neighbor who also owned Louisa, slave wife of Archer and the mother of his children. With his sale, he moved from St. Louis to St. Charles County. By 1863, Archer had heard sufficient talk about freedom to become convinced that he was entitled to it, and he ran from his St. Charles County owner. William Eliot and his family, then living on the western outskirts of St. Louis, eventually employed the fugitive slave. The runaway Archer was such a capable farmer and general handyman that his conscientious employer offered, through a third party, to buy him from his previous owner. The offer was refused. However, with the help

"Freedom's Memorial," Lincoln Park, Washington, D.C., by Thomas Ball (1876). The face of the sculpted bondman is that of Archer Alexander, subject of a book by William G. Eliot, president of Washington University and grandfather of T. S. Eliot. (Photograph by Abbie Rowe, 1958; courtesy National Park Service.)

of the military in the midst of the Civil War, Eliot prevented Archer's re-enslavement until the institution was officially abolished in Missouri in January 1865. Archer, whose wife had died, remained an Eliot family employee for several years after the Civil War. When he died in approximately 1880, according to Eliot, his friend, benefactor, and biographer, his last words were of thanksgiving that he did not die a slave. He was buried from the African Methodist Church in St. Louis, and the Reverend William Greenleaf Eliot officiated at Archer Alexander's funeral.[77] That Alexander as a runaway slave remained in Missouri was the exception; the great majority of the state's fugitives from labor did not.

As this chapter has shown, one of the most commonplace ways in which slaves received newspaper mention was by seeking their freedom through voluntarily leaving the territory and later the state. By 1860, a Missouri newspaper estimated the number of slaves who had successfully run from their American masters to Canada at 24,000.[78] This number was not based on any reliable figures, but that the country was a haven for escaping slaves, including those from Missouri, was fact. With one great river, the Missouri, flanking the state's northwestern border and running through it and an even greater river, the Mississippi, separating it from the free state of Illinois, little in Missouri's geography was favorable to the long duration of slavery. Any governing authority of it, be it French, Spanish, or American, was confronted with slavery's chief counterpart in any of the Border States, runaways. Neither severe nor mild treatment of the absconding slave prevented the departure of another, another, and yet another fugitive from the service of his/her master.

6

Slave John Anderson and Canadian-English Justice

Little is known about the later freedom of most slaves, whether featured in runaway ads or in news stories. However, the odds favor many having achieved permanent liberty by traveling from Missouri to the geographical beyond. This was so because of lax enforcement, in the free states, of the 1793 act concerning "Persons Escaping From the Service of their Masters" and because of immense controversy and opposition in these same states to the 1793 law's successor, the 1850 Fugitive Slave Act.

Equally important, in the slave's quest for freedom he may have eluded American slave catchers by slipping across an international boundary and entering a foreign country. Several bordered the United States, and no ocean, requiring navigational skills for travel upon an immense body of water, separated native from alien soil. These borders could be walked across. The runaway's imagined destinations can be tracked through the diplomatic efforts of the United States to reach agreement with various foreign countries for the return of fugitive slaves to their American masters. As early as 1790 the Washington Administration secured the cooperation of the Spanish government in closing its colony of Florida to slaves escaping primarily from Georgia.[1] Once Florida became a part of the United States by Spain's cession of it in 1821, American law, with its immense protections of slaveholding interests, governed Florida. No longer did a foreign country exist on the southern border of either Georgia or Alabama (a state that joined the Union in 1819).

However, runaway slaves could still flee the jurisdiction of the United States by crossing into Mexico. Efforts to close this escape route began during the administration of John Quincy Adams (1825–29). In 1828, under the guidance of Secretary of State Henry Clay, the United States secured a commercial treaty with Mexico. It contained an article that provided for both countries to return the fugitive slaves of the other. Though the U.S. Senate ratified this treaty in 1828, it was rejected in Mexico, a country with few slaves of its own and one that formally abolished slavery in 1829. After the admission of Texas to the Union as a slave state in 1845 and the resulting Mexican War of 1846–48, the U.S.-Mexican border shifted from its earlier location along the Sabine River 400 miles southwest to the Rio Grande River. Afterwards, any runaway found north of the Rio Grande was still in the United States and, if captured, no foreign law prevented his return to his owner. Nonetheless, some American bondpersons managed to escape to Mexico. Otherwise the State Department would not have resumed efforts in 1855 to secure an extradition treaty with that country for the return of any fugitive slaves. However, neither the efforts of the Secretary of State nor those of the two American ministers to Mexico succeeded. She refused to sign a treaty for the return of any runaway slave who managed to reach Mexican soil.[2]

Where did Missouri's runaways flee? It is almost unimaginable that any ever attempted to secure their liberty by traveling to Florida. It was both too far away and its Spanish governing authority too favorable to slaveholding interests. Probably few endeavored to obtain their freedom by escaping to Mexico. Geography did not favor such a journey. The fugitive who ventured southwest was required to cross either the slave jurisdictions of Arkansas, Louisiana, and Texas, or Indian Country (the present states of Kansas and Oklahoma) and then on to Texas. Nothing in Missouri's runaway ads, news stories, legislation, or court cases concerning fugitive slaves suggests that Mexico as a haven for persons escaping the service of their masters was a concern for slaveholding Missourians.

Their worries were about America's neighbor, Canada. In 1793 the parliament of Upper Canada, now Ontario, passed a law which prohibited the importation of slaves and freed those held in slavery at age 25. In addition, the parliament of Lower Canada, now Quebec, abolished slavery in 1800.[3] As a result, as early as Spanish rule of Missouri and at a time when the transfer of the Purchase from French to American hands was still in the future, a few of this area's runaway slaves ran, walked, rode, and limped their way to the safe haven of Canada. Mostly they traveled under cover of darkness, and their guide was the North Star.

Canada's freedom for blacks was not generally known until after the War of 1812, when returning American soldiers reported what they had seen of former American slaves fighting in Canadian regiments.[4] Many Missourians fought in this war against Canadians in both the Battle of River Raisin and the Battle of the Thames; these conflicts took place north of Detroit in Ontario. Veterans of the War of 1812, including homecoming Missouri soldiers, related their northern experiences of seeing black soldiers in Canadian regiments in the presence of both slave and free listeners. In addition, free blacks who served as cooks, waiters, and barbers with American forces in Canada continued those employments when their officers were reassigned to duty in posts such as St. Louis after the war.[5] In the town of St. Louis, slaves learned about freedom in Canada from the free African-Americans who cooked for, served food to, and shaved American officers during and after their northern duty tours. As these free blacks and transferred soldiers told and retold stories about slave freedom north of the United States, the numbers of Missouri's and other slave states' runaways who left for Ontario and other Canadian provinces significantly increased.

As early as 1819 James Monroe's secretary of state, John Quincy Adams, corresponded with Gibbs C. Antrobus, the British chargé d'affaires in Washington, about the return from Canada of several slaves from Tennessee who had run from their owners. Adams wrote, "The owners are anxious to know if any arrangements can be made by which permission could be obtained for them to go to Canada and reobtain possession of their property." He received this reply from Antrobus: "The Negroes have by their residence in Canada, become free, ... and should any attempt be made to infringe upon this right of freedom, these Negroes would have it in their power to compel the interference of the courts of law for their protection."[6] As a result, Secretary Adams never secured permission from Canadian authorities for any masters to retake their slave properties.

During John Quincy Adams's presidency, his secretary of state, Henry Clay, was sufficiently concerned about the presence of former American slaves in Canada to continue negotiation efforts. Just as this Kentucky cabinet member attempted to secure a treaty with Mexico which provided for the return of any fugitive slave who escaped south of the border, so also was he intent on obtaining an extradition treaty with the North American Possessions of His Britannic Majesty, as Canada was then known, for the return of runaways who escaped north of the border. In 1826, Secretary Clay protested that the country was receiving runaway slaves, and when he did not receive a satisfactory reply, he restated the American position in 1827. After a five-month delay, Canada responded that "It was utterly impossible to agree to a stipulation for the surrender of fugitive slaves." Clay made his last appeal in 1828, when the House of Representatives insisted that President John Quincy Adams make another attempt to secure an extradition treaty for the return of escaped American slaves then residing in Canada. All three attempts failed.[7]

In the late 1830s the law governing the return from Canada of fugitive slaves was further clarified in Jesse Happy's case. When Happy ran from his Kentucky master, he stole his owner's horse to aid his escape as he made his way to Canada. By the time he was in Canadian custody and a request for his extradition had arrived, four years had elapsed. Moreover, he both left his owner's horse in the United States and wrote his former master to tell him where he might find his equine property. Technically a slave who ran from his master committed a crime in most slave jurisdictions. His master owned his slave's clothes and even the chains with which he bound his recalcitrant bondpersons. Even if the fugitive ran away naked — and no ads suggest that this ever occurred — the fleeing bondperson committed the crime of "self-theft."

At this time, Canada was not an autonomous nation. Not until 1867 did the British North America Act give Canada dominion status and sovereign authority as a nation. Prior to that time any decision reached by any court in any British colony in North America, as each province was then known, could be appealed to a higher power in England, either executive or judicial. Not surprisingly, Canadian authorities submitted Happy's case to London for clarification of the applicable law. The English attorney general and his advisers decided that he should not be returned to the United States. Return of the fugitive must be based on an act which "would warrant the apprehension of the accused Party, if the alleged offence had been committed in Canada." As Robin Winks notes after quoting the above, "Since slavery did not exist in Canada the crime of escape could not exist there, and the use of the horse in Happy's case had been to effect escape and not for theft. Further, in future requests for extradition all evidence had to be taken in Canada, so that if it proved false, charges of perjury could be brought."[8] As a result, in 1838 Jesse Happy was set free. The precedent established in his case made clear that Canada would extradite a slave neither for "self-theft" nor for other criminal acts such as appropriating other personal property of the master incidental to the bondperson's departure from the service of his owner.

6. Slave John Anderson and Canadian-English Justice

In 1842, the United States and Great Britain were signatories to a treaty known as Webster-Ashburton. Its main purposes were to set the boundary between Maine and Canada and to bring about the "Final Suppression of the African slave trade." However it also specified the crimes for which either country would extradite an accused person from any country under the governance of the British Crown to the United States or the reverse. Clearly, British opposition to slavery had an immense influence on this treaty. As Jones observed, "Abolition sentiment, which had led to the emancipation of the slaves in the British Empire in 1833, had by 1842 settled down to a strong national feeling which permeated all classes of British society and all political parties." He continued, "The British people as a whole warmly supported their government's antislavery policy."[9] English abhorrence of slavery is plainly visible in the treaty's Article X, its list of extraditable offenses. These included "the crime of murder, or assault with intent to commit murder, or Piracy, or arson, or robbery, or Forgery, or the utterance of forged paper." There were restrictions on the return of persons charged with these crimes. It could only take place, as Article X specified, "upon such evidence of criminality as, according to the Laws of the place where the fugitive or person so charged, shall be found, would justify his apprehension and commitment for trial, if the crime or offense had been there committed." The extradition was further hemmed in by requiring a court order for the arrest of the fugitive so that "the evidence of criminality may be heard and considered." Finally, "the expense of such apprehension and delivery shall be borne and defrayed by the Party who makes the requisition and receives the fugitive."[10]

This treaty omitted several major crimes as extraditable offenses. Had it not been for intense anti-slavery sentiment in England, the document would have included the crime of rape. However, John Tyler was president when the treaty was signed and his home state of Virginia had no fewer than 73 capital offenses for slaves, only one of which, first degree murder, was also a capital offense for a white person. For the first offense of "attempting by force or fraud, to have carnal knowledge of a white female," Virginia provided no punishment for whites, but punished slaves convicted of the same with death.[11]

Further, with the exception of the state of Missouri, all slave jurisdictions punished the slave convicted of the rape of a white woman with death. What was the punishment for a white man's rape of a slave woman? There was no punishment. She was his possession, and he had the legal right to deal with her as he saw fit. The sexual liberties slave owners took with their black human properties were notoriously well-known in England and her North American possessions prior to the American Revolution, when anti-slavery writers such as Benjamin Rush in 1773 excoriated the peculiar institution as one in which "Husbands have been forced to prostitute their wives, and mothers their daughters, to gratify the brutal lust of a master." Clearly, England in 1842 wanted no part of American law concerning sexual offenses which gave everything to the owner and nothing to the owned.

Similarly, intense anti-slavery sentiment in England prevented larceny from being an extraditable offense under the treaty. This crime, now known as stealing or theft, consisted of taking and carrying away the personal property of another with the intent to deprive the owner of his property on a permanent basis. A dollar amount of the stolen property separates the misdemeanor of this crime (petit larceny) from the felony (grand larceny). Since all slaves were personal property, in American jurisdictions where running away was a crime the slave committed the offense of self-theft. Where running was not itself a crime, as in Missouri and as the next chapter explains, anyone who aided a slave in securing his liberty was chargeable with the felony of grand larceny. That the treaty did not include this crime — then and now stealing or theft is the most common of all offenses committed by all lawbreakers — is directly attributable to English determination to return neither fugitive slaves to their American masters nor abolitionists to criminal courts in slave states.

Finally, because of British anti-slavery feeling the treaty did not include all homicides other than those that were justifiable or excusable. Obviously, the treaty deliberately excluded manslaughter because the distinction between it and murder was already many centuries old in England when Webster-Ashburton was signed. The eighteenth-century commentator on English law, Blackstone, defined manslaughter as "arising from the sudden heat of the passions; ... it must be done without premeditation."[12] People knowledgeable about slavery knew perfectly well that whether or not a person committed manslaughter (never a capital offense) or murder (often a capital offense) depended on the race of the perpetrator and the race of the victim. When a slave killed a white the crime was murder; the circumstances of the killing were irrelevant. The law put the perpetrator to death if he or she did not die at the hands of a mob.

Under Canadian law in the twentieth century, attempted murder, manslaughter, larceny or theft, sexual assault, sexual assault with a weapon, threats to a third party, or causing bodily harm or aggravated sexual assault are all included on the list of crimes for which the government of Canada will extradite an accused person to, among other countries, the United States.[13] Missouri's U.S. senator Thomas Hart Benton complained of the 1842 treaty that all lands under British rule are places "where abolitionism is the policy of the government, the voice of the law, and the spirit of the people." An English abolitionist praised the treaty's list of extraditable offenses as "a pledge that we will not be slave catchers."[14] The treaty itself was simply silent regarding whether or not any country governed by English law would or would not extradite a runaway bondperson.

While this extensive tug and pull about slavery between the United States and her foreign neighbors was playing itself out, a slave was born in Howard County, Missouri. He was known as Jack or Jack Burton in Missouri, and as, among other names, John Anderson in the foreign countries in which his case later became a cause célèbre. His first owner was Moses Burton, a Howard County resident who, according to the 1830 federal census, was the owner of one female bondperson between the ages of 10 and 23 years. This young woman was Anderson's mother, and she may have been pregnant with him in 1830 when the census was taken. By the 1840 census, Burton owned three slaves: a female aged between 24 and 36 years, a female aged under 10 years, and a male aged between 10 and 24 years. We know nothing of the young slave girl; no subsequent account of Anderson's life mentions her as his sister, playmate, or the like. Burton's male slave aged between 10 and 24 years was Anderson, and his bondwoman aged between 24 and 36 years was Anderson's mother.

The slave youngster had no memory of his father, a mulatto servant on Mississippi River steamboats who escaped human bondage and made his way to South America. Almost certainly he heard this account of his father from his mother. According to Anderson, he lost his mother when he was about 7 years old: she gave some offense to her owner, and he punished her by selling her to a trader who transported her to New Orleans. Since slaves never knew their birth dates, their errors regarding the precise dates of other important events in their lives were highly likely. The 1840 census suggests that the sale and 800-plus-mile journey of his custodial parent orphaned him when he was about 10 years old, not seven.

Who raised him? The 1830 census enumerates a white female member of Moses Burton's household as being between ages 30 and 40, and that of 1840 lists one between 40 and 50 years of age. This woman was Mrs. Elizabeth Burton. She was aged 51 years in the census taken August 12, 1850. Anderson later recalled her with affection and gratitude. She took care of him after his slave mother's abrupt departure. He believed that she died when he was about 19 years old; probably, he was slightly older.

He lived as the agricultural bondman of Moses Burton, a tobacco farmer and a carpenter, and the young man became adept at the skills of his master. He also went a-courting when a Maria Tomlin caught his eye. She was a widow with children, aged 11 and 13 years; she and her offspring were slaves on the farm of Samuel Brown, located about two miles from the Burton farm. The 1850 slave schedule lists among the eight bondpersons of Samuel Brown a 25-year-old female, two girls ages seven and 10, and two boys 10 and 11. Most likely, the 25-year-old was Maria, and any two of the enumerated slaves aged between seven and 11 years were her children. Her father was Lewis Tomlin, a former slave who bought his freedom and that of his wife, and earned his living as a barber in Fayette, the county seat of Howard County. The 1850 census enumerates Lewis Tomlin as a 36-year-old free black male (most likely it should be a 46-year-old), then living with a 40-year-old free black female, presumably Maria's mother. The Tomlins, according to this same census, owned property worth $800, a sizable amount in 1850.

Anderson and Maria were "married" at Christmas in 1850, and in due course they became the parents of an infant. As long as she and Anderson resided on farms only two miles apart, all went well enough. However, in August 1853, for reasons never clarified, Moses Burton sold his slave Jack to Reuben E. McDaniel, a resident of Saline, a county across the Missouri River from Howard, whose farm was approximately 30 miles east of Samuel Brown's farm and Anderson's wife and child. Anderson later claimed that McDaniel paid Burton $1,000 for him; most likely his claim was accurate.[15] Harrison Trexler, an authority on the price of slaves in the state, wrote: "The golden age of slave values was the fifties. The prime male slave of Missouri in 1860 was worth about $1,300 and the negresses about $1,000."[16]

When Anderson requested a pass from his new owner to visit his wife and child, McDaniel refused him permission for such visits. He told Anderson that he must forget his Howard County family and choose a new slave "wife" from the available stock on his new master's farm. According to the 1850 slave schedule, Reuben E. McDaniel owned 27 slaves, and among these were three females, aged 15, 17, and 17, who by 1853 were aged 18, 20, and 20. Any offspring born of Anderson's union with any of these young women would become the property of his white owner. Anderson then and there quietly determined that he would not become the father of Reuben E.

McDaniel's bondbabies. Rather, he would escape slavery in Missouri and make his way to Canada.

Like the many runaway slaves discussed in the previous chapter, he carefully timed his departure. He began his journey in mild weather, and he chose a Sunday, a day which gave him considerable lead time before he was missed, because he would not have been at work in the fields on the Sabbath. Coincidentally, the very day he started for Canada, September 25, 1853, his owner was summoned to attend a church meeting about a fellow congregant who had whipped a slave to death.[17] To effect his escape, Jack took one of McDaniel's mules, some blankets, a 20-foot-long rope, and a bridle.

His first major obstacle was the Missouri River, a sizable body of water which separated Saline from Howard County. His attempt to secure passage across the river on a ferry was unsuccessful. The ferryman refused to transport him without a pass, and he had none. Nonetheless, he managed to find a small boat, and using a piece of bark as an oar, he crossed the river. He made his way to Fayette, to the residence of his father-in-law, Lewis Tomlin. The runaway son-in-law told him, no doubt without the eloquence of Patrick Henry, that he preferred death to remaining a slave. Tomlin offered him a pistol, but Anderson declined, telling him that he had a "dirk," a long straight dagger, with which to prevent his capture. Next, Anderson visited the slave quarters of Samuel Brown where he said goodbye to his wife and child, promising to get them and his stepchildren to Canada in due course. The runaway then returned to the residence of his father-in-law, and he probably slept there the night of Sunday, September 25, 1853.

By September 28, a Wednesday, Anderson was on the fourth day of his run for freedom. He happened to cross the farm of a Howard County slaveholder named Seneca T.P. Digges (a name subsequently and frequently misspelled Diggs). Digges, aged 46 years, was head of household to a family of 12 or 13 persons:[18] his unmarried sister, Ann, aged 63 years; his disabled brother, Robert, aged 55 years; his wife, Frances, aged 36 years; and eight or nine children. Perhaps Mrs. Digges was pregnant with their last child in September 1853. The approximate ages of the other children were: Thomas (18), Mary (15), William (13), Virginia (10), Benjamin (8), Frances (6), Cornelia (4), Seneca T.P. (2), and Sallie (unborn to six months of age). According to the 1850 slave schedule, Digges owned 15 slaves. At the time Anderson was traversing his farm, a property in an eastern section of Howard County, its owner, accompanied by his eight-year-old son Benjamin, was supervising several of his bondmen as they harvested the tobacco crop for drying in the barn.

Digges, like all Missouri slaveholders, had a duty as old as French ownership of his land to ascertain whether or not any unfamiliar colored person was a runaway. He properly asked Anderson to show him his pass. The black man had none, and when he refused Digges's order to accompany him to his house for some dinner, the slaveholder told the strange colored man that he was a runaway and his master would soon be able to reclaim him. Digges summoned the help of three of his own slaves and told them, "Catch that runaway, and I will give you the reward." At this time, Missouri law provided a 25-dollar reward for a fugitive slave captured in-state, plus whatever the owner offered. His slaves stood to collect at least $25 if they could apprehend Jack Burton.

Digges and eventually six of his slaves pursued Anderson; the chase was of several hours duration. According to Anderson, the white man had an ax which he threw at him, but it never hit him. Next, according to Anderson, his attempted catcher was armed with a club as were several of his slaves. The fugitive often showed his knife and made known that he had no intention of being taken alive. Under these harrowing circumstances, Anderson stabbed Digges with his dirk, and when he heard the white man exhort his slaves to continue their pursuit, he stabbed him a second time. Both thrusts of his knife were for the sole purpose of avoiding being captured and returned to the odious bondage which awaited him in Saline County. Equally important, his owner, Reuben E. McDaniel, had the option of making his ungovernable bondman's life even more unbearable by selling him to a slave dealer, as had happened to Anderson's mother. Digges's slaves briefly followed Anderson, but he told them to go back and say they could not capture him, and they left him and attended to their wounded master.

Anderson returned to Samuel Brown's slave quarters and told his wife of his encounter with the white man. She had already heard that a black man had stabbed a white; now she knew her husband was the culprit. Anderson got a few shirts from his wife. Shortly he left her, their child, and his two stepchildren, never to see any of them again.

He spent the next ten days making his way from Howard County to the eastern border of Missouri, a distance as the crow flies of at least 125 miles. His likely route took him through Monroe County, and at least one newspaper placed him there: "We understand the negro was seen in Monroe County, hotly pursued, and fired upon but succeeded in making his escape."[19] Very likely he traveled many extra miles as he dodged imagined and actual slave catchers. He had only $1.50 with him, moved largely at night, and mainly survived on nuts, raw corn, and raw potatoes. He helped himself to three chickens at one farmhouse, killed all of them, and ate two of them cooked. The third, uncooked, bird was his only source of food for the next two days. Thirteen days after he left the Reuben McDaniel farm on that September Sunday he found a boat on the western bank of the Mississippi River and managed to cross in it to the free state of Illinois during the night/early morning of October 8–9, 1853.

Once he reached Illinois he remained wary of being captured. He spent one night at the residence of an Englishman, where he ate an actual meal. When he left, his host gave him an ample supply of bread and apples. After buying a loaf of bread at another farmhouse and eluding what he believed were would-be captors, he found a branch of the Illinois River, crossed it, and came upon a railroad track. He followed it east until he came near Bloomington, a town in the middle of the state. He then traveled northwest to Rock Island by riding with some teams of horses en route to this town. When he reached it, a barber hired him as his assistant; but two days later, and with the active help of abolitionists who paid his fare, he traveled to Chicago. In this city he lived with a barber approximately three weeks. In late October/early November, he left Chicago and eventually arrived in Windsor, Ontario. He probably traveled east across Lake Michigan and the state of Michigan, and, like the Missouri slaves whom John Brown rescued from a western Missouri county several years later, crossed from Detroit into Windsor, Ontario. Once he reached this city, Anderson was no longer subject to, among other federal aids to slaveholders, the 1850 Fugitive Slave Act. Rather he was a free man in the colony of Upper Canada. Though Anderson's English biographer, Harper Twelvetrees, dates the black man's arrival in Windsor as September 1853, almost certainly it was early November of that year.

Meanwhile, Anderson was gone from but not forgotten in Missouri. A newspaper in Clay (four counties west of Howard) ran a story about "a strange negro" who belonged to Colonel McDaniel of Saline County inflicting two wounds upon Seneca T.P. Diggs, Esq., as he attempted to arrest him, "one in the breast near the heart and the other in the back.... Col. McDaniel was in Fayette at the time, in pursuit of the fugitive, and started immediately for the scene of the outrage."[20] Likewise, a Howard County newspaper carried this account of Anderson's knifing his would-be apprehender, Seneca Digges, under the headline "Negro Outrage": "Mr. Digges, who was stabbed by a runaway Negro last week ... was alive at last accounts, and hopes were entertained for his recovery. The negro ... was thought to be in the neighborhood. A large party of gentlemen started in pursuit of him Monday [October 3]. The citizens ... offer a reward for the apprehension of the negro."[21] This paper's next issue contained news of the death of Seneca T.P. Diggs, Esq. on October 11.[22] On October 17, less than a week after Digges's death, Missouri's governor, Sterling Price, offered a reward of $150 for the arrest and delivery of a Negro named Jack, who had murdered Seneca T.P. Diggs in Howard County on September 28, 1853.

Anderson or some of his abolitionist friends later claimed that the reward for his capture was $1,000. The amount seems excessive. The family of his victim had been deprived of its head of household and chief breadwinner, and his widow either had or would soon have nine children. Under these circumstances any money would be needed for raising them, not for reward purposes. The unspecified amount of the Howard County citizenry reward was almost certainly not $850. An examination of at least 100 Missouri newspaper ads for the capture of 200 runaways reveals only one reward of $1,000; otherwise, the largest was $200. Despite the later exaggerated claim of the compensation for his delivery to the Howard County sheriff, there is no doubt that Missouri authorities, from the governor on down, desperately desired his capture and return to them.

Meanwhile the citizens of Howard County took some action to avenge the death of one of their own, Seneca Digges. They held a mass meeting at the courthouse in Fayette on October 10, 1853, for the expressed purposes of suppressing "insubordination among slaves" and observing the "conduct of persons suspected of intermeddling with the slave population." (As Appendix 3 shows, Howard County juries twice sent a white man to the penitentiary for his abolitionist activities, one well before the death of Seneca Digges and one well after it.)

At the October 1853 meeting, a committee was appointed and several resolutions drafted in the belief that "the recent repeated outrages committed by the negro population ... are instigated by evil-disposed white persons." Included among the resolutions was the appointment of a nine-member committee for each of the county's seven townships. The duties of these committees included observing "the conduct of suspicious persons"; requesting that the "county court appoint a patrol company for each township"; and insuring that both the "vigilant committees and patrol companies ... take from ... all slaves all weapons, whether offensive or defensive such as knives, guns, pistols, walking canes, and clubs."²³ As Chapter 1 explains, most white Missourians believed that slaves were contented in their bondage unless meddlesome abolitionists turned them against their benevolent masters. There is no evidence that in his run for freedom Anderson had an iota of assistance from any white person in Missouri. Nonetheless, Howard County's slaveholders believed that one or more white abolitionists had somehow played a role in Anderson's escape and thus in Seneca Digges's death at the runaway's hand.

The indignation meeting held on October 10 produced no known results. However, shortly after it, the county court arraigned Lewis Tomlin, Anderson's father-in-law, "on charges of harboring the runaway that killed Mr. Digges." Missouri law then provided that if any "free negro or mulatto ... shall harbor ... any slave without the consent of his or her owner or overseer, ... a free negro or mulatto shall receive any number of lashes, not exceeding thirty."²⁴ The court, as the newspaper noted,

> $150 REWARD.
> PROCLAMATION.
> *By the Governor of the State of Missouri.*
> WHEREAS, it has been represented to me that a Negro man named Jack, did on the 28th, September 1853. murder Seneca P. Diggs in Howard county; and whereas it is further represented to me the said Jack, has fled from justice, and is now going at large, to the great detriment of the peace, good order, and dignity of the State: Now, therefore, I STERLING PRICE, Governor of the State of Missouri, do hereby offer a reward of one hundred and fifty dollars for the arrest and delivery of the said Jack to the Sheriff of Howard county.
> IN testimony whereof, I have hereto set my hand, and caused to be affixed the great seal of the State. Done at the office of Secretary of State, at the City of Jefferson, this 17th. October A. D. 1853,
> By the Governor, STERLING PRICE.
> JOHN M. RICHARDSON,
> Secretary of State.
>
> *Description of Negro man JACK.*
> Jack is about 23 years of age, copper color, about 5 feet 8 or 9 inches high; one shoulder a little lower than the other, which can redily be discovered by examination. • He will weigh about 165 or 170 lbs.

Governor Sterling Price's proclamation offering a reward of $150 for the arrest of John Anderson for the murder of Seneca Digges, published in the *Jefferson Inquirer* (Jefferson City), October 22, 1853, and located by Janice Toms, a descendant of Seneca Digges. (Used by permission, State Historical Society of Missouri, Columbia.)

"upon proof of the fact," ordered Tomlin to receive five lashes. Far more devastating than his flogging was the court's revocation of this free black barber's license to live in Missouri and its requirement that he leave the state by December 1, 1853.²⁵ By 1843 any offense a free black or mulatto was found guilty of, no matter how insignificant, carried with it the revocation of his license to live in-state and necessitated his leaving Missouri. Tomlin had allowed Anderson to spend the night at his home and had done so without Colonel McDaniel's permission. Such activity contained all the necessary elements of "harboring a slave."

Despite the indignation meeting and the cruel punishment of Lewis Tomlin, John Anderson remained at large. None of the local bustle effected his capture. He made steady progress in his goal to run for and live in Canada as Seneca Digges lay dying at a local doctor's home and other events resulting from his death unfolded in Howard County, at least 600 miles southwest of the colony of Upper Canada.

The Missouri runaway's first free employment was as a laborer on the Great Western Railway of Canada; specifically, he was hired on the section of the line between Windsor and Chatham, a town approximately 80 miles east of Windsor. Early in his Canadian residence, he found someone to write his father-in-law Lewis Tomlin and a free black shoemaker in Fayette named Allen. The contents of both letters were identical: he had arrived safely in Detroit. We can be sure that any letter with either a Michigan or a Canadian postmark addressed to the whipped and expelled Tomlin or any other free black such as Allen, once received at the post office in Fayette, Missouri, would have been opened and its contents carefully read by persons other than the addressee.

Meanwhile Anderson, desiring to better himself, bought some clothes and entered the school of William Bibb, a fugitive American slave now living in Windsor. Through his schooling he met a kind widow named Mrs. Evelyn. Soon she told him that a letter addressed to him had arrived in Windsor; it stated that his wife and children were waiting for him in Detroit, and he should meet them there. Mrs. Evelyn smelled a rat; she suspected that this piece of mail was a ploy to return him to the United States and the jurisdiction of the federal Fugitive Slave Law. Further, an extradition arrangement among the states, as old as the adoption of the Articles of Confederation in 1777, continued in the United States Constitution. Its Article IV, section 2 states: "A Person charged in any State with [a].... Felony ..., who shall flee from justice, and be found in another State, shall on demand of the executive Authority of the State from which he fled, be delivered up, to be removed to the State having Jurisdiction of the Crime." Mrs. Evelyn believed that Anderson's swift return to Missouri to stand trial for the death of Seneca Digges was a certainty if he set foot in Detroit.

She advised him to leave Bibb's school in Windsor, move to Chatham, and change his name. He did as she suggested; by the middle of April 1854 he had become a woodcutter in Chatham, and his new name was James Hamilton. This was a good choice because Hamilton was also the surname of another fugitive slave who resided in Chatham, and the other man was old enough to be Anderson's father. However, Missouri authorities persisted, and by late spring 1854 a rumor spread among the blacks in Chatham that Anderson was a wanted man and a reward was offered for his capture. He promptly saw an attorney, relating the circumstances of his departure from Missouri; the lawyer advised him to leave the town of Chatham and once more change his name.

He moved about Ontario for the next five years. He learned the trades of masonry and plastering, and he became sufficiently prosperous to settle in Caledonia and buy a house. This town was at least 100 miles east of Chatham and about 20 miles southeast of Brantford, Ontario. Up to this time, whomever Anderson told the true story of his escape from slavery had not betrayed him to the authorities. Then his luck ran out; in early 1860 he told a man named Wynne about Seneca Digges. Anderson broke the two rules of anyone wishing to avoid detection for a misdeed: do it alone and tell no one. Anderson and Wynne had a falling out, and shortly his confidant reported what he knew of Anderson to a justice of the peace in Brantford named William Mathews, who had

Anderson arrested. Perhaps this justice of the peace also reported the capture to interested parties in Howard County.

There followed for Anderson several imprisonments in the jail in Brantford and several releases from confinement. When no witnesses came forward against him by April 1860, he was let go. However, on April 30, he was rearrested on the information of a Detroit detective and professional slave catcher named Gunning. This man had communicated with either the Digges family or with Howard County authorities. Otherwise he could never have signed an affidavit with the specificity it contained, namely that he, James A. Gunning "verily believed Anderson had willfully, deliberately, and maliciously murdered Diggs, on 28th September 1853."[26] With the help of lawyers, Anderson was once again released, but by this time slave catcher Gunning, intent on obtaining the reward for Anderson's delivery to the sheriff of Howard County, bent every effort to effect the extradition of Anderson to the United States.[27] Several Missouri newspapers mentioned the fugitive slave's arrest and his discharge,[28] but subsequent developments are best followed in other sources.

Before there could be any thought of turning over Anderson to the custody of the sheriff of Howard County, provisions of the 1842 Webster-Ashburton Treaty came into play. The first move under it was that of the country seeking the return of any accused person. As a result, Lewis Cass, Secretary of State for President James Buchanan, requested that Her Majesty's Government extradite John Anderson, a man of color, to the United States to stand trial for murder in Missouri. Initially British officials were unaware that Anderson was a fugitive slave. Once his previous condition of servitude became known, the battle was joined. No decision reached by any mere justice of the peace would be the final Canadian word on whether or not John Anderson was returned to the state of Missouri.

Under precedent established in Jesse Happy's case in the late 1830s and continued by the Webster-Ashburton Treaty, the law required that the extradition proceeding be held in Canada. Accordingly and on September 27, 1860, a hearing began in Brantford before Justice of the Peace Mathews to determine whether or not Anderson should be returned to the United States to stand trial for the murder of Seneca Digges more than seven years earlier. The Court heard only prosecution witnesses; that side had the burden of proof: it had to provide the evidence. Four people, including two children of Seneca Digges, traveled from Howard County, Missouri, to Brantford, Upper Canada, in order to testify.

Among the witnesses which the prosecution put on was B. Hazelhurst, a resident of Brantford and a county constable. He took the stand and stated that Anderson had told him only what the prisoner had stated in an earlier hearing before Justice of the Peace Mathews. Hazelhurst said that Anderson told him that he was running away from slavery, and he cut an unknown white man. However, he had no knowledge that the man had died, and these events took place in Missouri. Regrettably, the printed case includes no summary of Anderson's earlier testimony.

J.A. Holliday, a Howard County attorney, took the stand as an expert witness of sorts. He explained to Mathews that under the 1845 Revised Statutes of Missouri any person may apprehend any Negro or mulatto suspected of being a runaway and take him or her before a justice of the peace. The JP in turn must take possession and deliver him or her to the owner. Of equal importance, the law declared that any slave found more than 20 miles from home was a runaway. Holliday also described the various statutory reward provisions for the capture of a slave who escaped the service of his master. He stated that all these laws were in effect in 1853 and they remained valid at the present time. The attorney was not certain that he had ever seen Anderson prior to shortly before the hearing in Brantford.

The prosecution's evidence also included the affidavit, not the person, of a slave named Phil. He had affixed his X to a written statement concerning his knowledge of the death of Seneca Digges and Anderson's role in it. At the time, Phil was one of 16 slaves that Frances Digges, widow of Seneca, owned. Had he come to the hearing in person, he would no longer have been a slave; his mere physical presence in Canada would have freed him. Further, his testimony might have been quite different in person than it was in the written form which the white witnesses against Anderson brought with them. Surprisingly, the attorney for Anderson consented to the admission into evidence of Phil's affidavit.

It stated that he and other bondmen attempted to capture Anderson at the command of their owner, Seneca Digges. He swore that he saw the runaway cut their master, and he attested that he and his fellow slaves were unable to catch the fugitive. Phil's written statement mentioned that he knew Anderson, had seen him the day before he killed Seneca Digges, and these events took place in Howard County, Missouri, in 1853. The defense's cross-examination of a live witness might have produced an interesting answer about Phil's seeing Anderson the day before their encounter on the Digges farm. His written statement mentioned that Anderson was owned in Saline County some 30 miles east of the Digges farm, and Missouri law, as the attorney Holliday clarified, provided that any slave seen more than 20 miles from his owner's property should be declared a runaway. Why did Phil not report the runaway's whereabouts to the proper authorities? His credibility might easily have been shaken had he come in person to the hearing in Brantford.

William C. Baker, a Howard County carpenter, also took the stand. He said that he first saw Anderson in the jail in Simcoe, a town approximately 47 miles south of Brantford. Baker viewed Anderson in a lineup with two other Negro men and immediately recognized him as a person he had known between 1844 and 1853, when Anderson was the slave of Moses Burton. On cross-examination, G. M. Wilson, Anderson's lawyer, established that Howard County had hired Baker to come to Brantford in order to identify the prisoner. In addition to his expenses, he was being paid $2.50 per day.

The testimony of Seneca Digges's son Thomas D. Digges, aged 25 in 1860 and 17 or 18 in 1853, is of interest chiefly because, for the most part, it is an exception to the rule prohibiting hearsay evidence, one known as a dying declaration. Thomas had no personal knowledge of the stabbing of his father because he was not present when it occurred. Rather, as the witness before Mathews in Brant County, the son testified to what his father told him about his encounter with an unknown black man a few days before his death. Thomas told the Court that his father said a runaway slave cut him in the wrist, stabbed him in the breast, and when the white man turned to leave, caught his foot and fell, the Negro stabbed him in the back. Had Thomas Digges testified in a Missouri court to what his father told him of the circumstances of his impending death, the court would almost certainly have ruled Thomas' evidence was admissible. Missouri courts, like others in the English-speaking world, usually admit dying declarations.[29]

The evidence of Benjamin F. Digges, the younger son of the deceased, was important; he was a witness to his father's encounter with a strange African-American. Since Benjamin was born in May 1845, though he was 15 years old when he took the stand in Brantford, he was eight years and five months old when he saw a stranger stab his father in Howard County. He testified that the assailant cut his father in the breast, and as the victim turned to run, he caught his foot in some vines, and the child saw an unknown person knife his father in the back with a long dirk knife. However, at the hearing in Upper Canada, this young witness could not identify Anderson.

From Benjamin's testimony we know about the medical care then available for the victim of stab wounds. The youngster helped wrap his father in quilts obtained from a neighbor who lived a quarter of a mile away. Next, a physician, Dr. Samuel Crewse, who lived one-half mile from the scene, was summoned. The victim was put in a horse-drawn sleigh and conveyed to the home of the doctor, and he remained there until his death 13 days later. He never returned home alive. As he lay wrapped in bandages, his head propped up with pillows, and covered with eiderdown, bacterial agents were spreading infection as they coursed through the body of Seneca T. P. Digges.

Once any victim of traumatic injury survives 24 hours, bleeding to death no longer poses a problem. Rather, sepsis or infection is the most likely cause of death, no matter what weapon caused the injury, be it stabbing, gunshot, barehanded attack, or any other source of injury. With infection comes fever, and prolonged fever affects cogency, rationality, and coherence.[30] Almost certainly as this husband and father of many children lay dying years before antibiotics became available, he faded in and out of consciousness. Any treatment his doctor might have offered him, such as morphine, opium, or brandy, could only have been a palliative. Such drugs would have increased, not lessened, the suffering patient's delirium. Nevertheless, Mathews received the testimony of Thomas, the witness to his cadaverous father's last words. The father's mental condition on his deathbed would not have caused a Missouri court that was hearing a witness relate the dying man's statements to exclude the testimony on grounds of its inherent unreliability. Not surprisingly, Digges's reflective capacity near the end of his life did not affect JP Mathews' decision, either.

The authorities in Howard County obviously took the affidavit of Slave Phil and sent it to Brantford with the four Missourians who made the trip in person. Once arrived, the Missourians probably interviewed B. Hazelhurst, the Brantford constable, and they saw his value as a witness. He testified to the recent admissions Anderson had made to him about cutting a man in Missouri seven years earlier. The prosecution used all this evidence to convince Mathews that John Anderson murdered Seneca Digges in Howard County, Missouri, and should be extradited to the United States.[31] All the parties understood that the crime of murder has no statute of limitations; hence no defense was available to the accused because his culpable act took place seven years earlier.

As Brode says, "Mathews had heard enough. To his mind, the facts indicated that a murder occurred. Mathews and two other magistrates ... signed the warrant of commitment. It only remained for the governor general to sign the order returning John

Anderson to the Missouri authorities."[32] However, no such order was signed. Canadian newspapers beat the drums against the return of Anderson to the United States, and Brode nicely documents the extensive press coverage of this case in his book-length study. Anderson's attorneys applied for a writ of habeas corpus so that the question of the former slave's extradition could be reviewed before the appellate judges who sat in Toronto on the Queen's Bench of Upper Canada.

After the fugitive slave lost his case in Brantford, his attorneys argued before the three-judge panel in Toronto that he should be discharged, that is, let out of jail. They reasoned that "According to our laws any attempt to deprive another of his liberty without legal process, would be illegal and might be legally resisted.... The [slave] is deprived of the right of dominion over himself.... His wife and children are not his own.... According to our law the homicide was justifiable, and in any view of the matter, it would not amount to murder."[33] The attorneys for the Crown replied that the prisoner should be returned to the United States. They argued that "Anderson is not claimed by the state of Missouri as a slave, but as a fugitive from criminal justice, as a murderer according to the laws of that state, as a murderer within the intent and meaning of an existing treaty."[34]

Between the hearing in September 1860 in which the witnesses testified before Mathews and the hearing in which the lawyers for both sides made their arguments, approximately two months elapsed. Prior to the appellate court's decision, newspapers voiced their opinions. One wrote that "the ultra Abolitionists, as also the negroes, are clamorous that he [Anderson] should not be given up.... The decision has not yet been rendered. I think the man will be given up."[35] The court announced its decision on Saturday, December 15, 1860, under dramatic circumstances. Landon noted that the "police stood about the court with muskets and ... a company of Royal Canadian Rifles were also under arms at the Government House."[36] The Canadian judges were ready for a violent reaction to a decision which they strongly suspected might prove very unpopular.

They did not reach a unanimous decision. Two were for returning him to the authorities in Missouri. They held that there might be sufficient reasons "to warrant [the Missouri] jury in taking a favorable view of the case, and to lead them to think it probable that the prisoner advanced toward the deceased and stabbed him under an apprehension that it was necessary, not merely to facilitate his own escape, but to save his life, or to avert threatened violence at the moment."[37] The dissent had no such pie-in-the-sky view of a Missouri jury sitting in judgment of a slave for the murder of a white man. It focused on two aspects of the prosecution's evidence: the inherent unreliability of Seneca Digges's dying declaration ("his body may have survived the powers of his mind") and the error in admitting the deposition of Slave Phil. It concluded, "Rejecting such portion [of the evidence] as is only hearsay and inadmissible, ... there is no testimony which establishes satisfactorily that the prisoner is the person who caused the death of Digges."[38]

The divided opinion of this court was not the end of the matter. An appeal from any decision it reached could be taken, and was. With the help of able counsel, Anderson obtained a writ from both the Court of Common Pleas in Toronto, Upper Canada, and a court in London, England. A person of total obscurity to most persons in the

English-speaking world, Louis Alexis Chamerovzow, Secretary of the British and Foreign Anti-Slavery Society in London, acting much like a jack-in-the-box, popped up with an affidavit wherein he stated that the life of John Anderson was "exposed to the greatest and immediate danger" unless the court at Westminster immediately issued a writ of habeas corpus. An attorney, Edwin James, presented Chamerovzow's affidavit, and on January 14, 1861, the court in London granted a writ which was directed "to certain gaolers ... in the province of Upper Canada, commanding them to bring up the body of A[nderson], a British subject, alleged to be illegally in their custody."[39] It was served on the sheriff of York and the keeper of the Toronto jail. As such these Canadian officials were under the order of a court thousands of miles away to produce the body of John Anderson before them in London, England. According to Reinders, the four judges in Westminster deliberated only 20 minutes before issuing the writ of habeas corpus,[40] an ancient and present-day means of testing the legality of any prisoner's confinement. However, back in Upper Canada, the Court of Common Pleas determined that Anderson should be discharged. Even had it not, Anderson had other appeals still remaining in Canada and in England. It was possible, Brode observes after noting the possible appellate processes for Anderson, "that these series of appeals would exhaust the resources of his pursuers."[41]

While Anderson remained in Canada, the British and Foreign Anti-Slavery Society experienced increased contributions because of all the English publicity about his case. In February 1861 the prestigious Juridical Society in London debated this question: "Is the Government of the United States of America entitled, under the Ashburton Treaty, to claim the extradition of the fugitive Anderson?" Most members believed that the fugitive's act was not an extraditable crime because "the offence with which he was charged is dependent altogether on the institution of slavery." Probably unaware that the state of Missouri had hanged a young slave woman, Celia, in 1855 because she killed her rapist-owner, another debater commented, "Suppose the law of that state had constituted it murder ... for a negress to kill a white man who was attempting to ravish her, England would be obliged to give up the party as a murderer." The majority of the Society's members were against the return of Anderson to the United States. However, one believed that extradition was proper. He stated: "All crime was in its nature local, and consequently to be determined by the law of the place where it is committed. It was useless to talk about the law of nature, that expression being nothing more than a collective name for a number of theories of various writers."[42] The odd man out was Sir James Fitzjames Stephen (1829–1894), later a judge and writer of considerable eminence as well as the grandfather of the writer Virginia Woolf.

While these learned fellows in London were debating the applicability of the Webster-Ashburton Treaty to John Anderson's case, on February 1, 1861, the chief justice of the Court of Common Pleas in Upper Canada issued a new writ of habeas corpus. Anderson appeared in his courtroom slightly over a week later. On February 16, these judges decided the crime with which Anderson was charged might contain only the elements of manslaughter, while the provisions of the treaty required that the offense must be murder. Therefore, this court ordered the release of the prisoner after he had spent eight months in jail. Though Anderson was freed by a Canadian court, he vividly remembered the doggedness of his chasers. He believed that as long as he remained in

Canada, somehow they might manage to return him to Missouri. Therefore, three months after his release, he sailed for Liverpool, England. He arrived in the middle of June, and after a short visit in that city he left for London.

On July 2, 1861, he appeared at a public meeting in London amidst a great assemblage of anti-slavery dignitaries at Exeter Hall. The chairman of this gathering was Harper Twelvetrees who would become, Anderson's biographer. Among many other speeches that night, a then-recent opinion of the U.S. Supreme Court, *Dred Scott*, was denounced: "No wonder then that from the judicial seat of that mighty Government came the shameful, disgraceful, wicked, and diabolical decision that 'No person along whose veins course one drop of African blood had rights that a white man need respect.'"[43] Most likely the highlight of the evening was Chairman Twelvetrees handing Anderson a small bottle of English soil, on which was inscribed, "John Anderson's Certificate of Freedom presented at Exeter Hall, London, July 2, 1861."[44] With another obvious reference to the ruling in *Dred Scott*, namely that the plaintiff was not a citizen and had no right of access to the courts, Twelvetrees addressed the guest of honor as "Citizen Anderson."

During the next few months, the former slave attended numerous meetings in and about metropolitan London. At them he told and retold the story of his life. He also seems to have enjoyed city life in a way that his supporters found displeasing. They decided he should leave London and go to the countryside in order to get an education. His benefactors chose a secluded place in the home of a gentleman who resided in the village of Corby, at least 100 miles from London. There Anderson supposedly refreshed his knowledge of reading, writing, and arithmetic. Much as he may have enjoyed his stay in a rustic setting, by the summer of 1862 his abolitionist friends decided that this former slave would best realize his full potential as a resident of the African Republic of Liberia, a country founded in 1822 by the American Colonization Society for freed slaves. Among America's enthusiastic supporters of Liberia as a home for freed Negroes was Tennessee Justice John Catron, the father of James Thomas. (As the chief justice on the Tennessee Supreme Court he upheld a Tennessee statute which conditioned the freeing of any slave on either the emancipator signing security bonds or transporting the former bondperson(s) out of the U.S., preferably to Liberia.) If the truth be known, it appears that John Anderson was no more welcome in England as a freed slave than he might have been had he lived in Tennessee.

With considerable fanfare and hyperbolic estimates from his many English abolitionist friends about his eventual social station in his new country, Anderson left London from Euston Station bound for Liverpool. From this port city, he sailed for Liberia on December 24, 1862, on the *Armenia*. His anti-slavery supporters described this country as one destined to be greater than Ethiopia, Egypt, and Carthage, and they told him that he might someday be its president. Once this former slave boarded his ship for his new country, however, he sailed into an unknown fate. No additional records about John Anderson survive; he simply disappeared. Moreover, as Winks writes about the document at the heart of any imagined return of Anderson to this country and to Missouri authorities, "No fugitive slave was ever surrendered to the United States under ... the Webster-Ashburton Treaty."[45]

While Anderson was enjoying his recent release from jail in Toronto, the Missouri

General Assembly passed a special law in March 1861 which gave to the witnesses who journeyed to Brantford, Ontario, in 1860 to testify about the murder of Seneca Digges $1,500 for their expenses in connection with his initial extradition hearing.[46] Other than this single reference in Missouri's session laws, there is no mention of Anderson elsewhere in either the statutes or case law of this state.

It is not difficult to imagine what would have happened had Canadian/English authorities determined that Webster-Ashburton required Anderson's return to the United States. His return to Howard County would have been swift. It is unlikely that a mob would have lynched him; there are no known extra-legal deaths of slaves in this county. Rather, he would have been tried before an all-white male jury in the courthouse in Fayette for the first-degree murder of Seneca T.P. Digges. Further, he would have been found guilty and sentenced to death by hanging. There is not one known slave in this state, male or female, adult or child, who, acting alone, caused the death of a white person, no matter what the circumstances, who was not sentenced to death. All except the few who managed to escape were dead persons walking as they mounted the scaffold in the respective counties wherein they were tried. Howard County executed four, all adult males, two in 1832 and two in 1837. Had Canadian and English judges reached a different interpretation of their extradition law, the known number of slave deaths by hanging in this county would be five.

Had the local authorities ever gotten Anderson in their custody, an account of him would appear in one or more of the Howard County histories. As it is, they make no mention of him. These compilations of events within the particular Missouri county describe the successful prosecution and hanging of slaves, not the ones who got away. One must go to out-of-state newspapers, books, law cases, and journal articles to learn what happened to John Anderson. However, despite the vast display of learning in one law review article containing 246 footnotes, the author misses the essence of this case. He concludes that Anderson's freedom "was won at the expense of a meddling slaveholder in Missouri."[47]

Seneca T.P. Digges was not concerning himself in the business of other people without being asked when he attempted to capture a runaway slave. So obsessed were Howard Countians with their love of slavery that they gave the man they believed to be threatening it one vote when he ran for president in 1860. In this same election Abraham Lincoln received 9,945 votes in St. Louis County.[48] Most obviously, Digges was a good citizen of a Missouri county that had a profound regard for the legality and the righteousness of slavery. He shared the beliefs of his time and place, and he acted on them. Doing so cost him his life, to the great sorrow of his wife and their nine children, and the lingering regret and bafflement of his grandchildren and their descendants.

As the next chapters demonstrate, the state of Missouri was protective of the property rights of its many slave owners throughout the existence of the peculiar institution. Its legislation enacted an ample body of law which criminalized the words and deeds of persons who attempted to help bondpersons gain their freedom. Antebellum Missouri was not a place strewn with messages encoded in quilts or one wherein signs were affixed to fences which aided the slave as he ran for freedom. Rather, it was an immensely dangerous environment for anyone who was believed, rightly or wrongly, to be aiding any runaway slave.

7

Abolitionist Prison Inmates

As early as 1830, the Ways and Means Committee of the Missouri General Assembly was issuing reports on a penitentiary; by 1833, an act for establishing the prison in Jefferson City had become law. In anticipation of the work being completed in October 1834 and the building(s) ready soon thereafter to begin receiving inmates,[1] in 1835 the legislature passed a major revision of the criminal code. Among many other provisions, the new law imposed penalties for persons, including free blacks, who either forged free passes or any other papers for slaves which eased their escape from their masters, or attempted to or actually did abduct or entice any slave from his owner.[2] Upon conviction of several variations of these slave-stealing crimes, the statute required that the perpetrator be confined in the penitentiary. In keeping with most of the state's legislation concerning slaves, the source of the newly enacted Missouri slave-stealing penalties was Virginia.

As in Missouri, so earlier in Virginia, once the state passed criminal statutes which included incarceration in the penitentiary as a punishment and completed its prison, it locked up slave stealers in its newly opened penal institution.[3] Some states in the Deep South punished this offense far more severely: Alabama, Florida, and South Carolina, for example, made stealing other men's human properties a capital offense, and the evidence suggests that these states carried out executions of slave thieves.[4] Though Missouri had a death penalty for slave stealers in territorial days, there is no known execution of any person for slave theft in Missouri's history. Moreover, as early as 1835, the stealing of any slave from his master or overseer was a non-capital felony in this state. Its punishments included a fine, up to 39 lashes, imprisonment in a county jail for up to ten years unless the slave was restored to his/her owner, and disqualification from voting, giving evidence, and serving as a juror.[5] Few records for this offense from early statehood years have been located; systematic recording in any available form awaited the arrival of inmates in the penitentiary.

By 1836, Missouri's newly completed prison began receiving persons convicted of, among other crimes, what its general citizenry believed was plain and simple "nigger stealing." Fellman describes people who aided and abetted runaway slaves from a respectable white Missouri citizen's point of view: "Underlying the ostensible purpose of destroying the institution of slavery raged northern white lust to couple with filthy black women.... In this vision, Northerners became in southern eyes subhuman beasts of the earth, who claimed infuriatingly that they were saints."[6] Most members of Mis-

124

souri's General Assembly believed that prison was the proper place for such hypocrites, and they passed the necessary legislation to lock up these meddlesome persons.

From its 1835 start and throughout slave-stealing times, the legislation specified that the minimum time in the penitentiary for any offense was two years. Unlike current law, under which Missouri's circuit court judges order and consult a pre-sentence investigative report about the convicted felon prior to sentencing him/her to Missouri's Division of Adult Institutions, antebellum law required that the jury assess the punishment for, among other offenders, slave stealers.[7] To be sure, judges could reduce or set aside the jury's punishment, but since white male voters elected circuit court judges, the evidence suggests that the state's trial judges infrequently, if at all, gave abolitionists less time in prison than the white male juries assessed. Persons tried for any aspect of enticing slaves to leave their masters were detested, some much more than others.

The Register of Inmates at the Missouri State Penitentiary between 1837 and 1865 documents a continuous presence of prisoners incarcerated for variations of the crime of slave stealing. Theirs is a little-known story worth telling. In all, 42 known convicts and others of Missouri's prison population may have been guilty of this same offense. According to the Register, four were imprisoned for "Grand Larceny." However, because of other sources regarding their cases, we know that they attempted to lead the state's bondpersons to freedom.

Missouri classified slaves as personal property, and this classification made them ideal subjects of larceny, or that crime committed when, with the felonious intent to deprive the owner permanently of his personal property, the perpetrator took it and carried it away by stealth as opposed to force or violence. In the antebellum period, the sum of $10 separated the misdemeanor of petty larceny from the felony of grand larceny. The former was at most an offense punished by time in a county jail, if not by a fine without jail time. However, Missouri law made the theft of any slave, regardless of his or her material value, a form of grand larceny, and anyone who "stole" any slave(s) in Missouri, and was caught and convicted of this offense in any of its multiple forms, was sent to the penitentiary in Jefferson City.

The prison received its first inmate on March 6, 1836. It is likely that, from its start, the register was kept by one or more literate inmates who, as the warden's clerical help and under his direction, recorded the essential facts of each new prisoner as he or she arrived. At a time when both photography and fingerprinting were in the future, this giant ledger, which reads from left to right, contained the following about each prisoner: (1) name, (2) age, (3) nativity, i.e. place of birth, (4) height, (5) length of foot, (6) complexion, (7) scars, (8) color of hair, (9) color of eyes, (10) trade & profession, (11) from what county sent, (12) for what offense charged, (13) sentence, (14) term of court, (15) when received, (16) remarks, and (17) when discharged. Most Missouri Penitentiary inmates discussed in this book were convicted of some aspect of slave stealing, and many of the particulars about each of the 42 are in Appendix 3, "Missouri's Slave stealer (Abolitionist) Prison Inmates."

With all these pieces of information, even though two men shared the same name and were convicted of the same crime, they are unlikely to be confused. Two abolitionists were named John Johnson, but because of the prison register's many specifics, one was not mistaken for the other. All prisoners can be identified with reasonable certainty. Moreover, from the opening of the state's prison through the Civil War period, blacks and women were such rarities as inmates that the keeper(s) of the ledger described any as "Negro," "Black woman," "Female," and the like.

Among other noteworthy aspects of the slave stealer offenders was the large number of states and foreign countries in which they were born and surely, in some cases, lived most of their lives until they came to Missouri, broke its laws, were found guilty in its courts, and became prisoners in its penitentiary. Included among this group's birthplaces were 14 jurisdictions within the United States and four foreign countries: Connecticut, District of Columbia, Illinois, Indiana, Kentucky, Maryland, Maine, Massachusetts, Missouri, New Hampshire, New York, Ohio, Pennsylvania, Virginia, Canada, England, Germany, and Ireland. The federal censuses of Missouri from these years are far less various. Excluding St. Louis County, the majority of Missouri's general population between 1830 and 1860 were born in Kentucky, North Carolina, Tennessee, Virginia, and Missouri,[8] all slave states. Though, unexpectedly, Virginia was the birthplace of six of the 42 inmates, most were not born in slave states. Indeed, 12, or more than 25 percent, were born in a foreign country which had earlier abolished slavery, if it ever sanctioned the institution. England, for example, had finally ended slavery in the West Indies in 1833, a few years before Missouri's penitentiary received the first of its abolitionist inmates.

Surely, most of them devoutly believed that ownership of human beings was a creature of the devil, and they came to Missouri with the same idealism that brought latter-day freedom riders on buses into the Deep South in the 1960s. Just as surely, most of the state's legislators, judges, jurors, slaveholders, and law enforcement officers from the Missouri counties in which these inmates were caught and convicted, believed with equal ardor that slavery was an honorable institution, ordained by God, sanctioned in the Bible, practiced by the Greeks and Romans; and that a man's property, human or other, was not to be tampered with, enticed away, stolen, or otherwise persuaded to leave its owner. The state's law was clear, and those who broke it and were caught paid the price. The chasm between the beliefs of these prisoners and those of the average citizen of the Missouri counties in which they were convicted was wide and deep. These different points of view would grow even more divergent as the Civil War neared, commenced, and raged.

The law itself was not quite as diversified as the prison records indicate. The basic offense was grand larceny, and the statute required imprisonment of no less than seven years upon conviction of one of its subdivisions, slave stealing. However, if the offender progressed no further in his criminal enterprise than an attempt to commit the crime, that is, if he did any act toward the commission of the offense but failed in the perpetration of it or was prevented or intercepted in executing it, the punishment was not to exceed "one half of the longest time prescribed upon a conviction for the offence so attempted."[9] By 1845 Missouri had refined its law intended to punish abolitionists, and had also eliminated the requirement of the evil intent of the larcenous taking of bondpersons. Instead of one statute, there were four, the basic crime of slave stealing and three others. One new law concerned persons enticing, decoying, or carrying away out of this state any slave belonging to another with the intent to deprive the owner of the services of such slave, or with the intent to procure or effect the freedom of such slave.

Another dealt with persons aiding or assisting in the above, and the third with persons attempting slave enticement. The penalty for slave stealing remained no less than seven years; the related offenses were punishable by imprisonment in the penitentiary for either "no less than five years" or "not exceeding five years."[10] By 1855 the law included, in addition to all the provisions of the 1845 statutes, criminal penalties for persons enticing, decoying, or carrying out of any state or territory of the United States any slave belonging to another, with the intent to effect the freedom of that slave brought into Missouri.[11]

As with this state's many changes in its legislation concerning fugitive slaves, so too in its counterpart concerning slave stealing: the many emendations over the years in these differing but interrelated laws make clear that slaves continued to run and dedicated abolitionists continued to assist their unauthorized departure from their owners. The papal bull which outlawed meteors no more ended shooting and falling stars than the plethora of laws against slaves' running away actually halted their search for freedom.

Despite the letter of these statutes, the men who assessed the punishments of Missouri's many convicted abolitionists were not bound by the length of the prison terms which the legislature specified. Most gave slave-enticing convicts less time in the penitentiary than the statutes required, and a few gave very long prison sentences. The Register of Inmates contained so many variations of the basic offense that one suspects the record-keepers at times wrote whatever entered their minds. In addition to "slave-stealing" and "grand larceny," persons were incarcerated in Missouri's State Penitentiary for "decoying slaves," "attempting to decoy a slave from his owner," "enticing off slaves," "assisting a slave to escape," "Negro stealing," "enticing slaves out of the state," and the like. One inmate was incarcerated for an "attempt to decoy a slave & stealing a mare." Presumably this two-part offense, which involved horse stealing, was committed in order to facilitate freeing the slave; however, the perpetrator was convicted of both crimes.[12]

Except for the kidnapping in Kansas of three suspected slave stealers which occurred after the U.S. Congress passed the Kansas-Nebraska Act in 1854, it is unlikely that these defendants were arrested out of state; rather, all were probably apprehended within Missouri's borders. This is so because the extradition of persons arrested elsewhere for violations of Missouri's crimes against property became a step in the criminal justice process only after the Civil War. During the antebellum period, as long as the proceeds of non-death-penalty criminal activity were confiscated, the wrongdoer who remained outside Missouri's borders was a benefit to the state's taxpayers, who thus did not have to pay for the escaped evildoer's imprisonment. As such, few if any of Missouri's abolitionist inmates actually succeeded in their slave-stealing offenses; probably most of them were guilty of the attempt to commit the crime, not the actual commission of it. Nonetheless, many were convicted of the substantive offense of slave stealing.

These inmates were tried in 21 different places. The most frequent trial location was St. Louis because its population was the largest in the state. However, the following additional counties were scenes of their conviction and prison sentences: Benton, Buchanan, Cape Girardeau, Chariton, Cole, Cooper, Franklin, Howard, Jackson, Lafayette, Lewis, Livingston, Macon, Madison, Marion, Monroe, Perry, Pike, St.

Charles, and Sullivan. The great majority bordered either the Mississippi, the Missouri, or both of these rivers, and most of the state's slaves lived in counties adjacent to those navigable waters.

One case concerning a 23-year-old defendant arose in Mississippi County, in the extreme southeastern section of the state. It involved one Thomas Hart, charged with attempting to entice away a male slave, Goliah, owned by Charles A. Shelby and valued at $600. The accused obtained a change of venue from Mississippi County to Cape Girardeau to its north. Hart's crime occurred in April 1850, but because he was not tried until May 1851, he was received at the prison in June 1851 or 14 months after he was arrested. Most of these cases involved far shorter lapses of time between the defendants' arrest and their arrival at the penitentiary. The prison records do not indicate changes of venue; information of this nature must be obtained from other sources. In Hart's case, court records confirm that the inhabitants of Mississippi County were so prejudiced against him that he was unable to obtain a fair trial in Charleston, its county seat. As a result, his case was transferred to Cape Girardeau, where he was convicted and sentenced to a three-year term, which he served in its entirety. Though he appealed his case to the Missouri Supreme Court, it refused review.[13]

Probably most abolitionists who were arrested put the county in which they were captured to the expense of a jury trial. Thoreau's "Civil Disobedience," published in both 1849 and 1850, celebrates passive resistance to unjust laws. It says, "When a sixth of the population of a nation which has undertaken to be the refuge of liberty are slaves,.... I think that it is not too soon for honest men to rebel and revolutionize."[14] Almost certainly this essay inspired some of Missouri's righteous law-breakers, and they insisted that they be afforded due process before they were imprisoned. Of the few known guilty pleas, the grand jury quickly indicted three of the four slave stealers, and these three hurriedly pled and were rushed off to prison to avoid a lynch mob. However, once any slave thief was discharged from the penitentiary, none was a repeat offender.

Those inmates who paid the greatest price for their abolitionist activities died in Missouri's prison. The youngest was John Johnson, aged 20 years, sentenced to a two-year term which commenced in March 1849; he died of cholera in August 1850. The oldest was John Gibson, aged 60 years, sentenced to a seven-year term, received at the prison in May 1858, who, as the register-keeper recorded of him without explanation, "died June 3, 1861."[15] Others who perished in the penitentiary included Peter Rusho, aged 55 years, sentenced to a two-year term which began in November 1843; he died in 1844 as a result of complications from "rheumatism" and "spasmodic affliction."[16] John Johnson, a 40-year-old Negro sentenced to a five-year term which commenced in April 1861, "died February 10, 1862";[17] and William Knapp, a 35-year-old sentenced to six years in March 1860, "died suddenly November 27, 1864."[18] That five abolitionists died while prisoners, that two deaths were explained and three, apart from the rapidity of one of them, were not, tell us only that Missouri's prison, like most of its time, was an unhealthy and dangerous place of misery. Apart from the 21-year-old, the mortality rate among these men was highest among the oldest inmates: the average age of those who died was 44.

The smallest demographic group, consisting of only two members, was also the group which served the shortest time, and these were the female abolitionist convicts. Marian Clements, a 31-year-old white, was received at the penitentiary with her husband, 36-year-old Samuel Clements, in September 1852. Both were sentenced to two years, and he served his full term. Eliza Shy, a 21-year-old black, sentenced to five years, became an inmate in June 1857. Both women served less than a year; the white was pardoned after three and one-half months and the black after eight months. No male prisoner, either white or black, convicted of any variation of slave stealing was released after such a short incarceration. If the penitentiary was not a good place for a man who wished to free slaves, it must have been totally unsuitable for any devout and saintly woman who committed the same crime, especially if she was already pregnant when she became an inmate.

In addition to the two women, Missouri imprisoned five free black males for abolitionist activity: Benjamin Savage, 50 years old, sentenced to 10 years, arrived at the prison in December 1850 and was released in June 1856, or after serving five and one-half years; George or Allen Pinks, a 21-year-old described as both Negro and mulatto, sentenced to seven years, became an inmate in January 1861 and was released in December 1864, after serving slightly less than four years; John Johnson, a 40-year-old Negro, already mentioned as one who died in prison, served only 10 months; and Isaac Johnson, a 50-year-old Negro sentenced to ten years and received at the prison in February 1862, was released in December 1864, having served slightly less than three years. None of the five free black males served his full term. Though their average sentence exceeded seven years, except for the one who died in the penitentiary, governors pardoned the other four after an average prison term of four years. The age of these black slave stealer inmates averaged almost 39 years when they entered prison and 43 when they were released. As such, they were considerably older than the typical runaway slave. Either younger free black male residents of this state were not inclined to abolitionist activity or they eluded their would-be captors and were never arrested in Missouri for their slave-stealing crimes.

The remainder of the abolitionist convicts were white males, and for the most part, these men were in their twenties and thirties, or the same sex and age as most of the runaway slaves. This group was also the most numerous, consisting of 30 prisoners. It included the one known abolitionist prisoner who left the penitentiary on his own: Richard Carrier, a 27-year-old sentenced to seven years, was the first slave stealer received at the prison in December 1838. As the register noted of him, he "escaped September 2, 1843."[19]

Apart from the prisoner who got away, these white males can be divided into those who served their sentences in their entirety and those whom various Missouri governors pardoned. Sixteen remained inmates through their full terms: on average, they were aged 26 years when they entered prison and aged 29 years when they were discharged after serving an average sentence of three years. Most likely, their relative youth encouraged their juries to give them comparatively light sentences. In addition, their age was also a major factor in their surviving the ordeal of imprisonment.

Those who served their full sentences included Andrew Baldridge, aged 18 years and the prison's youngest abolitionist inmate, sentenced to a three-year term which he served between 1855 and 1858; and Robert Maltby, aged 20 years, sentenced to three years which he served between 1858 and 1861. Fourteen others were received as inmates between 1846 and 1858 and discharged without benefit of a pardon between 1848 and 1861. Maltby was the last abolitionist to serve his full sentence. All who arrived at the prison after him obtained early release either through executive clemency or death.

Once the 1860s began, arrests, trials, convictions, and sentences for abolitionists, white, black, male, or female, slowed to a standstill. Except for St. Louis, armed conflict devastated the state during the Civil War. Guerrilla fighters and Union and Confederate Army troops battled for its turf and killed each other and civilians as they pillaged and burned homes, crops, and any personal property of value throughout Missouri's countryside.

In February 1862, the last person imprisoned for slave stealing in Missouri, Isaac Johnson, was taken to the penitentiary; his was a short journey because he was received from Cole County, and its seat, Jefferson City, also housed the prison. One of the earliest groups of abolitionist inmates to arrive, George Thompson, Alanson Work, and James Burr, traveled from Marion County's seat, Palmyra, in northeast Missouri, and their stagecoach trip in 1841 took three days.[20] Even with railroad service, such a hard and lengthy transportation of prison inmates was almost impossible during the war years.

Despite this bloodiest of conflicts in Missouri, no fewer than 15 abolitionists were inmates there at one time or another after the firing on Ft. Sumter in April 1861 began the Civil War. Moreover, nine were pardoned after President Lincoln issued the Emancipation Proclamation on January 1, 1863. Though the proclamation freed all slaves held in the Confederate states, Missouri had never left the Union, so slavery remained in place there for two more years; and the Union Army, which was by this time in charge of the prison, continued to hold the remaining slave stealer convicts until each was pardoned under the authority of the state of Missouri. The white inmates were released between February 9, 1863, and March 6, 1865. Both remaining free blacks were let out on the same date, December 13, 1864, or at a time when slavery was less than a month shy of being abolished in Missouri.

Had the last 11 of the 42 inmates served their full sentences, they would have remained prisoners after Lee's surrender to Grant at Appomattox Courthouse on April 9, 1865. The discharge of the defendant sentenced to 18 years in Buchanan County would not have taken place until September 1878. Though the prison records regarding these 42 abolitionists tell quite an ironic story, only one, 28- or 29-year-old John Andrews, a white, remained an inmate nearly three months after slavery in Missouri ended on January 11, 1865. Perhaps Andrews was forgotten until he personally wrote the governor and reminded him that he was the sole surviving slave stealer inmate, or he may have chosen to remain imprisoned until this state became Free Missouri because slavery in it had perished.

On average, those white males who were beneficiaries of executive clemency were aged 34 when they entered the prison and their actual sentences were more than seven and one-half years. As such they were, on the whole, more than eight years older than the white males who served their full average sentence of three years. Rather obviously, juries gave older abolitionists longer sentences than younger ones. However, because the governors pardoned these older men, on average they were prison inmates approximately the same amount of time as were the younger white abolitionists who served their full sentences.

Independent of the penitentiary records, other information survives about the crime of slave stealing. The Supreme Court of Missouri issued two decisions regarding it, both relatively early in the prison sentencing of abolitionists. In 1840, it affirmed the conviction of Joseph Kirkpatrick, the first inmate from St. Louis County incarcerated for slave stealing, who, as his case mentioned, was convicted of taking and carrying away a 20-year-old slave named John.[21] In 1841 it denied the petition to review the sentences of three persons convicted largely on the out-of-court statements of slaves,[22] and it probably denied review in other abolitionists' cases, such as that of Thomas Hart, the 23-year-old convicted of attempting to entice away Slave Goliah. In 1847 it held, in another St. Louis County case involving a free black, that an indictment for abducting and enticing a slave was defective because it did not allege that the slave, a woman named Mary owned by someone referred to only by his/her initials, W.S.S., was taken out of state.[23] Otherwise, Missouri's highest and its only appellate court during this time period issued no decisions regarding the larceny of slaves.

The juries or the judges of Missouri's circuit courts sentenced at least 42 abolitionists to the penitentiary over a 25-year period, from 1837 until 1862. No court action freed even one of these inmates. The executive effected the early release of 20 or more than one-half of those who lived through their imprisonment. Because there was no parole board in Missouri until long after the demise of slavery, the governor's pardoning power liberated all still-living convicts who left their cells legally before the expiration of their sentences. In all, eight different governors, each limited to a maximum term of four years, issued pardons for these slave stealer inmates between 1843 and 1865. No contemporary newspaper coverage of these instances of executive clemency was located because there appears to have been none.

With the exception of Robert M. Stewart (1857–1861), who was born and raised in New York, all Missouri governors who pardoned abolitionists were natives of states which retained slavery until the Civil War ended the institution. Thomas C. Reynolds (1840–1844) was born in South Carolina and moved to Virginia as a young child, where he remained until he graduated from the University of Virginia. John C. Edwards (1844–1848) was born in Kentucky and educated in Tennessee. Austin A. King (1848–1852) was born and grew to manhood in Tennessee. Virginia was the birth and rearing place of the following: Sterling Price (1852–1856), Hamilton R. Gamble (1861–1864), and Willard P. Hall (1864–1865). Thomas C. Fletcher (1865–1869) was the first elected governor of Missouri who was born in the state.[24] Each of these men effected the release of at least one of the abolitionist convicts.

Among most of these high officeholders' papers is preserved greater or lesser documentation concerning the pardons of the majority of the 20 slave stealers who obtained them. The thickest file is that of Alanson Work, James Burr, and George Thompson. Work was briefly a faculty member at Marion College in Palmyra, Marion County, Missouri. When enraged Missouri slaveholders ran the president of this college, Dr. David Nelson, out of state for advocating the abolition of slavery, Work went with him to Quincy, Illinois. Thompson and Burr were Work's and Nelson's Presbyterian divinity students at Mission Institute, a short-lived college near Quincy. In July 1841, Work and two of his students attempted to induce slaves of four different masters in Marion County to leave their owners and travel through Quincy and Chicago to freedom north of the United States. Because bondpersons were well taught that abolitionists were their worst enemies, the slaves only pretended that they wished to travel to Canada. On a pretext of getting their wives and children, they returned home and revealed the runaway plot to their owners who promptly devised a plan which resulted in the capture of the "nigger-stealers."

In September 1841, the three were tried in Marion County Circuit Court in Palmyra for grand larceny in "stealing and attempting to carry away certain slaves." A plaque in the courtyard in Palmyra commemorates their case. It reads: "In a noted trial here in 1841, three Illinois abolitionists, George Thompson, James Burr, and Alanson Work, were sent to prison for attempting to entice slaves to run away." Much of the evidence against them came from the out-of-court statements of the bondpersons, who were barred, under Missouri law, from testifying against whites, or at least from testifying in open court. As a result, white witnesses testified to what the slaves said they saw and heard regarding their would-be liberators. Despite the vigorous objections of the defense attorneys, the judge admitted this hearsay evidence against their clients. The jury found them guilty, and after various instructions from the judge, it assessed their punishment at twelve years. Among the members of the jury was John M. Clemens, father of Mark Twain, then five years old. The judge refused the three men's requests for both a new trial and an arrest of judgment, and the Missouri Supreme Court denied the petition to review their conviction. They were penitentiary bound.[25]

Alanson Work so totally admired the martyr abolitionist Elijah Lovejoy that he had earlier named his son Edwin Lovejoy Work, a naming which probably lengthened the father's imprisonment. According to George Thompson, one Missouri citizen said of Work's residence at the Missouri State Penitentiary, "He ought to stay there every day of his life for naming his children after such men."[26] With passion regarding their case at this level of ill will, the first governor to whom these men, their families, and supporters applied for a pardon, Thomas C. Reynolds, refused to consider their request. He was a cheerleader for slavery, and the three languished in prison during his administration.

Work, Thompson, and Burr's 12-year sentence in September 1841 was the second-longest given to any abolitionist in Missouri history, and the motivation behind such severity was the sparing of their lives at the hands of a lynch mob from Hannibal and Palmyra who had erected gallows, prepared ropes, and was ready to hang the defendants in the event of their acquittal or a light sentence. Despite this and their exemplary conduct as prisoners, each of the three served longer sentences than Missouri's average abolitionist inmate. None would recant his heartfelt belief that slavery was sinful, and one of Thompson's books, written while he was an inmate, makes clear that each would have been released from his confinement far sooner had he renounced his abolitionist beliefs.[27]

The size of their pardon file, 65 pages, is in itself remarkable. For the most part, the extant documentation concerning Missouri's slave stealer pardons is ten pages or less, and many files are only one or two pages long. Clearly their case became a cause célèbre in the American anti-slavery movement. Governor Edwards received many undated letters and multi-signatured petitions from a great diversity of groups; they appear to have been written between January 1845 and June 1846.[28] The female citizens of Indiana began their request for executive clemency by quoting Thomas Jefferson's famous words, "All men are created equal.... They are endowed by their Creator with ... Life, Liberty and the Pursuit of Happiness." Thompson, Burr, and Work, "citizens of the United States," the petition reminded the governor, "are now incarcerated in the state prison of Missouri on the charge of offering assistance to some persons endeavoring to avail themselves of these rights by escaping from bondage"; more than 100 women signed this letter. "Citizens of Indiana," both men and women, affixed at least 200 signatures to a request written after the three had served two years. After disclaiming "all right or wish to interfere in any manner whatever with the civil affairs of the state of Missouri," the Indiana petitioners requested that the governor remit the further execution of their sentence. Their request continued, "We believe that slavery is a violation of every principle of right, that God never made one man to be the slave of another."

The inhabitants of the Thirty-First Congressional District of New York asked that Governor Edwards effect "the pardon and speedy release of our fellow citizens, Work, Burr, and Thompson, ... for attempting to assist some slaves to recover their Liberty." In a letter sent to Thomas Hart Benton, one of Missouri's U.S. Senators, William Ware, probably the prominent New York Unitarian clergyman, asked Senator Benton to transmit his letter to Governor Edwards and urge these prisoners' pardon. Ware prophetically noted that "the practices [of slavery] are fast alienating the affections of one great portion of the American Family from the other." Citizens of Illinois, careful to "disclaim all connection with the abolition factions of the day," requested these inmates' liberation as former citizens of Illinois. Their release, argued another group from Quincy, Illinois, would have a "strong tendency to allay abolition movements in this vicinity and elsewhere."

More than 30 men, members of Missouri's General Assembly and citizens of the northeastern portion of the state, requested the release of the oldest of the three, Alanson Work. Their petition described him as "the dupe of others," ... not a "cold blooded fanatic." In a lengthy communication from Gilead Township, Marion County, Ohio, Phebe Work addressed the governor as "Dear Brother," and offered herself as a prisoner if her brother, Alanson, were freed. On January 20, 1845, Edwards pardoned Work on condition that he "returns East to the state of his former residence [Connecticut] & remains there." Work's later publication, in Hartford, Connecticut, of several of fellow inmate George Thompson's flowery books suggests that Work fully complied with the conditions of his pardon and never set foot in Missouri again. One year later, on January 20, 1846, the same governor pardoned the second of the trio, James Burr. His release of Burr and later of his fellow inmate, Thompson, was unconditional; specifically it did not require that in the future the two reside outside Missouri. There was no need to prohibit either from returning; both gladly left the state on their own.

Behind Edwards' pardon of Burr were several developments. In January 1844, this prisoner broke his right arm when he caught it in machinery which, before it could be stopped, wound his limb up halfway to his elbow. It was another eight months before he regained even partial use of it. A year later, in letter addressed to both the governor and the legislature, Burr wrote of the suffering he had endured as a result of his accident. He described himself, as, and underlined his words, *a cripple for life*. At this time he based his pardon request primarily on his impaired physical condition; but he also confessed his error and pledged never to engage in the like again. Of equal if not greater importance, Burr and Thompson certified in a joint letter which they wrote to the governor ten months later that they had undergone a material change in their minds and feelings regarding slavery. They acknowledged that "although we cannot feel that slavery is right, yet we ... can now exercise a charity for slaveholders which we did not before possess." They now considered their attempt to lead Missouri slaves to freedom as a "wild, imprudent, fanatical step," and pledged "never to enter the state again for any such purpose," and to "endeavor to prevent others from doing the like."

Missouri's Third Senatorial District then included Marion and Monroe counties, and its state senator, Carty Wells, had earlier observed the trial of these men. At the request of his constituents, he wrote the governor requesting Burr's and Thompson's pardon on grounds that influential citizens of Marion County, Missouri, and Quincy, Illinois, approved their release because these prisoners had repented and "the pardon of these men will more effectually allay the abolition excitement." In a postscript he added, "I have heard many persons speak of the pardon of Work and believe it met the approval of all." Wells's letter probably reached the governor immediately before he pardoned James Burr.

Only George Thompson, the articulate ringleader of the three, remained an inmate in 1846. His father, an acting justice of the peace in Ohio, petitioned for his son's release both in person, when he traveled to Jefferson City and met with the governor, and through at least two pathetic letters which he wrote him from Ohio. In them the senior Thompson discussed, among other matters, the relatively short prison terms of slave stealers in Maryland and Kentucky and the sufferings of Mrs. Thompson, the prisoner's grey-headed mother: "Dear Sir ... if you could hear [her] moans and see [her] tears." Joshua Mathiot of Newark, Ohio, also requested that his former colleague pardon Thompson. Mathiot had earlier served with then-Congressman John C. Edwards when both were members of the Twenty-Seventh Congress, 1841–43. His Ohio friend reminded Governor Edwards of their conversation regarding "young Thompson" when they were in Washington, D.C., advised him of "the high regard" which the former Ohio congressman entertained for the prisoner's parents, and requested that Edwards advise him about the matter. Thompson himself invited the governor to come see him at the prison, and Edwards accepted his invitation and visited him in his cell. This self-assured inmate explained his future plans to Missouri's chief executive. In January 1846 he wrote Edwards that if he were pardoned he intended to leave the United States and become a missionary in Africa. This young man had first considered such a career while a student of Dr. David Nelson at Mission Institute in Quincy, Illinois. Edwards minimized the political risk attached to this notorious trio's departure from prison when he spaced Work's and Burr's pardons a year apart, and, six months after Burr's release, on June 24, 1846, the governor pardoned Thompson.[29]

When he was released from "the slaveholder's prison in Missouri," as Thompson later referred to his residence of nearly five years, he returned to Ohio, and after less than two years in his native state, he left his wife and child with his family. In April 1848, he sailed from New York to Sierra Leone and worked for several years as a missionary at the Mendi mission. In this place, he came to know several of the former captives from the slave ship *Amistad* who eventually returned to their native land and lived at this mission after the U.S. Supreme Court decision in their favor in 1841.[30] In December 1852 Thompson again sailed from New York to West Africa, and this time his family accompanied him; he and his wife were missionaries until they returned to the United States in June 1856.[31]

Thompson had an extensive association with Oberlin College in Oberlin, Ohio. He was born in Madison, New Jersey, August 12, 1817, and moved to Licking County, Ohio with his parents when he was 15 years old. He first came to the college three years later, but after approximately a year of enrollment in the preparatory course, he left to study at Austinburg Academy in Austinburg, Ohio. After 18 months as a student there, he went to Mission Institute in Quincy, Illinois. By the time he reached Quincy, having heard lectures by Theodore Weld, author of the anti-slavery work *American Slavery As It Is* (1837), young Thompson was sufficiently influenced by Weld to have become an ardent abolitionist. When he was released from prison in Missouri, he returned to Illinois and there married his wife, to whom he was engaged before he began his abolitionist activity in Missouri. The Thompsons spent time as missionaries far from Oberlin, but they always returned to it. They became permanent residents there in 1879, and they did so to enable their four youngest children to attend the college; all were Oberlin College graduates. Both George Thompson and his wife, Martha Cook Thompson, died in Oberlin; he on February 4, 1893, aged 75 years, and she on March 2, 1917, aged 93 years.[32] That this man had been imprisoned in Missouri for his abolitionist activities was a badge of honor to him for the remainder of his long and eventful life.

Governor Edwards issued one additional slave stealer pardon. It effected the discharge of George Langston, an Englishman by birth and rearing, who was convicted in 1847 in Howard County Circuit Court of attempting to decoy a slave from his master and sentenced to two years in prison. More than 100 Howard County residents signed petitions in June and July of 1848 in favor of this prisoner's release. Their reasons included the fact that Langston was an Englishman by birth, not aware of his "great wrong ... at the time of doing the act," and "unacquainted with the laws and customs ... of this state." Further, "the punishment already inflicted ... is sufficient for the offence," and the inmate has a wife and child "of very respectable character now residing in this county and having no visible means of support except from the hands and daily labour of his said wife."

Several observers of the proceedings against Langston also wrote the governor. One, an attorney who watched Langston's arraignment, questioned the fairness of his trial, during which he had roomed with the circuit attorney who prosecuted the case. He advised the governor that the prosecutor doubted Langston's guilt at the time of the trial and believed that the jury might acquit him. Langston's former prosecutor signed a petition in favor of his pardon, and his letter to the governor contained this admission about Langston's case: "I have had the pleasure of convicting a great many criminals for almost all offences known to our laws and this is about the only man that I have convicted about whose guilt I have any doubt."

One trial spectator, also an attorney, wrote Governor Edwards that though the young lawyer who defended Langston had "done the best he could, it was adjudged a poor defence." In his letter to Edwards, another courtroom observer described the atmosphere in which Langston's case was tried: "The excitement again him was great ... the state of the public mind" was not conducive "to a trial on the merits of the case alone, free from passion and prejudice." On July 24, 1848, Governor Edwards pardoned George R. Langston, who by then had served slightly more than one and one-half years of his two-year sentence.[33] Despite the absence in his pardon file of any direct communication to the governor from the inmate's wife, Mrs. Langston, she was clearly the organizer of support among Howard County residents for her husband's early release from prison.

Though the two women abolitionists were not inmates at the same time and were pardoned by different governors, they both served short terms in the penitentiary for the same reason: its entire lack of facilities for them. In the case of Marian Clements, co-defendant and wife of Samuel Clements, an additional reason for her immediate release existed: she was pregnant. As an undated message from the members of the state senate and house Committees on the Penitentiary phrased her condition to Governor Price, "The prisoner is now enceinte and nearly arrived to the period of parturition."[34] At the request of the committee, on December 27, 1853, Price pardoned this woman about to give birth, who thus served only three and one-half months of her two-year sentence.

Slightly more than four years later, Governor Stewart pardoned four women inmates with one stroke of his pen on February 27, 1858. One of them was the African-American abolitionist, Eliza Sly. It is clear from the written-above-the-line space where her name appears that her release was an afterthought. What was important was ridding the prison of women inmates for whom there were no accommodations. As with Governor Price's pardon of Marian Clements, so too with Stewart's release of four women on the same day: all were freed on condition that, as the pardon document phrased it, they "leave the state and do not return during their natural lives."[35]

The files of free black male recipients of executive clemency highlight yet additional aspects of the conviction of abolitionists. Though the arrest of all accused slave stealers was apparently attended by a great deal of "excitement," as contemporary accounts would have it, public indignation was especially strong when the accused was black. As previous chapters have demonstrated, many respectable whites, including members of the Missouri Supreme Court, believed that free persons of color were public pests. They were believed to have a terrible influence on slaves. It should come as no surprise that juries gave blacks accused of tampering with, enticing off, or stealing slaves longer sentences than most whites convicted of these same crimes. The prison records make clear that the average sentence for a free black, male or female, found guilty of abolitionist activity was seven years; and the average sentence for a white accused of the same offense was slightly under five. Justice was apt to miscarry in any of these slave-stealing cases, but a wrongful conviction was more likely when the accused was black.

In September 1850, in St. Louis Criminal Court, the first free black, Phillip Harris, was convicted of "enticing away slaves." In January 1848 he had received his license to live in Missouri from the St. Louis County Court. He was then aged 31 years, and listed his occupation as cook. Less than two years later he became a convicted felon under the following circumstances. He happened to have crossed the Mississippi River from St. Louis to the Illinois side in a buggy on a ferry boat with a free black woman and returned to Missouri on that same day. Coincidentally and about this same time, one of Missouri's many slaves, a female whom a Mr. Gordon of St. Louis owned, ran away from her master. The dress of Harris's passenger resembled the outfit of the runaway; specifically, each wore a green veil. The state's evidence consisted of the testimony of white witnesses that the accused, in open day, "carried the girl in a buggy across the river." The defense put on the free woman of color who testified that she was with Harris that day, but the all-white male jury believed the state's witnesses, not the defendant's companion, and found him guilty.

Eyewitness testimony was and remains notoriously unreliable. Though a witness typically perceives the sex and the race of the person correctly, his/her mistakes greatly increase when the identification is cross-racial. The beholder sees the white, the black, the Asian, and the American Indian, not an individual who happens to be white, black, Asian, or American Indian. In Phillip Harris' case the state's witnesses saw Mr. Gordon's runaway in that buggy on the ferry. Just how unlikely they were to identify her correctly can be shown with reference to the Missouri census taken a few years earlier. By 1848 the population of St. Louis County was 73,391, including 868 free blacks and 4,327 slaves,[36] and this county's immense growth continued. As a result, the odds were overwhelmingly against any of the witnesses against Harris having ever met Mr. Gordon's runaway slave, and none could have seen a photograph of the particular runaway whom he was charged with enticing from her owner because there were none. Had any U.S. marshal or any of his deputies, or the runaway's owner, the owner's attorney, or the owner's agent been on the boat that day and believed Harris' passenger was a runaway, any of these individuals had the right to detain her under the auspices of the federal Fugitive Slave Act. Had anyone else, including a person like Seneca T.P. Digges, believed that Harris' passenger was a runaway, he/she had the legal right under Missouri laws to remove her from the buggy, hold her until the ferry returned to Missouri, and take her to her master's home or to any convenient jail in Missouri. Obviously, the state's witnesses against Harris included neither persons with specific duties to take fugitive slaves into custody nor any one else actually acquainted with Mr. Gordon's runaway.

As Harris' lawyer, Uriel Wright, advised Governor Price more than two years after his client's conviction: "The case was tried under some excitement natural to such accusation, and the jury found him guilty." As in George Langston's pardon, Harris' wife, Rosamond Harris, appealed to influential men who in turn wrote the governor regarding her husband. His attorney signed a petition, and in a letter of April 1853, wrote the governor: "The evidence cannot be reconciled by human reason, except on the hypothesis of the innocence of the accused." Two months later Sterling Price pardoned Phillip Harris,[37] a man who spent two and one-half years in prison because faulty eyewitness testimony identified his free black companion as a runaway slave.

In April 1856, the St. Louis jurors who more than five years earlier had given the free black Benjamin Savage ten years in the penitentiary, petitioned the governor to release him because statements made to them after his trial made them doubt his guilt.

Their letter also observed that "Phillip Harris, of color, has long since been pardoned." Equally important, as various letters in Savage's pardon file attested, "he had been a good man in the penitentiary ... a faithful and obedient convict ... a good hearted polite old man." Accordingly, in June 1856, Sterling Price pardoned Benjamin Savage for the crime of "enticing away slaves" after this prisoner, perhaps another innocent man, had served five and one-half years.[38] Earlier, Savage, a barber, was 47 years old when he obtained his license to live in Missouri from the St. Louis County Court in June 1847.

In December 1864, Governor Willard Hall pardoned three men: the remaining free blacks convicted of slave stealing, Isaac Johnson and George Pinks; and the white man given the longest sentence of any slave stealer in Missouri's history, Henry Hatcher. The only extant letter to the governor concerning their pardons was written by the Electors of President and Vice President of the United States for the State of Missouri, men who would soon meet with others to elect Abraham Lincoln to his second term. These petitioners favored the immediate release of these three named prisoners and the restoration to them of the "Liberty which they lost in endeavoring to bestow it upon others."[39]

The remainder of Missouri's pardoned slave stealers were white males, and, except for the case which arose in the Jackson county seat, Independence, the documents concerning their release from prison are meager. The files of John Wyland (pardoned by Governor Price in April 1856), Thomas Snider, and Benjamin Head (respectively pardoned by Governor Gamble in March and April 1863) each contain only one letter in support of clemency for the inmate. All were written at the request of the abolitionist, and they read much like other perfunctory recommendations: of Wyland, "has been an obedient and well behaved convict, and at his request I petition that you restore him to citizenship";[40] of Snider, "has conducted himself very well. He has for some months been in a position of some responsibility and has acquitted himself to my entire satisfaction";[41] and of Head, "His conduct has been very good since I have had charge of him. He has never been punished for neglect of duty or violation of the rules."[42] All three references were written in the same hand by a P.T. Miller. He wrote for Warden Cochran concerning Wyland's pardon, and as Warden Miller for Snider and Head. These bland letters tell us that these prisoners, like all other abolitionists locked up in Missouri of whom we have knowledge, were model inmates. Their continuing incarceration served no purpose, and like earlier imprisoned slave enticers, different Missouri governors uneventfully pardoned them.

Yet another inmate who secured early release was John H. Andrews, whose crime took place in St. Charles County, which bordered two rivers, the Missouri and the Mississippi, and the state of Illinois. Within less than two hours of the grand jury returning indictments against him, Andrews pled guilty to attempting to entice the slaves of two different owners out of state. As the former circuit attorney for the county wrote the governor in February 1865, the accused was "indicted on the evidence of excited men." The judge gave him three years for each attempted slave enticement, and since they were to be served consecutively, he sentenced Andrews to six years. This inmate's letter requesting clemency was dated January 16, 1865, or five days after the official end of slavery in Missouri. He probably delayed writing it until he could address it, as he did, to the "Governor of the State of Free Mo." It began, "Sir I take this liberty with you because I know you believe in the principles of Freedom in its broadest sense." It advises his "Excelency" of the release of other abolitionists in December 1864, and it observes, " I am the only one left in this prison on that same charge," and in the poor spelling but very moving writing of his entire letter, concludes, "I have a family and two children in the State of Ohio. Which are dear to me and they are left to the mercies of the cold world. Now I prey you to exorcise your clemency in my behalf. Most Respectfully Submited, I am your humble servt., John H. Andrews."

The man to whom this heartfelt letter was written, Thomas C. Fletcher, was an early supporter of Abraham Lincoln for president, a distinguished brigadier general in the Union Army, a strong opponent of slavery, and newly sworn in as Missouri's governor when he received Andrews' letter. Two months later he pardoned the state's last remaining abolitionist in March 1865.[43] Though Andrews' file contains no account of the circumstances which prompted his guilty plea within less than two hours of his indictment in September 1860, documents supporting pardons for inmates convicted in Jackson County raise a strong inference that a mob stood ready to lynch Andrews if he remained in the St. Charles County jail.

A newspaper account concerning another abolitionist incident says, "The negro thieves ... in Jackson County, pled guilty the other day, and were sentenced to the penitentiary for seven years. We guess by the time they get out they will come to the conclusion to let the negro question alone."[44] The pardon files of Henry McLothlin (or McLaughlin) and Thomas McGee contain a far more complete account of their guilty plea. These young white men and a free black, Alan Pinks, pled within two hours of their indictment in the town of Independence, Jackson County, to "attempting to entice a slave out of the state"; each was sentenced to seven years in the penitentiary. They waived their right to a jury trial to escape being lynched by a group of angry men intent on murdering them. The mob came from Clay County, on the north side of the Missouri River, on a ferry which crossed the river to Jackson, on the south side. The circumstances of the apprehension of these men were remarkably similar to that of Thompson, Burr, and Work in Marion County almost 20 years earlier: A slave who believed that abolitionists intended him harm told white persons about the young men's attempt to liberate him, and slaveholders and their supporters apprehended the slave's would-be rescuers.

Had their trial in Independence been conducted according to the law then in effect in the state of Missouri, the two whites would have been acquitted because blacks and mulattoes could not testify against whites. As an undated letter to Governor Gamble explained, the Clay County crowd was well aware of these facts: "A mob of lawless persons from the county of Clay crossed the river and came to Independence ... threatening to tear down the jail, and hang said prisoners who were therein confined.... Thereupon Judge Smart advised them, as a matter of personal safety to 'plead guilty'; which they did, and were immediately hurried off in the night to Jefferson City in order to escape said mob." Another petition to the governor, signed by 19 citizens and county officers in Independence and dated November 1863, advised him that these young men's guilty pleas were based on the best advice at the time of all of Independence's attorneys, the jailer, the sheriff, and the state's attorney. It noted, "In any other case than a negra [*sic*] case there probably would have been no excitement." Yet another file letter, signed by 28 men from Kansas, Missouri (now Kansas City), contained the additional information that both McGee and McLaughlin "were citizens of Kansas against whom great prejudice existed." As a final inducement for Governor Gamble to pardon them, two letters stated that these robust young men were willing to join the Union Army. Accordingly Missouri's governor pardoned the two whites, Thomas McGee and Henry McLaughlin, on February 10, 1863.[45] As noted earlier, Hall pardoned their free black co-defendant, George Pinks, in December 1864.

Many of the pardon files discussed in this chapter document the community's intense anger toward anyone accused of slave stealing. That rage bent the law and admitted, through the hearsay evidence of whites, the backdoor testimony of blacks against whites in the 1841 Marion County case. It helped to convict at least one innocent free black, perhaps two, in St. Louis. It was also an influence in sending two women to prison, one of whom was almost certainly visibly pregnant at the time of court proceedings regarding her and her husband. Slave enticement was no ordinary crime, and passions regarding it grew more heated, not less, as the controversy regarding slavery continued. As McGee's and McLaughlin's pardon papers illustrate, the savage indignation of proponents of the peculiar institution was particularly evident in the state's western counties.

8

Missouri's Western Front

On January 29, 1861, Kansas, the thirty-fourth state, was admitted to the Union, and it came in free, a place where slavery was prohibited. The depth of hatred between its residents and those of neighboring western Missouri, an area which counted much of its wealth in slaves, can be glimpsed in a series of events which occurred in the middle of the Civil War. In April 1863, Union Army General Thomas Ewing issued General Order No. 10, which stated that all men and women who willfully aided and encouraged anti-Union guerrillas would be arrested, tried, and sent to a Union Army prison which stood at 14th and Grand Streets, Kansas City (Jackson County), Missouri. Within three months this shabbily built three-story brick structure contained a number of female relatives of guerrilla fighters. On August 14 it collapsed; many women were injured, and four were killed, all of whom had close family ties to William C. Quantrill and his followers. The next day, in Jackson County, Quantrill and his men planned their infamous raid against a Unionist Kansas locale. It took place on August 21. In the course of it, they sacked and burned the town of Lawrence, Kansas, causing more than two million dollars in property damage, and killing at least 180 civilian men and boys, but no women because these bloodthirsty men considered themselves chivalrous.

In response, four days later on August 25, 1863, General Ewing issued General Order No. 11, which called for the civilian depopulation within 15 days of the northern half of Vernon and all of Bates, Cass, and Jackson counties, all of which places in wesern Missouri bordered Kansas. Fellman describes Ewing's General Order No. 11 as "the most drastic measure taken against civilians during the Civil War prior to General Sherman's march to the sea." He places the number of persons forced to evacuate their homes, most of which were burned down by Kansas troops, at 20,000.[1]

During this same period, no such ravages of war touched the strong Union city of St. Louis, 250 miles to the east. While Jackson County's population declined as a result of General Order No. 11, St. Louis so prospered that by 1870 it was the country's third-largest industrial city in terms of numbers of plants and value of products, behind only New York City and Philadelphia.[2] The demographics of the two locales explain the vast differences between life in Kansas City and that in St. Louis during the Civil War decade. Though Kansas City now rivals St. Louis in virtually all areas of endeavor and its geographical boundaries extend from Jackson into three other western Missouri counties (Cass, Platte, and Clay), such vitality and expansion were not its lot during the pre-Civil War period. Kansas City grew because it became a railroad center. However, the federal legislation necessary for building the first bridge across the Missouri River from Jackson County, a railroad structure named the Hannibal Bridge, was not passed until 1866.[3] The bridge itself was not completed until 1869. In the process of its construction, Kansas City became the second greatest railroad center in the United States, and its population mushroomed as a result. By 1870, the number of this city's residents was 32,286.[4]

In contrast, as early as 1848 the population of St. Louis was already 55,952; at the same time, Independence, the largest town in Jackson County, was 1,478.[5] By 1860, with a population of 162,000, St. Louis was the seventh largest city in the United States, ranking behind only New York, Philadelphia, Brooklyn, Baltimore, Boston, and New Orleans. It had the largest percentage of foreign-born residents of any American city: 60 percent, including 39,000 Irish and nearly 60,000 Germans. In the 1860 presidential election, Lincoln garnered 27,000 votes in the slave states, 17,000 of which came from St. Louis's German-American residents.[6] In 1860 the population of St. Louis County was 185,000, and that of Jackson County 22,000. The smaller county's largest towns included Kansas City, population 4,418; Independence, 3,164; and Westport 1,195.[7] However, both counties, one in extreme eastern Missouri and the other in extreme western Missouri, had approximately the same number of slaves, 3,250.[8] Those in St. Louis made up a very small part of the economy since they represented no more than one-tenth of one percent of the city's population and were in the main employed as maids, cooks, washerwomen, child- and horse-care providers, and butlers for the city's wealthiest residents. In Jackson County, a rural stronghold of slaveholders, that same number of bondpersons added up to 15 percent of its population. In other words, there were 160 more slaves for every free person in Jackson than in St. Louis County. These percentages created anxieties for slaveholders in the western portion of Missouri not present in the eastern section of the state. Then matters worsened.

On May 30, 1854, Congress passed the Kansas-Nebraska Act in the belief that it was enacting yet another piece of federal legislation conducive to the peaceful spread of slavery. The law established the separate territories of Kansas and Nebraska from what was earlier known as Indian Territory, a large and seemingly barren immensity of land west and north of the state of Missouri. The Act announced "the principle of non-intervention by Congress with slavery in the States and Territories," and did so as if the Continental Congress' Northwest Ordinance of 1787, which prohibited slavery north of the Ohio River, had never become the law of the United States. Previously, the Missouri Compromise, which Congress passed in 1820, had determined that, except for the state of Missouri, there should never be slavery north of latitude 36 degrees 30 minutes north, that is, the southern boundary of Missouri, or the Arkansas-Missouri border. With the behind-the-scenes help of one of Missouri's U.S. Senators, David Atchison, the western part of whose constituency was strongly pro-slavery, the 1854 act implicitly repealed the 1820 law by leaving the question of whether or not slavery should exist in Kansas and Nebraska to their settlers. The new law declared that its intention in the new territories was neither to "protect, establish, prohibit, nor abolish slavery." Senator Stephen Douglas of Illinois, chairman of the committee on Territories, marshaled the legislation through Congress and called the concept "popular sovereignty."

But abolitionists derisively termed it "squatter sovereignty." Douglas' hope that his territorial legislation would quiet the increasingly acrimonious debate over slavery was not realized. The law had no such ameliorative effect.

Instead, it turned a swath of land extending 70 miles west of the Kansas-Missouri border into a war zone for and against slavery. The Emigrant Aid Company was chartered in Massachusetts for the immigration to Kansas Territory of anti-slavery people; its members settled Lawrence and Topeka. Osawatomie was specifically settled by abolitionists, and they, like their Missouri State Penitentiary counterparts, believed that they were doing the Lord's work when they led or attempted to lead bondpersons to freedom. Pro-slavery factions immigrated to Leavenworth and Atchison (named for Senator Atchison), and after May 1854, nowhere in the United States was the conflict regarding slavery more violent than in the territory to Missouri's immediate west, a place which soon became known as "Bleeding Kansas."[9] Instead of the tranquil solution to an increasingly divisive issue which congressional backers of the Kansas-Nebraska Act envisioned when voting the measure into law, rage overran reason on the Missouri-Kansas border.

In July 1854, with the support of Senator Atchison, the Platte County Self-Defensive Association was formed in Weston, Missouri, a town in Platte County, then separated from Kansas Territory by the Missouri River. The group's purpose was to promote slavery in Kansas and rid the area of abolitionists; its membership eventually included over 500 of the county's most prominent citizens. At its first meeting a Judge Galloway told a large crowd "that the people of Platte county would not for a single day tolerate dishonest Abolitionists who came to steal negroes, destroy property and stir up strife and insurrection."[10] The full flavor of the association's aims can be illustrated by a public speech which Atchison made before its members in September 1854. Of his talk, he wrote his old friend, Jefferson Davis, then President Pierce's Secretary of War, that he advised "the people in Missouri, to give a horse thief, robber, or homicide a fair trial, but to hang a negro thief or abolitionist, without judge or jury; this sentiment met with almost universal applause."[11] In March 1855, now ex-Senator Atchison, whose term in the U.S. Senate had recently expired, led 80 angry men from Platte County to vote a pro-slavery ticket in a Kansas election. He said to them, "There are eleven hundred coming over from Platte County to vote, and if that ain't enough we can send five thousand — enough to kill every God-dammed abolitionist in the territory."[12] William Lloyd Garrison described him as "that lawless ruffian, the leader of the Missouri-Kansas bandits, David R. Atchison."[13] With such a demagogic leader in Platte County, anyone who publicly criticized vigilante activity ran the risk of mob retaliation.

An early target was *The Industrial Luminary*, a Platte County newspaper which no longer exists, published in Parkville, a place separated from Kansas Territory by the Missouri River. This village was named for the largest real estate owner in the county, a native of Grafton, Vermont, who laid out the town and founded the paper. In 1885, a Platte County history described this newspaper as holding "advanced views on the slavery question for that day, warmly opposing slavery."[14] After the March 1855 election fiasco in Kansas, Park and his fellow editor, W.J. Patterson, criticized the voter fraud in which Atchison and other Platte County residents had played a prominent role. Even earlier, Park had earned the border politician's wrath when his newspaper reported that Senator Atchison seemed to be "under the influence of liquor," when he claimed credit, rightfully to be given to Senator Douglas of Illinois, for introducing the Kansas-Nebraska Bill.[15]

On Friday evening, April 13, 1855, 200 members of Platte County's Self-Defensive Association rode into Parkville; most of them came from Atchison's hometown of Platte City, a distance of 13 miles. The mob seized *The Luminary* and dumped its press and type into the Missouri River. Contemporary newspaper coverage clarified that George Park only avoided the fate of Elijah Lovejoy, the eastern Missouri abolitionist martyr who was murdered in 1837, because a friend, himself a member of the Self-Defensive Association, had warned Park of the danger, and he escaped into Kansas Territory. The mob's intention regarding the newspaper's editors was to tar and feather them, tie them to their press, and drown them in the Missouri River. When the mob seized Patterson, Park's co-editor, he advised this rabble of cowards that he was a Canadian citizen, and his harm would result in an international incident. Equally important, the bigger fish, George S. Park, had already escaped. Instead of murdering anyone, the Platte County Self-Defensive Association offered various resolutions. It declared that *The Luminary* was a nuisance and should be abated; its editors were traitors to the state and county in which they lived and should be dealt with as such; and if within three weeks either Park or Patterson should be found in Parkville, "we will throw them into the Missouri River, and if they go to Kansas to reside, we pledge our honor as men to follow and hang them where we can take them."[16]

Though the actions of the cowards who destroyed Park's newspaper were punishable under Missouri law as "malicious mischief," no one was taken into custody for this pro-slavery violence. Hence it is not surprising, as Atchison's biographer Parrish notes, that "there is no evidence of [Atchison's] participation in the affair or its planning."[17] Evidence of community-approved criminal activity which incriminates its organizers usually remains uncollected, and in the aftermath of *The Luminary's* destruction, no one was so much as investigated, let alone arrested, prosecuted, and convicted. However, a St. Louis newspaper editor, B. Gratz Brown, later a governor of Missouri, believed that Atchison perpetrated the violence against the Parkville paper because it criticized the leading role the former senator played in the March 1855 voter fraud in Kansas. In one article about the destruction of Park's newspaper, Brown's paper wrote of the "infamous conduct of Atchison and his confederates."[18] In another it denounced Atchison as an aider and abettor of a "mob composed of hundreds, marching to attack the persons and property of two defenseless men."[19] In a lengthy letter to B. Gratz Brown, editor of the St. Louis *Missouri Democrat,* George S. Park blamed "Atchison and his organized bands" for the Platte County violence which destroyed his Parkville newspaper.[20]

After the Civil War, the former editor of *The Luminary* returned to his beloved Parkville, and in 1875, with the help of his fellow Presbyterian John McAfee, he founded Park College there, a school which still bears its founder's name. At his direction, after his death in Illinois in 1890, his body was returned to Parkville for burial. He is interred there in Walnut Grove Cemetery between his first wife, Eliza Ann, and his second, Mary Louise. Their tombstone contains no hint of the destruction of his newspaper and the failed lynching bee intended for his person 35 years earlier when the battle to extend or extinguish slavery engulfed the Missouri-Kansas border.

In 1855 worse happenings than reproaches from a Parkville newspaper editor lay in store for Missouri slave owners. Six months after the Platte County mob destroyed *The Luminary,* a Mr. John Brown (1800–1859) became a resident of Kansas Territory. Five of his sons had moved there somewhat earlier in order to lend their support to this territory entering the Union as a free state. Their father, a fanatical abolitionist who was born in Connecticut and spent his youth in Ohio, joined them in the fall of 1855; he lived in Kansas during three time periods: 1855–56, August–December 1857, and June 1858–February 1859. During his first stay he led a band of killers, including four of his sons, against pro-slavery people, and he and his followers murdered five men and mutilated their bodies. They split their heads, pierced their sides, and chopped off their fingers at the massacre of Pottawatomie Creek, Kansas Territory.[21] During his last stay in Kansas Territory, John Brown carried his violent abolitionist actions into Missouri.

In December 1858, he was staying in a cabin near Osawatomie, Kansas, with his brother-in-law, the Reverend Samuel Adair, a Congregationalist minister, and his wife, Florella Brown Adair, Brown's half sister. Both of the Adairs had been students at Oberlin College in Ohio, an early place of co-educational and bi-racial education and abolitionist sentiment. While living with the Adairs, Brown met Jim Daniels, a runaway from Bates County, Missouri, a locale which bordered Kansas Territory. The slave was seeking to prevent his sale, along with that of his wife, their two children, and another slave, as assets of an estate to the highest bidder. Brown resolved that he would rescue Daniels and his family and several slaves on nearby farms, and to accomplish these ends he organized two groups of raiders. There were eight men under Brown and seven under his trusted associate Aaron D. Stevens (who was wounded at Harpers Ferry and was hanged at Charlestown the next year).

The night of December 20, 1858, the two parties traveled south from the area of Kansas Territory which later became Miami County, and when they entered Missouri they separated. Brown and his followers went to the home of Harvey G. Hicklan, where Daniels, his family, and another slave were being held prior to their sale. With guns drawn, Brown and his band freed the slaves and looted Hicklan's home. The Brown party then proceeded less than a mile from the Hicklan residence to the home of John B. Larue, another slaveholder. At the Larue home, Brown gave the head of household this choice: "We have come after your Negroes and their property. Will you surrender or fight?" There he liberated five more slaves. From the two homes, in addition to ten slaves, the party also appropriated six horses, oxen, a wagon, bedding, clothes, boots, and supplies such as bacon, flour, meal, and the like.

Meanwhile, the Stevens party visited the Bates County farm of 60-year-old David Cruise with the intent of freeing a bondwoman who was a friend of the Daniels family. A member of Stevens' marauding group, Albert Hazlett, who also died a gallows death in 1860 because of his participation in the raid on Harpers Ferry, shot and killed Cruise in his home in cold blood. The Stevens party took the slave woman who belonged to their now-dead victim, two horses, mules, a yoke of oxen, and a wagon filled with provisions. This valuable property, appropriated by the liberators, Brown later sold piecemeal to finance his journey with the slaves whom he freed the five nights before Christmas 1858.

At daybreak December 21, the Brown and Stevens parties reunited at the Kansas border with 11 slaves and considerable booty. By Christmas Eve they had reached the Adair cabin near Osawatomie, 35 miles northwest of their slave-freeing raids in Bates County. The freed slaves were hidden in the Adair cabin from early December 21 through Christmas Day. Thereafter, they were temporarily hidden in an abandoned cabin on the south fork of Pottawatomie Creek near Osawatomie. By January 20, the freed party numbered 12 because one of the women had given birth to a girl; her mother named her Captain John Brown. In the dead of a cold winter, Brown and his party of slaves, who now called him their Moses, pushed on through Topeka, Lawrence, and Holton, all abolitionist towns, and on February 1 they spent their last day in Kansas. The party then entered Nebraska, and within another three days crossed the Missouri River into Iowa. By February 13, they had reached Grinnell, Iowa, and the home of Josiah Bushnell Grinnell, the state's most prominent abolitionist, where they remained several days. After additional travel in Iowa, Brown obtained a boxcar for the slaves on an express train which got him and his party to Chicago. In Chicago the famous detective, Allan Pinkerton, hid the slaves, raised over $500 for Brown, and obtained another boxcar for most of the party's remaining journey; in it they traveled through northern Illinois and Michigan to Detroit. Finally their liberator said good-bye to the 12 slaves, having given them funds for provisions, as the former Bates County, Missouri, bondpersons took the ferry from Detroit to Windsor, Ontario, and freedom in Canada. They had traveled for almost three months, from December 20, 1858, until March 12, 1859. Though their 2,500 mile journey followed a zigzag route, they and their Moses, Captain John Brown, always kept their eyes on the North Star. There were surely many other Missouri slaves who sought and achieved freedom in Canada, but only the journeys of Slave Jerry, who was hustled off to Ontario from Syracuse, New York, in 1851, John Anderson, and those whom John Brown liberated were traceable.

Even before Brown's farewell to the fugitives in Detroit, he was planning bigger and more daring slave liberations in the very heart of the confederacy, the Commonwealth of Virginia. He rented a farm near Harpers Ferry, Virginia (now West Virginia), and hoped that from it fugitive slaves and their abolitionist friends would go forth as torments and terrors to slaveholders. In October he and his followers captured the U.S. Arsenal at Harpers Ferry. The raid cost 17 lives, including that of two slaves. Colonel Robert E. Lee commanded a company of U.S. Marines which easily captured Brown and his party. Shortly, Brown and what remained of the men he led to Harpers Ferry were transported eight miles southwest under heavy guard to Charlestown. There the Commonwealth of Virginia put him on trial for murdering four whites and one Negro, conspiring with slaves to rebel, and committing treason against Virginia. He was found guilty on all counts and hanged December 2, 1859, in Charlestown, Virginia (now West Virginia).[22] He immediately became a martyr, the most famous in the abolitionist cause. Union Army troops marched to these poetic lines about him: "John Brown's body lies a moldering in the grave,/ His soul is marching on." Russell Banks's *Cloudsplitter*, a recent novel about him, illustrates the fascination which his life and deeds still hold for us. Regrettably, Banks's book contains only brief and inaccurate reference to this fiery abolitionist's Missouri slave-liberation raid.[23] Fortunately, John Brown has been the subject of many biographies.

At least three visual depictions of him, two statues and a mural, are currently located in eastern Kansas. The first was chiseled from marble in Italy, the sculptor working only from a photograph of Brown. The project's organizer was Bishop Abraham Grant of the African Methodist Episcopal Church, Kansas City, Kansas. At his urging blacks throughout the United States raised $2,000 in amounts which varied from a few pennies to $10. The result is a larger-than-life statue of Brown, formally attired in a shirt, vest, greatcoat, trousers, and shoes, which now stands at 27th and Sewell Streets in Kansas City, Kansas, formerly the town of Quindaro, a haven for runaway slaves from places such as Platte County, Missouri. Brown, who was hanged December 2, 1859, holds in his right hand a scroll of "The Emancipation Proclamation" which Lincoln signed into law on January 1, 1863. Despite the anachronism of the statue and the fact that the scroll and a part of Brown's nose are now missing, the work remains impressive. At its base is inscribed: "Erected to the memory of John Brown by a Grateful People." It was unveiled on June 8, 1911, at graduation ceremonies for what was then Western University, a black college. Among the dignitaries present was former Kansas Governor John P. St. John.

Statue of John Brown, Kansas City, Kansas. Erected with contributions made by African-Americans throughout the United States and dedicated in 1911, it stands at 27th and Sewell streets, in an area that was formerly the town of Quindaro. (Photograph by the author.)

Also included among the crowd of 3,000 spectators were members of the new National Association for the Advancement of Colored People (NAACP), formed in May 1910, and former slaves from places as diverse as Platte County, Missouri, and Jefferson County, West Virginia, the place where John Brown was hanged.[24]

In 1935, a $6,000 life-size figure of Brown in stone and bronze was erected in Osawatomie, Kansas; it was cast in the same foundry in Paris which made the Statue of Liberty. Its sculptor, George Fite Waters, undertook this project at the request of the Woman's Relief Corps, Department of Kansas Auxiliary to the Grand Army of the Republic. Waters' magnificent statue is of a small man in workman's clothing, trousers thrust in boots, with piercing eyes and a rifle slung over his right shoulder. It was dedicated on the 135th anniversary of Brown's birthday, May 9, in the presence of 5,000 spectators. Among the speakers at this unveiling ceremony was then Kansas Governor, Alfred Landon, who said, "Our institutions can best be safeguarded by recalling the courage of those who made them possible."[25]

In 1940 and 1941, the famous mural painter John Steuart Curry (1897–1946), born near Dunavant in Jefferson County, Kansas, created a 31' by 11½' mural in oils on the north wall of the second floor of the Kansas state capitol building in Topeka. Its centerpiece is John Brown. In his outstretched right hand, which extends west, he holds a rifle, and under Brown's right arm the artist placed a waving American flag and a fallen Union soldier clad in blue. In the distant western sky swirls a tornado. In Brown's outstretched left hand, which extends east or toward Missouri, he clasps an open Bible. Beneath Brown's left hand a Confederate flag flies, several slaves huddle, and a fallen Confederate soldier dressed in grey lies dead. Flames rage in the distant eastern background, and in the western foreground, free-soil fighters stand ready to do combat with their pro-slavery adversaries who face them, poised in firing position in the mural's eastern foreground. Dominating this apocalyptic scene of the carnage of the coming Civil War is the immense and towering figure of John Brown, clothed in buckskin. A sheathed knife is attached to one of his belts, and his head and face are wreathed in electrifying white hair. When Curry finished it, *Time* described his painting of Brown as "one of the most impressive murals to be seen anywhere in the U.S."[26] The artist himself believed *John Brown* to be his best work, and the *New York Times* termed his mural of the abolitionist "heroic" and "magnificent."[27] Its effect remains dazzling. All these monuments of a bearded Brown are fitting memorials to his prophetic place in Kansas-Missouri history between the passage of the Kansas-Nebraska Act in 1854 and the onset of the Civil War in 1861. However, it is no accident that all now stand on Kansas soil, in towns founded by people opposed to slavery.

Statue of John Brown, Osawatomie, Kansas. By George Fite Waters (1935), it stands in John Brown Memorial State Park. (Photograph by the author.)

The source of Brown's fame defies easy description. Much of it was the timing of both his successful and unsuccessful slave-liberation actions. If he had been captured in Missouri in December 1858, the odds are that he would be little known

Section of "Tragic Prelude — John Brown." Mural by John Steuart Curry (1937–42), north wall, second floor, Kansas State Capitol, Topeka. In its entirety this mural measures 11 ft. 6 in. × 31 ft. (Photograph courtesy the Kansas State Historical Society, Topeka.)

and uncelebrated today. Had he employed neither force nor any threat of force in his Bates County foray, he probably would have been sent to the Missouri State Penitentiary for some variation of slave stealing. The Register of Inmates would list his name after that of Robert Maltby, the last slave stealer who served his full sentence, and before William Drew, the first of a consistent series of abolitionist inmates who either died in Missouri's prison or were pardoned. Had Brown been tried and convicted for his first-degree robbery of the Bates County slaveholders, his minimum sentence would have been 10 years. Perhaps his jury and/or his judge would have given him a much longer prison term because of his old age. Had both the Stevens and the Brown parties been apprehended in Missouri after 60-year-old David Cruise was shot and killed, the odds are that at least the ringleader of the slave-liberation plot, John Brown, and the triggerman, Albert Hazlett, would have been tried for Cruise's murder, found guilty, and put to death. Instead of only one known pre-Civil War execution in Bates County, that of Dr. William Nottingham in 1855 for the murder of his second wife, Jewell, there would have been at least two additional antebellum hangings in this western Missouri county.

However, John Brown, who readily identified himself to his Missouri victims as "Old Brown" and "Osawatomie Brown," was never brought to justice for his crimes in Missouri. There were few law enforcement officers in its sparsely populated western sections, and the areas of Kansas Territory through which the slave robber (or rescuer) traveled were settled by people opposed to slavery. Expectedly, any bondpersons who happened to learn of Brown's slave-liberating activity were surely overjoyed. However, the reaction of Missouri's white citizens to Brown's criminal acts in Bates County was one of outrage. On January 6, 1859, Missouri's governor, Robert Stewart, sent a special message to the General Assembly concerning the new troubles in Kansas Territory, including those involving Brown's freeing of slaves in Missouri. The next day the abolitionist wrote a letter from Trading Post, Kansas, which he clearly intended to be widely publicized; he termed it his "parallels," and therein he acknowledged his role in the murder of David Cruise, the Bates County slave owner. Later that month, the *New York Times*, among other newspapers, published his letter; in it, Brown balanced the restoration of liberty to 11 slaves against the killing of "one white man (the master) who fought against the liberation."[28] On February 24, 1859, Missouri's General Assembly appropriated $30,000 to enable "the Governor ... to suppress and bring to justice the banditti on the western border of the state."[29] This law specified that the governor could use the money only to raise a military force and employ it near the scene of trouble in areas of Missouri adjacent to Kansas Territory.

Likewise, a bill was submitted to the Missouri legislature in January 1859, as reported in the Missouri press, which authorized the governor to offer $3,000 for the arrest and conviction of every person who "has been engaged ... in any offence committed on the western border of the state ... punishable by death or imprisonment in the penitentiary."[30] However, the legislature never passed this law. In the 1850s the maximum reward which any Missouri governor could give for the apprehension of any person charged with or convicted of a felony was $300; and in 2003 the governor's reward remains $300.[31]

Except for Stephen Oates, the most careful biographer of Brown, all writers about this fanatical abolitionist incorrectly state that Governor Robert Stewart offered $3,000 for his arrest and conviction. The Missouri legislature's anger with Brown's and his followers' law-breaking in the state manifested itself only in the appropriation of $30,000 to bring to justice any future criminals of their particular lawlessness. This, of course, was a very large sum of money for the state of Missouri to appropriate against the perceived threat of abolitionist slave robbers and murderers on the state's western border.

Despite the fact that there was never as much money on Brown's head as later writers about him claimed,[32] after his Missouri raid "Osawatomie Brown" was a wanted man. President James Buchanan offered $250 for his arrest and conviction, and, had the F.B.I. and its ten-most-wanted list existed in 1859, Captain John Brown would have been on that infamous list. The *New York Times* reported of his daring Missouri adventure that "Negroes have been freed by force, for the first time in the history of our Government. Captain John Brown publishes a letter, openly declaring himself the leader of the party that committed the deed, while a reward is offered for his head."[33]

Why were he and his human contraband not taken into custody? The failure of federal law enforcement officers to arrest him is best explained by detestation of the Fugitive Slave Act by citizens along Brown's route. As Oates describes Brown's journey, "All across northern Illinois and Michigan the signs were thrillingly auspicious; not a single peace officer dared to arrest Brown and his liberated Blacks because of widespread public resentment toward the Fugitive Slave Law."[34] After he saw the former Missouri slaves off to Canada, Brown went to Cleveland, Ohio, where he spent 10 days.

(Near Cleveland was Oberlin College, that hotbed of abolitionist sentiment dating back to George Thompson's days as a student there in the 1830s. He and his fellow abolitionists had nearly been lynched in Mark Twain's Marion County in 1841.) Because throughout Brown's slave-liberating journey he had bartered some livestock for others, during his Cleveland visit he sold the remainder of the booty obtained in Bates County, Missouri, what he termed "two abolitionist horses and a mule." He also conspicuously walked by the U.S. Marshal's office on each of those 10 days. Despite the marshal's sworn duty to arrest him because of his violation of criminal provisions of the Fugitive Slave Law, the marshal, according to Oates, "was apparently too intimidated by the angry mood in Cleveland to touch the bearded warrior."[35]

At 11:15 a.m., under heavy military guard, Brown's charmed existence dramatically ended on December 2, 1859. He was hanged under the authority of the Commonwealth of Virginia in Charlestown, Virginia, now West Virginia, and the particulars of his execution were reported nationwide, including in the newspapers of western Missouri. One published in Harrison County, which bordered the free state of Iowa, quoted the Associated Press account that Brown died "without any unusual excitement."[36] Another published in Clay County ran a similar AP story which emphasized that "no facilities will be extended to reporters.... No one will be allowed to be near enough to the place of execution to hear any remarks that may be made by Brown."[37] One Jackson County newspaper, Westport's, carried this account of his death: "Old Osawatomie Brown was yesterday hung by the neck until he was dead, dead, dead — may God have mercy on his guilty soul! The old man has gone to that Tribunal which has enunciated the command, 'Thou shalt not kill.' May he meet with more mercy than he showed to those whose blood he shed on Pottawatomie Creek."[38] Another in that county, a Kansas City paper, reported on its front page, "John Brown, alias Old Brown, alias Osawatomie Brown, is no more he is dead!... We wish our children to read a history that speaks of Brown as a villain dower'd with a nation's curse." So gleeful was this Kansas City newspaper's report of the abolitionist's death that it simultaneously ran an ad for a local merchant's dry goods establishment which began in large letters, 'OLD BROWN HUNG TODAY GREAT EXCITEMENT.... But this is nothing to be compared with the every day excitement of a business character that is witnessed by the customers of E.M. M'Gee & Co."[39] Such was the coverage of the death of a man who rose to a bad eminence in a section of a state where the institution of slavery was both honored and under siege.

When its enemy was hanged more than 800 miles east of the Kansas-Missouri border, Missouri's slave owners breathed a collective sigh of relief. They obviously hoped that soon its human property would be wholly secure. In actuality, Brown's demise provided little cause for any celebration among its slave-owning residents on the state's western front.

9

"The Excitement on It Continues"

On the very day that John Brown was executed, December 2, 1859, and just after his body was cut down from the Charlestown scaffold, a group of his abolitionist supporters in Lawrence, Kansas, adopted a number of resolutions, several of them honoring his intentions at Harpers Ferry. The Lawrence newspaper noted that the speakers praised "the integrity of virtue of [Brown's] past life, and gave lucid evidence that his character will be vindicated, and his memory honored when he has ceased to live." Because this meeting dealt with more immediate matters, Brown's death was only one of their concerns. Through one of its committees, these abolitionists also resolved "That we respectfully request our Legislature, at its next session, to pass such laws against kidnapping on our soil, as shall effectually protect the lives and liberties of all our citizens, irrespective of color."[1]

By December 1859, Missourians may have made several unauthorized captures of blacks in Kansas Territory, and the resolution may refer to several of those forays. One kidnapping from this time period is especially well-documented. On January 25, 1859, at least 35 miles west of the Missouri-Kansas border near Oskaloosa, Kansas Territory, a group of Missouri slaveholders apprehended 13 Negroes in the company of three abolitionists. These were Dr. John Doy, a physician formerly of Rochester, New York; his 25-year-old son Charles; and a young man named Clough. Dr. Doy knew John Brown; in January 1859 these men had spent an evening together in a home near Lawrence. During that evening Doy attempted to persuade Brown to join forces with him. However, his efforts did not succeed, and they went their separate ways.[2]

Unluckily for the Doys, when captured they were taken to their captors' home county, Platte. This was the locale of the pro-slavery violence in 1856 that involved the destruction of George Park's newspaper *The Industrial Luminary* in Parkville. Clough managed to escape from his would-be kidnappers and played no part in subsequent events. The *Platte Argus* ran an extra about the Platte County slaveholders' dramatic taking of Negroes. The capturing party numbered ten men and included some of Platte County's "best and most influential citizens." The story identified most of the 13 blacks by name, height, weight, owner, residence of owner, and the usual information contained in contemporary runaway-slave ads. It stated of two men, 21-year-old Wilson Hays and 24-year-old Charles Smith, "says he is free." For the most part, the slaves' surnames were those of their owners: 33-year-old Ransom Winston was an asset of the estate of Joseph Winston of St. Clair County; 38-year-old Dan Bright belonged to

Widow Bright of McGee's Addition to Kansas City (now a section of downtown Kansas City); 28-year-old Abe Rosbey, his wife, and two children, one five years old and the other 18 months, were owned by Rosbey of Westport; 22-year-old Ben Logan belonged to George Kirk of McGee's Addition to Kansas City; 22-year-old Malinda was owned by Mrs. S.M. Wilson of Clay County; 33-year-old Mary Russell was owned out-of-state by W.H. Russell, Leavenworth, Kansas; and 27-year-old Catherine West belonged to T.H. West, Kansas City.[3]

This last mentioned woman was probably the victim of rape by her owner and two of his sons. (Only three other women were among the captured blacks; one was owned by a woman, another had a husband and two small children, and the third was owned in Kansas.) As an anti-slavery paper in Kansas reported of the captured bondpersons, "One of these coloured women was sent to Kansas by her owner's wife because he and his two sons used her for the gratification of their lust. This Missouri wife and mother sent money with the poor slave woman and offered to pay her expenses to Canada." The story continued, "She has been recaptured and returned to the lustful embraces of her master and his sons!"[4] Annette Curtis identifies Thomas West as a Kansas City farmer who, according to the 1860 Slave Schedule, owned six bondpersons, including a 27-year-old female. Almost certainly she was Catherine West, the woman who escaped neither slavery nor the continuous unwanted sexual attentions of her owner and his sons.

Though the local newspaper identified a slave named Dick as owned by W.A. Newman, this 35-year-old man was actually owned by Ben Wood, mayor of Weston,[5] a town in Platte County. At a hearing on slave-stealing charges in Weston before two Platte County justices of the peace, bail for the two remaining white men was set at $5,000. Since they were unable to make bail, they were taken to the county jail in Platte City. Dr. Doy managed to send a letter from his confinement in Platte City to the editor of a Lawrence, Kansas, newspaper on February 7, 1859. In it, he identified, among others responsible for, as he phrased it, "this unparalleled outrage: Benjamin Wood, mayor of Weston, Mo."[6] The editor of the Platte County newspaper may have thought it unseemly to identify the mayor of Weston as a vigilante slave catcher in Kansas Territory.

News coverage of events became more biased. In late February 1859, a newspaper in St. Joseph, 30 miles north, ran a story which was reprinted in at least two other Missouri papers with this headline: "Lynching in Platte County." It recounted that a crowd of more than 300 men stormed the jail, took the Doys prisoner, and hung both from a tree two miles from town. The article contained this convincing detail: "The old man begged very hard for his life, but they would not hear him. The son was hung first." The story explained that this lynching was necessary because it was feared that the accused men would be found not guilty if tried in a court of law.[7] In fact, the Doys were not lynched in Platte County or anywhere else.

Dr. Doy's own narrative about his supposed Platte County lynching is a useful contrast to contemporary newspaper coverage of it. He wrote a book about his Kansas/Missouri experience, and in it he described his and his party's kidnapping near Lawrence, the revolvers which the Missouri men thrust in their faces, and their bitter denunciations of them as "nigger thieves." The captured abolitionists were taken from

Kansas Territory across the Missouri River on a ferry, the *Rialto*, and landed at Weston. There a mob greeted Dr. Doy with shouts of "'Hang him! Hang him! Hang him! Hang the d — d nigger-thief! Burn the c — d abolitionist!'" The next day, "the unwashed and unterrified Democracy of Weston," as Doy described the populace, shouted at him, his son, and Clough, "'Give 'em hemp! The rope is ready!'"[8] Obviously they were not lynched in Weston because from this Missouri River town they were transported seven miles to Platte City, the county seat, and remained inmates in the Platte County jail from January 28 until March 24, 1859.

There *was* a plan to lynch them, but a Platte City resident told the mob that he would defend the prisoners to the last. Specifically, he advised its members that they could only reach their intended victims over his dead body and that justice would be meted out to these abolitionists in a court of law. This man was Elijah Hise Norton, a judge on the Twelfth Judicial Circuit, which then included both Platte and Buchanan Counties (the latter yet another locale separated from Kansas Territory by the Missouri River). Doy noted that some Missouri newspapers carried a story that armed men took them from the jail and hanged them, and for a while their family believed the reports of their deaths and were greatly distressed.[9] The editor/publisher of the Platte City newspaper apparently learned of the lynching plan from one or more of its chief instigators, and his paper reported what the would-be lynchers *intended* to occur, in elaborate detail. From the Platte City paper's make-believe account, other Missouri newspapers mistakenly passed on the community's wish as accomplished fact.

On the advice of their lawyers, when the time came for their trial in Platte County on slave-stealing charges, the Doys applied for a change of venue to St. Joseph, the seat of Buchanan County. At their attorneys' request, on March 20, 1859, a magistrate came to the Platte County jail, and before him John and his son, Charles Doy, executed an affidavit. In it they stated their good-faith belief that they could not obtain a fair trial in Platte City, in Dr. Doy's words, "on account of the excitement,"[10] euphemistic language often used during this time period for a lynching, a serious threat of one, or some other civil disturbance.

When court opened, Judge Norton sat on the bench, and to him the Doys' attorneys presented their affidavit and made application for a change of venue for their clients. It was argued for and against, and once more the judge disappointed both the jury and courtroom spectators when he granted this defense motion. As Doy described that moment, "A low murmur ran through the crowd, and the jury looked daggers at us and each other ... when they saw their expected victims escape them."[11] The judge followed precisely the law, which allowed for a trial in another county "when it shall appear ... that the minds of the inhabitants of the county in which the cause is pending are so prejudiced against the defendant(s) that a fair trial cannot be had therein." He transferred their case, as the law provided as a first option, to the court of another county in the same circuit.[12]

Thus the same member of the judiciary who prevented the Doys' murder and granted them a change of venue also sat as judge when their case was transferred to Buchanan County. In describing their first trial in late March 1859, which lasted two and one-half days, Dr. Doy specifically praised Judge Norton's jury instructions as "quite fair and impartial."[13] The Buchanan County jury which heard the case could not agree on a verdict, and the judge declared a mistrial. The prosecuting attorney elected not to retry Charles Doy, and he entered a *nolle prosequi*, a formal declaration that a case will not be further prosecuted. However, because the prosecutor always has the option to retry any case whenever the jury cannot reach a unanimous verdict of either guilty or not guilty, he retried the senior Doy.

There may have been other Missouri judges who personally opposed lynch mobs, granted abolitionists changes of venue, and presided at their trials with sufficient even-handedness to enable them to obtain mistrials. However, we only know about the Doys' good luck as accused persons in the hands of a Platte County circuit court judge who dealt fairly with men charged with slave stealing, as Doy phrased it, "an offense considered the worst of all crimes in Missouri."[14] Who was Judge Norton and what became of him after the Doys' legal difficulties had ended? He was born in Kentucky on November 21, 1821, attended the public schools and Centre College in Danville, Kentucky, and graduated from the law department of Transylvania University in Lexington, Kentucky. He moved to Platte County in 1842, was admitted to practice law in 1845, elected county attorney in 1850, and elected judge of the circuit court in 1852, while still in his early thirties. Like other prominent persons of his time and place, he owned slaves. The 1850 Missouri Slave Schedule listed him as the owner of five: a 25-year-old woman and four children aged one, three, five, and seven, three boys and a girl. The 1860 Schedule also listed him as owning five slaves: a 35-year-old woman and four children aged 10, 11, 13, and 15, three boys and a girl. Norton appears to have made no purchases of slaves during the 1850s, and only a 7-year-old male in 1850 is unaccounted for in 1860.[15] The only adult bondperson at his residence, presumably the mother of the slave children he owned, apparently had one additional child after the 1850 census was taken. Because he owned only one woman and her children, his risk of their running away was a small one, and the censuses suggest that his household was a stable place. At the time he opposed the lynch mob and argued that it would have to kill him before it could obtain Dr. John Doy and his son Charles, Norton was 37 years old, married and the father of at least one child, a girl of three and one-half; and most of his career was ahead of him. His bravery, which saved the lives of a father and his son, never hindered his advancement in his profession.

After his terms as a circuit court judge from 1852 until 1860, he was elected as a Democrat to the Thirty-Seventh U.S. Congress, where he served from 1861 until 1863. In the 1860 election Norton defeated his opponent by 13,126 votes to 7,749, racking up solid majorities in both Platte and Buchanan Counties. While a member of Congress during these turbulent years, he argued against Missouri's secession from the Union; as a probable result, his bid for a second term of representing a strongly pro-slavery constituency was unsuccessful. However, he was a delegate to the Missouri Constitutional Convention in 1875, and in October 1876, Governor Hardin appointed him a judge on the Supreme Court of Missouri. In November 1878, he was elected to a ten-year term on the state's highest court, and he served as its chief judge in 1887 and 1888. At the age of 67, on December 31, 1888, he declined renomination, returned to Platte City, resumed the practice of law, and lived on his farm in Platte County until his death on August 6, 1914.[16] At present his portrait in oils adorns the west wall of the first floor of the Platte County Courthouse. He is buried in the Platte City Cemetery, and his tombstone, like his entry in two nationwide directories of famous Americans, is silent regarding his heroic opposition to a mob bent on murdering despised abolitionists. However, it contains this inscription from the Beatitudes: "Blessed are the pure in heart, for they shall see God." The surviving records make clear that Judge Norton, like the accused slave stealers who lived to appear before him, was a person of commitment and integrity.

Norton's duties as circuit judge involved presiding at Dr. Doy's second trial, which was also held in St. Joseph and began in June 1859. In requesting a change of venue from Platte City to St. Joseph, Doy's lawyers had moved his trial from a village of 800 to the largest city in western Missouri, a bustling place of over 8,000 inhabitants which by April 1860 would be home to the Pony Express. St. Joseph also had its own police department, a force of no fewer than six officers,[17] a number hopefully sufficient to protect any prisoners lodged in the Buchanan County jail from a lynch mob.

Doy's attorneys were more prominent than those of any other known persons prosecuted in Missouri for any form of slave stealing. The Kansas Territorial Legislature appropriated $1,000 to defray the expenses of his trial(s), and the governor of Kansas Territory, Samuel Medary, appointed both Wilson Shannon, a former governor of Kansas Territory, and the incumbent attorney general of Kansas Territory, A.C. Davis, as counsel for the Doys. In addition, Dr. Doy retained a Judge James Spratt of Platte City as a third member of his defense team.[18] Then as now, a local attorney, to assist in such matters as jury selection, is useful because he or she knows the potential jurors who will decide the facts regarding any client's case. Shannon, Davis, and Spratt represented the son, Charles Doy, at the first trial, and they represented the father, John Doy, at both trials. The state of Missouri was equally well represented. Its lawyers were General G. M. Bassett, State or District Prosecuting Attorney of Platte County; Colonel Silas Woodson of St. Joseph, W.H. Miller of Platte County, and Colonel John Doniphan of Weston. At Doy's second trial, in addition to these four prosecution attorneys, the Honorable James Craig, who then represented western Missouri in the Thirty-Sixth Congress, was a volunteer attorney for the state.[19]

At both trials, Doy was indicted for enticing Slave Dick from the state. This bondman, valued at between $1,500 and $2,000, was the one owned by Ben Wood, mayor of Weston. The Doys were not indicted for enticing any of the other slaves captured in their two-wagon caravan near Lawrence. This was because none of the runaways were apprehended within Platte or Buchanan Counties and the jurisdiction of the trial court did not include St. Clair, Clay, or Jackson Counties, or, for that matter, Leavenworth County, Kansas, all of which places were the residences of the owners of the other slaves captured with the Doys. Equally important, the town of Weston was then on the Missouri River, and the prosecution hoped that a jury would find it more credible that Doy had enticed a slave owned in this river town to leave the state than one owned in a landlocked county such as St. Clair, located at least 30 miles east of the Kansas border and as many as 100 miles south of Oskaloosa. Once a conviction was obtained for persuading Slave Dick to leave Missouri, Doy, the alleged serial slave enticer, could have been tried in any county in Missouri wherein the slave was either owned or was an asset of an estate. However, the prosecution wished to obtain a guilty verdict in Buchanan County before Platte County relinquished its abolitionist prisoner to another Missouri county such as Clay, Jackson, or St. Clair.

The state proved that Slave Dick ran away from his Weston, Missouri, owner on January 5, 1859, and was found on the 25th of that same month with 10 or 12 other Negroes in the company of Dr. Doy en route from Lawrence to Holton, Kansas Territory. The latter was a town in the northeastern portion of the territory through which runaways from Missouri would pass if they followed John Brown's route to Canada. The Westport paper reported that John Brown and his party were in fact only 14 miles north of Doy's wagons when Doy and his two-wagon caravan were apprehended.[20] Brown's biographer, Villard, places Brown just north of Lawrence on January 25,[21] the day Platte Countians stopped Doy in the belief, as another Missouri paper reported, that "Dr. Doy and his son ... undoubtedly intended taking [the slaves] through Nebraska and Iowa and thence by the nearest route to Canada."[22]

The defense argued that the presence of Slave Dick in their client's company on January 25 near Oskaloosa did not prove that Dr. Doy had enticed this slave or any other to leave Missouri 20 days earlier and at least 35 miles east of where Doy and his party were apprehended. Doy's witnesses, primarily his family members and neighbors, testified that between December 26, 1858, and January 11, 1859, he was not absent overnight. Further, he could not have been gone from the vicinity of Lawrence without their knowledge. In addition, a bookseller from Lawrence told the jury that from entries in his journal he was certain that Doy was in his store on several days in early January 1859 including the 5th of the month. A ferry operator whose craft crossed from Leavenworth to Missouri on January 5 also testified that John Doy was not one of his passengers on that date.

The person who knew best whether or not the defendant enticed Dick out of the state was the slave himself. However, under Missouri law, blacks and mulattoes were not competent witnesses for or against whites. Hence neither the prosecution nor the defense could put Dick on the stand as a witness for or against Dr. Doy. Though the 1850 Missouri Slave Schedule lists no one named Wood as a Platte County owner of slaves, the 1860 Slave Schedule suggests that Dick's owner, Ben Wood, sold him prior to the June 1860 census. It lists B. Wood of Weston as owning a 30-year-old female and five children, two boys aged three and 12 years, and three girls aged five, seven, and eight years. The spaces beside Wood's name for "No. of Fugitives" and "No. Manumitted" are blank.[23] That the 30-year-old female was Dick's wife and the children his seem reasonable inferences, but the absolute truth of this can no more be ascertained than can exactly how Dick came to be a passenger in a two-wagon caravan north of Lawrence on January 25, 1859.

As a part of its vigorous prosecution of the Doys at the first trial, the state's closing arguments included these comments: W.H. Miller told the jury, "We stand here as the representatives of an outraged people. Dr. Doy ... believes we have no property in niggers." He attempted to discredit all of the Doys' witnesses by saying, "I would select a man blindfolded in this courtroom and take his testimony sooner than that of a thousand Kansas witnesses." Colonel Doniphan also reminded the jury, "If we allow our negroes to be stolen with impunity, our fair-skinned daughters will be reduced to performing the contemptible drudgery of the kitchen." Likewise at both trials, at the prosecution's request, Judge Norton gave the jury this instruction: "If the jury believe from the evidence that Doy aided in decoying Dick from Platte County with the intent to effect his freedom, they must find him guilty, although they may believe that said prisoner was never within the limits of the state of Missouri."

In its closing, the defense stressed that Doy was about his legitimate business of common carrier in Kansas Territory when he was kidnapped. To the jury at the Doys' first trial, the defense argued convincingly that the state of Missouri could not prove Doy's agency in Dick's crossing the Missouri River into Kansas. It obtained these favorable jury instructions from Judge Norton: (1) "The transporting of slaves from one point to another within the Territory of Kansas is no offense against the laws of Missouri"; (2) "Unless the jury believe that the defendant was present in person, or was near enough to give aid, counsel, encouragement, or assistance to those engaged in slave enticement, they will acquit"; and (3) "If the jury believe from the evidence that the Negro Dick crossed the Missouri River into Kansas without the agency of Defendant, they will acquit, though they may believe that Defendant did assist said Negro in Kansas Territory, in removing there from."[24]

At Doy's first trial, the jury stood all but one in favor of acquitting him because of the prosecution's inability to connect him with enticing Dick, or any other slave within the jurisdiction of the court, to leave the state. At his second trial with the same attorneys and the same witnesses but a different jury, Doy was found guilty as charged, and his jurors assessed his punishment at five years in the Missouri State Penitentiary. In late June 1859, Judge Norton upheld Doy's five-year sentence, but, at the request of his attorneys, allowed the prisoner to remain in the Buchanan County jail while the Missouri Supreme Court heard his appeal. On July 1, the *St. Joseph Gazette* commented of Doy's second trial, "This is the first conviction for Negro-stealing that has fallen under our observation in this quarter of Missouri, and we trust it will have a wholesome influence."[25] The newspaper assumed that the Supreme Court of Missouri would uphold Doy's conviction and he would soon join the other abolitionist inmates at the prison in Jefferson City.

Since the Missouri Supreme Court reversed no conviction for any variation of slave stealing, most probably it would have upheld Doy's five-year sentence. Almost certainly at issue in his conviction would have been the legality of his kidnapping in Kansas territory, that is, the manner in which the state of Missouri obtained jurisdiction of his person. At least three times since the Civil War and as recently as the 1990s the U.S. Supreme Court has upheld the power of a court to try a person for crime who has been brought within the court's jurisdiction by a "forcible abduction" in either a foreign country or another state.[26] Therefore, it seems almost certain that Missouri's only appellate court at the time would have upheld Doy's conviction despite the fact that unauthorized parties had forcibly abducted him in Kansas Territory. However, Missouri's slave owners had no such good fortune; the Supreme Court of Missouri never reviewed Doy's conviction.

On a Saturday, July 23, 1859, some of his abolitionist friends from Kansas arrived at the Buchanan County jail about midnight. They awakened the jailer and asked him to take into custody a horse thief whom they had captured in Andrew County, a rural area north of St. Joseph. The story seemed credible to the jailer, and he eventually admitted the three men, one of whom was the play-acting horse thief and the other two his supposed guards. However, as soon as Doy's keeper opened the door, one of the men he admitted drew a pistol and announced that they intended to rescue Doy or die in the attempt. The jailer, a Mr. Brown, realized that he was in the power of three heavily armed men and tried to persuade Doy to try for a new trial in which he could be honorably acquitted. His prisoner told him that he preferred to leave with his friends; they assured Jailer Brown that he must not attempt to leave the jail because if he did he would be shot. By the time the beleaguered jailer notified the sheriff, and the sheriff in turn assembled a sufficient force to recapture Dr. Doy, he and his rescuers had crossed the Missouri River and safely returned to Kansas Territory. In the aftermath of Doy's successful escape, the white citizens of St. Joseph were so angry that the editor of the Republican St. Louis newspaper, the *Free Democrat,* was asked to leave St. Joseph for his own safety. The *St. Joseph Gazette* ominously reported of Doy's escape, "This is a[n] outrage and ... most unfortunate for the peace of the border between Kansas and Missouri. If the laws are to be thus disregarded..., it will not be strange if in the future persons charged with Negro theft should be hung up to the nearest tree, without the benefit of trial.... Nothing has ever occurred in our city which has created so much indignation."[27] The *Free Democrat* reported that, following Doy's rescue, the citizens of St. Joseph passed "resolutions in which they expressed great respect for law and order, and great contempt for jailbreakers, nigger thieves, and rescuers of criminals."[28]

Despite the Buchanan County sheriff's offer of a $1,000 reward for Doy's re-arrest, he was never recaptured. His rescuers took him from St. Joseph to Lawrence, and from this abolitionist town he traveled through Iowa and soon was back in the Northeast.[29] By the time his friend John Brown was being tried and executed in Charlestown, Virginia, Doy was on a lecture tour in the North where he aroused considerable indignation in his audiences as he described his first-hand experiences of slavery in Missouri.[30] By 1860, his book about this matter was published in New York and Boston. The New York edition carried an advertisement for a photograph of Doy and his Buchanan County jail rescuers; this "fine likeness" of these men was obtainable from a New York City post office address at a cost of 25 cents. In 1862, a portion of his narrative, *Aventures d'un Abolitioniste du Kansas dans le Missouri,* was published in a French translation in Paris.

Since Doy never wavered in his belief that he had been kidnapped near Oskaloosa, Kansas Territory, on January 25, 1859, he had no qualms about leaving Buchanan County's jail with the extralegal help of his friends. In his book and presumably throughout his late-1859 lecture tour, he insisted that he had played no part in Slave Dick's running away from his owner Ben Wood, the mayor of Weston. Doy thought, as did his lawyers, that the guilty verdict was contrary to both the law and the evidence because he first met the runaway slave Dick when this fugitive had been living in Lawrence for several weeks. He stated this when an admission to the contrary, i.e., that he did break Missouri law, would neither compromise his liberty nor endanger his safety.

In large part, Doy credited his second jury's guilty verdict to jury tampering by U.S. Congressman James Craig. This volunteer attorney for the state carried a number of messages between the prosecutors and the jury during the second trial, and he also ate meals with its members during the day and night it deliberated its verdict. Doy

The ten men who rescued John Doy (seated) from the Buchanan County jail in St. Joseph, Missouri, and transported him to Lawrence, Kansas. Photograph provided by Martha Parker. (Photograph courtesy the Kansas State Historical Society, Topeka.)

noted of Craig's meddling with his jury, "Such an interference would not have been allowed in any of the Northern States,"[31] or, for that matter, under current Missouri law. Doy was surely gratified when he learned, after the publication of his book, that the Democratic Party of Missouri had denied James Craig, who served in the Thirty-Fifth and Thirty-Sixth Congresses, its renomination for election to the U.S. House of Representatives; instead it nominated Judge Elijah Norton, who easily won the general election and represented western Missouri in the Thirty-Seventh Congress.[32]

When Judge Norton granted Dr. Doy a change of venue from Platte to Buchanan County, he followed the law, but he did not give the defense an unfair advantage. Buchanan was not a slave-poor county. Though its population in bondage was approximately 11 percent, as compared to Platte County, where slaves made up 17 percent of the population, nonetheless Buchanan's slaves represented considerable wealth. By 1860 there were over 2,000 Buchanan County bondpersons, and by 1862, their appraised value was $325,180.[33] Their owners were persons of importance, and the fate of the next known person charged with slave stealing in Buchanan county was surely influenced by all the trouble and expense the former New York physician had caused the county. What happened to an obscure abolitionist, Henry Hatcher, slightly more than one year after St. Joseph's famous jailbreak, suggests that Hatcher's jury sought vengeance for the permanent escape of the "nigger stealer" whom Buchanan County tried twice for slave enticement but who served no time in the state prison in Jefferson City, Dr. John Doy.

Details of Hatcher's arrest, trial, and conviction are unknown because of the lack of any discovered newspaper coverage about his case and any packet materials pertaining to Buchanan County's criminal records from this early time period. His jury assessed his punishment at 18 years, the longest sentence given to any known person in Missouri's history for his abolitionist activities. The Register of Inmates recorded that he was a 44-year-old white man born in Canada, and both the circuit court and prison records indicate that he was convicted of grand larceny in September 1860. His judge was the recently-sworn-in Silas Woodson, one of Doy's prosecutors. Woodson, who upheld Hatcher's jury-assessed punishment of 18 years, was later governor of Missouri from 1873 to 1875. He appointed the attorneys Slayback and Baugh to represent this defendant; the trial took only one day. Twelve good and lawful men, residents of Buchanan County, found this Canadian native guilty and assessed his punishment at 18 years.[34]

The only other known abolitionists tried for grand larceny in Missouri were Alanson Work, James Burr, and George Thompson in Marion County almost 19 years earlier, and their jury assessed their punishment at 12 years. Their sentence, apart from Hatcher's still more severe prison term, was the longest given any abolitionist inmates in Missouri's history. Unlike attempted or completed slave enticement, which had maximum penalties of five and ten years, from 1835 on Missouri law provided no upper limit for grand larceny when the stolen property was a slave. Juries could not give less than seven years, but they were free to assess extremely long penalties as exemplified by this 1841 Marion County case and the 1860 Buchanan County case. From George Thompson's book, we know that in 1841 a mob from Hannibal and Palmyra stood ready to lynch the accused men should the jury not return a sentence which met with its approval. Absent any surviving account of the matter by Henry Hatcher, any extant contemporary newspaper coverage of his case, and any detail in the surviving circuit court records about him, one can only infer that his arrest, trial, and conviction were also accompanied by considerable excitement.

It is primarily from Governor Willard Hall's pardon papers that Hatcher can be positively identified as an abolitionist. However, since Missouri law only punished grand larceny with no less than seven years when the object of it was a slave as opposed to a horse or some other personal property, the length of Hatcher's sentence also identifies him as a slave enticer. In December 1864, the Missouri Electors of Abraham Lincoln to a second term wrote Hall concerning the release from confinement of three inmates, one of whom was Hatcher. The governor pardoned all three in December 1864.

George (or Allen) Pinks was released from prison with Hatcher, and this previously discussed young man's case also arose in western Missouri. One of the chapters in Doy's book is entitled "Allen Pinks." In his narrative, Doy explains that this 20-year-old mulatto was born in Pittsburgh, Pennsylvania, had a German grandmother, and until mistaken for a fugitive slave in Weston and jailed in Platte County, where he met Doy, Pinks was a cook and headwaiter on steamboats on the Mississippi and Missouri Rivers. He carried free papers with him, but thinking that they were wearing out, he registered and deposited them with the Jackson County Clerk's office in Independence. During the time Pinks was a Platte County jail inmate, he could find no one to travel the 30 miles between Platte City and Independence to ascertain that he was not a runaway slave. His biracial skin color was prima facie evidence of slavery; Pinks had to prove that he was free; the person or persons who asserted that he was a slave need not present any evidence.

After six months in jail, Pinks escaped and worked for a brief while on a steamboat until it docked in Weston. There he was recognized and re-incarcerated for an additional five months as a presumed runaway. Had he remained in the Platte County jail one more month, a cruel fate awaited him. Missouri law stated that, after one year of being locked up, a presumed runaway slave could be sold by the sheriff to the highest bidder at a courthouse-door auction to recover the costs of his keep. But the resourceful young Pinks once more escaped from the Platte County jail. The second time, he secured his freedom by swimming across the Missouri River from Missouri into Kansas, north of Leavenworth. In September 1859, another copy of Pinks's free papers arrived from Pittsburgh, Pennsylvania, in Lawrence, Kansas, where he was employed at a hotel. The last time Doy saw him, the young mulatto believed that he would live either in Mexico or Haiti; he hoped that in these places his skin color would not lead to his jailing.[35] A year later, Pinks was still living in Lawrence: its newspaper carried a story about him being shot on the street but not fatally because his unknown assailant's bullet glanced off his skull and lodged in his neck.[36]

Less than four months later, Pinks waived his right to a jury trial in Independence, Missouri, on a charge of "attempting to entice a slave out of state." He did so, as did his two white co-defendants, Thomas McGee and Henry McLothlin, to avoid being lynched by a Clay County mob. The three were received at the Missouri State Penitentiary from Jackson County on January 7, 1861, and remained inmates until pardoned: the whites in February 1863 and Pinks in December 1864. Had they been arrested on similar charges in St. Louis in 1860, a capable municipal police force would have assured their right to a jury trial without jeopardy to their lives prior to their imprisonment. Within the city of St. Louis, an actual lynching or the serious threat of one had not occurred since 1836. Unluckily for Pinks and his friends, they were apprehended in Jackson, not St. Louis, County.

Pinks was one of a number of free blacks in considerable danger of being enslaved in western Missouri after the mid-1850s. Doy related the experience of two others, Wilson Hayes and Charles Smith, captured with him near Oskaloosa, Kansas Territory, in January 1859. Despite the fact that both were free, they too were locked up as presumed runaways in the Platte County jail. An unsavory character named Jake Hurd came there several times and ordered them to admit that they were slaves. Despite Hurd's savage beatings, they insisted that they were free. Nonetheless, according to Doy, Hurd removed these men, citizens of Ohio and Pennsylvania, from the Platte City jail and sold them in Independence for $1,000 each.[37]

Similar stories of free blacks being kidnapped in Kansas Territory, taken to several jails in Missouri, including Buchanan County's in St. Joseph and Jackson County's in Independence, and forced to admit that they were slaves appeared in the press in August 1860. One newspaper related that the free papers found in the possession of captured blacks and mulattoes were useless because the kidnappers immediately destroyed their captives' proof of freedom. It wrote that "The Negro is whipped into an admission that he is a runaway slave and … he is ready for a Southern slave market."[38] Another related the misfortunes of other free Negroes in Kansas whom the notorious Jake Hurd and his henchmen lured into Missouri, jailed on charges of being runaways, and attempted to sell as slaves "to the dank, lone rice swamps of the South."[39]

After Congress passed the Kansas-Nebraska Act, St. Louis, Missouri, or its eastern neighbor, Madison County, Illinois, were far safer places to live as free blacks and mulattoes than any locale 250 to 300 miles to their west. After May 1854 and throughout the remainder of slavery's tenure in this state, slaveholders in western Missouri remained skittish about the frequency with which slaves ran from their owners. Free persons of color on the Kansas-Missouri border were at high risk of being mistaken for runaways.

Earlier, western Missouri had not been an especially dangerous place to own other human beings because of its proximity to Indian Territory: fugitive slaves from Missouri who ran west were in grave danger of being re-enslaved by various Indian tribes. The Indians knew the terrain and were skilled hunters, and some of the tribes emulated the darker side of the whites who first befriended them, then betrayed them, and pushed them farther west to make way for white settlers. Beginning as early as the late eighteenth century, American Indians began enslaving blacks, mainly runaways from southern plantations.[40] The Cherokees, for example, adopted a slave code between 1839 and 1842 which meted out different punishments for Cherokees and blacks who broke the same laws. It resembled Virginia's slave code adopted as Missouri law in 1804; poles-apart sentences for whites and African-Americans convicted of the same criminal conduct were the rule. Likewise, under the Cherokee Code, Indians convicted of rape were given 100 lashes; blacks found guilty of this same offense against "any free female, not of Negro blood" were hanged.[41]

From the 1850s on, the Cherokee, among other tribes, principally inhabited the lands south of Kansas; the area's northeastern tip bordered Missouri. Besides Cherokees, members of the Seminole, Choctaw, Chickasaw, and other slaveholding tribes sympathetic to secessionist sentiment occupied the region west of Arkansas. In late 1861 the Confederate government negotiated a treaty with these various tribes which made them Confederate allies during the Civil War.[42] In the 1850s, Indians lost their slaves both to the enticements of abolitionists and to seizures by southerners under the pretense that blacks and mulattoes were their runaway slaves. Before free-soil settlers moved to Kansas and Nebraska, Indians roamed as far north as Nebraska, but once forced out of these lands, they primarily resided in what is now the state of Oklahoma.[43] Though the presence of slaveholding Indians in Nebraska, Kansas, and Oklahoma deterred Missouri's slaves from running west to freedom, that presence in these regions did not prevent slaves from leaving their western Missouri masters.

Ads concerning fugitive slaves owned in Jackson County appeared as early as the 1830s. A 21-year-old left the residence of her owner in Sibley in October 1837. Significantly, her owner, who placed his ad for her in a St. Louis newspaper, believed that she had already reached St. Louis and "may now be living in one of the neighboring towns of Illinois."[44] Other ads for runaways from Jackson County appeared in the 1840s. One concerned a slave named Stephen who ran from his Westport master in May 1848. The fugitive was described as "speak[ing] the Shawnee language well." Perhaps he had been owned by one of the nearby Shawnee tribesmen: a few of the more opulent Shawnee Indians owned Negro slaves very near Westport at the Shawnee Methodist Mission during this time period.[45] Stephen's companion, a free black named John Scott, had "been lurking for some time in the neighborhood of Westport." The ad advised that they "took with them a sorrel mule, two horses, and two men saddles, one of which is of Spanish make, from the Methodist mission."[46]

Since Westport, Missouri, was less than two miles from the Shawnee Methodist Mission, a pro-slavery establishment in Indian Territory, what better place for a man who may recently have been in bondage there to steal necessities before beginning a long journey? Stephen's owner indicated no direction of flight for his runaway property and his free Negro companion. However, he offered $50 for either, $100 for both, and $150 if they were taken out of state; he surely assumed that they would travel 260 miles east to the state of Illinois. Westport, now a section of Kansas City, Missouri, borders the state of Kansas. A residential street, State Line Road, marks a border laid out prior to Missouri's statehood; what is now this street is all that separated Missouri from Kansas Territory, or, earlier, Indian Territory. A proffered fee of $150 is an unimaginable sum for any slave-catching immediately west of Missouri, an area virtually in the backyard of the slaveholder's residence in Westport.

Likewise, a runaway ad from 1849 offered $25 if Slave Anthony was apprehended within four miles of Weston and $100 if taken out of state.[47] This ad's Platte County subscriber never imagined that his escaped slave would cross the Missouri River into Indian Territory. Since Weston was then on the river, a distance as short as several city blocks separated this village from what is now the state of Kansas. This owner, like other western Missouri slaveholders, assumed that his runaway had traveled east. An 1829 advertisement from a Clay County owner offered $10 for each of three runaway slaves if taken within the state and $20 each if taken out of state. Their owner placed his ad for them in two newspapers published in eastern Missouri and two in western Illinois towns: Jackson and St. Louis in Missouri, and Galena and Vandalia in Illinois.[48] Since the distance between Liberty, seat of Clay County, and what is now the state of Kansas is 25 miles or less, this ad's subscriber was confident that his slaves would not travel west. An 1851 runaway ad concerning a slave owned in Clay County offered $20 for him if he were taken in the county, $40 if apprehended in the state, and $100 if taken out of state.[49] Once more the owner assumed eastern, not western travel.

From an early stage in Missouri's history, Illinois was the route to the promised land of Canada. Significantly, the Missouri legislature required that runaway-slave ads be placed in Illinois newspapers as early as 1845. Though they may also have appeared in Kansas and Iowa papers, the Missouri General Assembly never required such advertising and never appropriated funds for it as it did for Illinois newspaper advertisements. All the evidence gleaned from the runaway ads placed by western Missouri slaveholders in early statehood years suggests that the mass exodus of slaves from Missouri was not to Iowa, or to Indian Territory; it was to Illinois.

The Shawnee Methodist Mission, from which Westport-owned Slave Stephen stole his means of transportation, is now in Fairway, Kansas. Founded in 1839 by a Virginia native, the Reverend Thomas C. Johnson, it is in one of the two Kansas counties that border Kansas City, Missouri. Abel describes the Reverend Johnson as an "ardent pro-slavery advocate" and writes of him, "By far the best instance of missionary activity in behalf of slavery among the northern Indian immigrants is to be found in the case of the Reverend Thomas Johnson's work at the Shawnee Mission."[50] Other views of him include "vulgar, illiterate, and coarse, ... a violent pro-slavery partisan, ... pathetic,

... [and] pompous."[51] The records of his mission show that in 1853 he bought two Negro girls for $550: one was eight-year-old Jane and the other was two-and-one-half-year-old Mary. In 1855 he paid $700 for Harriet, a 14-year-old Negro girl. In 1856, he paid $800 in Westport for 15-year-old Martha. All of these youngsters were warranted to be "sound in body and mind and ... slave[s] for life."[52] In 1858, their owner moved from the mission in Johnson County, Kansas (named for him when it was organized in 1855), to a fine home near Westport, at what is now 35th and Agnes Streets in Kansas City, Missouri. Either these young girls remained behind at the mission or the Reverend Thomas C. Johnson evaded his taxes on slaves, because neither the 1850 nor the 1860 Missouri Slave Schedule lists him as a Jackson County slave owner. The continuing presence of slaves in Johnson County, Kansas, after passage of the Kansas-Nebraska Act in 1854, makes clear that this county was not a safe route for Missouri' runaways headed for freedom. Fortunately for the young slave girls and women, Jane, Mary, Harriet, and Martha, when the Reverend Johnson was murdered at his Missouri place on January 2, 1865 (nine days before slavery was abolished in Missouri), none of them were suspects. His assassin was never captured, however, and his death remains an unsolved Jackson County homicide.

Despite pro-slavery sentiment in areas such as Johnson County, Kansas, the Kansas-Nebraska Act changed the general direction of flight for slaves owned in western Missouri. After its passage, slaveholding Indians no longer inhabited eastern Kansas; they had been moved south to Oklahoma, and some of their free-soil replacements were abolitionists in and near such towns as Osawatomie, Topeka, Lawrence, and Holton, Kansas Territory. Runaways who now traveled west, but not too far west, on their way to Canada, escaped the dangers of recapture in Missouri and the equally great dangers of re-enslavement by new Indian owners in western Kansas Territory.

Once the threat of re-enslavement by Indians in certain sections of eastern Kansas Territory was removed, runaways from Missouri could reach either a permanent or a temporary safe haven across Missouri's western state line if they avoided locales such as Johnson County. Unlike Missouri's eastern bordering areas of Illinois, Kentucky, and Tennessee, where the Mississippi River formed the boundary, Missouri's western border was only partially natural. The Missouri River separated at least the first 75 miles of Missouri from Nebraska in the north and a sizable stretch of Kansas. However, when this river flowed to the southern boundary of Platte County, it turned east, traversed the state, and became a tributary of the Mississippi River in St. Louis. Once the Missouri River no longer separated Missouri from Kansas, the border became a straight line separating western Missouri and Arkansas from eastern Kansas and Oklahoma. During Kansas' territorial period, large trees, meandering creeks, and unmarked prairie land inhabited by wild animals and birds were on this wholly artificial dividing line which separated the slave state of Missouri from Kansas Territory. Anyone could walk or be carried across this border, and many slaves made their way west from Missouri by putting one foot in front of the other. South of the river, this border was as easy to cross as any in the United States. According to the 1856 census of Missouri, there were 11,438 slaves north of the Missouri River in counties adjacent to Kansas Territory, and 5,677 south of the river in counties which bordered this same territory.[53] Stated another way, twice as many slaves were required to cross the Missouri River to reach Kansas as could walk from Missouri into Kansas south of that river.

The river was then far wider than it is now, but travel across it from counties such as Platte to Kansas Territory posed no great problem. Many easily-built means of conveyance were readily at hand. The sort of raft which Huck and Jim used in *Huckleberry Finn* to travel down the Mississippi River was surely available for any enterprising slaves who lived north of the Missouri River in western Missouri and wished to cross it in order to reach Kansas. The canoe, mackinaw, bullboat, keelboat, and steamboat were all in use as watercraft on these rivers prior to the Civil War. The canoe was the easiest to fashion because it could be made by hollowing out a cottonwood log, the most common tree which grew on the Missouri River's banks. Work on it, felling a 15- to 30-foot tree, hewing and shaping,[54] and otherwise readying it for its fugitive slave crew and passengers, could be easily disguised. The unfinished canoe could be hidden among the trees, brush, dead logs, and other refuse along the river bank.

A man of the value of Dick, the slave whom John Doy was convicted of enticing out of state, did not require an abolitionist to help him cross the Missouri River. Perhaps he walked across a frozen river in January 1859, as Paxton reported a number of Platte County's slaves did in February 1863, when they left Missouri to join the Union Army in Kansas.[55] Perhaps he reached it in a canoe or other watercraft which he built himself. He may have been either a stowaway or a passenger on a steamboat which regularly crossed from Weston to Kansas Territory. Any 35-year-old male worth between $1,500 and $2,000 was both a skilled worker and an intelligent person who knew the ways of the river because he lived near it.

The most telling evidence regarding the presence of free borders as an enticement for slaves to flee their bondage can be found in Appendix 4. Insofar as bondpersons were locked by land or sea in their servitude, as were the slaves of the Carolinas, Mississippi, Alabama, and Georgia, and lacked a great seaport city such as New Orleans, their percentage of the population in these states between 1820 and 1860 either remained steady or increased. For example, South Carolina's slaves made up 52.8 percent of its residents in 1820 and 58.6 percent in 1860. Likewise, Arkansas, a place without any free borders, increased the percentage of its population which was enslaved from 15.5 percent in 1820 to 25.6 percent in 1860. Tennessee, surrounded by eight other slave states, increased its slave population from 19 percent in 1820 to 25.5 percent in 1860. Only Texas, admitted to the Union in 1845, was a slave state with both free borders and an increase in the percentage of its population slave in 1860. Congress created New Mexico Territory, adjacent to northwestern Texas, in 1850, and the language of the federal statute establishing it was identical to the law which created Nebraska and Kansas Territories in 1854; the territory "shall be received into the Union with or without slavery" as its constitution provided at the time of admission.[56] Mexico, the neighbor of Texas to the south, had abolished slavery in 1829. The District of Columbia, originally made from small portions of both Virginia and Maryland, technically had no free borders. However, its proximity (48 miles) to the Pennsylvania line explains the continuous decline in our nation's capital of the percentage of its population that was enslaved. Pennsylvania's Quaker citizenry made it one of the earliest areas of abolitionist activity in American history. Runaway slaves from the District of Columbia received many a helping hand in their quest for liberty once they reached Pennsylvania's southern boundary.

All other states with a declining percentage of their population as slaves between 1820 and 1860 had free borders, and the greater the free adjacent geographical area, the more precipitous the decline in the percentage of bondpersons within that jurisdiction's boundaries. Virginia's slaves ran north to Pennsylvania and Ohio; Maryland's headed for New Jersey and Pennsylvania, as did Delaware's. The percentage of Virginia's, Maryland's, and Delaware's slave population decreased. Kentucky's bondpersons ran north to Ohio, Indiana, and Illinois; the Ohio River, which formed the natural boundary between Kentucky and these free states, was an obstacle for slaves, but it was not insurmountable. The percentage of slave populations in all of these border states grew smaller from one federal census to the next.

Coming in last of all 16 slave jurisdictions for the percentage of its population which remained bondpersons in 1860 was Missouri. It dropped from 18.3 percent slave in 1820 to 10 percent in 1860. Surely this state's four free borders, Kansas, Nebraska, Iowa, and Illinois, which represented approximately 75 percent of all of Missouri's borders, made it the runaway capital of American slavery.

After the passage in May 1854 of the Kansas-Nebraska Act, countless slaves left their Missouri owners by traveling west to Kansas and then north to Nebraska and east to Iowa and beyond. Among them were Mr. and Mrs. Samuel Harper, liberated by John Brown in Bates County, Missouri, in 1858. They were photographed in Windsor, Ontario, by the Murdoch brothers in November 1894, either in the Harper home or in the photographers' studio. How silly now seems the heartfelt belief of most white Missourians that the imprisonment of abolitionists actually prevented the departure of slaves owned within the state's borders. Mr. and Mrs. Harper, Slave Dick, and countless others needed no enticement; freedom itself beckoned, and they and their brothers and sisters answered its call. The myth that slaves were contented unless outsiders excited them underlay the trial of John Doy and all other abolitionists who were prosecuted for any variation of Missouri's slave-stealing crimes. To be sure, help was available to those escaping slavery in areas bordering Missouri, and in due course, a catchall name for that assistance became the Underground Railroad.

10

The Underground Railroad on Missouri's Borders

The total separation of myth and fact regarding the Underground Railroad is difficult, if not impossible. In a 1928 biography of Mary Todd Lincoln, her niece, Katherine Helm, related that the trusted family slave "Mammy" confided to the Todd children, who always kept her secret, that she had marked a fence in such a way that runaway slaves knew "vittles," such as cornbread and bacon, were available. Helm quoted Mammy as saying, "All of 'em knows the sign, I have fed many a one."[1] The odds are that Mammy fed few, if any, runaways. Had her owner, Robert Todd, detected her, at best she would have been sold, if for no other reason than to insure that Mary's father remained on good terms with his fellow Kentucky slave owners, including my own great-great-grandfather, Thomas Buford Johnston (1774–1853), of Adair County.

More than 70 years later, a best-selling book, *Hidden in Plain View: A Secret Story of Quilts and the Underground Railroad*, makes equally fanciful claims about slaves creating quilts with messages hidden in them, messages which enabled other slaves to make their way north to freedom. However, John Anderson, to cite but one example, knew without viewing a quilt with a "Monkey-Wrench" pattern that he needed to gather a few items before he left his master. Further, all the runaway ads suggest that the season of the year was a crucial factor in most runs for freedom. Since the great majority of bondpersons were field hands, they had intimate knowledge of the seasons for planting, growing, harvesting, and, if life as a slave proved unbearable, running away. Though it cannot be documented through the newspaper advertisements for their apprehension, the day of the week must have been an important factor in their departure. Probably most runaways left their masters and mistresses on either Saturday evening or early Sunday morning. Since slaves did not labor on Sundays, they gained considerable time before they were missed by scheduling the start of their runs for weekends. Likewise, when making their escapes, slaves already knew that an irregular course was necessary to avoid apprehension in their home states. They had no need to view the "Drunkard's Path" quilt pattern to learn that they must be artful dodgers to avoid detection in their flight for freedom. Similarly, they knew independent of the "Northern Star" pattern that they must follow the North Star when attempting to reach Canada from a slave state. All the evidence suggests that bondpersons needed no quilts, coded or otherwise, hanging in or near slave cabins to tell them how, when, or where to run for freedom. Their assistance came from other sources, if it came at all, in the places where their flights originated.

A reviewer of *Hidden in Plain View* writes, "Quilt codes are not mentioned in contemporaneous accounts of the underground railroad, and the code doesn't reach the systematic nature of, say, the symbols scrawled on fences by tramps a century ago to set apart friendly farms from hostile ones."[2] Katherine Helm may have attributed tramp-marking of fences many years after slavery to the Todds' Mammy in the 1820s and 1830s. Likewise, the later book's authors, Jacqueline L. Tobin and Raymond G. Dobard, may confuse what is pleasing to believe was the truth with its reality. She is a professor of women's studies and he an art history professor and African-American quilter. Since their bibliography contains neither statutory nor case law, their research for this appealing book apparently did not include an examination of what the legislatures of the various slave states devised as punishment for those caught and convicted of attempting to help slaves attain their freedom. At their most severe, the laws allowed a death sentence for slave-enticement activities, and as noted earlier, the evidence suggests that some states actually executed abolitionists. There may be a grain of truth in what Helm, Tobin, and Dobard have written about those who secretly aided runaway slaves, but it is only a grain.

What we actually know is that the phenomenon of blueprinted aid to fleeing bondpersons was neither a railroad nor underground, though in childhood we believed it was both. We were fascinated by it, and we still remain immensely interested in it. The phrase *Underground Railroad* tells us that any significant organized assistance for those escaping the service of their masters came relatively late in this country's experience of slavery. Before the metaphor of a subterranean means of transportation for persons fleeing bondage could become a part of American English, an above-ground railroad had to exist. Further, the vehicle had to have reached a stage of development where it was no longer horse-drawn, as in its earliest forms. Neither speed nor any widespread availability of this means of travel was possible for either passengers or freight until a locomotive, meaning an engine that moves under its own power, replaced beasts of burden as movers of railway cars. By the early 1830s, the word *railroad* meant "a track consisting of parallel lines of iron or steel rails for the conveyance of cars drawn by a locomotive."[3] By this time, slavery had more than 300 years of growth in an English colony such as Virginia and more than 200 in the French settlements that eventually became the states of Louisiana, Arkansas, and Missouri. As noted in Chapter 2, written opposition to American slavery can be found as early as 1688, or more than 150 years before the phrase *Underground Railroad* became a part of American English. It is not credible that no helping hands were extended to fleeing bondpersons prior to the 1830s. However, such assistance as was earlier available was scattered, isolated, and without political power. Mainly, it was no threat to the owners of slaves. In colonial times, slave owners gained, retained, and wielded immense influence in the many slave jurisdictions which endured until the Civil War years. Likewise, from the start of the United States, the dominion of slaveholders was and would remain secure for many years in all three branches of the federal government.

Then came the crusading spirit of the 1830s, fueled by a religious fervor which included actual belief in the equality of human beings. The use of the word *abolition-*

ist as meaning one who agitates for the compulsory and immediate emancipation of American slaves became a part of American English, and the American Anti-Slavery Society was organized in Philadelphia in 1833. Among its principal founders was William Lloyd Garrison, who almost two years earlier had begun publication of his newspaper, the *Liberator*, an organ for the total, immediate, and uncompromised abolition of slavery. Its editor unrelentingly published this paper on a weekly basis for the next 35 years, or until after the 13th Amendment to the U.S. Constitution, abolishing slavery, became a part of American law.

Theodore Weld, another leading crusader, drew dedicated disciples to the anti-slavery cause, including several who were abolitionist inmates in the Missouri state penitentiary. Weld's book *American Slavery As It Is* (1836) was a powerful argument against any form of human bondage. He and Garrison used much the same methods: they showed slavery for what it was by reprinting news stories and advertisements about the subject from slave-state newspapers, doing so in a way the Southern editors and publishers never intended, for ironic effect. Yet another important event in the abolitionist cause was the move of Elijah Lovejoy to St. Louis in 1833; there he edited the *Observer*, a Presbyterian weekly which advocated the emancipation of slaves. His views were so detested by most of St. Louis' residents that he was forced to move across the Mississippi River to Alton, Illinois. There, mobs attacked his presses, and he was murdered in 1837 while guarding a new press. He immediately became the martyr abolitionist, and his death advanced the cause of ending slavery.

It is only by chance that an important advance in transportation (the railroad in the 1830s) occurred at the same time that anti-slavery sentiment became an organized force. It seems wholly logical that this particular advance in moving persons and goods faster and cheaper became a metaphor for the movement of persons of color from slavery to freedom. Had aviation reached the stage of development by 1830 that it did a century later, airplanes might have been identified with escaping bondpersons. Instead of conductors there would be flight attendants, terminals instead of depots, pilots instead of engineers, and layovers, hubs, passenger agents, and a variety of other terms associated with flight in the sky would be identified with escaping bondpersons.

Surprisingly, the phrase *Underground Railroad* seems not to have been invented by abolitionists. Wilbur H. Siebert, author of the most comprehensive and detailed history of this subject, mentions a Kentucky slave owner who in approximately 1831 tracked his runaway across the Ohio River, managing to keep him in sight until he reached the state of Ohio, where the fugitive simply disappeared. When the master was unable to find his property after a long and arduous search, he supposed "the nigger must have gone off on an underground road." From the word *road* evolved *railroad*, according to Siebert, "as an apt title for a mysterious means of transporting fugitive slaves to Canada."[4] In *Uncle Tom's Cabin* (1852), Stowe's dialogue about the secret means of getting slaves up to Canada is not abolitionist chitchat. It is a slave trader who says of Eliza's escape from Kentucky to Ohio, "I know the way of all of em,— they make tracks for the underground," and a slave catcher says of her disappearance, "The gal's been carried on the underground line up to Sandusky."[5] This Ohio city was an important terminus because it was on Lake Erie and a relatively short distance from Canada.

We find an apparently familiar use of the metaphor of railroads in the *Weston*

Argus' account of the capture of Dr. Doy and his son in Kansas in the company of 13 Negroes. The paper's headline mentions, "Men, Women, Children, belonging to citizens in ... Mo. In the charge of two Underground Railroad agents from Lawrence to Iowa." In the text of this paper's account of the Doys' capture, "valuable negroes" are in the company of "white conductors."[6] Likewise, the *Richmond Inquirer*, a Virginia newspaper, complained in 1860 that "The Republican party insists that slavery where it now exists, shall be surrounded by a cordon of free States, infested by Abolitionists, Liberty shriekers, underground railroads, and border ruffians."[7] A year earlier, the *New York Times* used the headline "Underground Railroad" when describing an association of Canadian persons of color who were erecting a "depot for the reception of passengers over the Underground Railroad from the slave states."[8]

The Fugitive Slave Law was both a cause of increased help on the part of abolitionists for escaping slaves and a product of the considerable assistance these dedicated anti-slavery persons had already given such fugitives. Henry Clay, U.S. Senator from Kentucky, was one of the chief sponsors of the 1850 legislation, which as its multiple circumlocutions stated, was "for the more effectual execution of the third clause of the second section, fourth article of the Constitution of the United States." Approximately four months before the Fugitive Slave Bill became law, he spoke on the floor of the Senate about the difficulties each of four Kentucky citizens had experienced when attempting to reclaim his slave "of very great value.... These slaves have taken refuge in the State of Ohio, and ... it is in vain for [their owners] to attempt to recapture them.... Within the last six weeks, by the long-continued unlawful acts, mischievous controversies, and impertinent intermeddling ... persons residing in non-slaveholding states, have induced [Kentucky slaves] to escape into the state of Ohio."[9] Senator Clay was complaining about the especially effective assistance that dedicated conductors on the Ohio branch of the Underground Railroad had been providing fugitive slaves for a number of years prior to 1850; they would continue to give runaways superb help in achieving freedom until slavery was no more.

It is expected and fitting that the most complete account of the clandestine assistance abolitionists provided escaping bondpersons was written by a history professor at Ohio State University in Columbus. Wilbur H. Siebert published his detailed account in 1898, early enough that a number of abolitionists were still alive and could tell him their stories. His index to his *Underground Railroad* expectedly contains more entries under *Ohio* than any other state. It was the first state to be carved out of the Northwest Territory and the first free state admitted to the Union (March 1, 1803) which bordered any slave state. Siebert's map of "Underground" routes to Canada shows more lines in Ohio than any other state. This jurisdiction is almost synonymous with secret help for those escaping slavery. From his book and other sources, a great deal of valuable material is available about the importance of the U.G.R.R. in a number of Ohio towns. For example, anti-slavery sentiment in the small town of Salem, Ohio, was so pronounced that one of its newspapers was the *Anti-Slavery Bugle*. This paper began publication on June 20, 1845, and continued until May 4, 1861.[10]

At present, the federal government is the most important source of current information about clandestine aid for fleeing slaves. On November 28, 1990, the U.S. Congress passed legislation which required the National Park Service to "study the

Underground Railroad, its routes and operations in order to preserve and interpret this aspect of American history." The law specified that the "National Park Service ... conduct a study of alternatives for commemorating and interpreting the Underground Railroad, the approximate routes taken by slaves escaping to freedom before the conclusion of the Civil War.[11] In 1995, the Park Service published several books about its findings. One is a useful comparison with Siebert's work of almost 100 years earlier.[12] Both the 1898 and 1995 studies contain maps of U.G.R.R. sites and routes; Siebert's are the more detailed. (When the particular source is relevant, it will be mentioned.) Both Siebert and the Park Service are at their most specific and detailed in pinpointing sites and routes in Ohio, Pennsylvania, and New York, two of which states, Ohio and Pennsylvania, bordered places of slavery. When locating sites in Missouri and on her borders, the more general the listing by Seibert, the Park Service, or both, the more likely that no evidence survives that this locale was on the U.G.R.R. The paucity of detail also suggests that any connection between the named place and the Underground Railroad may be no more than make-believe.

It should come as no surprise that for most of its history, Missouri had no known U.G.R.R. stations. Though the Park Service lists six Missouri towns as Underground Railroad sites, four are without any corroboration. One of the Park Service's undocumented places in this state is Bethany, the county seat of Harrison County, which borders Iowa. However, the Bethany public librarian, born and raised in Bethany, had never heard that her town had any connection with the U.G.R.R. Obviously a meaningful investigation must start with what lay on or just outside this state's borders. My discussion of U.G.R.R. sites will begin near southeastern Missouri, come north along the Mississippi River the entire length of the state, cross over to Iowa, and travel north to Illinois. I will then investigate Kansas City, Missouri, cross over into Kansas, and eventually travel north to Nebraska, and traverse Iowa west to east.

Because the states of Ohio, Indiana, and Illinois all bordered slave jurisdictions, Siebert accurately termed them "the most favorably situated of all the Northern states to receive fugitive slaves" (134). The last named bordered Missouri. Siebert tentatively dated the first U.G.R.R. near Missouri as 1819 and 1820 and placed it in Bond County, Illinois, two counties east of St. Louis. Its workers were the followers of a Presbyterian minister, one who came from the branch of this denomination opposed to slavery. However, Siebert went no further than to list this Illinois place and time as "may be considered probable ... and must remain without corroboration" (41). Randolph County is the southernmost area in Illinois which Siebert mentioned as a depot; it is an area adjacent to the Mississippi River and near Ste. Genevieve, the earliest known French settlement (1750). He dated the earliest U.G.R.R. activity in this county as 1844 and as organized by Covenanter congregations, another anti-slavery offshoot of Presbyterianism. Siebert wrote of the Randolph County "Covenanters" that they "kept a very large depot wide open for slaves escaping from Missouri" (14–15). The Park Service lists a number of Illinois locales, and Siebert had earlier identified many of these.

Neither Siebert nor the Park Service in 1995 listed any persons living in or near St. Louis as associated with the Underground Railroad. More recent efforts to find St. Louis conductors on the line name Mary Meachum, widow of John Berry Meachum who died in 1854, as a dedicated helper of runaways from Missouri. In November 2001, the National Park Service, the state of Missouri, and St. Louis officials dedicated a site on the St. Louis riverfront and called it the "Mary Meachum Freedom Crossing." It is the first addition in Missouri to the National Park Service's National Underground Railroad Network to Freedom. This site officially became a part of the network on September 30, 2001.

The story behind this belated recognition for Mary Meachum concerns her arrest on May 21, 1855, for assisting eight or nine runaway Missouri slaves who crossed the Mississippi River from St. Louis to Illinois, where waiting law enforcement officers and several slave owners apprehended at least five of them. Mrs. Meachum was arrested because she had allowed several of the fugitives to meet at her St. Louis apartment (a place subsequently torn down and now a paved parking lot). She and a man named Isaac were charged in St. Louis criminal court with helping the fugitives escape. Charges against Isaac were dropped, and precisely what punishment, if any, Mary Meachum received is unclear.[13] On May 31, 2003, almost 100 people re-enacted the scene of a sheriff and several slave owners preventing Mary Meachum from leading her people to freedom. The re-enactment took place at the spot dedicated almost two years earlier as the "Mary Meachum Freedom Crossing."[14] This locale remains this state's only official Underground Railroad site.

This much about Mary Meachum is clear; she never became an inmate in the Missouri State Penitentiary. St. Louis County sent nine persons to prison for their abolitionist activity, including a black female, Eliza Sly, who arrived at the Jefferson City prison in 1857. This is a greater number than any other Missouri county; it is mainly explainable by St. Louis being by far the most populous county in the state during these years. Mary's sex may have been a factor in keeping her out of prison. An equally likely explanation may have been that she was the widow of John Berry Meachum, a famous black preacher who managed to get along with white authorities.

Equally important, St. Louis's enthusiasm for slavery was waning by the time Mrs. Meachum was arrested. In 1859, a Miss Bates of St. Louis, sister of Edward Bates, later Lincoln's attorney general, emancipated the last of 32 slaves she had inherited; her brother Edward had earlier freed the last slaves that he owned.[15] The same year Miss Bates freed the last of her slaves, Pierre Chouteau, a member of Missouri's most powerful slave-owning family, complained that a St. Louis jury of white males, from prejudice of birth and education, were unable to decide fairly whether or not slavery existed in Lower Canada (Quebec) in 1768. The St. Louis jury, as Chapter 3 clarifies, decided slavery was illegal in Lower Canada by this date. As a result Chouteau lost, and his slave Charlotte won her suit for freedom. Unlike a county such as Howard, which remained a bastion of slavery until the institution was abolished in 1865, mid-1850s St. Louis was not a secure place of human bondage. It is entirely appropriate that a spot near the Mississippi River in this city should become the first official site on the Underground Railroad in Missouri.

Traveling north from St. Louis, the next Missouri locale associated with the Underground Railroad is Hannibal, Mark Twain's hometown. The National Park Service's September 1995 publication lists a cave near this city as one associated with "URR activities" (169). Contemporary proof of this is found in a letter written from Hannibal by one Missouri brother to another. On December 31, 1862, William Sausser, among other mostly military matters, wrote, "The General Depot of the Underground R.R. is now established at the post, and in offering every facility for passengers is doing a flourishing business. Negroes are flowing in from all directions constantly & they disappear. One half of Mr. Fugua's [a Marion County man listed in the 1860 Slave Schedule as owning 11 slaves] left—the balance choose to remain yet."[16] A Union Army post in Hannibal, a location on the Mississippi River, made it a likely spot for assistance for fugitive slaves during the war years. The day after William Sausser wrote his brother about abolitionist activity in and near Hannibal, was January 1, 1863, the date President Lincoln announced the Emancipation Proclamation.

Continuing a few more miles north on the Mississippi River, one finds an early locale for Underground Railroad activity in and near Quincy, Illinois, a place immediately across the river from Palmyra, county seat of Marion County. Siebert identified Quincy as "the starting-point of four or five lines," and he explained that this proliferation was constructed to confuse slave owners and their agents who searched areas in and near Quincy for their missing bondpersons (141). The National Park Service in September 1995 lists two: the first is the Richard Eells house, 415 Jersey St., Quincy, built 1835–36, and it states that "Eells was an abolitionist, who was arrested in 1842 for helping a slave escape." Its second listing is the Nelson House, east of Quincy (161–62).

Dr. David Nelson (1793–1844) was a special irritant for Marion County slave owners. He was a Tennessee native who began practicing medicine as a surgeon with an American force which invaded Canada during the War of 1812. He gave up the practice of medicine and became an evangelist and a Presbyterian minister. In 1831 he founded and became president of Marion College, an institution "for the training of pious young men" near Palmyra, Missouri. In 1836, from the pulpit of his Presbyterian Church in Palmyra, he exhorted the slaveholders in his congregation to free their slaves. He was promptly expelled as Marion College's president, and a mob forced his immediate departure from Missouri. He took up residence across the river and slightly north of Palmyra in Quincy, where he founded a short-lived college, Mission Institute, whose purpose was the education of Christian missionaries for Africa, the West Indies, and other locales. Dr. Nelson also became active as an anti-slavery lecturer in western Illinois and worked to help slaves escape until his health broke in 1840. His Quincy students regularly crossed the Mississippi River and tapped stones together on the Missouri side; from the woods runaway slaves emerged to be guided across the river and sent 16 miles inland to a barn, which, until it was burned to the ground, served as a "waiting room" of the Underground Railroad.[17] Fugitive slaves from Missouri traveled east with the help of Nelson and his followers. The portion of their route from Quincy to Chicago was later followed by the Chicago, Burlington, and Quincy Railroad.[18] From Chicago, runaways journeyed to Detroit, to Canadian towns such as Dresden, Amherstburg, and Collingwood, Ontario, and farther north to Montreal, Quebec. The most famous of Dr. Nelson's followers were George Thompson, James Burr, and Alan Work, all of whom were convicted of grand larceny for their abolitionist activities in Marion County Circuit Court. They were sentenced to 12 years in the Missouri State Penitentiary; their case is discussed in Chapter 7.

Siebert's map of U.G.R.R. routes through southeastern Iowa indicated that Denmark, a town presently of 400 persons in Lee County, Iowa, adjacent to Clark County, Missouri, contained a safe house for escaping slaves. More than 50 years after Siebert labeled Denmark as containing a U.G.R.R. waiting room or depot, the remodeling of an old farmhouse yielded a wonderful surprise. The house was built by an antebellum deacon in the Congregationalist Church and a known abolitionist, a Mr. Trowbridge. When the new owners began replacing the roof, they discovered a secret room under the south section of the roof. In it were a number of strewn items in decrepit condition, a boot, a blanket, and the like; but one newspaper was in sufficiently good condition to be readable: a copy of the Salem, Ohio, *Anti-Slavery Bugle*, dated November 15, 1851. This paper indicates that for at least 10 years before the Civil War began, escaping Missouri slaves were hidden in a concealed room, which the deacon, a skilled plasterer, had fashioned at the top of the stair. A sizable board could be lifted so that a person could squeeze into the room; no suggestion of this hidden chamber's existence showed from any place outside the house. Old-timers in Denmark had always believed that Deacon Trowbridge's home on the south side of town had a secret place in it for fugitive slaves. In 1955, his house was confirmed as a U.G.R.R. station to aid runaways from Missouri as they made their way to Canada.[19] An anniversary publication of the Denmark Congregational United Church of Christ (1988) contains a photograph of the Trowbridge home as it exists today, and it identifies the structure as a place where slaves were hidden. The *Lee County [Iowa] History* identifies the Reverend Asa Turner, pastor of the Denmark Congregational Church, as a leader of U.G.R.R. activities in the area.[20]

John Anderson mentioned in his narrative that he was assisted by an unnamed abolitionist in Rock Island, Illinois, a city on the Mississippi River approximately 93 miles northeast of Denmark. Most likely the fugitives whom Deacon Trowbridge and Asa Turner assisted traveled on northeast until they too reached Rock Island, received assistance from the group of conductors who aided John Anderson as he and others made their way to Chicago, and continued from there east and north to Canada.

Siebert does not mention Kansas City, Missouri, as in any way associated with the U.G.R.R. The 1995 National Park Service publication does, but only as a dot on a map. Most likely, its mark represents a section of the city known as Westport. Through its founding in 1848 until its annexation by Kansas City in 1897, Westport, Missouri, was a separate town. The Ewing-Boone Building, 500 Westport Road, now called "Kelly's Westport Inn," an extremely well-known bar, is the oldest building in what is now Kansas City, Missouri. Construction began in 1850, and it was completed in 1851. Its builders, George W. and William Ewing, Indian traders, sold it to Albert Gallatin Boone, grandson of Daniel Boone, in January 1854, and he sold the store in 1860 and moved to Denver.[21] Local legend has it that this building was both a stop on the U.G.R.R. and a place where slaves were shackled in its basement. Lifelong residents of Westport heard these stories from their parents and grandparents. The likelihood is small that Kelly's was ever a U.G.R.R. stop. Westport was never inhabited by abolitionists; equally important, its close proximity to Kansas Territory, no more than one mile away, makes it an unlikely waiting room for fugitive slaves. They would find safe haven just outside Missouri, not within its borders in a vehemently pro-slavery town. Another urban myth regarding Westport seems more likely. My neighbor's Uncle John told her that what is now Pioneer Park, a traffic island at the intersection of Westport Road and Broadway Streets, was once a slave market. We know that the Reverend Thomas Johnson came to Westport from his Shawnee Methodist Mission and there paid $800 for 15-year-old Martha. He traveled at most three miles to make his purchase, and he may have bought other promising children in Westport. Very likely he inspected the merchandise and made his purchase(s) at what is now Pioneer Park, immediately east of The Corner Restaurant. This much is certain: there is no documentation of any kind now extant that Westport, Missouri, or any other area of what is now Kansas City, Missouri, was a place of U.G.R.R. activity.

Once the state line is crossed which separates Missouri from Kansas, the prospects of discovering houses of and routes on the Underground Railroad become more likely. Since Chapter 8 covers the journey of John Brown in some detail, only brief mention will be made of certain safe houses where he and his fugitive slaves spent time.

The existence of the town of Quindaro, Kansas Territory, from 1856 until 1862 is a certainty, and its importance as a site of Underground Railroad activity is also well-established; the National Park Service lists the Quindaro Ruins as a U.G.R.R. site (164). It is now mainly vanished rubble within the city of Kansas City, Kansas, but its recent addition to the National Register of Historic Places will make the use of it as a landfill or golf course much more difficult.[22] It was once a town with about 5,000 residents and 100 businesses, directly across the river from Parkville, Platte County, Missouri, the place where pro-slavery violence drove the town's founder, George Park, into hiding. Quindaro served as a haven for runaways from Platte County. Its principal founder was Abelard Guthrie, who established it as a port of entry for free-soil immigrants to Kansas; he named it for his Wyandot wife, Nancy Quindaro Brown. The Missouri River then ran west of its present boundaries, and the town became an Underground Railroad station for slaves escaping from Platte County who crossed the river either in small boats or on the Parkville-Quindaro Ferry. Phillip Murray took his grandson, Orrin Murray, then eight years old, to the 1911 unveiling of John Brown's statue near what was once Quindaro at 27th and Sewell, Kansas City, Kansas. The grandfather was a former Platte County slave who with his family made his way across the river from Platte County to Quindaro.[23] In February 1983, Orrin Murray, then aged 80 years, recalled that his father was the only one of his paternal grandfather's children who was born free because he was born in Kansas City, Kansas, not as a slave in Platte County, Missouri.[24]

James Johnson, archeologist and anthropologist, and the great-great-grandson of a Missouri slave, has investigated his ancestor's past. His great-great-grandfather, George Washington, was born in 1840 on a Virginia plantation. His owner, Daniel Jones, Sr., gave him to his daughter, Margaret A. Jones, as a wedding gift when she married Lewis M. Waller, and they brought him with them when they moved to Platte County, Missouri, in 1841. Lewis M. Waller died soon after they arrived in Platte County, but in 1848, Mrs. Margaret Waller married Jesse Miller, and Jesse Miller inherited his wife's property, including his slave George Washington, an illiterate farm laborer on the farm which grew hemp, corn, and other cash crops near the present location of Kansas City International Airport. The slave's primary business was planting, weeding, and harvesting various profitable crops for more than 20 years. One very cold night in January 1862, he simply walked across the frozen Missouri River from the state of Missouri to what had recently become the state of Kansas. He found safe haven in Quindaro. He soon heard that the North was recruiting slaves as soldiers in Leavenworth, Kansas. There he joined the Union Army and served in the 1st Regiment Kansas Colored Volunteers, later termed the 79th U.S. Colored Troops. After the Civil War, he became a farmer in Douglas County, Kansas; he lived there until his death in 1931. He is buried at a family plot in the Clinton (Douglas County), Kansas cemetery.[25]

Douglas County is the most extensively documented of the abolitionist strongholds in Kansas. It gained its anti-slavery settlers after the Kansas-Nebraska Act of 1854. One abolitionist resident of its county seat, Lawrence, estimated the value of the human property as "No less than one hundred thousand dollars' worth of slaves passed through Lawrence on their way to liberty during the territorial period."[26] The National Park Service lists four specific locations in Lawrence now home to the University of Kansas, as U.G.R.R. sites. One of these is Joel Grover's Barn, 2819 Barn Terrace, 23rd Street (164).[27] This place is now a fire station, and courteous on-duty firemen welcome visitors and pass out literature which makes clear that John Brown spent the night at this location with his Bates County, Missouri, slaves, including Mr. and Mrs. Sam Harper, en route from slavery to freedom in Windsor, Ontario.

The Clinton Abolitionist Museum, southwest of Lawrence, is a preserve of multiple artifacts and photographs of abolitionists; it is in effect an Underground Railroad gallery. Two recent books document the importance of Douglas County as center of abolitionist activity: Richard B. Sheridan's *Freedom's Crucible: The Underground Railroad in Lawrence and Douglas County, Kansas, 1854–1865* [28] and Martha Parker's *Angels of Freedom*.[29] Parker also details the importance of Topeka, Kansas, as a place of several Underground Railroad sites. Most important of these was 429 Quincy St., a little stone house of which its owner, John Armstrong, stated in 1913 that he estimated that in all 300 slaves stayed there: "every one of them was taken north and eventually reached Canada."[30] Other locales are perhaps more legend than fact in Topeka.

Both publications contain a map of what was known as the Lane Trail, a route that John Brown traveled with his cargo of slaves as did a number of other conductors on the line. This trail ran from Topeka to Holton, to Powhattan, to Sabetha, Kansas, and on into Falls City, Nemaha City, and Nebraska City, Nebraska. The National Park Service lists no specific areas in Nebraska. Local legend and a gift shop at John Brown's Cave (a cave which has changed location several times in this century) are the most prominent features of the U.G.R.R. in Nebraska.

From Nebraska, the Underground Railroad went northeast to Tabor, Fremont County, Iowa, approximately 20 miles north of the northwesternmost county in Missouri, Atchison. Tabor was settled in 1852 by three men, all of whom had been students at Oberlin College. The most important of these was the Rev. John Todd, a Congregationalist minister whose house became a major U.G.R.R. station after the passage of the Kansas-Nebraska Act in May 1854. Tabor, Iowa, unlike pro-slavery Westport, Missouri, was 100 percent abolitionist. Slave owners knew that they would receive no help in tracking any fugitives in this town of approximately 200 persons in the 1850s. From Tabor, slaves who spent either a day or a night, most likely at the Todd residence, went on to the home of the Rev. George B. Hitchcock, a friend of John Todd's who lived in

Mr. and Mrs. Sam Harper, runaway slaves from Bates County, Missouri, whom John Brown transported to Windsor, Ontario, Canada, in 1858–59. They were photographed in December 1894 in Windsor by the Murdoch Brothers, probably at their studio, Curry Block. Mr. Harper holds a walking stick and his wife an umbrella. She is wearing mitts (fingerless gloves), and their accessories are fashion statements. (Photograph courtesy the Kansas State Historical Society, Topeka, Kansas.)

Lewis Cass County (now simply Cass County) Iowa, northeast of Fremont County.[31] Siebert also lists the Rev. John Todd of Tabor as an important U.G.R.R. conductor (43 and 98). The National Park Service lists eight specific places in Iowa, including John Todd's house in Tabor and the Rev. George B. Hitchcock's house in Lewis Cass County (163). From these Iowa locations, fugitive slaves made their way east and north to Chicago; there they may have mingled with runaways who had earlier traveled, as John Anderson did, through Illinois to Chicago, then probably to Detroit, and on into Canada.

Finally, on January 11, 1865, there was no longer any need for an Underground Railroad on Missouri's borders. A constitutional convention here declared that human bondage had ended in the state. The attitude toward the demise of the peculiar institution in rural Missouri can be illustrated by the comments of a Clay County, Missouri, newspaper:

> The negroes are all free now, and forever, and we rejoice in it most sincerely as a punishment to the rebels.... The negroes having no owner to care for them — no one owning property in them; they will cease to increase in numbers. They will gradually become extinct.... What an admission for abolitionists! If all this be true, the abolition of slavery at the South was one of the most cruel things that darken the pages of history.[32]

What a surprise it would be for this paper's editor, publisher, and readers in 1865 if they could look about today.

Appendix 1

1771 Spanish Census of Missouri

		Whites				Slaves		
		Up to 14 yrs. inclusive	From 14 to 50 yrs.	From 50 upwards	Total number of whites of all ages	Useful for work	Useless for work	Total number of slaves of both sexes
St. Louis	Males	7	9	1	17	8	4	12
	Females	8	7	1	16	4	2	6
Ste. Genevieve	Males	7	9	1	17	8	4	12
	Females	8	7	1	16	4	2	6

Source: Louis Houck, ed. *The Spanish Regime in Missouri*, 1:53.

Appendix 2
1794–95 Spanish Census of Missouri

	Whites						Free Mulattoes						Free Negroes					
	Men			Women			Men			Women			Men			Women		
Names of the Villages	1st Age	2nd Age	3rd Age	1st Age	2nd Age	3rd Age	1st Age	2nd Age	3rd Age	1st Age	2nd Age	3rd Age	1st Age	2nd Age	3rd Age	1st Age	2nd Age	3rd Age
St. Louis	120	209	39	119	126	23	12	8		11	6		1			1	4	
St. Charles	61	103	34	71	63	5												
San Ferdinand[1]	25	43	8	35	41	5												
Carondelet[2]	35	59	6	39	35	8												
Ste. Genevieve	97	200	15	110	111	4	2	3		5	1		2	3	1	2	1	
New Bourbon[3]	26	68	6	17	31	2												
Totals	364	682	108	391	407	47	14	11		16	7		2	4	1	3	5	

	Mulatto Slaves						Negro Slaves					
	Men			Women			Men			Women		
Names of the Villages	1st Age	2nd Age	3rd Age	1st Age	2nd Age	3rd Age	1st Age	2nd Age	3rd Age	1st Age	2nd Age	3rd Age
St. Louis	25	26		23	19	4	31	55	24	17	60	13
St. Charles							5			1	2	3
San Fernando												
Carondelet											1	
Ste. Genevieve	9	13		12	7		46	91	12	18	84	
New Bourbon											3	
Totals	34	39		35	26	4	82	146	36	36	150	16

Source: Louis Houck, ed. *The Spanish Regime in Missouri*, 1:324–25.

[1] Now Florissant, Missouri, a St. Louis suburb.
[2] Incorporated into St. Louis in 1876.
[3] This village was two miles south of Ste. Genevieve. It ceased to exist in 1856.

Appendix 3
Missouri's Slave-Stealer (Abolitionist) Prison Inmates, 1838–1865

	Name	Age	Place of Birth	Co. Con.	When Received	Sentence	How Discharged
1	Carrier, Richard	27	MO	Benton	Dec. 1838	7 years	Escaped Sept. 1843
2	Kirkpatrick, Joseph	50	KY	St. Louis	Oct. 1840	7 years	Pardoned Jun. 1843
3	Work, Alanson	42	CT	Marion	Oct. 1841	12 years	Pardoned Jan. 1845
4	Burr, James	28	NY	Marion	Oct. 1841	12 years	Pardoned Jan. 1846
5	Thompson, George	23	OH	Marion	Oct. 1841	12 years	Pardoned Jan. 1846
6	Rusho, Peter	55	Canada	Chariton	Nov. 1843	2 years	Died 1844
7	Whitman, John	23	VA	Perry	May 1846	2 years	SFS May 1848
8	Langston, George	38	England	Howard	Dec. 1846	2 years	Pardoned July 1848
9	Spinkel, George	30	VA	Macon	Dec. 1848	2 years	SFS Dec. 1850
10	Johnson, John	20	MO	St. Louis	March 1849	2 years	Died Aug. 1850
11	Brownville, Andrew	54	PA	Perry	May 1849	4 years	SFS May 1853
12	Stain, William	22	DC	St. Louis	Jan. 1850	4 years	SFS Jan. 1854
13	Savage, Benjamin, B	50	PA	St. Louis	Nov. 1850	10 years	Pardoned Jun. 1856
14	Harris, Phillip, B	33	MO	St. Louis	Dec. 1850	5 years	Pardoned Jun.1853
15	Hart, Thomas	23	England	Cape G.	Jun. 1851	3 years	SFS Jun. 1854
16	Brown, Thomas	27	Ireland	Lafayette	Dec. 1851	2 years	SFS Dec.1853
17	Clements, Samuel	36	MA	Lafayette	Sept. 1852	2 years	SFS Sept. 1854
18	Clements, Marian, WF	31	ME	Lafayette	Sept. 1852	2 years	Pardoned Jan. 1853
19	Wyland, John	34	Germany	Franklin	April 1853	3 years	Pardoned April 1856
20	Men, Francis	24	Canada	Cooper	March 1854	5 years	SFS March 1859
21	Taney, William	20	MO	St. Charles	Oct. 1854	2 years	SFS Oct. 1856
22	Baldridge, Andrew	18	MO	St. Charles	June 1855	3 years	SFS June 1858
23	Shepperd, Charles	19	MO	Sullivan	Oct. 1855	3 years	SFS Oct. 1858
24	Pritchard, James	24	Ireland	Monroe	Nov. 1855	3 years	SFS April 1858
25	Brown, Thurman	19	Canada	Jackson	April 1856	2 years	SFS April 1858
26	Smith, William	41	KY	St. Louis	Dec. 1856	5 years	SFS Dec. 1861
27	Sly, Eliza BF	32	VA	St. Louis	June 1857	5 years	Pardoned Feb. 1858
28	Gibson, John	60	Ireland	St. Louis	May 1858	7 years	Died June 1861
29	Goodwin, Ferris	22	IN	Livingston	Aug. 1858	3 years	SFS Aug. 1861
30	Maltby, Robert	20	England	Howard	Sept. 1858	3 years	SFS Sept. 1861
31	Drew, William	30	IL	Lewis	April 1859	4 years	Pardoned Jan. 1861
32	Knapp, William	35	NH	Pike	March 1860	6 years	Died Nov. 1864
33	Grounds, William	38	KY	Madison	April 1860	5 years	Pardoned July 1864
34	Snider, Thomas	36	KY	Madison	April 1860	5 years	Pardoned March 1863
35	Head, Benjamin	45	KY	Lewis	April 1860	5 years	Pardoned March 1863
36	Andrew, John	24	VA	St. Charles	Sept. 1860	6 years	Pardoned March 1865
37	Hatcher, Henry	44	England	Buchanan	Sept. 1860	18 years	Pardoned Dec. 1864
38	McLothlin, or McLaughlin, Henry	21	VA	Jackson	Jan. 1861	7 years	Pardoned Feb. 1863

	Name	Age	Place of Birth	Co. Con.	When Received	Sentence	How Discharged
39	McGee, Thomas	23	Ireland	Jackson	Jan. 1861	7 years	Pardoned Feb. 1863
40	Pinks, George or Allen B	21	PA	Jackson	Jan. 1861	7 years	Pardoned Dec. 1864
41	Johnson, John	40	PA	St. Louis	April 1861	5 years	Died Feb. 1862
42	Johnson, Isaac B	50	VA	Cole	Feb. 1862	10 years	Pardoned Dec. 1864

B=Black; WF=White Female; BF= Black Female; Co. Con.= County of Conviction; SFS= Served Full Sentence

Appendix 4

Slave Population as a Percentage of Total Population in American Slaveholding Jurisdictions, 1820–1860

	Area	1820	1830	1840	1850	1860	Adjacent Free Jurisdictions
1	South Carolina	52.8	55.6	56.4	58.9	58.6	None
2	Mississippi	44.1	48.4	52.3	51.2	55.3	None
3	Louisiana	51.8	58.5	55.0	50.7	49.5	None
4	Alabama	33.2	38.5	43.3	44.7	45.4	None
5	Florida	.....	47.1	48.7	46.0	44.6	None
6	Georgia	44.4	42.6	42.0	42.4	44.0	None
7	North Carolina	34.4	35.9	35.6	36.4	36.4	None
8	Virginia	43.4	42.7	40,2	37.1	34.4	Two: PA & OH
9	Texas	....	....	....	27.5	30.3	Two: Mexico & NM
10	Arkansas	15.5	11.7	20.9	22.7	25.6	None
11	Tennessee	19.6	21.4	22.7	24.5	25.5	None
12	Maryland	36.1	34.9	32.3	28.3	24.9	Two: NJ & PA
13	Kentucky	22.9	24.7	24.3	22.5	20.4	Three: OH, IN, & IL
14	Missouri	18.3	15.9	15.6	13.2	10.0	Four: IL, IA, NE & KS
15	District of Columbia	19.0	15.0	11.0	7.0	4.0	None but PA 48 miles
16	Delaware	6.0	4.2	3.3	2.5	1.6	Two: NJ & PA

Percentages figured from raw numbers in *U.S. Department of Commerce, Negro Population, 1790–1915*, 57.

Abbreviations

BDAC: *Biographical Directory of the American Congress, 1774–1996.* Alexandria, VA: CQ Staff Directories, 1997.

DAB: *Dictionary of American Biography.* 11 vols. New York: Charles Scribner's Sons, 1964.

FHC: Family History Center, Church of Jesus Christ of Latter-Day Saints, Independence, MO.

Laws: Laws of a Public and General Nature of the District of Louisiana.

L.T.: *Liberty Tribune* (Liberty).

MHS: Missouri Historical Society, St. Louis, MO [YEAR].

MORE: *Missouri Republican* (St. Louis).

MSA: Missouri State Archives, Jefferson City, MO.

R.C.: *Randolph Citizen* (Huntsville).

WHMC: Western Historical Manuscript Collection, Columbia, MO.

Laws of Missouri (1804–2003) includes every enactment of the legislative authority from shortly after the Louisiana Purchase in 1804 through 2003. Missouri Revised Statutes are printed every ten years, and they include only the laws which remain in effect as of each successive printing.

Chapter Notes

CHAPTER 1

1. Mark Twain, "Jane Lampton Clemens," *Huck Finn and Tom Sawyer Among the Indians*, 87–88.
2. Benjamin Quarles, *Black Abolitionists*, 70.
3. Andrew E. Murray, *Presbyterians and the Negro—A History*, 69.
4. *L.T.*, Sept. 28, 1849, 1:1.
5. *Ibid.*, May 9, 1856, 2:1.
6. *Ibid.*, Dec. 2, 1859, 2:2.
7. Quoted in Gilbert Osofsky's Introduction to *Puttin' On Ole Massa: The Slave Narratives of Henry Bibb, William Wells Brown, and Solomon Northup*, 33.
8. William Wells Brown, "Narrative of William Wells Brown," *Puttin' On Ole Massa*, 211.
9. "Acts Relating to Slaves," No. 670, *The Statues at Large of South Carolina*, 7:413.
10. 1819 Va. Acts 424–25.
11. *U.S. v Rhodes*, 27 Fed. Cas. 785, 793 (C.C.D. Ky. 1866) (No. 16, 152).
12. Catterall, *Judicial Cases Concerning Slavery*, 3:614–15.
13. 1837 Mo. Laws 3.
14. Stephen B. Oates, *The Fires of Jubilee: Nat Turner's Fierce Rebellion*, a wholly factual and well-documented narrative, is the basis for my account of Nat Turner.
15. See Henry Mayer, *All on Fire: William Lloyd Garrison and the Abolition of Slavery* and *DAB*, s.v. Garrison, William Lloyd.
16. Wendell Phillips Garrison and Francis Jackson Garrison, *William Lloyd Garrison*, 1:240–48.
17. 1833 Va. Laws 244–47.
18. *Missouri Intelligencer* (Columbia) Sept. 17, 1831, 2:4.
19. *Ibid.*, Sept. 24, 1831, 2:1.
20. *Ibid.*, Dec. 3, 1831, 3:3.
21. 1845 Mo. Laws 117.
22. 1847 Mo. Laws 104–05.
23. *Negro Population*, 57.
24. Oates, *The Fires of Jubilee*, 144.
25. Mo. Rev. Stat., chap. 50, secs. 1–13 (1835).
26. *California News,* Oct. 13, 1860, 2:5.
27. *Brunswicker*, Feb. 2, 1856, 2:7.
28. See "Phoenix Life Insurance Company of St. Louis" tables in *L.T.*, March 29, 1850, 3:2 and June 4, 1850, 4:5.
29. *Twenty Censuses: Population and Housing, 1790–1980*, 8–17.
30. *Springfield Advertiser*, April 21, 1849, 2:1.
31. *L.T.*, May 11, 1860, 2:1.
32. Twain, *Huckleberry Finn*, 221–22.
33. Twain, "Jane Lampton Clemens," 89.
34. *R.C.*, Jan. 30, 1858, 3:2.
35. *Springfield Advertiser*, March 7, 1846, 2:1.
36. Lois Stanley, George F. Wilson, and Maryhelen Wilson, *Death Records of Pioneer Missouri Women, 1808–1853*, 22.
37. Stanley, Wilson, and Wilson, *Death Records from Missouri Newspapers, January 1854–December 1860*, 191.
38. *California News*, May 5, 1860, 2:3.
39. *Missouri Intelligencer* (Columbia), Aug. 22, 1835, 2:2.
40. *Ibid.*, Sept. 19, 1835, 4:1.
41. *L.T.*, Aug. 19, 1853, 4:1.
42. Twain, *Complete Humorous Sketches and Tales*, 91.
43. Frederick Douglass, *Narrative of the Life of Frederick Douglass*, 41.
44. Wilma King, *Stolen Childhood: Slave Youth in Nineteenth-Century America*, 10.
45. *Independent Patriot* (Jackson), June 22, 1822, 1:4.
46. *L.T.*, Feb. 19, 1858, 1:7.
47. *Ibid.*, Nov. 23, 1860, 1:7.
48. *Weekly Observer* (Boonville), July 30, 1859, 1:8.
49. *Liberator* (Boston), July 24, 1834, 1:6.
50. *Missourian* (St. Charles), Dec. 6, 1821, 3:5.

51. *Missouri Statesman* (Columbia), July 4, 1845, 1:4.
52. *L.T.*, Sept. 12, 1856, 1:5.
53. *R.C.*, April 17, 1858, 2:2.
54. *L.T.*, Sept. 12, 1856, 1:5.
55. *Kansas City Enterprise*, Nov. 22, 1856, 2:2.
56. *California News,* Nov. 19, 1856, 2:2.
57. *L.T.*, Nov. 30, 1860, 3:1.
58. *Ibid.*, March 8, 1861, 2:2.
59. *California News*, March 31, 1860, 2:2.
60. Erich Fromm, *Escape From Freedom*, 134 and 165–66.
61. *Missouri Daily Democrat* (St. Louis), April 9, 1861.
62. *Ibid.*, April 12, 1861, 3:3.
63. Trexler, *Slavery in Missouri*, 206, and Sheridan, "From Slavery in Missouri to Freedom in Kansas," *Freedom's Crucible*, 37.
64. 13 Stat. 11.
65. 13 Stat. 200.
66. Fellman, *Inside War,* 69.
67. Trexler, *Slavery in Missouri*, 207.
68. Brown, "Narrative of William Wells Brown," 175–223; Farrison, *William Wells Brown*, passim; *DAB s.v.* Brown, William Wells; and Brown's obituary, *Boston Evening Transcript*, Nov. 8, 1884, 1:2.
69. *Liberator* (Boston) Sept. 3, 1:5; Sept. 17, 2:6; Oct. 1, 2:3; Oct. 8, 1847, 2:6 and 3:6, Jan. 21, 2:4 and Feb. 11, 1848, 2:6.
70. Brown, "Letter to Sidney Howard Gay," Jan. 13, 1845, 541–42; and Brown, "Letter to William Lloyd Garrison," May 17, 1853, 545.
71. Margaret Sanborn, *Mark Twain*: *The Bachelor Years*, 57.
72. Mark Twain, "Jane Lampton Clemens," 89.

Chapter 2

1. Louis Houck, *A History of Missouri*, 1:282.
2. Charles L. Dufour, *Ten Flags in the Wind: The Story of Louisiana*, 229–30.
3. John Duffy, ed., *The Rudolph Matas History of Medicine in Louisiana,* 1:135.
4. Eugene M. Violette, "The Black Code in Missouri," 288.
5. Arthur Hertzberg, *The French Enlightenment and the Jews*, 12.
6. John B. Dillon's *A History of Indiana*, 31–43, contains an English translation of the Black Code in its entirety. All textual citations of its Preamble and its Articles, 1–55 are from this translation.
7. Article 6 encouraged marriage between free blacks and slaves. The influence of religion is evident in this article. Marriage was and is one of Catholicism's seven sacraments, and from an early date, holy matrimony was more important to the Church than subjugating an entire race. In addition, the Code's Article 51 freed slaves whom masters appointed guardians of their children. The influence of these two provisions helps explain that by 1830 Louisiana had a larger percentage of its Negro population free than any other slave jurisdiction with the exception of Maryland, another primarily Catholic colony and state. In addition, in 1830 more free persons of color owned slaves in Louisiana than elsewhere in the U.S.: 946 as opposed to one in Arkansas and four in Missouri. Most owned members of their own families. As Woodson demonstrated, a husband might own a wife or vice versa, and a free black male who married a slave became the owner of any children born of the union. The purpose was not, on the whole, to accumulate wealth; it was philanthropic. Bondpersons were freed after they were taught a trade and capable of supporting themselves. See Carter G. Woodson, ed., *Free Negro Owners of Slaves in the United States in 1830*, v and 6–15.
8. In 1967, the U.S. Supreme Court ruled that the miscegenation statutes, which remained law in 16 Southern states, including Missouri, were unconstitutional. Writing for a unanimous Court, Chief Justice Warren stated, "Under our Constitution, the freedom to marry, or not marry a person of another race resides with the individual and cannot be infringed by the State," *Loving* v. *Virginia*, 388 U.S. 1, 12.
9. See Jerry A. Michelle, "From Law Court to Local Government: Metamorphosis of the Superior Council of French Louisiana," 85–107.
10. Duffy, ed. *The Rudolph Matas History of Medicine in Louisiana*, 1:78.
11. Derek Kerr, *Petty Felony, Slave Defiance, and Frontier Villainy*, 38–42.
12. Duffy, ed. *The Rudolph Matas History of Medicine in Louisiana*, 1:127.
13. "Indian Slaves at Ste. Genevieve," May 28, 1770, and "Indian Slaves at St. Louis," July 12, 1770, in Lawrence Kinnaird, ed., *Spain in the Mississippi Valley*, 2:167–70, 172–79.
14. Liliana Obregon, "Black Codes in Latin America," 246.
15. Kerr, *Petty Felony*, 12–14.
16. Gustavus Schmidt, *Louisiana Law Journal*, Aug. 1841, 1–65, contains an English translation of O'Reilly, "Ordinances and Instructions." All textual citations are cited from this translation.
17. Henry Charles Lea, *A History of the Inqui-*

sition of Spain, 1:29 and 2:282. In *Candide* (1759), Voltaire satirizes the "Holy Hermandad" when they bury the Grand Inquisitor in "a beautiful church" and "toss [another dead man] on the dump," 25.

18. Kerr, *Petty Felony*, 138.

19. Morris S. Arnold, *Colonial Arkansas, 1686-1804*, 65.

20. Kerr, *Petty Felony*, Appendices I-V, 215-317. Textual citations on the following pages are from these records.

21. Annie H. Abel, *The American Indian as Slaveholder and Secessionist*, 155.

22. See Jack D.L. Holmes, "The Abortive Slave Revolt at Pointe Coupée, Louisiana 1795," 341-62.

23. Charles Montesquieu, *The Spirit of Laws*, trans. Thomas Nugent, 282.

24. Alonford James Robinson Jr., "Suriname," 1806-09.

25. Voltaire, *Candide,* 55. See also Edward Derbyshire Seeber, *Anti-Slavery Opinion in France During The Second Half of The Eighteenth Century*, and Claudine Hunting, "The Philosophes and Black Slavery: 1748-1765," 405-418.

26. Roger Bruns, in *Am I Not a Man and a Brother*, explains of the Mennonites, "Exiled to America, they perceived slavery as the same kind of horror that their own people had suffered at the hands of the hated Turks." (3) This excellent anthology contains excerpts from nearly 100 American protests against slavery written between 1688 and 1788. Page numbers follow quoted material in the text.

27. The terminology requires explanation. The Louisiana Purchase consisted of the territories of Orleans and Upper Louisiana. The latter included the present states of Missouri and Arkansas. In 1812 Congress admitted the Territory of Orleans to the Union as the state of Louisiana, and to avoid confusion changed the name Upper Louisiana to Missouri Territory. In 1819 what had been a county in Missouri, New Madrid, became the Territory of Arkansas, and just as Missouri was pair-admitted to the Union with Maine in the early 1820s, the state of Arkansas was pair-admitted to the Union with Michigan in the mid-1830s.

28. Joseph J. Ellis, *Founding Brothers*, 90.

29. July 4th was an important date in these states for freeing slaves. By a New York statute passed in 1817, all Negroes born before July 4, 1799, were to be freed after July 4, 1827. A New Jersey law of 1804 provided that every child born of a slave after July 4, 1804, should be freed but should remain the servant of the owner of the mother until the age of 25 in cases of males and 21 in cases of females. Helen Catterall, *Judicial Cases Concerning American Slavery and the Negro*, 4:319-20 and 352.

30. George F. Willison, *Patrick Henry and His World*, 266-67, 485-86.

31. James Boswell, *Life of Johnson*, 876-78.

32. 1 Stat.4-9 contains the Articles of Confederation in their entirety.

33. Don E. Fehrenbacher, *The Slaveholding Republic*, 25.

34. *DAB*, s.v. Dane, Nathan.

35. 1 Stat. 53. On August 7, 1789, the First U.S. Congress reenacted the Northwest Ordinance of 1787.

36. Catherine Drinker Bowen, *Miracle at Philadelphia*, 204.

37. William M. Wiecek, "The Witch at the Christening: Slavery and the Constitution's Origins," 167-84.

38. Fehrenbacher, *The Slaveholding Republic*, 136.

39. Cited in Henry Mayer, *All on Fire*, 313 and 397.

40. Ellis, *Founding Brothers*, 93.

41. Paul Finkelman, *Slavery and the Founders*, 34-5.

42. Gaillard Hunt, ed., *Journals of the Continental Congress*, 26:246-47.

43. David McCullough, *John Adams*, 137-38. James Thomas Flexner, *George Washington: Anguish and Farewell*, 131, lists the number of slaves that Washington owned by 1786 at 216.

44. McCullough, *John Adams*, 347.

45. *Ibid.*, 347.

46. Quoted in Joseph J. Ellis, *American Sphinx: The Character of Thomas Jefferson*, 258.

47. Eric S. Lander and Joseph J. Ellis, "Founding father," 13-14, and Eugene A. Foster et al, "Jefferson fathered slave's last child," 27-28.

48. Finkelman, *Slavery and the Founders*, 151.

49. Ellis, *Founding Brothers*, 81-119.

50. Cited in Fehrenbacher, *The Slaveholding Republic*, 76.

51. Stoddard to William Henry Harrison, June 3, 1804, Amos Stoddard papers.

52. "Treaty of Cession," art. 3 (1803), *Laws of a Public and General Nature of the District of Louisiana, of the Territory of Louisiana, of the Territory of Missouri, and of the State of Missouri Up to the Year 1824*, 2. Hereafter cited as *Laws*.

53. 2 Stat. 287.

Chapter 3

1. Louis Houck, *The Spanish Regime in Missouri*, 1: 84.
2. *Ibid.*, 2: 365–386.
3. *Ibid.*, 1:324–25.
4. *Ibid.*, 2:414.
5. *Ibid.*, 1:16.
6. "Emancipation given by Jean Louis de Noyon to an Indian Woman named Jeanette," Oct. 29, 1779, trans. Sylvie L. Richards. F19, Collection 3636, WHMC.
7. Houck, *The Spanish Regime in Missouri*, 2:221.
8. David D. March, *The History of Missouri*, 1:79.
9. Frederic L. Billon, *Annals of St. Louis in Its Early Days*, 39–40.
10. Judith A. Gilbert, "Esther and Her Sisters," 19.
11. Billon, *Annals of St. Louis in Its Early Days*, 102.
12. Gilbert, "Esther and Her Sisters," 14–23.
13. Persons of color who owned property in St. Louis under Spanish rule are listed in at least the following appellate decisions, all concerning disputed land-ownership claims. *Berthold* v. *McDonald*, 63 U.S. (22 How.) 334 (1859), states, "Under the Spanish Government, there was a common field near the town of St. Louis, called the common field of the Prairie des Noyers. In this common field were two lots, owned respectively by two negresses, one of whom was named Florence Flore, and the other named Jeannette, or Jeannette Flore." *St. Louis Public Schools* v. *Risley's Heirs*, 40 Mo. 356, 367 (1867), says, "The defendant introduced a concession by the Spanish Governor, dated March 1, 1788, to the free negro Charles Leveille for a lot in St. Louis of 60 by 150 feet." *St. Louis Public Schools* v. *Schoenthaler's Heirs*, 40 Mo. 372, 373 (1867), notes of a particular property, "Charles Leveille and his wife lived on this lot until the death of the old man, which occurred in 1809 or 1810. His widow lived on it until her death in 1826." *The Schools* v. *Risley*, 77 U. S. (10 Wall.) 91, 93 (1869), specifies of land in controversy, "On the north side of this block, for many years prior to the cession of 1803, one Madame Charleville had been settled, inhabiting and cultivating it; and on the south side, a free negro, named Charles Leveille." The page in the U.S. Supreme Court Reporter which lists this information about Madame Charleville and Charles Leveille also contains a map of their block with their separate properties clearly marked on it. Esther as a St. Louis property owner appears in at least two Missouri Supreme Court decisions and at least four of the U.S. Supreme Court.

Hill v. Wright, 3 Mo. 243, 244 (1833), notes that Joseph Brazeau's land is "bounded towards the S.S.E. by the concessions granted to a free mulatress named Esther." *Magwire* v. *Tyler*, 40 Mo. 406, 408 (1867), mentions, "In the year 1793, the Spanish government conceded or granted to one Esther, a free mulatress, a tract or parcel of land situate on the border of the Mississippi River." *Landes* v. *Brant*, 51 U.S. (10 How.) 348, 350 (1850), contains, "Jacques Clamorgan, assignee of Esther, mulatress, assignee of Joseph Brazeau, assignee of Gabriel Dodier, claiming one by 40 arpents of land... adjoining the town of St. Louis... a transfer from Gabriel Dodier and Joseph Brazeau to Esther, dated 4th November, 1793; from Esther to claimant, dated 2d September, 1794." *West* v. *Cochran*, 58 U.S. (17 How.), 403, 409 (1854), mentions that the Lt. Governor of Upper Louisiana on June 10, 1794, put Joseph Brazeau "in possession of the parcel of land... in the S.S.E. bounded by the land granted to the free mulatress Esther." *Magwire* v. *Tyler*, 75 U.S. (8 Wall.) 652, 654 (1869), holds that "the governor formally concede to the donee [Joseph Brazeau] a tract of land,... of which one end is to be bounded by the concession to one Esther, a free mulatto woman." *Tyler* v. *Magwire*, 84 U.S. (17 Wall.) 253, 293 (1872), states of Esther's land, "the northern boundary of the said Esther survey, to the northwest corner of the said Esther survey."

14. Lois Stanley, George F. Wilson, and Maryhelen Wilson, *Death Records of Missouri Men, 1808–1854*, 32.
15. William E. Foley, *The Genesis of Missouri*, 72.
16. Gilbert, "Esther and Her Sisters," 15–18.
17. Julie Winch, ed., *The Colored Aristocracy of St. Louis by Cyprian Clamorgan*, 23.
18. *Ibid.*, 24.
19. The refusal of early Missouri writers to discuss Jacques Clamorgan, his concubines, and their descendants is illustrated by the copious detail about him available in a U.S. Supreme Court case decided in 1850 and the omission of his very name from subsequent histories of the state, such as Scharf's *History of Saint Louis City and County*, 2 vols., 1883; Hyde and Conard, eds. *Encyclopedia of the History of St. Louis*, 6 vols., 1899; and Conard, ed. *Encyclopedia of the History of Missouri*, 6 vols, 1901. *Landes* v. *Brant*, 51 U.S. 348, 351–52 (1850), contains, "Jacques Clamorgan... devised all his estate to his natural children, St. Eutrope, Apoline, Cyprian Martial, and

Maximin.... Apoline was never married, and her children were illegitimate; Cyprian Martial and Apoline were mulattoes." Attorney and historian Louis Houck's *A History of Missouri*, 3 vols., 1908, discusses the public Jacques Clamorgan, and his *The Spanish Regime in Missouri*, 2 vols., 1909, states of Clamorgan's personal life only that "He never married," 2:149. Foley's *History of Missouri, 1673–1820*, 1971; *The First Chouteaus: River Barons of Early St. Louis*, 1983; and *The Genesis of Missouri: From Wilderness Outpost to Statehood*, 1989, discuss the public aspects of Clamorgan. Greene Kremer and Holland's *Missouri's Black Heritage*, 1980, mentions Cyprian Clamorgan and his authorship of *The Colored Aristocracy of St. Louis*, but is silent about his grandparents and his mother. Until Gilbert's and Winch's accounts in the 1990s of Esther and of Jacques Clamorgan's other women of color, as progenitor and emancipator, he was an invisible man in Missouri's history. The *Dictionary of Missouri Biography*, eds. Christensen, Foley, Kremer, and Winn, 1999, contains entries about Esther, Jacques Clamorgan, and his grandson Cyprian Clamorgan.

20. Harrison Trexler, *Slavery in Missouri*, 220.
21. City of St. Louis Recorder of Deeds, Book B, 368–72.
22. Houck, *A History of Missouri*, 2:70, and Billon, *Annals of St. Louis in Its Territorial Days from 1804 to 1821*, 9.
23. All material quoted from these handwritten court records is taken from *Esther, Free Mulatto v. Jacques Clamorgan*, October 1809, Case 13, Box 24, F.14 and 15, MSA.
24. Gilbert, "Esther and Her Sisters," 19.
25. Winch. *The Colored Aristocracy of St. Louis*, 26.
26. Ibid., 26–27.
27. U.S. Dept. of Commerce, *Negro Population 1790–1915*, 57.
28. *Laws* (1804), chap. 3, sec. 23, 31–32.
29. Winch, *The Colored Aristocracy of St. Louis*, 25.
30. *Private Laws of the U.S. Congress, 1789–1845*, 65–66.
31. Stephen E. Ambrose, *Undaunted Courage*, 457–58.
32. Washington Irving, *The Western Journals*, 82.
33. *Missouri Gazette* (St. Louis), March 30, 1816, 3:4.
34. *Missouri Gazette*, April 21, 1819, 3:2.
35. George Rogers Clark Papers, Box 7, F. 3, MHS.
36. Mo. Const., art. 3, sec. 26, in Thorpe, *The Federal and State Constitutions*.
37. Robert Betts, *In Search of York*, 123.

38. See "Black voices from 1800s emerge in freedom suits," *Kansas City Star*, April 16, 2003, F 4:1.
39. *LaGrange (alias Isidore), a Man of Colour v. Pierre Chouteau*, 29 U.S. (4 Pet.) 287 (1830) and *Pierre Chouteau, senior v Marguerite (a woman of colour)*, 37 U.S. (12 Pet.) 507 (1838).
40. *Marguerite v. Chouteau*, 3 Mo. 540 (1834).
41. James Curtis Ballagh, *A History of Slavery in Virginia*, 60–61.
42. William E. Foley, "Slave Freedom Suits before Dred Scott: The Case of Marie Jean Scypion's Descendants," 1–23.
43. *Charlotte (of color) v. Chouteau*, 33 Mo. 194, 195, and 200 (1862).
44. All material quoted from these handwritten court records derives from *Matilda, a black girl v. Isaac Van Bibber*, Sept. 1816–Sept. 1817, Box 41, F 35 and Box 43, F 26, MSA.
45. Houck, *A History of Missouri*, 3:266.
46. Billon, *Annals of St. Louis ... From 1804 to 1821*, 49.
47. 3 Stat. 548.
48. Stanley, Wilson, and Wilson, *Death Records of Missouri Men, 1808–1854*, 99; Houck, *A History of Missouri*, 3:66; and Billon, *Annals of St. Louis...From 1804 to 1821*, 277–78.
49. *La Grange (alias Isidore) v. Pierre Chouteau*, 2 Mo. 20, 22 (1828).
50. *Theoteste (alias Catiche) v. Chouteau*, 2 Mo. 144 (1829).
51. *Nat (a man of color) v. Ruddle*, 3 Mo. 400, 401 (1834).
52. *Winny (a free woman held in slavery) v. Whitesides alias Prewitt*, 1 Mo. 472, 474–75 (1824).
53. *Merry v. Tiffin and Menard*, 1 Mo. 725, 726 (1827).
54. Ill. Const., art. 6, sec. 2 (1818), in Francis Thorpe, ed., *The Federal and State Constitutions*, 2:980. See also Paul Finkelman, "Evading the Ordinance," 58–80.
55. *Vincent (a man of color) v. Duncan*, 2 Mo. 214 (1830).
56. *Menard v. Aspasia*, 30 U.S. (5 Pet.) 505 (1831).
57. *Ralph (a man of color) v. Duncan*, 3 Mo. 194 (1833).
58. *Julia (a woman of color) v. McKinney*, 3 Mo. 270, 271 and 273–74 (1833).
59. *Rachael (a woman of color) v. Walker*, 4 Mo. 350, 354 (1836).
60. *Anderson v. Brown (of color)*, 9 Mo. 646 (1845).
61. *Emmerson* [sic] *v. Harriet (of color)*, 11 Mo. 413 (1848) and *Emmerson* [sic] *v. Dred Scott (of color)* 11 Mo. 413 (1848).
62. 1849 Mo. 4.

63. *Scott (a man of color)* v. *Emerson*, 15 Mo. 576, 586 -87 (1852),
64. *Ibid.*, 583.
65. *Ibid.*, 586.
66. Art. III, sec. 2 [1].
67. *Dred Scott* v. *Sandford* [sic], 60 U.S. (19 How.) 393, 407 (1857).
68. *Ibid.*, 453.
69. *Ibid*, 526–27.
70. Cited in David Herbert Donald, *Charles Sumner and the Rights of Man*, 180–81.
71. Don Fehrenbacher, *The Dred Scott Case*, 421 and 568–69.

Chapter 4

1. *Laws* (1804), chap. 3.
2. For example, see Chapter 7, "Free Sailors and the Struggle with Slavery," in W. Jeffrey Bolster, *Black Jacks: African American Seamen in the Age of Sail*, 199–214, for a thorough discussion of legislation which authorized the jailing of free black sailors in southern American ports during the antebellum period.
3. *Charlotte* v. *Chouteau*, 11 Mo. 193, 200–01 (1847).
4. Mo. Const., art. 3, sec. 26.
5. U.S. Dept. of Commerce, *Negro Population, 1790–1915*, 57.
6. Mo. Rev. Stat., "Free Negroes and Mulattoes" (1835). Section numbers precede the quoted material.
7. See Mary E, Seematter, "Trials and Confessions: Race and Justice in Antebellum St. Louis," 36–47.
8. Mo. Rev. Stat., chap. 123, "Negroes and Mulattoes" (1845). Section numbers precede the quoted material.
9. Mo. Rev. Stat., Chap 115, "An Act Respecting Slaves, Free Negroes and Mulattoes," approved Feb. 16, 1847 (1855).
10. *Glasgow Times*, March 15, 1860, 2:1.
11. *Kansas City Enterprise*, Nov. 24, 1855, 2:5.
12. *Stoner* v. *State*, 4 Mo. 614 (1837).
13. *Carroll* v. *The City of St. Louis*, 12 Mo. 444, 447 (1849).
14. Tiffany Collection, Box 63, F. 7, MHS.
15. *Ibid.*, Box 63, F. 7, MHS.
16. *Ibid.*, Box 62, F. 6, MHS.
17. "List of Free Negroes," Tiffany Collection, Box 63, F 6, MHS.
18. Jeremy Noakes and Geoffrey Prudham, eds., *Documents on Nazism, 1919–1945*, 463–68.
19. Fehrenbacher, *The Dred Scott Case*, 349.
20. Thomas P. Lowry, *The Story the Soldiers Wouldn't Tell*, 81.
21. *St. Louis City Directory*, 1859, 592.
22. Julie Winch, ed., *The Colored Aristocracy of St. Louis*.
23. Winch's excellent annotations identify most of these learned references, but not *Romeo and Juliet, A Midsummer Night's Dream*, "Elegy Written in a Country Churchyard," or "Benito Cereno."
24. The only successful slave revolt in the Western Hemisphere occurred in 1791 in Haiti, where at least 500,000 Africans vastly outnumbered the French colonists. This was on the island called, in English, San Dominick; in French it was St. Domingue and in Spanish Santo Domingo.
25. Herman Melville, "Benito Cereno," *Selected Tales and Poems*, ed. Richard Chase, 49–51.
26. *Oxford Classical Dictionary*, 248.
27. Patrick Hanks and Flavia Hodges, *Dictionary of First Names*, 264.
28. *Merry* v. *Tiffin and Menard*, 1 Mo. 725, 726 (1827).
29. *Western Watchman* (St. Louis), March 24, 1922, 13:3.
30. *St. Louis Post-Dispatch*, March 22, 1922, 3:7–8.
31. *St. Louis Argus*, March 24, 1922, 1:4. See also *Church Progress* (St. Louis) for the date and place of her funeral: March 23, 1922, at St. Thomas of Acquin's Church.
32. *Fisher's Negroes* v. *Dabbs*, 14 Tenn. (6 Yer.) 119, 126–31 (1834).
33. Loren Schweninger, ed., *From Tennessee Slave to St. Louis Entrepreneur:* 28–30.
34. *Ibid.*, Appendix 1, 197–99.
35. *St. Louis Post-Dispatch*, Dec. 18, 1913, 26:7.
36. *Western Watchman* (St. Louis) Dec. 18, 1913, 20:3.
37. *Church Progress* (St. Louis), Dec. 25, 1913, 3:5.
38. Quoted in Winch, *Colored Aristocracy*, 73.
39. Loren Schweninger. *From Tennessee Slave to St. Louis Entrepreneur*, 11–16. Subsequent page numbers follow quoted material.
40. N. Webster Moore, "John Berry Meachum (1789–1854): St. Louis Pioneer, Black Abolitionist, Educator, and Preacher," 96.
41. *Meechum* [sic] v. *Judy, alias Julia Logan, A Woman of Color*, 4 Mo. 361 (1836).
42. [Summary of circuit court trial,] Transcript, *Berry Meachum* v. *Judy, alias Julia Logan*, May 20, 1836, MSA.
43. *Dictionary of Missouri Biography*, s.v. Turner, John Milton..
44. 1 Stat. 468.
45. 2 Stat. 666.
46. Moore, "John Berry Meachum (1789–

1854)," 96–103. See also s.v. Meachum, John Berry in *Dictionary of Missouri Biography*.

47. Jennifer Fleischner, *Mrs. Lincoln and Mrs. Keckly*, 134.

48. *Ibid.*, 29.

49. Elizabeth Keckley, *Behind the Scenes*, 236–37.

50. Keckley, *Behind the Scenes*, 101.

51. David Herbert Donald, *Lincoln*, 335.

52. Jean H. Baker, *Mary Todd Lincoln: A Biography*, 212. See also s.v. Keckley, Elizabeth in *Dictionary of Missouri Biography*.

53. Fleischner, *Mrs. Lincoln and Mrs. Keckly*, 316.

54. Dorothy Porter, "Introduction," *Behind the Scenes*, n.p.

55. Keckley, *Behind the Scenes*, 189.

56. *Ibid.*, 301.

57. Steven Lubar and Kathleen M. Kendrick, *Legacies: Collecting America's History at the Smithsonian*, 232.

58. *Jefferson Republican*, Dec. 17, 1836, 3:2–6 and *L.T.*, Jan. 26, 1849, 1:6.

59. Robert Samuel Fletcher, *A History of Oberlin College*, 1: 528.

60. Carl Sifakis, *The Encyclopedia of American Crime*, s.v. Dalton Brothers: Outlaws, and Younger Brothers: Outlaw Band.

61. Annette W. Curtis, *Jackson County, Missouri in Black & White: Census of Slaves, Their Owners and "Free Colored," 1850 and 1860*, lists Charles Younger as the owner of 30 slaves, including a 17-year-old female in the 1850 Slave Schedule. Almost certainly she would have been Elizabeth. Curtis also enumerates the free colored in Jackson County by family name, age, color, occupation, and township residence in both 1850 (41 persons) and 1860 (70 persons). Included among the free colored of Jackson County were Hiram Young, a successful blacksmith, and Emily Fisher, the county's first black businesswoman. See William J. Curtis, *A Black History of Independence, Missouri*.

62. Stanley, Wilson, and Wilson, *Death Records from Missouri Newspapers January 1854–December 1860*, 260.

63. *Younger v. Judah*, 111 Mo. 303, 312, 19 S.W. 1109, 1111 (1892).

64. *Plessy v. Ferguson*, 163 U.S. 537 (1896).

65. Becky Carlson, "'Manumitted and Forever Set Free': The Children of Charles Lee Younger and Elizabeth, a Woman of Color," 16–31. This superb article is the source of all information regarding this subject unless otherwise indicated. It is research at its best.

66. *Kansas City Star*, August 25, 2002, 1:2.

Chapter 5

1. Derek Kerr, *Petty Felony*, 138.

2. *Ibid.*, 140–42.

3. See *Sarah Pickens v. Pascal Cerré*, Box 5, F 7; *Sarah Pickens v. Antoine Soulard*, Box 5, F 8; and *U.S. v. John Pickens*, Box 5, F 6, MSA.

4. *Missouri Gazette* (St. Louis), May 24, 1809, 1:2, and Aug. 30, 1809, 1:3 and 3:3.

5. The language "lurking in swamps, woods and other obscure places" of Missouri law derives from a Virginia statute. Compare chap. 3, sec. 13 *Laws* (1804) with *Va. Code*, chap. 41, sec. 20 (1792), 125.

6. William M. Wiecek, "The Origins of the Law of Slavery in British North America," 1711, 1785.

7. Marvin L. Michael Kay and Lorin Lee Cary, *Slavery in North Carolina, 1748–1775*, 63–66.

8. *Ibid.*, Table 3.1, 246–48.

9. *Laws* (1817), chap. 187, sec. 1–3, 499–500.

10. *Missouri Gazette*, Dec. 26, 1809, 2:1–3.

11. The language "found strolling about from one plantation to another" is Virginia law. Compare *Laws* (1822), chap. 422, sec. 1, 991 with *Va. Laws* 1819, chap. 242, sec. 3, 288.

12. Betty Harvey Williams, "Patrol Companies Appointed in Ralls County, Missouri," 121–24.

13. *L.T.*, Dec. 21, 1860, 3:1.

14. Compare *Va. Code*, chap. 131, sec. 4, 347 (1792) in *All Such Acts of the General Assembly of Virginia*, 2nd ed. (1814) with *Mo. Rev. Stat.*, art. 4, sec. 20 (1835).

15. *L.T.*, Nov. 24, 1848, 2:1.

16. Compare *Va. Code*, chap. 241, secs. 6–8 (1819), 286 with *Mo. Rev. Stat.*, chap. 168, sec. 9 (1845).

17. *Mo. Rev. Stat.*, chap. 268, sec. 9 (1845).

18. William L. Heckman, *Steamboating: Sixty-Five Years on Missouri's Rivers*, 27.

19. 1825 Mo. Laws 747.

20. *Mo. Rev. Stat.*, art 1, sec. 35–36 (1835); chap. 167, secs. 31–32 (1845); and chap. 150, secs. 30–31 (1855).

21. *Eaton v. Vaughan*, 9 Mo. 743, 748 (1846).

22. *Withers v. Steamboat El Paso*, 24 Mo. 204, 211 (1857).

23. Mark Twain, *Life on the Mississippi*, 142–43.

24. 1855 Mo. Laws 169–70.

25. *Welton v. Pacific Railroad Co.*, 34 Mo. 358 (1864); *Rogers v. Pacific Railroad*, 35 Mo. 153 (1864): *McClure v. Pacific Railroad*, 35 Mo. 189 (1864); and *Harris v. Hannibal and St. Joseph Railroad*, 37 Mo. 307 (1866).

26. *Missouri Gazette*, Dec. 28, 1808, 3:3.

27. "Acts Relating to Slaves," No. 314, 474, and 586 in *The Statutes at Large of South Carolina*, 7:355–97.
28. Catterall, "*State v. Doctor James,*" *Judicial Cases Concerning Slavery*, 2:280.
29. *Va. Code*, chap. 131, sec. 2 (1792), 347 in *All Such Acts of the General Assembly of Virginia*, 2nd ed. (1814).
30. 1 Stat. 302–05.
31. *Missouri Gazette*, March 23, 1816, 2:2; *St. Louis Enquirer*, Nov. 3, 1819, 2:1; Dec. 11, 1819, 2:4; May 10, 1820, 2:2; *Missouri Herald* (Jackson), June 17, 1820, 2:4; and *St. Louis Enquirer*, Sept. 30, 1820, 3:5.
32. Theodore Weld, *American Slavery As It Is*, 9.
33. *Missouri Gazette*, March 23, 1816, 2:2 and Oct. 3, 1820, 4:5.
34. *St. Louis Enquirer*, Sept. 12, 1821, 1:4 and June 24, 1822, 4:1; *Independent Patriot*, Sept. 17, 1825, 3:5; *L.T.*, July 5, 1850, 3:1; and *Missouri Argus* (St. Louis), April 2, 1839, 4:6.
35. *Oxford Classical Dictionary*, 469.
36. Patrick Hanks and Flavia Hodges, *A Dictionary of First Names*, 21.
37. *Louisiana Gazette* (St. Louis), Sept. 5, 1812, 1:2; *Missouri Gazette*, March 23, 1816, 2:2; *Independent Patriot*, Oct. 12, 1822, 3:3; *MORE*, May 10, 1827, 1:3; *Missouri Argus*, Oct. 18, 1837, 3:2 and April 12, 1839, 4:6; *L.T.*, May 26, 1848, 3:1; *MORE*, Aug. 22, 1825, 1:2; *Missouri Intelligencer* (Columbia), June 28, 1834, 3:5; *St. Louis Enquirer*, May 10, 1820, 2:2; *L.T.*, June 21, 1850, 3:4; and *Missouri Gazette*, Oct. 3, 1820, 4:5.
38. *Louisiana Gazette*, May 30, 1812, 4:4; Sept. 26, 1812, 3:4; and May 7, 1814, 3:4.
39. *Missouri Gazette*, June 27, 1811, 3:4 and Sept. 2, 1815, 4:3.
40. *Louisiana Gazette*, Feb. 8, 1810, 3:4; *Missouri Gazette*, Oct. 11, 1817, 3:5; *Louisiana Gazette*, June 21, 1810, 3:4 and Aug. 22, 1811, 2:1; *Missouri Herald*, June 17, 1820, 2:4; *Louisiana Gazette*, Aug. 23, 1810, 3:4; *Missouri Gazette*, June 27, 1811, 3:4 and Dec. 18, 1818, 4:4; *St. Louis Enquirer*, Oct. 20, 1821, 2:3; *L.T.*, June 21, 1850, 3:4; *Independent Patriot*, April 1, 1826, 3:4; *L.T.*, Dec. 19, 1851, 3:1 *Missouri Gazette*, July 12, 1820, 4:1; and *Missouri Intelligencer* (Fayette), Jan. 4, 1827, 2:5.
41. *U.S. v. Catherine*, July 17, 1811, Manuel Lisa Collection, Box 2, MHS
42. *Louisiana Gazette*, May 30, 1812, 4:4; Sept. 26, 1812, 3:4 and May 7, 1814, 3:4.
43. *St. Louis Enquirer*, June 24, 1822, 4:1 and May 10, 1820, 2:2; *Missouri Intelligencer* (Columbia), June 28, 1834, 3:5; *MORE*, Dec. 23, 1828, 4:4; and *Louisiana Gazette*, May 7, 1814, 3:4.
44. *Louisiana Gazette*, Jan. 25, 1809, 4:3; June 27, 1811, 3:4 and Sept. 5, 1812; and *L.T.*, June 21, 1850, 3:4.
45. *St. Louis Enquirer*, May 10, 1820, 2:3; Dec. 11, 1819, 2:4 and May 10, 1820, 2:2; *Missouri Gazette*, Oct. 21, 1812, 1:2; *Missouri Argus*, March 18, 1826, 2:6; *MORE*, Sept. 16, 1828, 1:3; and *St. Louis Enquirer*, Oct. 29, 1821, 2:3.
46. *Louisiana Gazette*, March 28, 1811, 3:4; *St. Louis Enquirer*, May 24, 1820, 2:2; *Salt River Journal* (Bowling Green), Sept. 26, 1840, 4:1; *St. Louis Enquirer*, June 24, 1822, 4:1; and *MORE*, Dec. 23, 1828, 4:4.
47. *Louisiana Gazette*, Oct. 3, 1811, 1:2; Sept. 26, 1812, 3:4; April 2, 1814, 2:1; May 7, 1814, 3:4; *Missouri Gazette*, Nov. 5, 1814, 3:4; and *MORE*, Aug. 22, 1815, 1:2.
48. *MORE*, Dec. 23, 1828, 4:4 and *Missouri Argus*, April 19, 1839, 3:6.
49. W. Jeffery Bolster, *Black Jacks*, 95.
50. Kay and Cary, *Slavery in North Carolina, 1748-1775*, 133 and 349.
51. *Missouri Argus*, April 12, 1839, 4:6.
52 *Missouri Gazette*, July 23, 1814, 3:4 and Sept. 2, 1815, 4:3; *Independent Patriot*, Jan. 26, 1822, 1:2; *Louisiana Gazette*, Sept. 5, 1812, 1:2; *St. Louis Enquirer*, Nov. 3, 1819, 2:1; *Independent Patriot*, July 14, 1821, 3:4; *Missouri Gazette*, March 30, 1816, 3:4; March 22, 1817, 1:2; July 29, 1815, 4:3; *St. Louis Enquirer*, May 10, 1820, 2:2; *Missouri Gazette*, June 22, 1816, 3:2; Oct. 20, 1819, 3:5; *St. Louis Enquirer*, May 10, 1820, 2:3; *Missouri Gazette*, Nov. 1, 1820, 4:2; and *Louisiana Gazette*, April 25, 1811, 3:4.
53. *MORE*, Dec. 23, 1828, 4:4 and *Missouri Argus*, April 19, 1839, 3:6.
54. *MORE*, Sept. 3, 1861, 3:2.
55. *Missouri Argus*, April 12, 1839, 4:6.
56. *L.T.*, Oct. 1, 1854, 4:1.
57. *MORE*, Sept. 3, 1861.
58. *R.C.*, Sept. 27, 1855, 1:6.
59. Stanley, Wilson, and Wilson, *Death Records of Missouri Men, 1808–1854*, 31.
60. *R.C.*, Aug. 9, 1855, 1:6.
61. *Ibid.*, Sept. 27, 1855, 1:6.
62. *R.C.*, July 30, 1857, 2:1 and *L.T.*, July 31, 1857, 1:5.
63. *R.C.*, Dec. 10, 1857, 2:7.
64. *L.T.*, Nov. 25, 1859, Dec. 10, 1857, 2:1.
65. *Louisiana Journal*, June 7, 1860, 3:2.
66. *Ibid.*, Feb. 28, 1861, 2:2.
67. *Prigg v. Pennsylvania*, 42 U.S. 539 (1842).
68. 9 Stat. 462.
69. *Ibid.*
70. 13 Stat. 200.
71. *New York Times*, July 25, 1859, 3:1.

72. *L.T.*, April 19, 1861 and May 19, 1861, 2:1.
73. *L.T.*, Aug. 30, 1861, 2:6.
74. Stanley W. Campbell, *The Slave Catchers*, 154–56 and *L.T.*, Feb. 3, 1860, 2:1.
75. After concluding his life of Archer Alexander, the author joins to it "Slavery in the Border States." In this filler-piece, he mentions that he initially moved to St. Louis in November 1834. One of the "first things [he] heard was of a colored girl who had been whipped so severely by a 'gentleman' who lived not far from where I lodged, that she died." He continues that the accused obtained a change of venue from St. Louis to St. Charles County where he was found not guilty. Eliot quotes a letter dated June 17, 1880, about a "Major _____" and his indictment for either manslaughter or murder, probably murder. Since the letter writer is describing events which took place 46 years earlier, he no longer recalls the precise crime charged. William G. Eliot, *The Story of Archer Alexander*, 91–93. Eliot's discussion of the *never-named* defendant concerns Major General William Selby Harney (1800–89) who was then still alive. My extensive investigation of extant St. Charles County Circuit Court records of 1834–36 uncovered no mention of him. See Frazier, *Slavery and Crime in Missouri*, 135–39, for the particulars of then-Major Harney's crime and the absence of any punishment.
76. Eliot, *The Story of Archer Alexander*, 11.
77. *Ibid.*, 87. See also *DAB, s.v.* Ball, Thomas, and Eliot, William Greenleaf, and *Dictionary of Missouri Biography, s.v.* Alexander, Archer.
78. *L.T.*, Feb. 3, 1860, 2:1.

CHAPTER 6

1. Fehrenbacher, *The Slaveholding Republic*, 98.
2. *Ibid.*, 101.
3. Sharon Cosner, *The Underground Railroad*, 13.
4. Henrietta Buckmaster, *Let My People Go*, 35.
5. Conversation with Betty Harvey Williams.
6. Fehrenbacher, *The Slaveholding Republic*, 102.
7. Buckmaster, *Let My People Go*, 42–43.
8. Robin W. Winks, *The Blacks in Canada*, 171.
9. Wilbur Devereux Jones, "The Influence of Slavery on the Webster-Ashburton Treaty," 49.
10. Avalon Project: "The Webster-Ashburton Treaty. 1842:": http://www.yale.edu/lawweb/Avalon/19th.htm
11. George Stroud, *A Sketch of the Laws Relating to Slavery*, 78.
12. William Blackstone, *Commentaries on the Laws of England*, IV, 190–91.
13. Revised Statutes of Canada, IV, Chap. E-23 (1985).
14. Both opinions of the Webster-Ashburton Treaty are cited in Winks, *The Blacks in Canada*, 173.
15. The 1863 *Life of John Anderson* edited by Harper Twelvetrees incorrectly identified Anderson's new owner as *McDonald* and his county as *Salem*.
16. Harrison Trexler, *Slavery in Missouri, 1804–1865*, 39.
17. A decade earlier, a Saline County owner, Thomas B. Finley, whipped his slave, Rachael, to death. Frazier, *Slavery and Crime in Missouri*, 139–41.
18. Stanley, Wilson, and Wilson, *Death Records from Missouri Newspapers, January 1854–December 1860*, 60, lists the death of "Digges, Sallie W., daughter of S.T.P. and F.A., *Glasgow Times*, 29 February 1856." This child appears in neither the 1850 nor the 1860 census. She was not born when the 1850 was taken, and she died before that of 1860. She was probably the Digges' ninth and last child.
19. *Glasgow Times*, Oct 13, 1853, 2:5.
20. *L. T.*, Oct. 8, 1853, 2:5.
21. *Glasgow Times*, Oct. 6. 1853, 3:2.
22. *Ibid.*, Oct. 13, 1853, 2:5.
23. *Ibid.*, Oct. 20, 1853, 2:3.
24. *Mo. Rev. Stat.*, Chap. 167, sec. 25 (1845).
25. *Glasgow Times*, Oct. 27, 1853, 3:3.
26. *In the Matter of John Anderson, Committed Under the Extradition Treaty with the United States*, 24 Upper Canada Queen's Bench Reports, 124, 125 (1860). Hereinafter cited UCQBR.
27. My summary of John Anderson's life is taken from Harper Twelvetrees, ed., *The Story of the Life of John Anderson*.
28. *L. T.*, Sept. 28, 1860, 3:1 and *Missouri Telegraph* (Fulton), March 1, 1861, 4:3. The *Fayette Banner* probably closely followed this case; unfortunately, this newspaper is not extant.
29. Harriet C. Frazier, "'Like a Liar Gone to Burning Hell': Shakespeare and Dying Declarations," 166–180.
30. Frazier, "Burns, Abortions and Dying Declarations," 344.
31. My summary of the affidavit of Slave Phil and the testimony of the live witnesses against John Anderson is taken from *In the Matter of John Anderson, Committed under the Extradition Treaty with the United States*, 24 UCQBR 124 (1860).

32. Patrick Brode, *The Odyssey of John Anderson*, 31.
33. *In The Matter of John Anderson, Committed Under the Extradition Treaty with the United States*, 24 UCQBR, 124, 135 (1860).
34. *Ibid.*, 144.
35. *New York Times*, Nov. 29, 1860, 8: 2.
36. Fred Landon, "The Anderson Fugitive Case," 239.
37. *In The Matter of John Anderson*, 24 UCQBR 173.
38. *Ibid.*, 183.
39. *Ex Parte Anderson*, 121 English Reports 525 (1861).
40. R.C. Reinders, "Anglo-Canadian Abolitionism: The John Anderson Case, 1860–1861," 82.
41. Brode, *The Odyssey of John Anderson*, 65.
42. "Judicial Society — Anderson's Case," *The Jurist*, Feb. 23, 1861, 73.
43. Harper Twelvetrees, *Life of Anderson*, 91.
44. *Ibid.*, 113.
45. Winks, *The Blacks in Canada*, 174.
46. 1861 Mo. Laws, 545.
47. Paul Finkelman, "International Extradition and Fugitive Slaves: The John Anderson Case," 810.
48. *Glasgow Times*, Nov. 22, 1860, 3:4.

Chapter 7

1. In *Missouri Intelligencer* (Columbia), Dec. 11, 1830, 3:1 and *Jefferson Republican* (Jefferson City), June 16, 1833, 2:1.
2. Mo. Rev. Stat., art. 3, sec. 31 (1835).
3. Va. Code, chap. 111, secs. 28–31 (1819).
4. See *State v. Brown*, Jan. 1837, wherein the Alabama Supreme Court upheld a death sentence for slave-stealing, in Catterall, *Judicial Cases Concerning Slavery*, 3:242; and *L.T.*, which reported: "Three men, named Flowers, Black, and Smith have been sentenced to be hung in Florida for negro stealing" (Nov. in Cheraw, S. Carolina on [Oct. 28,, 1846] for negro stealing, was found guilty and sentenced... to be hung on the first Friday in January [1847]" (Nov. 28, 1846, 2:2).
5. Mo. Rev. Stat., "Crimes and Misdemeanors," Sec. 32 (1835).
6. Michael Fellman, *Inside War*, 19.
7. Mo. Rev. Stat., art. 7, sec. 3 (1835) (1845); Art 7, sec 4 (1855).
8. Walter H. Ryle, *Missouri: Union or Secession*, 2.
9. Mo. Rev. Stat., art. 9, sec. 1 (1835).
10. Mo. Rev. Stat., art. 3, secs. 31–34 (1845).
11. Mo. Rev. Stat., art. 3, sec. 30 (1855).
12. Missouri State Penitentiary, Register of Inmates, 1837–1862.
13. *State v. Hart*, Cape Girardeau County Circuit Court Records, 1850–51.
14. Henry David Thoreau, *Walden* and "On the Duty of Civil Disobedience," 248–85.
15. Register of Inmates, Reel 1, Second Series, 146.
16. *Ibid.*, Reel 1, n.p. nos.
17. *Ibid.*, Reel 2, 150.
18. *Ibid.*, Reel 2, 210.
19. *Ibid.*, Reel 1, 13–14.
20. George Thompson, *Prison Life and Reflections*, 131.
21. *Kirk, alias Kirkpatrick v. State*, 6 Mo. 469 (1840).
22. Thompson, *Prison Life and Reflections*, 95.
23. *State v. Rector*, 11 Mo. 28 (1847).
24. *Encyclopedia of the History of Missouri*, 2:354, 472–73, 552–53; 4:155, 537; 5:229–31, 339–40; and 6:79; and *DAB*, *s.v.* Fletcher, Thomas C.; Gamble, Hamilton R.; King, Austin; and Price, Sterling.
25. *History of Marion County, Missouri*, 256–58; *Quincy Herald-Whig*, June 5, 1944, B1:1; and Thompson, *Prison Life and Reflections*, 39, 91, and 191. In *Moore v. Dempsey*, 261 U.S. 86 (1923), the U.S. Supreme Court reversed the first state criminal trial in the high court's history in a case involving six blacks sentenced to death in Arkansas for the murder of whites. The Court held that any mob-dominated trial violates the Due Process Clause of the 14th Amendment. Unfortunately for some of Missouri's slave stealers, this amendment first became federal law after the Civil War in 1868, and its use to invalidate the conviction in a trial atmosphere similar to Work, Burr, and Thompson's took another 55 years.
26. George Thompson, *Prison Life and Reflections*, 222.
27. My summary of the case is based on Thompson, *Prison Life and Reflections*, 17–415.
28. Pardon Papers, Box 3, F 21, MSA.
29. *Ibid.*
30. George Thompson, *Thompson in Africa*, 1, 128–30 and 188–89. This book also contains a brief account of "a vessel called the *Amistad*." Appendix, 335–37.
31. George Thompson, *Palm Land or West Africa*, 13.
32. *Oberlin News*, Feb. 9, 1893, and Oberlin College Archives, Group 28 Alumni Records, Series former Students — A, Box 2542, F Thompson, George.

33. Pardon Papers, Box 4, F 13, MSA.
34. Pardon Papers, Box 4, F 13, MSA.
35. Pardon Papers, Box 10, F 2, MSA.
36. *L.T.*, Jan. 26, 1849, 1:6.
37. Pardon Papers, Box 6, F 20, MSA.
38. Pardon Papers, Box 8, F 67, MSA.
39. Pardon Papers, Box 18, F 26, MSA.
40. Pardon Papers, Box 8, F 2, MSA.
41. Pardon Papers, Box 16, F 21, MSA.
42. Pardon Papers, Box 16, F 20, MSA.
43. Pardon Papers, Box 19, F 8, MSA.
44. *Glasgow Times*, Jan. 24, 1861, 1:4.
45. Pardon Papers, Box 16, F 8, MSA.

Chapter 8

1. Michael Fellman, *Inside War*, 95.
2. *Ibid.*, 246.
3. The federal law provided "That any company authorized by the legislature of Missouri may construct a bridge across the Missouri River at the city of Kansas." 14 Stat. 245.
4. *Encyclopedia of the History of Missouri*, 4:489.
5. *Springfield Advertiser*, Feb. 24, 1849, 1:6.
6. *Boonville Weekly Observer*, Feb. 16, 1861, 2:6 and Fellman, *Inside War*, 5 and 8.
7. Conversation with Annette Curtis.
8. *Louisiana Journal*, Oct. 4, 1860, 1:2.
9. 10 Stat. 277. See also Alice Nichols, *Bleeding Kansas*, for a Missouri-Kansas–border emphasis on the results of the federal legislation, and James A. Rawley, *Race & Politics*, for a dual focus, the border and the national causes of and reaction to the Kansas-Nebraska Act.
10. *History of Clay and Platte Counties, Missouri*, 634.
11. Rawley, *Race & Politics*, 86.
12. *Ibid.*, 88.
13. Louis Ruchames, ed. *Letters of William Lloyd Garrison*, 4:359.
14. *History of Clay and Platte Counties, Missouri*, 834.
15. Roy V. Magers, "The Raid on the Parkville Industrial Luminary," 42.
16. *L.T.*, April 22, 1855, 2:1. See also Magers, "The Raid on the Parkville Industrial Luminary," 39–46; W.M. Paxton, *Annals of Platte County, Missouri*, 198–99; and David D. March, *History of Missouri* 2:842–45.
17. William E. Parrish, *David Rice Atchison of Missouri, Border Politician*, 175.
18. *Missouri Democrat* (St. Louis) April 30, 1855, 2:1.
19. *Ibid.*, May 4, 1855, 2:1.
20. *Ibid.*, May 18, 1855, 2:2.
21. Rawley, *Race & Politics*, 134.
22. Stephen B. Oates, *To Purge This Land with Blood*, 261–358; Jules Abels, *Man on Fire*, 216–33; and *DAB*, s.v. Brown, John.
23. *Cloudsplitter's* 758 pages contain only one paragraph about Brown's liberation of 11 Missouri slaves, 418, and the novelist incorrectly places the raid in Vernon County, Missouri, not Bates.
24. *Kansas City Times*, June 9, 1911, 3:1; *Kansas City Post*, June 9, 1911, 1:8; and Susan Greenbaum, *The Afro-American Community in Kansas City, Kansas*, 93–95.
25. *New York Times*, May 10, 1935, 23:3. See also *Kansas City Star*, May 9, 1935, 22:3.
26. *Time*, July 13, 1942, 49–50.
27. *New York Times*, Aug. 30, 1946, 1:1.
28. *Ibid.*, Jan. 28, 1859, 2:4.
29. 1859 Mo. Laws 8.
30. *L.T.*, Jan. 28, 1859, 2:3.
31. Mo. Rev. Stat., chap. 127, sec. 22 (1855) and Mo. Rev. Stat. 544.245 (1999).
32. James Redpath, *The Public Life of Capt. John Brown*, 221; Oswald Garrison Villard, *John Brown 1800–1859*, 371; *DAB*, s.v. Brown, John; and Abels, *Man on Fire*, 219.
33. *New York Times*, Jan. 28, 1859, 2:3.
34. Oates, *To Purge This Land with Blood*, 265.
35. *Ibid.*, 267.
36. *Bethany Star,* Dec. 15, 1859, 2:3.
37. *L.T.*, Dec. 9, 1859, 2:2.
38. *Border Star* (Westport) Dec. 3, 1859, 2:1.
39. *Western Journal of Commerce* (Kansas City), Dec. 8, 1859, 1:5 and 3:5.

Chapter 9

1. *Lawrence Republican*, Dec. 8, 1859, 2:2.
2. Villard, *John Brown*, 380.
3. *L.T.* Feb. 4, 1859, 1:5.
4. *Lawrence Republican*, Feb. 3, 1859, 2:2; emphasis in the original.
5. *L.T.*, Feb. 4, 1859, 1:5.
6. *Lawrence Republican*, Feb. 17, 1859, 2:4.
7. *California News*, March 5, 1859, 2:2, and *Observer* (Boonville), March 5, 1859, 2:3 ran identical stories which came from a St. Joseph newspaper. They obtained the story of the Doys' lynching from a Platte City paper. Neither a St. Joseph nor a Platte City newspaper is extant from this time period.
8. John Doy, *Thrilling Narrative of Dr. John Doy*, 31–38.
9. *Ibid.*, 26–49.

10. *Ibid.*, 77.
11. *Ibid.*, 77.
12. Mo. Rev. Stat., chap. 127, sec. 17 (1855).
13. Doy, *Thrilling Narrative*, 88.
14. *Ibid.*, 85.
15. Ronald V. Jackson, ed., *Missouri 1850 Slave Schedule*, 193, and *Missouri 1860 Slave Schedule*, 222.
16. See *History of Clay and Platte Counties, Missouri*, 747–51, and *L.T.*, Aug. 24, 1860, 2:5, for Norton's county-by-county vote tallies in his 1860 election to Congress; and *BDAC* and *DAB*, *s.v.* Norton, Elijah Hise.
17. Chris L. Rutt, ed., *History of Buchanan County and the City of St. Joseph*, 81.
18. Doy, *Thrilling Narrative*, 74–75.
19. *Ibid.*, 86–106.
20. *Border Star* (Westport), Feb. 11, 1859, 4:2.
21. Villard, *John Brown*, 677.
22. *California News*, Feb. 5, 1859, 2:1.
23. *Missouri 1860 Slave Schedule*, 225.
24. *Daily Democrat* (St. Louis), March 31, 1859, 1:6, and Doy, *Thrilling Narrative*, 105–07.
25. *L.T.*, July 1, 1859, 1:3.
26. See *Ker* v. *Illinois*, 119 U.S. 436 (1886): abducted in Peru, tried for larceny in Illinois; *Frisbie* v. *Collins*, 342 U.S. 519 (1952): seized in Illinois, tried for murder in Michigan; and *U.S.* v. *Alvarez-Machain*, 504 U.S. 655 (1992): kidnapped in Mexico, indicted for kidnapping and murder in a federal court in Texas.
27. Doy, *Thrilling Narrative*, 110–14; *L.T.*, July 29, 1859, 2:5; and *New York Times*, Aug. 1, 1859, 1:4.
28. *Free Democrat* (St. Joseph), Aug. 13, 1859, 2:6.
29. Doy, *Thrilling Narrative, passim*.
30. Villard, *John Brown*, 106.
31. Doy, *Thrilling Narrative*, 106.
32. *BDAC*, *s.v.* Craig, James.
33. "Census of Missouri—1856" lists the number of each county's slaves, whites, and their total in *R.C.*, March 12, 1857, 1:2 and *Morning Herald* (St. Joseph), July 10, 1862, 2:5.
34. *State* v. *Hatcher*, Buchanan Circuit Court Records, Order Book, No. 6, Sept. 18, 1860, 102–03, FHC.
35. Doy, *Thrilling Narrative*, 65–72.
36. *Lawrence Republican*, Sept. 17, 1860, 2:1.
37. Doy, *Thrilling Narrative*, 50–52.
38. *New York Times*, Aug. 2, 1860, 2:6.
39. *Lawrence Republican*, Aug. 16, 1860, 1:4.
40. Daniel F. Littlefield, *Africans and Seminoles: From Removal to Emancipation*, 5.
41. *Ibid.*, 78–79.
42. *Ibid.*, 180–84.
43. Annie Heloise Abel, *The American Indian as Slaveholder and Secessionist*, especially "The Indian Country, 1830–1860." See also Gary R. Kremer, "For Justice and Fee," in *James Milton Turner and the Promise of America*, 131–54, which concerns Turner's efforts in the 1880s to aid the Indians' former slaves who remained in Oklahoma territory after the Civil War.
44. *Missouri Argus* (St. Louis), April 19, 1839, 3:6.
45. Martha B. Caldwell, compiler, *Annals of Shawnee Methodist Mission*, 62.
46. *L.T.*, May 26, 1848, 3:1.
47. *Ibid.*, May 18, 1849, 3:1.
48. *MORE*, Nov. 3, 1839, 3:5.
49. *L.T.*, Dec. 19, 1851, 3:1.
50. Abel, *The American Indian as Slaveholder*, 22.
51. Cited in John W. Ragsdale, Jr., "The Dispossession of the Kansas Shawnee," 229.
52. Caldwell, *Annals of Shawnee Methodist Mission*, 76, 86, and 95.
53. *R.C.*, March 12, 1857, 1:2.
54. James R. Kyle, "The Way West: A Short History of Man and the Missouri River," Parts 1 and 2, the Internet.
55. Paxton, *Annals of Platte County*, 337–38.
56. 9 Stat. 447; 10 Stat. 277; and 10 Stat. 284.

Chapter 10

1. Katherine Helm, *The True Story of Mary, Wife of Lincoln*, 40.
2. *New York Times*, Feb. 18, 1999, F 11:1.
3. William A. Craigie and James R. Hulbert, *A Dictionary of American English on Historical Principles*, 4: 1885.
4. Wilbur H. Siebert, *The Underground Railroad*, 45–46. Additional references to this work follow the cited material.
5. Harriet Beecher Stowe, *Uncle Tom's Cabin*, 59 and 73.
6. Reprinted in *Lawrence Republican*, Feb. 3, 1859, 3:2.
7. Craigie and Hulbert, *A Dictionary of American English on Historical Principles*, 4: 2389.
8. *New York Times*, March 28, 1859, 5:3.
9. *Congressional Globe*, 31st Congress, April 22, 1850, 793.
10. See for more information Sister Kay Paumier's 1955 term paper on "The Underground Railroad in Salem, Ohio," her hometown. She read numerous successive issues of the *Anti-Slav-*

ery Bugle to write it for her course on "History of the United States and Pennsylvania" at Mount Mercy College, Pittsburgh, PA (the name was changed to Carlow College in the late 1960s).

11. 104 Stat. 4495–96.

12. U.S. National Park Service, *Special Resource Study/Management Concepts/Environmental Assessment: Underground Railroad*. Additional references to this work follow the cited material.

13. *St. Louis Post-Dispatch,* Nov. 12, 2001, B1:1.

14. *Ibid.*, June 1, 2003, D14.

15. *Free Democrat* (St. Joseph), Aug. 6, 1859, 2:3.

16. Hamilton R. Gamble Papers, ALS William Sausser, Hannibal, Mo. 12–31–1862, MHS.

17. See *DAB s.v.* Nelson, David; Buckmaster, *Let My People Go.*, 98–99; and *Quincy Herald-Whig* (Quincy, Illinois), June 5, 1994, 3B:1.

18. *Quincy Herald-Whig,* April 11, 1971.

19. Vertical file, Underground Railroad, *Kansas City Star,* 10-2-1955, MHS. The date of this newspaper account could not be confirmed by checking the *Kansas City Star* for either Oct. 2 or Feb. 10, 1955.

20. Packet of materials provided by the Fort Madison Public Library, Fort Madison, Iowa, July 11, 2003.

21. http://www.westporthistorical.org/tours.html

22. *Kansas City Star,* June 12, 2002, B3:1.

23. Susan Greenbaum, *The Afro-American Community in Kansas City, Kansas,* 95.

24. Quindaro Newspaper Clippings, Kansas City, Kansas Public Library.

25. *Kansas City Star,* Feb. 24, 1994, and James Johnson, "The Life and Times of George Washington (1840–1931)" 12–16.

26. Richard B. Sheridan, "From Slavery in Missouri to Freedom in Kansas," 28, 31; and Richard B. Sheridan, ed. and compiler, "Lizzie and the Underground Railroad," *Freedom's Crucible: The Underground Railroad in Lawrence and Douglas County, Kansas, 1854–1865,* 75.

27. The National Park Service lists Joel Grover's Barn as located in Kansas City. It is in Lawrence.

28. Lawrence: University of Kansas, Division of Continuing Education, 1998.

29. Lawrence: Published by the Author, 1999. It is available at the Clinton Abolitionist Museum, Clinton, Kansas.

30. *Topeka Capital,* Aug. 13, 1913, cited in Parker, *Angels of Freedom,* 67.

31. Conversation with Wanda Ewalt, President, Tabor Historical Society, Tabor, Iowa.

32. *L. T.,* Dec. 22, 1865, 3:2.

Bibliography

BOOKS

Abel, Annie Heloise. *The American Indian as Slaveholder and Secessionist.* Cleveland: Arthur H. Clarke, 1915. Rpt. Lincoln: Univ. of Nebraska Press, 1992.
Abels, Jules. *Man on Fire: John Brown and the Cause of Liberty.* New York: Macmillan, 1971.
Ambrose, Stephen E. *Undaunted Courage: Meriwether Lewis, Thomas Jefferson, and the Opening of the American West.* New York: Touchstone, 1996.
Arnold, Morris S. *Colonial Arkansas, 1686–1804: A Social and Cultural History.* Fayetteville: Univ. of Arkansas Press, 1991.
Baker, Jean H. *Mary Todd Lincoln: A Biography.* New York: W.W. Norton, 1987.
Ballagh, James Curtis. *A History of Slavery in Virginia.* Baltimore: Johns Hopkins Press, 1902. Rpt. New York: Johnson Reprint, 1968.
Banks, Russell. *Cloudsplitter.* New York: HarperCollins, 1998.
Betts, Robert B. *In Search of York: The Slave Who Went to the Pacific with Lewis and Clark.* Rev. ed. Boulder: Univ. of Colorado Press, 2000.
Billon, Frederic L. *Annals of St. Louis in Its Early Days Under the French and Spanish Dominations, 1764–1804.* St. Louis: Published by the author, 1886.
_____. *Annals of St. Louis in Its Territorial Days from 1804 to 1821.* St. Louis: Nixon-Jones, 1888.
Blackstone, William. *Commentaries on the Laws of England, A Facsimile of the First Edition of 1765–1769.* Vol. 4. Chicago: Univ. of Chicago Press, 1979.
Bolster, W. Jeffrey. *Black Jacks: African American Seamen in the Age of Sail.* Cambridge: Harvard Univ. Press, 1997.
Boswell, James. *Life of Johnson,* ed. Geoffrey Cumberlege. London: Oxford Univ. Press, 1953.
Bowen, Catherine Drinker. *Miracle at Philadelphia: The Story of the Constitutional Convention, May to September, 1787.* Boston: Little, Brown, 1986.
Brode, Patrick. *The Odyssey of John Anderson.* Toronto: Univ. of Toronto Press, 1989.
Brown, William Wells. "The Slave Narrative of William Wells Brown," *Puttin' On Ole Massa,* ed. Gilbert Osofsky. New York: Harper & Row, 1969.
Bruns, Roger, ed. *Am I Not a Man and a Brother: The Antislavery Crusade of Revolutionary America 1688–1788.* New York: Chelsea House, 1977.
Buckmaster, Henrietta. *Let My People Go: The Story of the Underground Railroad and the Growth of the Abolition Movement.* Columbia: Univ. of South Carolina Press, 1992.
Caldwell, Martha B., compiler. *Annals of Shawnee Methodist Mission,* 2nd ed. Topeka: The Kansas State Historical Society, 1977.
Campbell, Stanley W. *The Slave Catchers: Enforcement of the Fugitive Slave Law, 1850–1860.* Chapel Hill: Univ. of North Carolina Press, 1968.
Catterall, Helen, ed. *Judicial Cases Concerning American Slavery and the Negro.* 5 vols. New York: Octagon Books, 1968.
Christensen, Lawrence O., William E. Foley, Gary R. Kremer, and Kenneth H. Winn, eds. *Dictionary of Missouri Biography.* Columbia: Univ. of Missouri Press, 1999.
Conard, Howard L., ed. *Encyclopedia of the History of Missouri,* 6 vols. St. Louis: Southern Historical Press, 1901.

Cosner, Sharon. *The Underground Railroad*. New York: Franklin Watts, 1991.
Craigie, William A., and James R. Hulbert. *A Dictionary of American English on Historical Principles*, 4 vols. Chicago: Univ. of Chicago Press, 1940.
Curtis, Annette W. *Jackson County, Missouri in Black & White: Census of Slaves, Their Owners and "Free Colored," 1850 and 1860*. Independence, MO: Published by the author, 1995.
Curtis, William J. *A Black History of Independence, Missouri*. Atlanta, GA: Traco, 1985.
Dictionary of American Biography. 11 vols. New York: Charles Scribner's Sons, 1964.
Donald, David Herbert. *Charles Sumner and the Rights of Man*. New York: Alfred A. Knopf, 1970.
____. *Lincoln*. New York: Simon & Schuster, 1995.
Douglass, Frederick. *Narrative of the Life of Frederick Douglass: An American Slave Written by Himself, with Related Documents*, ed. David W. Blight. Boston: Bedford/St. Martin's, 2003.
Doy, John. *The Thrilling Narrative of Dr. John Doy of Kansas: Slavery As It Is, Inside and Out*. Boston: Thayer & Eldridge, 1860.
Duffy, John, ed. *The Rudolph Matas History of Medicine in Louisiana*. Vol. 1. Baton Rouge: Louisiana State Univ. Press, 1958.
Dufour, Charles L. *Ten Flags in the Wind: The Story of Louisiana*. New York: Harper & Row, 1967.
Eliot, William G. *The Story of Archer Alexander: From Slavery to Freedom*. Boston: Cupples, Upham, 1885. Rpt. Westport, CT: Negro Universities Press, 1970.
Ellis, Joseph J. *American Sphinx: The Character of Thomas Jefferson*. New York: Random House, 1998.
____. *Founding Brothers: The Revolutionary Generation*. New York: Random House, 2002.
Farrison, William Edward. *William Wells Brown: Author and Reformer*. Chicago: Univ. of Chicago Press, 1969.
Fehrenbacher, Don E. *The Dred Scott Case: Its Significance in American Law and Politics*. New York: Oxford Univ. Press, 1978.
____. *The Slaveholding Republic: An Account of the United States Government's Relations to Slavery*. Completed and edited by Ward M. McAfee. New York, Oxford Univ. Press, 2001.
Fellman, Michael. *Inside War: The Guerrilla Conflict in Missouri During the American Civil War*. New York: Oxford Univ. Press, 1990.
Fleischner, Jennifer. *Mrs. Lincoln and Mrs. Keckly: The Remarkable Story of the Friendship Between a First Lady and a Former Slave*. New York: Broadway Books, 2003.
Fletcher, Robert Samuel. *A History of Oberlin College From Its Foundation Through the Civil War*. 2 vols. Oberlin, OH: Oberlin College, 1943.
Flexner, James Thomas. *George Washington: Anguish and Farewell (1793–1799)*. Boston: Little, Brown, 1972.
Foley, William E. *The Genesis of Missouri: From Wilderness Outpost to Statehood*. Columbia: Univ. of Missouri Press, 1989.
____. *History of Missouri, 1673–1820*. Columbia: Univ. of Missouri Press, 1971.
____, and C. David Rice. *The First Chouteaus: River Barons of Early St. Louis*. Urbana: Univ. of Illinois Press, 1983.
Frazier, Harriet C. *Slavery and Crime in Missouri, 1773–1865*. Jefferson, NC: McFarland, 2001.
Fromm, Erich. *Escape from Freedom*. New York: Holt, Rinehart, and Winston, 1964.
Garrison, Wendell Phillips, and Francis Jackson Garrison. *William Lloyd Garrison, 1805–1879: The Story of His Life Told by His Children*. Vol. 1. New York: Century, 1885.
Greenbaum, Susan. *The Afro-American Community in Kansas City, Kansas*. City of Kansas City, Kansas, 1982.
Greene, Lorenzo J., Gary R. Kremer, and Anthony F. Holland. *Missouri's Black Heritage*. St. Louis: Forum, 1980.
Hanks, Patrick, and Flavia Hodges. *A Dictionary of First Names*. New York: Oxford Univ. Press, 1993.
Heckman, William L. *Steamboating: Sixty-Five Years on Missouri's Rivers*. Kansas City, MO: Burton, 1950.
Helm, Katherine. *The True Story of Mary, Wife of Lincoln by her Niece*. New York: Harper & Bros., 1928.
Hertzberg, Arthur. *The French Enlightenment and the Jews*. New York: Columbia Univ. Press, 1968.
History of Clay and Platte Counties, Missouri. St. Louis: National Historical, 1885.
History of Marion County. St. Louis: E.F. Perkins, 1884.
Houck, Louis. *A History of Missouri*. 3 vols. Chicago: R.R. Donnelley & Sons, 1908.
____, ed. and trans. *The Spanish Regime in Missouri*. 2 vols. Chicago: R.R. Donnelley & Sons, 1909.

Hyde, William, and Howard L. Conard, eds. *Encyclopedia of the History of St. Louis.* 6 vols. St. Louis: Southern History, 1899.
Irving, Washington. *Western Journals,* ed. John Francis McDermott. Norman: Univ. of Oklahoma Press, 1944.
Jackson, Ronald Vern, ed. *Missouri 1850 Slave Schedule.* North Salt Lake City, UT:Accelerated Indexing Systems, 1988.
_____, ed. *Missouri 1860 Slave Schedule.* North Salt Lake City, UT: Accelerated Indexing Systems, 1990.
Kay, Marvin L. Michael, and Lorin Lee Cary. *Slavery in North Carolina, 1748–1775.* Chapel Hill: Univ. of North Carolina Press, 1995.
Keckley, Elizabeth. *Behind the Scenes: Thirty Years a Slave, and Four Years in the White House.* New York: G.W. Carleton, 1868. Rpt. Arno Press and The New York Times, 1968.
Kerr, Derek N. *Petty Felony, Slave Defiance, and Frontier Villainy: Crime and Criminal Justice in Spanish Louisiana, 1770–1803.* New York: Garland, 1993.
King, Wilma. *Stolen Childhood: Slave Youth in Nineteenth-Century America.* Bloomington: Indiana Univ. Press, 1995.
Kremer, Gary R. *James Milton Turner and the Promise of America.* Columbia: Univ. of Missouri Press, 1991.
Lea, Henry Charles. *A History of the Inquisition of Spain.* Vols. 1 and 2. New York: Macmillan, 1922.
Littlefield, Daniel F., Jr. *Africans and Seminoles: From Removal to Emancipation.* Westport, CT: Greenwood, 1977.
Lowry, Thomas P. *The Story the Soldiers Wouldn't Tell: Sex in the Civil War.* Mechanicsburg, PA: Stackpole Books, 1994.
Lubar, Steven, and Kathleen M. Kendrick. *Legacies: Collecting America's History at the Smithsonian.* Washington, DC: Smithsonian Institute Press, 2001.
March, David D. *The History of Missouri.* 4 vols. New York: Lewis Historical, 1967.
Mayer, Henry. *All on Fire: William Lloyd Garrison and the Abolition of Slavery.* New York: St. Martin's, 1998.
McCullough, David. *John Adams.* New York: Simon & Schuster, 2001.
Melville, Herman. *Selected Tales and Poems,* ed. Richard Chase. New York: Rinehart, 1957.
Montesquieu, Charles, Baron de. *The Spirit of Laws,* trans. Thomas Nugent. New York: D. Appleton, 1900.
Morrison, Toni. *Beloved.* New York: Alfred A. Knopf, 1987.
Murray, Andrew E. *Presbyterians and the Negro: A History.* Philadelphia: Presbyterian Historical Society, 1966.
Nichols, Alice. *Bleeding Kansas.* New York: Oxford Univ. Press, 1954.
Noakes, Jeremy, and Geoffrey Prudham, eds. *Documents on Nazism, 1919–1945.* New York: Viking, 1975.
Oates, Stephen B. *The Fires of Jubilee: Nat Turner's Fierce Rebellion.* New York: Harper & Row, 1985.
_____. *To Purge This Land with Blood: A Biography of John Brown.* New York: Harper & Row, 1970.
Oxford Classical Dictionary, ed. M. Cary et al. Oxford: Clarendon, 1968.
Parker, Martha J. *Angels of Freedom.* Lawrence, KS: Published by the author, 1999.
Parrish, William E. *David Rice Atchison, Border Politician.* Columbia: Univ. of Missouri Press, 1961.
Paxton, W.M. *Annals of Platte County, Missouri.* Kansas City, MO: Hudson-Kimberly, 1897.
Quarles, Benjamin. *Black Abolitionists.* New York: Oxford Univ. Press, 1969.
Rawley, James A. *Race & Politics: "Bleeding Kansas" and the Coming of the Civil War.* Philadelphia: Lippincott, 1969.
Redpath, James. *The Public Life of Capt. John Brown.* Boston: Thayer and Eldridge, 1860.
Ruchames, Louis, ed. *Letters of William Lloyd Garrison: From Disunion to the Brink of War, 1850–1860.* Vol. 4. Cambridge: Belknap Press of Harvard Univ. Press, 1975.
Rutt, Chris L., ed. *History of Buchanan County and the City of St. Joseph.* Chicago: Biographical, 1904.
Ryle, Walter H. *Missouri: Union or Secession.* Nashville: George Peabody College for Teachers, 1931.
St. Louis City Directory. St. Louis, MO, 1859.
Sanborn, Margaret. *Mark Twain: The Bachelor Years.* New York: Doubleday, 1990.
Scharf, J. Thomas. *History of Saint Louis City and County.* 2 vols. Philadelphia: Louis H. Everts, 1883.
Schweninger, Loren, ed. *From Tennessee Slave to St. Louis Entrepreneur: The Autobiography of James*

Thomas. Columbia: Univ. of Missouri Press, 1984.
Seeber, Edward Derbyshire. *Anti-Slavery Opinion in France During the Second Half of the Eighteenth Century*. New York: Greenwood, 1969.
Sheridan, Richard B., ed. and compiler. *Freedom's Crucible: The Underground Railroad in Lawrence and Douglas County, Kansas, 1854–1865: A Reader*. Lawrence: Division of Continuing Education, Univ. of Kansas, 1998.
Siebert, Wilbur H. *The Underground Railroad: From Slavery to Freedom*. New York: Macmillan, 1898. Rpt. New York: Arno Press and The New York Times, 1968.
Sifakis, Carl. *The Encyclopedia of American Crime*. New York: Smithmark, 1982.
Stanley, Lois, George F. Wilson, and Maryhelen Wilson. *Death Records from Missouri Newspapers, January 1854–December 1860*. Greenville, SC: Southern Historical Press, 1990.
____, ____, and ____. *Death Records of Missouri Men, 1808–1854*. Greenville, SC: Southern Historical Press, 1990.
____, ____, and ____. *Death Records of Pioneer Missouri Women, 1808–1853*. Greenville, SC: Southern Historical Press, 1990.
Stowe, Harriet Beecher. *Uncle Tom's Cabin*. New York: Harper & Row, 1965.
Stroud, George M. *A Sketch of the Laws Relating to Slavery*. 1856. Rpt. New York: Negro Universities Press, 1968.
Thompson, George. *Palmland or West Africa, Illustrated: Being a History of Missionary Labors and Travels with Descriptions of Men and Things in Western Africa. Also a Synopsis of All the Missionary Work on that Continent*. Cincinnati, 1858. Rpt. London: Dawsons of Pall Mall, 1969.
____. *Prison Life and Reflections, or A Narrative of the Arrest, Trial, Conviction, Imprisonment, Treatment, Observations, Reflections and Deliverance of Work, Burr and Thompson Who Suffered an Unjust and Cruel Punishment in Missouri Penitentiary for Attempting to Aid Some Slaves to Liberty*. Antioch, OH: James M. Fitch, printer, 1847.
____. *Thompson in Africa, or An Account of the Missionary Labors, Sufferings, Travels, Observations of George Thompson in Western Africa at the Mendi Mission*. New York: Printed for the Author, 1852.
Thoreau, Henry David. *Walden and On the Duty of Civil Disobedience*. New York: Rinehart, 1948.
Tobin, Jacqueline, and Raymond G. Dolsard. *Hidden in Plain View: The Secret Story of Quilts and the Underground Railroad*. New York: Doubleday, 1999.
Trexler, Harrison. *Slavery in Missouri, 1804–1865*. Baltimore: Johns Hopkins Press, 1914.
Twain, Mark. *The Adventures of Huckleberry Finn*. New York, Rinehart, 1956.
____. *The Complete Humorous Sketches and Tales*, ed. Charles Neider. New York: Hanover House, 1961.
____. *Huck Finn and Tom Sawyer Among the Indians and Other Unfinished Stories*. Berkeley: Univ. of California Press, 1989.
____. *Life on the Mississippi*. New York: Penguin, 1984.
Twelvetrees, Harper, ed. *The Story of the Life of John Anderson, The Fugitive Slave*. 1863. Rpt. Freeport, NY: Black Heritage Library Collection, 1971.
Villard, Oswald Garrison. *John Brown 1800–1859: A Biography Fifty Years After*. Boston: Houghton Mifflin, 1911.
Voltaire. *Candide*, ed. and trans. Donald M. Frame. Bloomington: Indiana Univ. Press, 1961.
Weld, Theodore Dwight. *American Slavery As It Is: Testimony of a Thousand Witnesses*. New York: American Anti-Slavery Society, 1836. Rpt. New York: Arno Press and The New York Times, 1968.
Willison, George F. *Patrick Henry and His World*. Garden City, NY: Doubleday, 1969.
Winch, Julie, ed. *The Colored Aristocracy of St. Louis by Cyprian Clamorgan*. Columbia: Univ. of Missouri Press, 1999.
Windsor City Directory. Windsor, ON, 1894.
Winks, Robin W. *The Blacks in Canada: A History*. New Haven: Yale Univ. Press, 1971.
Woodson, Carter G., ed. *Free Negro Owners of Slaves in the United States in 1830*. Washington, DC: Assoc. for the Study of Negro Life in America, 1924. Rpt. New York: Negro Universities Press, 1968.

Articles

Brown, William Wells. "Letters, Sept. 24, 1844–Nov. 12, 1857." *J. of Negro History* 10 (July 1925): 533–67.

Carlson, Becky. "'Manumitted and Forever Set Free': The Children of Charles Lee Younger and Elizabeth, a Woman of Color." *Missouri Historical Review* 96 (Oct. 2001): 16–31.

Finkelman, Paul. "Evading the Ordinance: The Persistence of Bondage in Indiana and Illinois." *Slavery and the Founders: Race and Liberty in the Age of Jefferson*. 2nd ed. Armonk, NY: M.E. Sharpe, 2001: 58–80.

_____. "International Extradition and Fugitive Slaves: The John Anderson Case." *Brooklyn J. of International Law* 18 (1989): 765–810.

Foley, William E. "Slave Freedom Suits before Dred Scott: The Case of Marie Jean Scypion's Descendants." *Missouri Historical Review* 79 (Oct. 1984): 1–23.

Foster, Eugene A., M.A. Jobling, P.G. Taylor, P. Donnelly, P. de Knijffs, Rene Mieremet, T. Zerjal, and C. Tyler-Smith. "Jefferson fathered slave's last child." *Nature* 396 (5 November 1998): 27–28.

Frazier, Harriet C. "Burns, Abortions and Dying Declarations." *Medicine and Law* 5 (1986): 431–40.

_____. "'Like a Liar Gone to Burning Hell': Shakespeare and Dying Declarations." *Comparative Drama* 19 (Summer 1985): 166–80.

Gilbert, Judith A. "Esther and Her Sisters: Free Women of Color as Property Owners in Colonial St. Louis, 1765–1803." *Gateway Heritage* 17 (Summer 1996): 14–23.

Holmes, Jack D.L. "The Abortive Slave Revolt at Pointe Coupée, Louisiana, 1795." *Louisiana History* 11 (Fall 1970): 341–62.

Hunting, Claudine. "The Philosophes and Black Slavery: 1748–1765." *J. of the History of Ideas* 39 (1978): 405–18.

Johnson, James. "The Life and Times of George Washington (1830–1931)." *Platte County Missouri Historical & Genealogical Society Bulletin* 47 (1994) 12–16.

Jones, Wilbur Devereux. "The Influence of Slavery on the Webster-Ashburton Treaty." *J. of Southern History* 22 (1956): 48–58.

"Juridical Society — Anderson's Case." *The Jurist* 7 (new series) (Feb. 23, 1861), 73.

Kyle, James R. "The Way West: A Short History of Man and the Missouri River." Part I and 2. Missouri River Heritage Corridor: www.mid-mo.net/bigmuddy.

Lander, Eric S. and Joseph J. Ellis, "Founding father." *Nature* 396 (5 November 1998): 13–14.

Landon, Fred. "The Anderson Fugitive Case." *J. of Negro History* 7 (July 1922): 233–42.

Magers, Roy V. "The Raid on the Parkville Industrial Luminary." *Missouri Historical Review* 30 (Oct. 1935): 39–46.

Michelle, Jerry A. "From Law Court to Local Government: Metamorphosis of the Superior Council of French Louisiana." *Louisiana History* 9 (1968): 85–107.

Moore, N. Webster. "John Berry Meachum (1789–1854): St. Louis Pioneer, Black Aboltionist, Educator, and Preacher." *Bulletin of the Missouri Historical Society* 19 (Jan. 1973): 96–103.

Obregon, Liliana. "Black Codes in Latin America." *Africana: The Encyclopedia of the African and African American Experience*, eds. Kwame Anthony Appiah and Henry Louis Gates. New York: Basic Civitas Books (1999): 245–49.

Ragsdale, John W., Jr. "The Dispossession of the Kansas Shawnee." *UMKC Law Review* 58 (winter 1990): 209–56.

Reinders, Robert C. "Anglo-Canadian Abolitionism: The John Anderson Case, 1860–1861." *Renaissance and Modern Studies* 19 (1975): 72–97.

Robinson, Alonford James, Jr. "Suriname." *Africana: The Encyclopedia of the African and African American Experience*, eds. Kwame Anthony Appiah and Henry Louis Gates. New York: Basic Civitas Books (1999): 245–49.

Seematter, Mary E. "Trials and Confessions: Race and Justice in Antebellum St. Louis." *Gateway Heritage* 12 (fall 1991): 36–47.

Sheridan, Richard B. "From Slavery in Missouri to Freedom in Kansas: The Influx of Black Fugitives and Contrabands into Kansas, 1854–1865." *Kansas History* 12 (Spring 1989): 28–47.

Time 40 (July 13, 1942): 49–50.

Violette, Eugene M. "The Black Code in Missouri." *Proceedings of the Mississippi Valley Historical Association* 6 (1912–1913): 287–316.

Wiecek, William M. "The Origins of the Law of Slavery in British North America." *Cardozo Law Review* 17 (May 1996): 1711–90.

———. "The Witch at the Christening: Slavery and the Constitution's Origins." *The Framing and Ratification of the Constitution*, ed. Leonard W. Levy and Dennis J. Mahoney. New York: Macmillan, 1987: 167–84.
Williams, Betty Harvey. "Patrol Companies Appointed in Ralls County, Missouri." *Missouri State Genealogical Assoc. J.* 13 (Summer 1993): 121–24.

NEWSPAPERS

Bethany Star
Boonville Weekly Observer
Border Star (Westport)
Boston Evening Transcript
Brunswicker (Brunswick)
California News
Church Progress (St. Louis)
Free Democrat (St. Joseph)
Glasgow Times
Independent Patriot (Jackson)
Jefferson Inquirer (Jefferson City)
Jefferson Republican (Jefferson City)
Kansas City Enterprise
Kansas City Post
Kansas City Star
Kansas City Times
Lawrence Republican (Lawrence, KS)
Liberator (Boston)
Liberty Tribune
Louisiana Gazette (St. Louis)
Louisiana Journal
Missourian (St. Charles)
Missouri Argus (St. Louis)
Missouri Daily Democrat (St. Louis)
Missouri Gazette (St. Louis)
Missouri Herald (Jackson)
Missouri Intelligencer (Fayette and Columbia)
Missouri Republican (St. Louis)
Missouri Statesman (Columbia)
Missouri Telegraph (Fulton)
Morning Herald (St. Joseph)
New York Times
Quincy Herald-Whig (Quincy, IL)
Randolph Citizen (Huntsville)
Salt River Journal (Bowling Green)
Springfield Advertiser
St. Louis Argus
St. Louis Enquirer
St. Louis Post-Dispatch
Western Journal of Commerce (Kansas City)
Western Watchman (St. Louis)

GOVERNMENT DOCUMENTS

Biographical Directory of the American Congress 1774–1996. Alexandria, VA: CQ Staff Directories, 1997.
Congressional Globe, April 22, 1850.
1850 U.S. Census (Slave Schedule), Missouri; National Archives Microfilm Series, M-432.
1860 U.S. Census (Slave Schedule), Missouri; National Archives Microfilm Series, M-653.
Hunt, Gaillard, ed. *Journals of the Continental Congress, 1774–1789*. Vol. 26. Washington, DC: Government Printing Office, 1928.
Kinnaird, Lawrence, ed. *Spain in the Mississippi Valley*. Vol. 2. Annual Report of the American Historical Association for the Year 1945. Washington, DC: 1946.
Miller, Hunter, ed. "Webster-Ashburton Treaty, 1842." *Treaties and Other International Acts of the United States of America*. Vol. 4. Documents 80–121, 1836–1846. Washington, DC: Government Printing Office, 1934.
National Park Service. *Special Resource Study/Management Concepts/Environmental Assessment: Underground Railroad*. Washington, DC: Government Printing Office, Sept. 1995.
Official Manuals, State of Missouri. Jefferson City: Office of Secretary of State, 1977–78–2001–02.
Thorpe, Francis N., ed. *The Federal and State Constitutions, Colonial Charters, and Other Organic Laws of the States, Territories, and Colonies Now or Heretofore Forming the United States of America*. 7 vols. Washington, DC: Government Printing Office, 1909.
Twenty Censuses: Population and Housing, 1790–1980. Washington, D.C.: Bureau of the Census, 1979.
U.S. Department of Commerce. *Negro Population, 1790–1915*. Washington, DC: Government Printing Office, 1915.

Archival Material

Family History Center, Church of Jesus Christ of Latter-Day Saints, Independence, MO: Circuit Court Records, State of Missouri.
Missouri Historical Society, St. Louis, MO: Clark, George Rogers, Papers; Gamble, Hamilton R., Papers; Lisa, Manuel, Collection; Lovejoy, Elijah, Vertical File; Stoddard, Amos, Papers; Tiffany Collection; Underground Railroad, Vertical File.
Missouri State Archives, Jefferson City, MO: *Esther, Free Mulatto* v. *Jacques Clamorgan*, Box 24, Folders 14 and 15; *Matilda, a Black Girl* v. *Isaac Van Bibber*, Boxes 41–43, Folders 26 and 35; *Berry Meachum* v. *Judy, alias Julia Logan* [Summary of circuit court trial], Box 152 Folder 15.
John Pickens, U.S. v. Box 5, Folder 6.
Sarah Pickens v. *Pascal Cerré*, Box 5, Folder 7.
Sarah Pickens v. *Antoine Soulard*, Box 5, Folder 8.
Missouri State Penitentiary: Register of Inmates, 1836–1865.
Pardon Papers, 1837–1865.
Western Missouri Manuscript Collection, University of Missouri, Columbia, MO: Ste. Genevieve District and County Court Records, Collection 3636.

Statutory Law

Canada (1985).
Code Noir, 1724, in John B. Dillon, *History of Indiana*, Laws of Indianapolis: Bingham & Douglas, 1859, 31–43.
Missouri, Laws of (1804–2003).
South Carolina, "Acts Relating to Slaves," *The Statutes at Large of South Carolina* (1842).
[Spanish Colonial Law] O'Reilly, Don Alejandro. "Ordinances and Instructions," trans. Gustavus Schmidt, 1 *Louisiana Law J.* (Aug. 1841): 1–65.
United States, Statutes at Large (1789–1990).
U.S. Congress, Private Laws of the 1789–1845.
Virginia, Laws of (1619–1831).

Handwritten Court Records, Missouri Counties

Buchanan:
    Hatcher, State v. (1860).
Cape Girardeau:
    Hart, State v. (1850–51).
St. Louis:
    City of St. Louis Recorder of Deeds, Book B.

Printed Court Records

Missouri

Anderson v. *Brown (of color)*, 9 Mo. 646 (1845).
Carroll v. *The City of St. Louis*, 12 Mo. 444 (1849).
Charlotte v. *Chouteau*, 11 Mo. 193 (1847).
Charlotte (of color) v. *Chouteau*, 33 Mo. 194 (1862).
Eaton v. *Vaughan*, 9 Mo. 743 (1846).
Emmerson [sic] v. *Dred Scott (of color)*, 11 Mo. 413 (1848).
Emmerson [sic] v. *Harriet (of color)*, 11 Mo. 413 (1848).

Hill v. *Wright*, 3 Mo. 243 (1833).
Julia (a woman of color) v. *McKinney*, 3 Mo. 270 (1833).
Kirk, alias Kirkpatrick v. *State*, 6 Mo. 469 (1840).
La Grange (alias Isidore) v. *Pierre Chouteau*, 2 Mo. 20 (1828).
Harris v. *Hannibal and St. Joseph Railroad*, 37 Mo. 307 (1866).
Magwire v. *Tyler*, 40 Mo. 406 (1867).
Marguerite v. *Chouteau*, 2 Mo. 71 (1828).
Marguerite v. *Chouteau*, 3 Mo. 540 (1834).
McClure v. *Pacific Railroad*, 35 Mo. 189 (1864).
Meechum [sic] v. *Judy, alias Julia Logan, A Woman of Color*, 4 Mo. 361 (1836).
Merry v. *Tiffin and Menard*, 1 Mo. 725 (1827).
Nat (a man of color) v. *Ruddle*, 3 Mo. 400 (1834).
Rachael (a woman of color) v. *Walker*, 4 Mo. 350 (1836).
Ralph (a man of color) v. *Duncan*, 3 Mo. 194 (1833).
Rector, State v. 11 Mo. 28 (1847).
Rogers v. *Pacific Railroad*, 35 Mo. 153 (1864).
Scott, a man of color v. *Emerson*, 15 Mo. 576 (1852).
St. Louis Public Schools v. *Risley's Heirs*, 40 Mo. 356 (1867).
St. Louis Public Schools v. *Schoenthaler's Heirs*, 40 Mo. 372 (1867).
Stoner v. *State*, 4 Mo. 614 (1837).
Theoteste (alias Catiche) v. *Chouteau*, 2 Mo. 144 (1829).
Vincent (a man of color) v. *Duncan*, 2 Mo. 214 (1830).
Welton v. *Pacific Railroad*, 34 Mo. 358 (1864).
Winny (a free woman held in slavery) v. *Whitesides alias Prewitt*, 1 Mo. 472 (1824).
Withers v. *Steamboat El Paso*, 24 Mo. 204 (1857).
Withers v. *Steamboat El Paso*, 24 Mo. 358 (1864).
Younger v. *Judah*, 111 Mo. 303, 19 S.W. 1109 (1892).

Tennessee

Fisher's Negroes v. *Dabbs*, 14 Tenn (6 Yer.) 119 (1834).

Federal

Alvarez-Machain, United States v., 504 U.S. 655 (1992).
Berthold v. *McDonald*, 63 U.S. (22 How.) 334 (1859).
Dred Scott v. *Sandford*, 60 U.S. (19 How.) 393 (1857).
Frisbie v. *Collins*, 342 U.S. 519 (1952).
Ker v. *Illinois*, 119 U.S. 436 (1886).
LaGrange (alias Isidore), a Man of Colour v. *Pierre Chouteau*, 29 U.S. (4 Pet.) 287 (1830).
Landes v. *Brant*, 51 U.S. (10 How.) 348 (1850).
Loving v. *Virginia*, 388 U.S. 1 (1967).
Magwire v. *Tyler*, 75 U.S. (8 Wall.) 652 (1869).
Menard v. *Aspasia*, 30 U.S. (5 Pet.) 505 (1831).
Moore v. *Dempsey*, 261 U.S. 86 (1923).
Pierre Chouteau, senior v. *Marguerite (a woman of colour)*, 37 U.S. (12 Pet.) 507 (1838).
Plessy v. *Ferguson*, 163 U.S. 537 (1896).
Prigg v. *Pennsylvania*, 41 U.S. 539 (1842).
Rhodes, United States v. 27 F. Cas. 785 (C.C.D.Ky 1866) (No. 16, 152).
Schools v. *Risley*, 77 U.S. (10 Wall.) 91 (1869).
Scott v. *Sandford*, 60 U.S. (19 How.) 393 (1857).
Tyler v. *Magwire*, 84 U.S. (17 Wall.) 253 (1872).
West v. *Cochran*, 58 U.S. (17 How.) 403 (1854).

Canadian

Anderson, In The Matter of, Committed under the Extradition Treaty with the United States, 24 Upper Canada Reports: Court of Queen's Bench 150 (1860).

English

Anderson, Ex parte, 121 English Reports 525 (1861).

Index

African Americans, free: imprisoned for abolitionist activity 129, 161–62; mention in appellate case law 45; pardons of for same 136–38, 161–62
Alexander, Archer 103–5
Anderson, John 110–23
Anti-Slavery Bugle (Salem, Ohio) 171, 175
Articles of Confederation, attitudes toward slavery in 36–37
Atchison, Senator David 142–44

Bates County 145–46
Bill of Rights: bars branding in territories 94; bars mutilations of runaways, in territories 89
biracial children 24, 71, 72–76, 80–84
Black Code (Code Noir) 23–28, 44, 46
Blow, Taylor 60–61, 67
branding, runaways 93–94
Brown, John 145–51; mural in state capitol 148–49; statuary in Kansas 147–48
Brown, William Wells: appearance in London, England 21; runaway from Missouri 7, 19, 21
Buchanan County: number and value of bondpersons in 1860 160; trials of abolitionists in 156–58, 160–61
Burr, James 131–34
Burton, Moses: original owner of Jack Anderson 110–11

Campbell, Jessie McCanse 84, 85
Canada: abolition of slavery in 107; appeal of unfavorable verdict regarding John Anderson, to England 120–21; Brantford and Toronto hearings concerning John Anderson 117–121; destination of runaways 174; John Anderson's imprisonment in 117; John Brown travels to, with slaves from Bates County, MO 146; residence in 116; run to 113; unwillingness to return runaways to U.S. 108
Catherine, runaway 97
Catholicism: *Colored Aristocracy of St. Louis* 68–72; relationship to French and Spanish slavery in Louisiana 24, 28–29
Catron, John: U.S. Supreme Court Justice's concurrence in *Dred Scott* 60; father of biracial son 72–73
Census, federal: African Americans in Arkansas 19; African Americans in Missouri 10, 48, 142; comparisons between African Americans and whites 112, 142
Census, Missouri, slaves and whites 18, 137, 142
Census, Spanish, 1770, of St. Louis and Ste. Genevieve 42
Census, Spanish, 1794–95, of Upper Louisiana 43
Census, Spanish, 1800, of Upper Louisiana 43
Chouteau, August 41
Chouteau, Pierre 51, 55
Chouteau family: as slaveowners 51, 53
churches: attitudes toward slavery 5, 172

Clamorgan, Cyprian 47, 68–72, 74
Clamorgan, Jacques 45–48
Clark, William 49–50, 56; runaways from 101
Clemens, John (father of Mark Twain) 132
Clemens, Samuel (Mark Twain) 5, 12–14, 21
The Colored Aristocracy of St. Louis 47, 68–72
compensation: for death of slaves, French and Spanish in Louisiana 28–29, 87
concubinage 43–44, 80–81
Craig, Congressman James 159–60
crimes by slaves, under Spanish rule of Louisiana 28–32
curfew: for free Negroes and mulattoes in Kansas City, MO 65
Curry, John Steuart 148–49

death of abolitionists, in prison 128
death penalty, for abolitionist activity 124
Denmark, IA 174–75
Dick (runaway slave from Platte County, MO) 156–58
diet, of runaways 113
Digges, Benjamin 119
Digges, Frances 112
Digges, Seneca T.P. 112–23
Digges, Thomas 118–19
District of Columbia: attitudes and laws concerning slavery 9
Doy, Dr. John, abolitionist: captured in KS by MO slave owners 152; change of venue from Platte to Buchanan County 154; escape from jail 158–59; metaphor of Under-

211

ground Railroad used to describe capture of 171; trial on slave-stealing charges 156–58
Edwards, Governor John C. 134
Eliot, William Greenleaf 103–5
emancipation, earliest record of Missouri slaves 45
Emancipation Proclamation 18
England: anti-slavery sentiment in 109–10, 121–22; appearance of William Wells Brown in London 21; residence of John Anderson in London and Corby 122
"Equal Protection of the Law," Simpson Younger suit under 82
Esther (free mulatto) 45–47

fines 65–66
free papers 91
free states 35, 58
freedom suits of slaves: failure of 55–61; success of 53–54, 56–61
Fromm, Erich 17
Fugitive Slave Law of 1793 94, 102, 110
Fugitive Slave Law of 1850 17, 94, 102–03, 110; Senator Henry Clay from Kentucky, one of chief sponsors of 171

Garrison, William Lloyd 9, 10, 15, 20–21, 39, 170
Georgia, attitudes and laws concerning slavery 8–9
Ginny, question of ownership 88

Haiti 7, 23
Hannibal, MO 5, 21; associated with Underground Railroad 173–74
Harper, Mr. and Mrs. Sam 177–79
Harris, Phillip 137–38
Hatcher, Henry 160–61
Henry, Patrick 35
Howard County: birthplace of John Anderson 110; civil suit concerning runaway 92; indignation meeting in 114–15; pardon of abolitionist convicted in 131–35; residence of Seneca T.P. Digges and family 112

Illinois: slaves' run through to freedom 20, 113; Underground Railroad in 172
Indians: as slave owners 28, 30, 50–51, 163
Industrial Luminary (newspaper) 143–44
intermarriage of whites and blacks 24
Iowa, route of runaways 174–75
Irving, Washington 49–50

Jackson County: early runaway ads 163–64; guilty pleas and pardons of abolitionists 139–40, 160–61; murder of Thomas C. Johnson 165; number of slaves in, 1860 142; press coverage of John Brown's execution 151
Jefferson, Thomas: attitudes toward slavery 39–40
Johnson, the Rev. Thomas C.: buys promising slave children in MO 164–65; founds Shawnee Methodist Mission, KS 164–65; murdered in Jackson County, MO 165

Kansas: abolitionist stronghold 146–49; Indian country 163; Quindaro, haven for runaways 147
Kansas-Nebraska Act 142–43; changes direction of runaway flight 165
Keckley, Elizabeth 76, 78–80

Langston, George 135–36
"Law Respecting Slaves" (1804) 48
Liberty, MO: city of, formation of patrol considered 90
licenses: requirements of, for free Negroes and mulattoes to live in MO 66–67; revocation of Lewis Tomlin's 115
life insurance, on slaves 11–12
"List of Free Negroes, Licensed [in]... St. Louis County" 67–68; Elizabeth Keckley 76, 78–80; probable children of John Berry Meachum in 76–78
Logan, Julia: freedom suit against John Berry Meachum 76–77
Louisiana: French rule of 23–28; Spanish rule of 28–32
Lower Canada (Quebec): abolition of slavery in 107
lynch mob: presence influencing sentences of abolitionists 128, 132, 139, 162; successful opposition to, by judge 155
Lyons, Nancy 107, 1922, 71–72, 74

Marion County 132
Marronnage 87
Matilda, freedom suit of 53–54
McCanse, Jeremiah 84–85
McGirk, Mathias 54–57
Meachum, John Berry 76–78
Meachum, Mary 172–73
Mennonites, attitude toward slavery 33
Mexico, abolishes slavery, 1829 106
Missouri, 1820 Constitution of, attitudes toward slavery 62
Missouri, legislation: free Negroes and mulattoes 62–65; runaways 88–89, 91–93; slave stealing 124–27; special law to compensate witnesses against John Anderson who traveled to Canada 123; Western border security 150
Missouri, Supreme Court of: decisions regarding slave stealing 131; freedom of Indian slaves 28; freedom suits 55–59; hostility toward free Negroes and mulattoes 65; pro-slavery attitudes of 58–59
Missouri Compromise: declared unconstitutional 59; enactment of 54
Montesquieu, Charles 32
mutilations, of runaways 89, 93–94

National Park Service 172
Nelson, Dr. David 131, 174
newspapers: advertisements for runaways, 93–101; coverage of Seneca T.P. Digges' homicide 114
North Carolina, attitudes and laws concerning slavery 9–10, 88–89
Northwest Territory 53–60
Norton, Elijah Hise: appointed

judge and chief judge on Missouri Supreme Court, 155; elected to Congress 155, 160; presides at Doy's trial 156–58; prevents lynching, 155

Oberlin College (Oberlin, OH) 80–81, 82, 135, 145
occupations, free Negroes and mulattoes 67–68, 70
Ordinance of 1787: abolition of slavery by 36–37; allowed owners to recapture runaways in 94; declared unconstitutional 59–60; increased slavery elsewhere 40–41
Osawatomie, KS, Adair Cabin 146

pardons: abolitionist prison inmates 130–40; last abolitionist pardon after slavery abolished in Missouri 138–39
Park, George S. 143–44
patrols: Liberty, formation of considered 90; ordinance regulating in St. Louis 90; Ralls County 90
Phil (slave of Frances Digges) 118–19
Pickens, John 87–88
Pinks, George (or Allen) 161–62
Platte County: destruction of *Industrial Luminary* 143–44; jailing of John Doy, abolitionist 153.
Press, Missouri, attitudes toward slavery 10–12, 13, 15–18

Quakers, attitudes toward slavery 20, 33–35, 40
Quindaro, KS: haven for runaways 147; station on Underground Railroad 176

Rachael, freedom suit 57
railroad: means of transportation for runaways 93; slave owner suits against concerning runaways 93; Underground, metaphor for slave flight 169–71
Ralls County, patrols in 90
Register of Inmates, Missouri State Penitentiary 125–130
rewards: capture of John Anderson 115; capture of runaways 89, 91, 112
runaways, punishment of 26–27, 31–32
Rush, Benjamin 35

St. Louis: Catherine, a runaway from 97; *Colored Aristocracy of...* 47, 68–72; Mary Meachum aids runaways in 172–73; most frequent trial location for abolitionists 136–38; number of slaves in, 1860 142; ordinance regulating patrols in 90; press, sympathetic attitude toward escaping slaves 17–18; safe haven for runaway slaves 100
Saline County 112
Scott, Dred: English reaction to decision regarding 121; freedom suit 57–61, 67
Scott, Harriet 57–61, 67–68
Scypion, Marie Jean 50–51
self-theft 108
Sewall, Samuel 33
Shawnee Methodist Mission, KS 164
slaves: absence of names in press accounts of accidental deaths and those by non-contagious diseases 13; anecdotes about birth and longevity 13–15; behavior peculiarities of, described in newspaper ads 98–99; clothing, described in ads 99; color of, described in ads 98; disfigurements, described in ads 95; male and female, contrasting descriptions in ads 98–100; mother's status determines whether slave or free 15; names and nicknames 95; rewards for capture of runaway 89, 91, 112; runaway, moral deficiencies of, alleged in ads 98; special skills, mentioned in ads 96–97; speech defects described in ads 98–99
South Carolina, attitudes and laws concerning slavery 7–9, 88
Spring Hill, KS: residence of freed slave Jeremiah McCanse and his family 84–85
steamboats: civil suits of slave owners against 92–3; means of transportation for runaways 92
Stoddard, Amos 41
Stowe, Harriet Beecher 5, 21, 170

Tabor, IA, station on Underground Railroad 177, 179
Taney, Roger 59–60
Thomas, James 72–76
Thompson, George: abolitionist convict in Missouri State Penitentiary 34, 131–35; associated with Oberlin College 135
Tomlin, Lewis: free black father-in-law of John Anderson 111; treatment of 115
Turner, Nat 8–9

United States Constitution: amendments abolishing slavery and establishing the equal protection of the law in 60–61; attitudes toward slavery in 37–40; extradition of persons charged with crimes in 116; requirements of, favorable to slavery 94
U.S. Supreme Court: denial of jurisdiction in freedom suits 56; Dred Scott case 60
Upper Canada (Ontario), abolition of slavery in 107

Violence: encounters between runaways and pursuers in 1850s 101–2
Virginia, attitudes and laws concerning slavery 10, 88, 94
Voltaire, on slavery 32

Washington, George (slave) 176–77
weather and climate: influenced start of runaway's departure 100–1, 112
Webster-Ashburton Treaty 109–10; interpretation of concerning John Anderson, 117–22; list of extraditable crimes under 110
Weld, Theodore 34, 95, 170
Westport, MO 18, 163–65; unlikely as Underground Railroad station 175–76

Windsor, Ontario 113: residence of Mr. and Mrs. Sam Harper 177–79
women: abolitionist inmates, Missouri State Penitentiary 129, 136; less likely to be runaways 93, 95, 99
Work, Alanson 131–33

York (slave, of Lewis and Clark expedition) 49–50, 52, 56
Younger, Catherine 80–84
Younger, Charles Lee 80–81
Younger, Simpson 80–82, 84

www.ingramcontent.com/pod-product-compliance
Lightning Source LLC
Chambersburg PA
CBHW081555300426
44116CB00015B/2885